Sharon Tate was throwing a party. Sal Mineo was walking from his car to his apartment. Bob Crane was asleep in a motel room. Rebecca Schaeffer opened her front door. And moments later they were dead.

Sometimes it is obsession, sometimes jealousy or greed, sometimes fear. Whatever the reason, our celebrities — from show business, politics, sports, or those whose names are simply in the news — become targets, living in fear of the time when someone is going to step out of the dark and bring their lives to a sudden end.

But our fascination with their lives, with wanting to know what happened and why, never ends. Whether the celebrity is the victim, the accused, or just a witness, we want to know more.

Here are the stories. . .

CELEBRITY MURDERS

Edited by
ART CROCKETT

PINNACLE BOOKS
WINDSOR PUBLISHING CORP.

EDITOR'S NOTE

All the stories in CELEBRITY MURDERS appear as they did when first published. Results of trials or subsequent investigations have not been included for this volume.

PINNACLE BOOKS

are published by

Windsor Publishing Corp.
475 Park Avenue South
New York, NY 10016

First Pinnacle Books printing: November, 1990

Printed in the United States of America

Bloody Bludgeoning Climaxed the Playgirl's Sexcapades, *Master Detective:* February, 1985
Murder of the World's Champion, *True Detective:* June, 1942
Glamorous Model, A Wheeler-Dealer & Death by Torture, *True Detective:* August, 1979

Rolling Stones Rock Festival Murder Case, *True Detective:* August, 1970

Arnold Rothstein: The Gambler Who Was Too Smart To Live, *Master Detective:* June, 1976

America's No. 1 Murder Mystery, *True Detective:* August, 1968

Day of Reckoning for Sal Mineo's Murderer, *Official Detective:* July, 1979

Murder at Madison Square Garden, *Inside Detective:* December, 1980

A Rage to Destroy the Pristine Screen Beauty, *Offical Detective:* August, 1990

How Success Killed the Lennon Sisters' Dad, *True Detective:* February, 1970

How I Would Have Handled The Taylor Case, *True Detective:* June, 1924

The Sharon Tate Sex Cult Massacre, *Official Detective:* March, 1970

Show Business Beauty Hammered to Death, *Inside Detective:* June, 1979

Riddle of the Bludgeoned Gay's Double Life, *Inside Detective:* February, 1984

The Truth About Ramon Novarro's Murder, *True Detective:* January, 1969

A Most Likely Candidate for Murder, *True Detective:* May, 1976

The Texas Killing Caused A Political Earthquake, *Official Detective:* July, 1981

Kid McCoy's *Own Story* of the MORS Death Mystery, *True Detective:* May, 1925

Murder of Bob ("Hogan's Heroes") Crane, *Inside Detective:* May, 1979

Murder of the Beloved Actor, *True Detective:* November, 1988

The Unpublished Truth about the Thelma Todd Extortion Case, *True Detective:* March, 1936

Killing of the Scarsdale Diet Doctor, *Official Detective:* July, 1980

Actor Tom Neal's Fight to Prove He Didn't Murder His Wife, *Official Detective:* March, 1966

CONTENTS

Bloody Bludgeoning Climaxed The Playgirl's Sexcapades!

by Chris Edwards

Was she murdered because she had a lot of dirt on a number of prominent people, or was her death the result of a petty little man's sexual frustrations? Here's what L.A. detectives turned up and what the jury decided . . .

The pitiful whimpering of a sleek Doberman Pinscher broke the early morning stillness of a luxurious apartment house complex in the North Hollywood area of Los Angeles, California. The dog was stretched on the bedroom floor, his muzzle resting on his forepaws, his attention focused on the still form of the attractive young woman on the bed.

Beside her was a wooden baseball bat of the size used by Little League ball players. But in this case it had been a cruel bludgeon that had been used to smash the life out of Vicki Morgan, a bit-part actress, a model, and a playgirl who traveled in Hollywood's fast lane.

No one knew how long she had been dead before she was found murdered on July 7, 1983. It was later determined that her teenage son had not been home with her that night and that the bat had been seen at the nearby home of his grandmother.

It didn't take long to come up with Vicki Morgan's

identity, and when it did it would become apparent why . more than one person might want to kill her.

For 12 years Vicki had been the mistress of Alfred Bloomingdale, founder of the prestigious Diners Club, a member of the Bloomingdale department store family, and a member of President Ronald Reagan's "kitchen cabinet."

The Bloomingdales moved in the most exclusive circles in the nation's capital, hardly the sort of places where Vicki Morgan would be invited — or welcomed.

But her skeleton could be found in the Bloomingdale closet, where her presence was known by many but discussed by few.

Alfred Bloomingdale couldn't care less about the tragic end of his one-time paramour, who was murdered in 1983. Cancer had taken his life in August, 1982 at the age of 66.

A week before her lover's death, Vicki, 30, filed a 231-page sworn deposition in an $11 million "palimony" suit in the Los Angeles Superior court naming the Bloomingdale estate as plaintiff when Vicki's $18,000 monthly support checks suddenly stopped coming.

She charged that Bloomingdale had promised to support her for life, and told her he would give her a palatial home in return for her services to him as a confidante, traveling companion and advisor in real estate matters. The usual palimony support suit declared that one of her duties had been to serve as a therapist to help Bloomingdale overcome his Marquis de Sade complex.

Anyone with any knowledge of sex knows that the Marquis wrote about guys who got their kicks by abus-

10

ing lovers.

The deposition was full of kinky nonsense, but Vicki swore it was all true. She once said, "Alfred was two people. He was a Jekyll-and-Hyde in that personality of his which is the sexual part. Alfred was strange. I don't mean a fantasy. I mean a sickness."

According to the deposition, Vicki said she met Bloomingdale for the first time in 1970, when she was 17 and he was 54. She said he had telephoned her as often as 20 times a day until she agreed to have lunch with him. But on that "first date" she was accompanied by another woman — a friend of Bloomingdale.

Vicki said this woman told her, "Alfred has a real interest in you and I'm here to tell you that he is going to beat you up when he gets you up to the house (in the Hollywood Hills). He does that to all the hookers he sees."

The woman reportedly told Vicki, "He'll probably tie you up. He wants me to let you know that you are special to him and he'll make some special allowances."

Vicki declared in the deposition that Bloomingdale wanted her to be his mistress and she agreed.

The second-hand proposition didn't seem to offend Vicki as long as the price was right. Nor did she object to being treated like a whore. In her deposition, Vicki said she got a chance to see what she would be in for once she surrendered to Bloomingdale's offer. The funky sessions took place sometimes several times a week over a long period of time.

According to Vicki, Bloomingdale would sometimes strip nude, and beat her. Other women were sometimes in the room with the couple and she would watch as he would lash their buttocks with a belt after he had tied

11

their hands with expensive silk ties.

At the end of these orgies, Vicki said, Bloomingdale would ask her, "Wasn't that fun?" And Vicki said she would agree. "Alfred had a look in his eyes. And believe me when I say it. And his face. It scared me to death. He was a different person," she said.

Continued Vicki: "I was scared to death to say anything but 'Yes' and you better believe I said, 'Sure, this is fun.'" Vicki said that when she had intercourse with him after the orgies she could expect him to give her a bare-bottom spanking. Asked why she didn't break off this strange relationship with Bloomingdale, she replied, "I was scared to leave at that point. At the same time Alfred was the most fascinating man I had ever met in my whole life. There was no one like him in the world. Every day having lunch with him, going out with him. He's fun. He's childlike. He is a little arrogant — but not rude arrogant. He was so worldly."

The deposition declared that after Bloomingdale beat Vicki and other women in one of their orgy sessions he would single her out and have straight intercourse, but only with her.

Again in the deposition, Vicki said she served as Bloomingdale's therapist, getting her experience by watching her lover bind up women with ties after they'd stripped. Then he would strip, force the women to get down on their hands and knees, sit astride them and order to ride him around the room like horses while he drooled on their backs.

Morgan also testified that her lover shared with her "secret and delicate matters," such as the amount of his campaign contributions to Reagan, his presidential appointments and his role in the President's kitchen cabinet.

In her deposition, Morgan said that she eventually tired of the beatings, the horseplay and the spankings, so she left Bloomingdale in 1975 and married her second husband. But that marriage lasted only a brief period and Vicki once more went back to Bloomingdale.

She said she returned to Bloomingdale only after he agreed to give up his sadistic practices and allow her to serve as his therapist. She said she helped him by "watching" his activities and warning him when he was hurting a client. "I mean, when he got too rough with other women in the private group sessions," she said, "I would give him the 'look,' because I could see he was hurting—I mean seriously hurting someone—and he would calm down."

Eventually, she said, the sadistic sex slowed, and, to the best of her knowledge, it ceased.

On September 28, 1982, Los Angeles Superior Judge Christian E. Markey dismissed the bulk of the $11 million palimony suit Vicki had filed seeking a lifetime income and branded her 12-year affair with Bloomingdale as "adulterous, immoral, bordering on the illegal."

He added, "A thorough consideration of the material facts leads inescapably to the conclusion that the relationship between Morgan and Bloomingdale was no more than that of a wealthy, older paramour and a young, well-paid mistress."

The judge declared that "their relationship was explicitly founded on meretricious sexual services." A meretricious sex relationship involves sex for hire, such as prostitution. It is automatically illegal in California and on those grounds the suit was denied.

13

Except for a few minor points in her favor, the court ruling left Vicki Morgan destitute and faced with the problem of supporting herself and her son. Sugar Daddies were hard to come by and she was forced to sell her Mercedes Benz to pay the rent on her $1,000-a-month apartment in North Hollywood or face eviction.

What she really needed was another Bloomingdale.

At about 3:30 a.m. on the morning of July 7, 1983, a shabby looking 33-year-old man warily entered the North Hollywood police station and asked to talk to a detective. Detective Bill Welch asked the man if he had witnessed a crime. The man shook his head, hesitated for a short time and then replied to Welch's question, "No . . . I didn't." and then he added:

"I just killed someone.

"I beat her to death with a baseball bat."

The man identified himself as Marvin Pancoast, a clerk in a Hollywood talent agency, and said the woman he killed was Vicki Morgan, with whom he had been living for a short time in a North Hollywood apartment.

The late mistress of Bloomingdale had found another roommate. No Bloomingdale, to be sure, but a chance to keep afloat financially. But she picked a loser—like herself—who couldn't keep his own head above water.

Uniformed officers were dispatched to the apartment, where they found Vicki's battered body on her bed, dressed in her nightgown. On the bed beside her, the officers found the bloody club that had killed her.

Pancoast told detectives he was quarreling with Vicki over money the morning he killed her. Pancoast was taken into custody and held on $250,000 bail after his so-called confession about his part in her murder.

14

Ten days after the killing of Vicki Morgan, Robert K. Steinberg, a Beverly Hills criminal attorney, called a press conference to announce that through some mysterious channel he had received three pornographic videotapes of 40 minutes in duration.

He described them as portraying sado-masochistic orgies featuring the late Alfred Bloomingdale, one unnamed U.S. Congressman, four unnamed Reagan Administration appointees—and last but not least—Vicki Morgan.

In another version of the story, Steinberg told the Beverly Hills police he got the tapes from a woman who did not identify herself but who allegedly told him the tapes might help in the defense of Pancoast, who Steinberg said he represented briefly.

Steinberg said other persons had seen the tapes and could corroborate their content and the identities of those who took part in them. But the lawyer declined to identify these "other persons."

If Vicki Morgan had a role in the sex tapes she probably knew who else took part in the orgies. It was possible she had been trying to blackmail the other party-goers who, in turn, could have killed Vicki or had her killed.

Pancoast's attorneys, including Steinberg, argued that the real motive of Morgan's murder was not her argument with Pancoast over a few dollars, but that someone else killed her to keep from being blackmailed.

But Pancoast's confession to the police was hard to discount.

There appeared to be more interest in the elusive sex tapes than in the death of Vicki Morgan. But the existence of these tapes depended on the word of Steinberg, who admittedly didn't even know how he got them — if, indeed, he did have them.

The tapes eventually vanished in a snarl of contradictions and were never found. Steinberg had been subpoenaed to produce them, and then another strange thing happened — the tapes were stolen from Steinberg's office, he said. And they haven't been seen since.

Steinberg was indicted on a misdemeanor charge of filing a false report, but he has not yet been prosecuted.

At this point, Steinberg said, an attorney in the Justice Department — who was not named — suggested that the best thing to do would be to destroy the tapes, but Steinberg said he would offer the tapes to the White House first, to determine whether it would embarrass the Administration should they surface. So far they have not.

If there were such a blackmail plot in connection with the sex tapes, no one in Washington or in the White House knew anything about it.

Then another personality entered the picture.

Nan Clark, 32, told the press that the videotapes — which she says she never saw — may have been filmed at one of a series of semi-weekly sex orgies at locations in the San Fernando Valley.

She didn't attend these parties, but she said she had been invited to them by none other than Marvin Pancoast. She turned him down, she said, adding, "I wasn't interested. I'd rather read a magazine."

Clark said in a newspaper interview, "Marvin (Pancoast) said there were a lot of prominent people involved in these parties. He made it sound like they took place a couple of times a week."

Clark said that she was a friend of both Pancoast and Steinberg, and that Steinberg got involved in the case at her request. After she heard that Pancoast had been arrested for killing Morgan, Clark phoned Steinberg and told him that Pancoast needed a lawyer and asked him to take part in the case.

After visiting Pancoast in jail, Steinberg claims he was visited by an unidentified blonde who dropped off the tapes at his office and left.

Clark said, "Bob (Steinberg) called me back and said he had some tapes and he said the people in them were very, very prominent in government. He was very excited . . . He was phasing out . . . But he didn't name anyone who was in the tapes. One guy was in the Justice Department."

On July 20, 1983, Pancoast pleaded not guilty and not guilty by reason of insanity to the murder of Vicki Morgan. Pancoast was held on $250,000 bail and his preliminary hearing was set for July 23, 1983, by Municipal Judge Robert Swasey.

The prosecutor was District Attorney Stanley M. Weisberg and Pancoast's lawyers were Arthur Barens and Charles T. Matthews. By, this time, Steinberg had faded out of the picture.

Despite the confession Pancoast made when he surrendered to the police and directed them to the body of Vicki Morgan, he entered a simple plea of not guilty and not guilty by reason of insanity, which in effect says, "I didn't kill her but if I did it is because I was insane."

The suspected killer stood quietly with his hands in his pockets during his arraignment. The only word he uttered was, "Yes," when asked if he understood the nature of the proceedings against him.

On July 29, 1983, Pancoast appeared in court, where his attorneys argued unsuccessfully that the murder suspect be released for lack of evidence. Encino Municipal Judge James E. Satt ordered the defendant held without bail after hearing police testimony that Pancoast had confessed.

Detective Welch said that when Pancoast walked into the police station on the morning of the murder he declared voluntarily, "I did it! I did it! I killed Vicki. I did it with a baseball bat."

The coroner's report indicated that the young woman died from multiple skull fractures and hemorrhages resulting from at least half a dozen blows to the head.

Welch testified that no fingerprints were found on the bat, nor were there any fingerprints at the scene to prove Pancoast had been there.

The defense attorneys contended that the uncertain mental condition of Pancoast would have rendered him incapable of understanding what he was doing when he waived his right to be silent and made his confession. The full text of Pancoast's statement was recorded on a 40-minute tape, police officers testified.

Earlier, in an interview with a reporter from the *Los Angeles Times,* Pancoast, an admitted homosexual, said he had a "special love" for Vicki, but that didn't keep him from smashing her skull.

In the county jail, where he had been placed to keep from killing himself, Pancoast wept as he recalled some of the events leading to the murder.

"I just wanted her to go to sleep," Pancoast told the *Times.* "I just wanted her to go to sleep and leave me

18

alone that night. I wasn't angry. I just was tired. I'd been working with her, trying to get her moved."

Asked why he had been talking so freely to Los Angeles newspapers and wire services, Pancoast replied, "I guess I feel guilty. I was here in jail and I had to talk to somebody. I hadn't seen anybody. I've got to talk to somebody. I feel like I've been buried under the ground and the dirt's on top of me but I'm still breathing. I'm still alive and I feel ashamed. I feel sorry for Vicki's fourteen-year-old son."

Pancoast continued, "I'm very scared and I'm so confused."

An attorney for Pancoast said his client had been confined to mental institutions on at least four occasions and that he was under mental care at the time of the killing.

The attorney said, "The guy just had a complete psychotic shock. He is just a very sick boy."

Pancoast had told the press that he met Morgan in 1979 when they were both patients in the mental treatment center at Cedars-Sinai Hospital in Los Angeles. He said that he and Morgan had always been good friends and that he knew all about her relationship with Bloomingdale.

Said Pancoast: "Our friendship got closer and closer and I was staying at her condominium. I was there off and on and then I would go back to my mother's in Encino.

"Alfred used to visit us at the hospital and bring us pastries and sweet rolls all the time," he said.

Pancoast said, "I loved Vicki as a sister. She has

helped me more than anybody."

Pancoast's trial got under way on June 12, 1984. Testimony indicated that before the murder of Morgan, Pancoast had told the young woman's mother that he was a homosexual but nonetheless he was in love with her daughter.

Vicki's mother testified that on the night before her daughter's death, Pancoast had been to her apartment and when he left he took her grandson's Little League bat from her home and put it in his car. It was found by the boy at the murder scene on the following morning.

The defense argued that the police who neglected to test for fingerprints on the bat were either grossly negligent or engaged in an unspecified cover-up. When the bat was examined after sitting in an evidence locker for nearly three weeks, no fingerprints were found. Said Defense Attorney Charles Matthews, "I submit to you there is no valid basis on which you can conclude this bat is the murder weapon."

The defense attorney added, "There is no proof at all that Marvin Pancoast did anything at all except to say he killed Vicki Morgan."

During defense arguments, Pancoast's attorneys said Pancoast's confession was an "illusion" brought on by his masochistic urge to take the blame for someone else's crimes.

Mathews suggested that Morgan was killed by someone other than Pancoast—someone who wanted Morgan dead because she knew who took part in the sex taping and that material included "some very influential and powerful people." No names were mentioned in that connection.

The prosecution argued, "This is a simple case with

simple facts."

Prosecutor Weisberg told the jury that they should simply believe what Pancoast told the police—that he had just smashed Vicki's head with a ball bat and directed the cops to the apartment where they found the dead woman and the bat.

"This is murder in the first degree," said the prosecutor.

He declared that Pancoast had killed Morgan with malice and premeditation because he had become frustrated with her domineering treatment of him and her inability to make decisions about their future together.

Pancoast's attorneys repeated that Morgan was killed because she had in her possession material which could have damaged some influential people.

As he was led from the courtroom he turned angrily on a news photographer and snarled, "Leave me alone!" Asked to comment on the verdict that was reached after four and a half hours of deliberation, the prosecutor declared that he was delighted.

When the jury resumed its deliberations on the sanity issue of the trial, Pancoast was declared to be legally sane when he beat the model to death with a ball bat.

Pancoast sat quietly at the counsel desk with tears streaming down his cheeks. The first judgment brought down a penalty of 26 years in prison. The second verdict declared Pancoast to be legally sane and fit to serve his sentence.

The jury foreman told the press, "We felt that he was legally sane before, during and after. We wish Pancoast well. We all held hands and said a prayer for Marvin. We have gotten to know Marvin Pancoast well during the trial. Better than if we had known him all his life."

21

She said the nine other women and two men on the jury held hands and prayed for Pancoast at the time they found him guilty of the killing.

The jurors agreed that Pancoast's confession that he murdered Morgan, which he later repudiated, weighed in their decisions on the issues of both guilty and sanity.

Defense Attorney Barens addressed the court and said, "I think this has been a miscarriage of justice. I am stunned that the jury said Pancoast was sane in the light of his long history of his mental illness."

Deputy District Attorney Weisberg said he was not at all surprised by the decision and felt the evidence in the case established that Marvin Pancoast knew right from wrong.

On September 14th, Superior Court Judge David Horowitz sentenced Pancoast to serve 25 years to life for the murder of Vicki Morgan.

The defendant rocked nervously in his chair as Judge Horowitz imposed the prison term and denied defense motions for a new trial or reduction of sentence.

Editor's Note:

Nan Clark is not the real name of the person so named in the foregoing story. A fictious name has been used because there is no reason for public interest in the identity of this person.

Murder of the World's Champion

By Francis C. Preston

The long freight train steamed into Kansas City. Hoboes riding the rods dropped to the ground and, like silent shadows, disappeared into the heavy evening fog that had fallen over the city.

One hobo — he was only a boy of fifteen — looked out warily from his precarious perch just over the wheels. He made sure no railroad bulls were about before he swung lightly to the road-bed and moved off toward the town.

The then youthful wanderer is now known in every section of the globe where sporting men gather. He is one of the most popular figures in ring annals. His name is Jack Dempsey.

The Manassa Mauler whose pugilistic prowess was to bring him the World's Heavyweight Boxing Championship, had but two interests in life on this dreary night of October 15th, 1910.

One was dodging the railroad cops who were out to get him. For at this tender age Dempsey was referred to in almost every railroad police office as "Tiger Man." He got the name after a husky pair of bruised and battered bulls showed up and reported that a hobo whom they were hustling none too gently out of a freight-yard had turned on them and, fighting with the fury of a tiger, had administered a sound drubbing. Ashamed to admit that a mere boy had been able to do this, they described him as "a wild-looking guy, about thirty." The railroad police were never able to catch up with him.

Young Dempsey's second interest was the prize-ring.

His hands were thrust deep in his pockets, his shoulders hunched, as he shuffled along the dismal streets. He passed a newsstand which stood under a cluster of overhead lights that looked yellow in the dreary dusk. An excited newsboy was shouting: *"Extra! Read all about it. Murder of the World's Champ!"*

The young hobo's interest quickened and he hurried across the street and eagerly scanned the headline. For a moment he blinked his eyes. No, it wasn't possible. The handsome, reckless, romantic fighter whose indomitable spirit in the ring had won for him the World's Middleweight Boxing Championship and the admiration of the nation's millions, the man who could fight his weight in wildcats—no opponent was ever able to keep him down.

Yet here, splashed in heavy black type across the paper was the news that Stanley Ketchel was down for the count—for keeps. The champ—Jack Dempsey's first idol of the ring—had gone down before a carefully aimed bullet from a high-powered rifle.

There was a lump in his throat as the future champion dug a copper out of his pocket and handed it over to the newsboy and got a paper. He eagerly scanned the story. Ketchel had been spending a brief vacation at the Ozarks mountain ranch of R. P. Dickerson, a well-known sportsman, when he was murdered by an assassin whose identity was as deep a mystery as was the motive for the murder. The only reason for the shocking act that suggested itself to the reporters on the scene and

24

to the boxing authorities throughout the country was that the popular fighter had refused to play ball with a crooked gambling syndicate. Being the top-heavy betting favorite in every fight, it would have been enormously profitable for an unprincipled combine to back the underdog if Ketchel could be induced to take a dive.

But Ketchel was honest. He couldn't be bought at any price and dozens of editorials were now being written extolling him for his sterling character even in advance of the solution of the crime.

Dempsey carefully folded the newspaper, stuck it under his arm. His face was grim as he continued walking toward the heart of the city.

The murder of Stanley Ketchel was the kind to stir the feelings of men and this was as it should be. He had lived a quick-paced and hard life — and he had lived it cleanly. There could be no doubting his might, but he never used it to try to prove that might is right. There was an inspirational quality in his life.

But looking backward now that he lay cold in death, it was easy to see that each step in his life that brought him closer to fame and wealth was bringing him closer, also, to his doom. For a better understanding of the crime that rocked the sport of boxing, let us go back to the first step that was to lead him out of obscurity.

The Eldorado dance hall was a honky-tonk place on the main street of the wide open town of Butte, Montana. It depended on dance-hall girls to lure the miners and others into its precincts and separate them from their hard-earned cash. Goldie was the prettiest girl in the place and, when her singing stint was over, she could generally be found seated at a table in the corner of the bar in the company of the free spenders. She was a blue-eyed, blonde-haired girl whose beguiling, if somewhat calculating smile, was found irresistible by the men in this woman-scarce town.

Joe the bouncer was in love with Goldie and it was an open secret that she was his girl. One of the waiters was in love with her, too, although in a somewhat different way. He was only a seventeen-year-old youth and the least important man in the place, but, just as a peasant may love a queen, so this waiter, whose name was Ketchel, looked up to Goldie, his brown eyes filled with devotion.

This was the setting and part of the cast of characters when Fate, on this autumn night in 1904, first beckoned to the young waiter. On this particular night three burly miners had rolled into the bar. They were in high spirits. One of them, a dark, bearded giant of a man, knew exactly what action he would find most diverting and he was liquored up just enough to have the courage to do it.

Walking in the lead he made directly for the table at which Goldie was seated. Joe the bouncer looked the men over with an appraising eye and, sensing trouble, edged toward his girl.

Without a word the miner grabbed Goldie about the waist, lifted her easily off her feet and held her in a crushing embrace. The dance-hall girl struggled, her small fists beating a futile tattoo on the miner's chest as he tried to plant a kiss on her lips.

The bouncer jumped forward, but he wasn't quick enough. A white-aproned waiter grabbed him by the arm, pushed him aside.

"This is my table," the seventeen-year-old future ring champion said quietly. "I'll take care of it."

The bouncer's eyes opened in momentary amazement. Being a man of direct action he knew what he had to do and arguing with a brash youth was not one of these things. He lashed out a heavy-booted kick at the young waiter's groin.

This was a bit of rough and tumble tactics at which Joe the bouncer was particularly adept. This time, surprisingly, it proved ineffective, for young Ketchel, his lithe movements like poetry in motion, had side-stepped the kick, grabbed the heavy boot by heel and toe, and had given a quick twist and heave. The bouncer flew through the air and crashed headlong into the far end of the bar. He lay face down in the sawdust, stunned.

During the excitement the miner had relaxed his grip and Goldie managed to twist from his grasp, although her spangled dress was badly torn. Having lost the girl, the miner turned on Ketchel and, with a roar, leapt at him.

The youth ducked under the outstretched arm, stepped to the left and shot a terrific right into the miner's midsection. It was a short punch, but it had the kick of a mule. The miner, stopped momentarily, then dropped as a smashing uppercut from Ketchel's left caught him flush on the button.

The second miner hurled himself at the waiter. A sharp left jab to the stomach brought down his guard and a right cross to the side of the jaw, struck with tigerish fury, laid him alongside his partner. The third miner was too bewildered by these swift events to do more than raise his hands defensively. Ketchel, in a cold fury, was upon him. Four sledge-hammer blows to the midsection finished him.

So quickly was the fighting over that this minor free-for-all had no chance to become a riot. The owner ar-

rived hurriedly. Four men — one of them his bouncer —
lay on the floor. His first reaction was one of anger and
he would have fired the young waiter on the spot had not
one of the customers intervened.

He was Maurice Thompson, a welterweight boxer of
note, who was Butte's leading citizen so far as the sporting fraternity was concerned. He was training for a fight
with Sid La Fontise and was badly in need of sparring
partners. Here was one made to order for him. He led
Ketchel aside for a quiet talk. He learned that the young
waiter had a Polish father and mother, a large family of
sisters and brothers back in Grand Rapids, Michigan,
that his name was Stanislaus Kiecal. (This name for
professional purposes was later changed to Stanley Ketchel.) He had left home a few months before to come
West in order to become a cowboy. He rode the rods to
Montana and worked as a ranch-hand for a while, but
the lure of city life — Butte being considered a metropo-
lis — had brought him to the Eldorado.

Thompson told the youth that he was impressed by
the manner in which he had acquitted himself in a difficult situation; that he felt a future in the ring awaited
him if he applied himself to it.

The waiter said that he had never worn a pair of boxing gloves in his life and was dubious about the matter.
Thompson liked his honesty and modesty. Thus began a
lasting friendship.

Through the intercession of Thompson, Ketchel was
elevated to the job of bouncer. He began putting in all
his spare time at Reilly's training quarters where
Thompson was working out. Day after day he went
through the grueling grind so necessary to put a fighter
in top condition. His benefactor taught him all the tricks

of the game.

Thompson won his fight from Sid La Fontise and now turned his full attention to his young protégé. Ketchel, he felt, was the closest approach to a natural born fighter that he had ever seen.

He walked into the Eldorado one day and said to Ketchel, "You're ready for your first trial."

Ketchel replied, "All right, if you say so."

"I've got you matched with Kid Tracy for Thanksgiving night. You'll be the opening bout on the card."

"I won't let you down," answered the youth.

Thompson mused, rubbing his chin reflectively. "What'll we call you?"

The youth looked puzzled. "What's wrong with my name?"

Thompson shrugged. "That's no name for a fighter." he said. "Suppose we make it Stanley Ketchel, then the fight fans will be able to pronounce it."

The rickety stands were jammed that night in Butte even before the preliminary fights. Kid Tracy and Stanley Ketchel were introduced to the crowd, sent to their corners, and at the sound of the bell came out fighting. Ketchel was in the peculiar half-crouch that was later to characterize him in his big bouts.

As the fighters met in the center of the ring, Ketchel's left jabbed out with the speed of lightning. His right crashed home a split second later. Kid Tracy dropped heavily to the canvas. The entire thing had required just 30 seconds.

The spectators were stunned. The very speed with which Ketchel had terminated the bout raised doubts in the minds of many of the onlookers. For the remainder of the night arguments waxed fierce as to whether it was a lucky punch or skill that was responsible for the quick victory. The local match-maker was quick to see the advantage in this discrepancy in views and he speedily matched Ketchel with Mose La Fontise, brother of Sid, the fighter whom Maurice Thompson had beaten. It was to be a finish fight.

Old-timers in Butte still speak of that battle. Ketchel, the young novice, went into the fight an underdog, for Mose — a hard-hitting French-Canadian boxer — was one of the top-ranking welterweights of the day.

From the opening gong Ketchel pressed his opponent hard. For twenty-four rounds Mose stood off the battering punches before going down in a bloody heap. It wasn't even necessary for the referee to count. There could be no doubting the fact that La Fontise was completely out.

Five more fights in which Ketchel scored knock-outs were chalked up and Montana had a new fistic idol. From the shy boy of seventeen he blossomed out into a self-confident, free-spending extrovert. He became the best-dressed man in Butte, his taste running to wide-brimmed Stetson hats, two-colored boots of hand-tooled leather which cost fifty dollars the pair, silk shirts and handkerchiefs. His earliest ambition had been to be a cowboy and now, since he seemed destined not to be one, he determined to dress the part, anyway. Despite these tendencies he maintained a rigid training schedule.

Goldie looked upon him differently now that he was an important personage and, during his infrequent appearances at Frank's Bar, she could be found at his side clinging to his arm in a possessive manner.

30

Ketchel's close friendship with Maurice Thompson faced an acid test the year after it began. It was inevitable that Ketchel and Thompson, both top-notchers in the same division, should some day meet. It was, as the sporting fraternity put it, a natural. Thompson was fast and a shrewd ring general who knew all the ins and outs of the game. Ketchel was stronger, less experienced, but with a wallop that was like a charge of dynamite.

They faced each other in the main bout, a six-round affair, in the Butte Stadium. Ketchel didn't have his heart in the fight. It wasn't right for him to knock down the man who was responsible for his rise to fame — a man who had taken him as an unknown waiter and raised him to a boxer or prominence.

As they squared off in the center of the ring, Ketchel, whose usual style was to leap out of his corner with a furious two-fisted attack, now broke out slowly and fell into a clinch.

"I can't do it," he whispered in Thompson's ear.

"You've got to," Thompson replied. "Get set, Stan, for I'm going to pin your ears back."

"No hard feelings?" Ketchel asked.

Thompson shook his head and danced back.

Ketchel crouched down and began throwing the terrific punches which had subdued every opponent he had met thus far. But somehow Thompson wasn't at the receiving end. Like an elusive phantom he managed to duck and weave, parry and block the heavy ones, at the same time countering with a left that flicked with the speed of a serpent's tongue. For six rounds Ketchel tried to hang up a finishing wallop without success. When the final gong sounded, the referee raised Thompson's hand, signifying him to be the winner.

It can honestly be said that this was a fight Stanley Ketchel did not regret losing, even though he tried his hardest to win. He met Maurice Thompson in a second encounter on Labor Day, 1905. This was a ten-round battle and the result was precisely the same. When the referee raised Thompson's hand once again, he rushed over to Ketchel's corner and embraced him.

"I'll never fight you again, Stanley," Thompson said. "I've licked you twice, but I'll never be able to do it again. There isn't a man on earth who's going to stop you from being the next World Champion."

These fights taught Ketchel a valuable lesson. There was no harder puncher in the game, but this punch power was valueless if he didn't back it up with real boxing ability. During the next two years he concentrated on his style until he felt he had it perfect. He scored thirty-two knockouts in thirty-six contests.

His fame spread beyond the borders of Montana. Sportswriters in New York City, Chicago and San Francisco began calling him *The Michigan Assassin*. He was ready for greener pastures and San Francisco, a fight-crazy town if ever there was one, raised a beckoning finger.

Joe Thomas was World Champion in the welterweight division. He had defeated every opponent in the field with more or less ease until finally there wasn't a man to stack up against him.

There wasn't, that is, until word seeped out of Montana concerning the whirlwind Michigan Assassin. In the public mind a battle between these two loomed as a certainty. The match-makers arranged the bout with Thomas's title at stake for July 4th, 1907, at Coffroth's

Arena on Mission Street in San Francisco.

Taking leave of Butte was not a simple matter to stanley Ketchel. There were the hundreds of friends he had made — Maurice Thompson, for example — whom he was leaving behind. Then, also, there was Goldie, the dance-hall girl at the Eldorado in whose company he was usually to be found.

The affair between them had been a strange one from the very outset. It began with the respectful love-from-a-distance of a shy, seventeen-year-old boy, with the blonde singer, ten years his senior, accepting it merely as a manifestation of the power of her beauty. But as the fame of Stanley Ketchel spread, she tried to show him that she reciprocated, to a certain extent, his emotions. This belated attempt did not have quite the force it might have had. A curious change had taken place in the personality of Ketchel. His feelings toward the individual were crowded out by his feeling toward the mob. He, himself, became more a symbol than a person. It is a condition that is not uncommon and is to be found among movie stars, ranking politicians, and others who have large personal followings.

Although Stanley went around with Goldie, the dance-hall girl knew that he was a far different person from the boy waiter at the Eldorado. It was hard for him to say goodbye to her. She wanted to go with him — hinting first and asking later — but Stanley refused her.

At the station a large crowd of admirers were present to bid him Godspeed. Goldie was in that crowd, resentful. With smoldering eyes she watched him go, knowing in her heart that each mile he traveled would widen the chasm between them until it could never be bridged.

The first Thomas-Ketchel bout was declared a draw.

33

The verdict was a highly unsatisfactory one and the old argument as to who was the better man gained added momentum. Was it Thomas, older, the superior ring general, or was it the younger Ketchel fighting with abandon, absorbing with a smile every punch Thomas could throw, and dealing out fewer but harder wallops?

The champ and the contender were matched to meet once more at Coffroth's Arena, this time on Labor Day.

This amazing fight has already gone down in boxing history. Never had frenzied fight fans seen such a grueling exhibition, witnessed such a display of "guts" in a pair of opponents. Ketchel jumped out of his corner at the opening bell in the familiar crouch. He didn't waste a minute setting out after Thomas. The champ shrewdly backed away, peppering the challenger's handsome face with a steady tattoo of stinging lefts. The smile never left Ketchel's face as he absorbed the punishment and kept boring in. When the bell sounded ending the first round, he still hadn't landed a single clean blow.

Thomas' strategy was apparent from the first. He would not slug with his opponent. Instead he would box, using guile to overcome the advantage of the stiffer punching.

In the sixth round Thomas saw his opening. Ketchel had been wild with a left. It had left him off balance momentarily and in that split second the champ lashed out with a right that had every ounce of his power behind it. The blow caught Ketchel on the side of the jaw, literally raised him off his feet and sent him sprawling face forward on the canvas. At the count of six the challenger was on his knees shaking the cobwebs out of his brain. At the count of nine he stood groggily on his feet, hanging on until the bell sounded.

The minute rest was all he needed for a complete recovery. Once more he set after Thomas, caught up with him in a neutral corner at the close of the round. Thomas was short with a left lead and Ketchel was on him like a fury, whipping out his famous one-two — left hook to the mid-section and right uppercut to the jaw. The champion went down like a log, but the bell saved him. His handlers had him in shape when the gong sounded again and Thomas managed to stay away from Ketchel's blows, gaining strength throughout the succeeding rounds. But Ketchel caught up with him again and again just as the champ managed to break through his weak defense. For thirty-two punishing sessions the fight went on. Stanley Ketchel lay on the bloody canvas twenty times while the champion went down thirty-one times.

It was in the thirty-second round of a fight scheduled to go to the finish that Ketchel, the fighter with a lion's heart, put an end to that great battle. Thomas, who was tiring fast, no longer had the strength in his left to hold off the aggressive challenger. It was the one-two that did the job, a hard left to the midsection and a smashing right upper-cut to the side of the jaw. Thomas sank to the canvas and lay still. He was out for the count. Stanley Ketchel was crowned the Welterweight Boxing Champion of the World.

It was a puzzle to most people who knew Ketchel how a mild, shy youth, as he was outside the ring, could turn into a savage, ruthless fighter inside the ropes. His manager later explained the strange mental trick which Ketchel used to perform this transformation.

Ketchel had an overpowering love for his mother, Julia Oblinki Kiecal. In the absence of any fighting fury he would conjure up a belief that the man before him had insulted Julia. It usually took him half-a-round to get it clear in his mind, but once he made himself believe it he would have the fans on their feet cheering wildly.

Still not twenty-one years of age, his character and personality underwent considerable change. Once uncertain of himself, now he had a strong feeling of self-confidence. It went even further than that. He felt that he was invincible in the ring—not only in his own weight but in all weights. His burning ambition was to hold the crown in all classes, from welterweight to heavyweight inclusive. In this he was encouraged by the celebrated wit, Wilson Mizner, who acted as his manager.

Ketchel's clothing was distinctive. His suits were of Western cut, hats broad brimmed, shirts flashy. He wore a large diamond stickpin in his tie. Despite these changes in apparel he remained the same likable fighter whose reckless courage had endeared him to fight fans everywhere. An example of the affection people felt for him could be found in the strange notice that appears in San Francisco's newspapers year after year down to the present day. On each anniversary of the champion's death the death notices contain the following:

KETCHEL, STANLEY—in loving memory of Stanley Ketchel, died October 15th, 1910. (signed) O.

For a time the identity of "O" was a mystery, but it has come out recently that this is Olga Harting, a woman who, from her early youth in San Francisco where her father was a boxing timekeeper, looked up to Ketchel as a knight in shining armor. The hero worship she felt then has lasted through the years.

Stanley Ketchel was an active champion. He fought all comers. But soon there wasn't a single challenger in his weight who could stand up to him. It can be said that necessity helped him make his first move toward accomplishing the ambition that sports experts said was impossible. He challenged middleweight champion Billy Papke, known as the *Illinois Thunderbolt,* to a title match in the heavier class.

It was generally conceded that the fight against Thomas would be a picnic compared to the one against Papke, since the latter, every bit as good a fighter as Thomas, was a 160 pounder, while Ketchel weighed only 145 pounds. Billy Papke went into the fight a favorite. Ketchel whipped the middleweight champ decisively and so became the world's champion in two divisions — welterweight and middleweight. The man who lost his title demanded an opportunity to win it back and Ketchel, never one to side-step any challenge, agreed to another fight.

This one was held in Los Angeles. As the fighters moved to the center of the ring at the opening bell, Papke belted the champ a terrific right across the bridge of the nose. Ketchel was blinded. For twelve rounds he sought futilely to hold off the savage onslaught while he tried to regain his sight. He took the worst beating that any fighter had ever suffered before sinking to the canvas. The sporting fraternity was stunned. Ketchel, the iron man with the lion's heart, had been knocked out.

The sports authority, Edward Dean Sullivan, said of this fight: "Ketchel lost his title to Papke in a trick fight that started when Papke hit Ketchel a terrific blow on the bridge of the nose the moment the referee told them to shake hands at the beginning of the bout. Blinded and in agony, Ketchel fought on for twelve rounds, then went down for the count."

There was many a sad shake of the head as people said, "Well, even the best of them have to lose sometime."

Ketchel, a hero and world's champion at nineteen, was already being considered a has-been at twenty-two.

In his hotel room that night, his face puffed and raw, he said to his manager that he wanted an immediate rematch with Papke. Wilson Mizner shook his head slowly.

"I think we'd better wait a while," he counseled.

"I'm a better man than he is," Ketchel argued.

"You took a terrible beating tonight."

"What round did he knock me out in?" Ketchel asked.

"The twelfth."

"All right, then," Stanley Ketchel said and there was a smile on his bruised lips, "I'm going to lay him away in the eleventh and you can write that down in your book."

Seventy-seven days after having received the beating at the hands of Billy Papke, Stanley Ketchel stepped into the ring with him again. He was, as on the occasion of his first fight, the underdog. True to his word, he terminated the fight in the eleventh round. He caught his heavier opponent with the crushing one-two punches early in the first round, carried him along until the eleventh round before delivering the knock-out wallop. Once again he was dual champion.

One of the qualities that endeared Ketchel to the followers of the sport was that he was never static. You could never anticipate what he would do next.

He relinquished his claim to the welterweight crown, came East to New York with his manager and proceeded to lick a long line of middleweights. It was during this period in his career that attempts were made by the underworld to have him throw an occasional fight. Having the reputation of being incorruptible, he would never be suspected of taking part in a crooked deal. The crowd with which Mizner, a Broadway luminary, traveled had in it a singularly sinister individual named Arnold Rothstein, underworld banker, fixer and gambler. A. R.'s personable, suave exterior masked the cunning mind which engineered the plot to fix a baseball World Series. Although there were a number of men, so-called impeccable characters, in many walks of life including boxing, who succumbed to Rothstein's blandishments, Stanley Ketchel was not one of them.

The fixer and gambler had two arguments to induce recalcitrant persons to do his bidding. The first was the lure of money. This had no effect on Ketchel, who had sufficient funds for his own needs and who was more concerned with having his name go down as one of the greatest boxers of all time. Rothstein's second argument was force, which meant that the person refusing to do his bidding could expect a visitation from the strong-arm squad. This also failed, because Ketchel's courage was such that he feared no man or group of men.

Having established himself firmly as champion of the middleweight division by defeating a long list of competitors, he cast his eye at the heavyweight class. Here he was confronted with as formidable an obstacle as ever faced any man.

Jack Johnson, the colored giant, was firmly entrenched as the title holder. The ebony-skinned fighter was a big heavyweight, topping six feet and weighing 220 pounds. Alongside of him, Stanley Ketchel, weighing less than 160 pounds, appeared like a midget.

Fearful lest this tremendous difference in size deny him a crack at the heavyweight crown, Ketchel took to wearing high-heel boots, jackets and coats with heavily padded shoulders, and high bowler hats so that in photographs taken of Johnson and himself there appeared to be only a slight difference in size between them.

This ruse, aided considerably by the fact that the boxing world was seeking anxiously for a "white hope" to retake the title, worked and the match was made. It wasn't until the pair stepped into the ring on October 16th, 1909, at Colma, California, that the David-and-Goliath difference between them was so apparent. Being outweighed by almost sixty pounds didn't mean a thing to the plucky middleweight. He fought his usual fight, boring in, never taking a backward step.

Johnson was a great defensive fighter. He also packed a knock-out punch in either fist. He kept them cocked as he backed away, watching for an opening.

Ketchel found one first. In the eleventh round be feinted with his left and Johnson's guard dropped to protect his midsection. With perfect split-second timing Ketchel threw a right hook with everything he had behind it. The blow caught the heavyweight champion behind the left ear and Johnson went down.

A mighty roar rose from the throats of the thousands of onlookers. The mighty Johnson was on the canvas. It was incredible, but there it was before their very eyes.

At the count of six Johnson was on one knee shaking his head. It was easy to see that he was badly hurt. At the

40

count of nine he was up. Ketchel swarmed over him like a tiger, throwing punches from every angle, but the heavyweight champ managed to hold him off until the gong rang. He was greatly refreshed when he came up for the twelfth. Ketchel, anxious to finish off the colored champion in that frame, rushed out of his corner in a fury. Johnson parried a left jab, blocked a right lead and then threw a looping right hook that had in it every ounce of strength in his 220-pound frame of bone and sinew.

It caught Ketchel on the side of the jaw as he came in, and he dropped like a log. His jawbone was shattered.

Johnson was the winner and still heavyweight champion of the world.

In Ketchel's dictionary there was no such word as defeat. He came East with his manager, fought a string of middleweights and light heavyweights, beating them all.

Once again Rothstein and his clique worked on the fighter, trying to get him to throw some battles. Ketchel ignored them.

In the early fall of 1910, Ketchel told his manager that he wanted another try at Jack Johnson. Wilson Mizner shook his head slowly.

"I'm afraid he's too big for you, Stanley."

Ketchel smiled. "What round did Johnson knock me out in?"

"The thirteenth."

"All right then. Write this down in your book. I'm going to knock him out in the twelfth. Now, do I get the match?"

"Put some weight on and the fight is yours."

Coming from someone else, this might have looked like a boast, but the memory of a certain similar occasion was enough to allay that feeling. In fact, Mizner said to himself, "I'll be darned if he won't, too."

Mizner brought his fighter along slowly, matching him against opponents whose weights increased as one succeeded another. It was thus that he was booked into one of the most thrilling fights of his career against the clever boxer, Philadelphia Jack O'Brien, at the National Sporting Club in New York.

It was a fight between a boxing master and a fighting demon. Never once breaking up, Ketchel took all that the shifty and hard-hitting O'Brien could give him — up to the last eight seconds of this furious fight. Then he uncorked a pile-driver right that stretched O'Brien cold on the canvas.

There was in Ketchel's entourage a friend, a millionaire sportsman named R. P. Dickerson, who felt toward the young fighter as does a father for a son. On numerous occasions Dickerson invited the young fighter to spend as much time as he cared to at the Dickerson ranch in the Ozark Mountains. Being miles away from Broadway, it was a perfect spot for a fighter in training. It was located in an isolated spot near the village of Conway about forty miles from the city of Springfield, Missouri.

Ketchel accepted the invitation. Certain sportswriters professed to see in his trip to this lonely place a desire to get out of the reach of the gunmen who had been ordered by a gambling syndicate to get him. This may have been the case, although there is no evidence to support it.

Closer to the truth, and supported by a letter which

the champ wrote to his manager less than a week before his death, is the fact that, added to the excellence of the Dickerson estate as a place to train, Ketchel loved ranch life and welcomed every opportunity to live it. He wrote to Wilson Mizner:

Dear Bill:

More than ever before I'm stuck on this farming thing and I guess I'll be here for life. I have bought 3,300 acres and I intend to incorporate for about $300,000, put in a saw mill and lumber it off. It will give me one of the finest farms in the world.

If I do any more fighting, Bill, I think it will be for fun or charity. This is the place for me.

Write to me with all the news and give my best to Will Lewis, the best little fellow in the world.

Your farmer pal, Stanley.

Whatever the reason, Stanley Ketchel left Broadway and each mile that carried him closer to the Ozarks brought him that much closer to Death. Being far from an ordinary person, he was destined to go out in no ordinary manner.

At the large ranch-house Ketchel wasted no time before getting into training. On Saturday morning, October 16th, he awoke at six o'clock, stood before the open window and expanded his chest as he breathed in the brisk and stimulating air. He went through a series of exercises, dressed in a sweat suit, and ran over the country road for an hour. On his return he took a cold plunge and dressed. A ranch-hand escorted him to the main house.

"The cook'll rustle up anything you ask for," the hired

man said, leading the champion into the kitchen, "unless it's some of that Eastern *filet tripe* you'll be wanting."

The woman standing behind the stove was about thirty-five years old, although she looked much older. Her hair was streaked, showing plainly that it had once been bleached blonde. She looked up quickly as the two men entered, then turned away and stared resolutely at the frying pan in front of her.

The boxer's eyes widened when he saw her and the ranch-hand noticed this. Ketchel opened his mouth as though he were about to say something, but he closed it without speaking.

The hired hand said, "This is Mr. Ketchel, our famous boxing champion, and this is Goldie. Tell her what you'll have for breakfast."

The hired hand could feel the strain in the room though he couldn't tell what caused it. He told Goldie that the guest would have an order of ham and eggs, toast and coffee. Then he led the fighter onto the sun-drenched, open porch on which a small table covered with a white cloth had been set for one person. The host was at his town house at Springfield, and wasn't expected back until that evening.

Ketchel sat with his back to the house, looking out at the sun as it rose in a slow arc over the rounded hill-tops whose foliage was touched by autumnal flame. As the sizzling platter of ham and eggs was laid before him, he looked up at Goldie and smiled.

"That's an appetizing dish," he said.

The woman's eyes were fixed in an expressionless stare. She merely nodded her head, turned on her heel and walked back into the house.

The boxing champion dug into the dish. The silence

44

that surrounded him gave no hint of impending tragedy. A stealthy shadow within the house crept toward the open door that led to the porch. Closer and closer crept this nameless menace until it stood but a few feet from the broad, unsuspecting back of the ring idol.

"Stanley Ketchel," the voice said ominously.

The champion twisted his head, saw an evil-visaged man with a rifle aimed directly at him. Ketchel pushed back from the table, faced the intruder. He saw the grim, purposeful look on the unshaven face, read the deadly intent in the tightening trigger finger. Every muscle in his body went taut. The mind had no opportunity to read any reason into the assault. He had to act — and act fast if he were to save himself from death. Almost unconsciously his body dropped into a half crouch as he leapt forward.

There was a roar of rifle fire. Ketchel stopped short for a moment as the slug smashed into his chest, but with the courage he had shown in countless ring battles he moved on, hands grasping out. The killer backed away a step, fired again. The boxing champion went down in a bloody heap just inside the door. The killer smashed him over the face and shoulders with the butt of the rifle then, apparently satisfied that his deadly work was done, slipped past the kitchen and out the back door.

Goldie was in the kitchen all this time. She heard the shots, but made no move. There was still a spark of life in the wounded man. He groped blindly to his feet, blood pouring down his white shirt front, staggered to the steps and crawled up the stairs. With his last ounce of strength he stumbled into his room and fell across the bed.

The ranch foreman, C. E. Bailey, was working in the harness shop some distance from the house when he heard the sound of the shots. Rifle fire in the country is not an unusual thing but Bailey, out of curiosity, decided to investigate. Wiping his hands on his blue jean trousers, he walked over to the main house. He found the porch splattered with blood. He followed the drops into the house, up the steps and into Ketchel's room. The champion lay stretched on his back, his arms and legs spread-eagled. The foreman bent over him and the champion stirred.

"They got me," Ketchel said in a faint whisper.

"Who was it?" Bailey asked. "Tell me."

The champ tried to raise his head. "Di—I tried to—he shot me."

The effort to talk was too much for the boxer. The foreman threw open a window and shouted to a passing ranch-hand to telephone for a doctor, that the boxing champion had been shot. Then he raced down the steps and ordered another hired man to "hitch up the fastest team and get ready to drive Mr. Ketchel to Conway." Then he telephoned Mr. Dickerson.

Hearing that there was still a spark of life in his guest, Dickerson got three doctors and nurses in Springfield, put them aboard a special train and raced for Conway, but he was too late.

Stanley Ketchel's gallant heart had given out. He had fought his last fight. Standing at his friend's bedside, the wealthy sportsman vowed that he would never rest until the killer was caught and had been made to pay for the crime.

News of the murder traveled swiftly and from miles

around curious ranchers drove toward the Dickerson house. Sports fans were stunned by the news. The murder crowded all other events off the front pages. For weeks sports scribes wrote of nothing else. Such outstanding commentators as Ned Brown, boxing expert for the New York *World,* summed up the feelings of American fans when he said that lovers of true sport had suffered their keenest blow and that whether or not the investigation showed that the Arnold Rothstein gambling mob was responsible, Ketchel's relentless fight against all forms of crookedness in the sport would be an inspiration to those who followed in his footsteps.

In San Francisco, a pretty, black-haired schoolgirl, Olga Harting, read the headlines and wept. In Kansas City a young man named Jack Dempsey heard the news from the lips of excited newsboys and felt that he had suffered a personal loss. In Grand Rapids, Michigan, the parents of the brave fighter broke down in grief. In New York City, Wilson Mizner, the fighter's manager, heard the news as he sat in on a poker game in a Broadway hotel.

He looked up from his cards and said, "Tell them to start counting to ten. Ketchel will get up."

Although Mizner loved himself better than any person, living or dead, those who knew him — as did boxing expert Ned Brown — say that he was truly grief-stricken when he was finally convinced that the great fighter was dead.

Sheriff C. B. Shields of Wright County, Missouri, lost no time in climbing into a buckboard wagon with two of his deputies, and rushing to the Dickerson ranch. It will be remembered that this was in a day when there were few scientific devices for the detection of crime, and a police officer was dependent on common sense and a healthy suspicion.

Foreman Bailey was waiting for the officers when they arrived. He told them the little he knew about the crime, that he was working in one of the barns when he heard the rifle shots and, more out of idle curiosity than concern, had sauntered over to the main house and there saw drops of blood on the porch; how he followed the blood spots up the stairs to Ketchel's room where he found the dying fighter; he reported the few brief words Ketchel spoke before consciousness left him.

There was little in this information that proved helpful. The fact that Ketchel had spoken to Bailey before losing consciousness and had not given the name of his slayer could mean any one of three things. Either Ketchel did not know the identity of the killer, or he desired to hide it, or, finally, he knew it and was too confused give it.

How it was possible for an outsider to reach this isolated ranch was a puzzle. It had to be an all powerful motive to bring a murderer all the way out to the ranch on foot. This was evident since the approach of a wagon would have been instantly noted. Escape, therefore, had also been effected on foot. One of the strange elements in the murder was that $500 in cash and the diamond stickpin Ketchel always wore were missing from his person, giving rise to the theory that robbery was the motive.

The deputies went about rounding up all the help for questioning. This was not at all difficult, for most of them were already gathered at the main house, their chores momentarily forgotten in the excitement. When they were together, they were checked against a list supplied by Mr. Dickerson. It was found that one hired hand, a man named Walter Dipley, was missing. While one of the deputies went looking for him, Sheriff Wright faced the assemblage and asked all those who had heard the rifle shots to step forward.

Foreman Bailey stepped out of line. Nobody else stirred.

"There must have been somebody else who heard the shots," the sheriff said.

"To tell you the truth," the ranch foreman said, "none of the men were around the house and I heard the shots pretty faintly myself, because they must have been fired from inside the house and that deadens the sound."

"Who was in the house at the time?" the Sheriff asked.

The foreman replied, "Goldie was."

The Sheriff crooked his finger at the cook. Goldie stepped forward. Her lips were set in a grim line and her eyes fixed in a belligerent stare. She was taken into the house.

"You heard the shots?" the Sheriff asked.

"Yes," Goldie replied.

"Then why did you try to hide the fact?"

"Because there was nothing I could tell you about the murder."

"You saw Stanley Ketchel shot, didn't you?"

"No."

"Wasn't it unusual for someone to be firing a rifle inside the house?"

"Yes."

"And you didn't bother to investigate?"

"No."

It was obvious to Sheriff Wright that Goldie was lying, but what it was that she was trying to conceal was still a mystery.

When the Deputy Sheriff arrived to say that Dipley was nowhere to be found, a search was made in the missing man's room. In a battered valise that was pulled out from under the bed, Sheriff Wright found a group of photographs. One of them showed Dipley in the uniform of a sailor in the United States Navy. Another photograph, of far greater importance, was one which showed the ranch-hand in an affectionate pose with Goldie, the cook. It was fairly evident now, why Goldie was covering up. It was known about the ranch that she and the missing man were sweethearts. For some reason Stanley Ketchel's presence must have stirred up resentment.

It was Dickerson who supplied the information that early in the boxing champion's life there had been a woman named Goldie who had, he believed, been an entertainer in a honky-tonk bar in Butte, Montana. He had no way of knowing, either, whether Goldie the entertainer and Goldie the cook were one and the same person. An inkling that this might be so was furnished by one of the ranch hands who told the Sheriff of the strange reaction he had noticed in Ketchel when he met the cook.

If it turned out that the missing Dipley was actually the killer, then two things could more or less be taken for granted. First, it would be logical to assume that Goldie the cook had, years before, been the object of Stanley Ketchel's first love. Second, that it was this affair and not his battles with Rothstein's racketeers, that was responsible for his murder.

Dickerson offered a reward of $5,000 for the capture and conviction of the person or persons who had killed his friend. Posses were hurriedly formed and bloodhounds set out on the trail of Dipley.

It was almost midnight, two days after the brutal slaying, that Thomas Haggard, a farmer living in a small cabin in the lonely vastness of the Ozark Mountains heard a knock on his door. He picked up a kerosene lamp, walked to the door and opened it. Framed in the pale yellow glow of the lamp stood a man gripping a rifle firmly in both hands. The stranger's clothing was torn by briers and his face bore bloody streaks from thorn cuts.

"I'm lost," he said in a weak voice. "If you could give me something to eat and a place to sleep I would gladly pay you for it."

"Come in," the farmer said. "I'll be glad to take care of you during the night. There's no charge for hospitality here."

The stranger squatted on a stool before the open fireplace, glanced nervously about the room. Every move he made seemed to indicate that he was in great fear. When Haggard asked him if he cared to wash, he said no and it appeared to the farmer that the only reason for the refusal was that to wash would have meant relinquishing his hold on the rifle.

There was something queer about this and Haggard determined to look further into the matter. After the stranger had retired — fully clothed and with the rifle beside him — Haggard managed to slip out through a window and race away to the cabin of his brother, Joseph. After listening to the recital, Joseph felt certain that the stranger was the man named Dipley who was being sought as the slayer of Stanley Ketchel.

In order to confirm this the two brothers hurried to the cabin of a neighbor, Seit Murphy, who had a telephone. From there they got in touch with a Springfield newspaper and obtained the description of Dipley.

The three men armed themselves and hurried back to Tom Haggard's cabin. Slipping up quietly they peered through a window, saw that the stranger was still asleep. In single file they crept up to the sleeping man. Tom Haggard rammed the muzzle of his rifle into the stranger's side while his brother jerked the rifle away from him.

The man jumped up with a start. "What's the idea?" he demanded.

Tom Haggard said: "Roll up your right sleeve."

The stranger slowly peeled back the sleeve of his shirt. On the forearm was tattooed in red ink: "Hong Kong, China."

"So you are Walter Dipley," Haggard said.

At first the stranger tried to deny it, but the farmer cut him short by telling him that the entire nation was on the look-out for that tattoo mark.

Sheriff Wright brought Dipley to the county seat for questioning. The latter denied that he was in any way responsible for the killing, but, when it was proved that the rifle which he carried was the murder weapon, he broke down and confessed, saying that the reason for the act was that Ketchel had made improper advances toward Goldie.

Goldie was arrested and charged with murder. Under questioning she denied that she was the Goldie who had figured earlier in Ketchel's life. Instead she supported her sweetheart's story that the boxing champion had tried to make love to her and that she had told Dipley about it.

The trial was a lengthy one and at its conclusion the judge instructed the jury that Goldie Smith should be found guilty if she had encouraged the killing or had knowledge that it was going to take place. The jury was out a short time and returned with a verdict which found both Dipley and Goldie guilty of first-degree murder and the penalties were fixed at life imprisonment in the Missouri State Penitentiary.

The verdicts were appealed and the life sentence of the trigger man in the slaying was affirmed while the verdict against Goldie was upset and she was set free.

The strange woman who was the spark which set off the conflagration in which two men were consumed, disappeared from view and nothing more has been heard concerning her in the intervening thirty-two years. Whether she still lives or is dead is not known to this writer.

Down through the years Dickerson fought all attempts made by Dipley to obtain a parole, but on May 19th, 1934, Governor Guy B. Parks of Missouri granted Dipley his release from prison after he had served twenty-four years.

The body of Stanley Ketchel is buried in a cemetery near the Grand Rapids home in which he was born and the graveyard remains to this day a shrine where all true lovers of the boxing game still pay homage.

Glamorous Model,
A Wheeler-Dealer
& Death by Torture!

by George Carpozi, Jr.

When two New York homicide squads suddenly discovered they were working on the same killing, they pooled their information and narrowed their focus.

He is the first cousin of Patrice Jacobs, who with husband Louis Wolfson, wrote racing history last year with triple-crown winner Affirmed. Howard "Buddy" Jacobson himself had shaped some important marks on the thoroughbred turf in his time as the nation's Number One horse trainer. He had even surpassed his celebrated uncle, Hirsch Jacobs, Patrice's father.

Until 1970, the fast-talking, 39-year-old horseman stood on top of the racing world, after having come in with more winners than anyone in 1963, 1964, and 1965 — 509 first-places in that period alone.

But the Brooklyn-born Buddy Jacobson was never one to kneel at the altar of any four-legged critter. In his characteristic bluntness he'd say: "I don't like horses. Horses are dumb and I have no respect for them. In fact, I hate horses. I just like winning races with them . . . "

His reputation as a trainer ultimately catapulted Buddy to the presidency of the New York Division of the Horsemen's Protective and Benevolent Association.

The year was 1969. This would have been a propitious

time for Buddy to have suffered lockjaw as he served in that prestigious office. Instead, he cackled quite loudly that backstretch employees at the state's tracks were being shortchanged on pension benefits. So Jacobson called them out of their barns for a nine-day strike at Aqueduct Racetrack in New York City's borough of Queens.

Before the year was out, Jacobson was sorry he'd taken such precipitate action. The Establishment got his neck. But it would have been too obvious to have put the noose on Buddy for pulling the walkout. So they stuck the spurs into him in Maryland for allegedly misrepresenting the sale price of horses that had gone on the block and which he'd bought for his owners.

No sooner had he been suspended in the state where Spiro Agnew had practiced a few peccadillos of his own, than poor Buddy was put down by the New York Racing Association for 45 days. That, however, was not the real zonk. The NYRS also denied him stall space at the track — a major setback for Jacobson.

For all intents and purposes, that was the end of Buddy's racing days. For, without a barn to harbor a horse, well — would the Holiday Inn put up Seattle Slew in a bedroom for two if he was deprived of a stall at Santa Anita?

Although his career in racing was now at an end, Jacobson didn't leave the Sport of Kings poverty-stricken. He was well-heeled, so he went forth with his bundle, investing in real estate all over the landscape. Before long he discovered that apartment buildings churn up far better paydirt than horses' hooves. As he gobbled up land and buildings like a mad speculator, he was suddenly stalled in his tracks by the sight of a tawny, auburn-haired, eye-catching aspiring model named Melanie Cain — sweet, beautiful, only 18, and fresh out of high school in Naper-

55

ville, Illinois.

She had migrated to Fun City, as New York was called then in pre-Big Apple days, to launch her career. They met in Manhattan just after Buddy Jacobson's marriage of more than 20 years had busted up.

By now Buddy had acquired, among many other properties, a luxury seven-floor town house which he converted to apartments. He established himself in one of the two top-floor penthouses and rented the other one. In time, a businessman, John "Jack" Tupper, who had been living on the fifth floor, moved into the penthouse across the hall from Jacobson's.

That didn't happen, however, until early last summer, by which time Buddy and Melanie had established a long-standing relationship in their private and professional lives.

The first step Jacobson took after meeting Melanie was to bring her to live in his penthouse. Then she headed out in search of a job, but didn't welcome the blisters from walking, the cattle calls at the model agencies, and the rest of the hassle.

So Melanie and Buddy extended their private partnership on the seventh floor to a professional partnership into a vacant shop on the first floor. They opened a model agency and called it "My Fair Lady."

But the agency never went far. The major magazines, the fashion houses, and those others who call on agencies for models were never overly impressed with it. Melanie Cain, who'd made the cover of Redbook and had other successes, was the agency's top asset.

Buddy Jacobson wasn't concerned about the agency's lack of business. He was still pulling down thousands a month from his many properties. In fact, he was now on the verge of making it even bigger in real estate. For he had just recently bought the 10-story Park East Hospital after it closed, and he was converting it to residential apartments.

The building on East 83rd Street, between Lexington and Park Avenue, was a block away from his town house at 155 East 84th Street, lying between Lexington and Third Avenues.

In early July of last year, not long after Buddy's newest real estate acquisition, something happened in his relationship with Melanie. She packed her clothes and other belongings and moved out. But she didn't have far to go, for she took her things into the 34-year-old Jack Tupper's penthouse down the hall.

This arrangement continued until early Sunday morning of August 6th. That was when Melanie kissed Tupper goodbye and went off to look at an available apartment nearby. Object: rent it so she and Jack could move away from Jacobson. They didn't want to be near him because, they told friends, he was annoying them.

"He's been miserable to us," Melanie had told one of the downstairs tenants.

She had not explained in what way Buddy was getting on their nerves. And none of the tenants seemed to be concerned with the difficulties Melanie and Jack claimed they were having with Jacobson — until a few short hours after the model returned to the town house from her apartment-hunting excursion.

Melanie got off the elevator on the seventh floor and almost tripped over Jacobson, who was on his knees cutting a section of carpeting in front of the lift. It was spattered with fresh white paint.

"What happened?" asked Melanie, who was still on speaking terms with Buddy despite the tensions between

57

them.

"Some son of a bitch painter spilled his can and ruined the carpet. I'm taking it up. There's no way to clean it."

Melanie entered Tupper's penthouse and called his name. He didn't answer. She looked around, didn't find him, and decided he had probably gone jogging.

But after an hour had passed, she became concerned. She went downstairs and spoke to some of the other tenants, many of them models like herself. They had been discussing the mysterious death of a model who lived in the town house.

At 2:30 a.m. that Sunday, 20-year-old Cheryl Corey and her boyfriend, 22-year-old Scott Shepard, both fell from a 17-floor roof setback in an apartment building at 400 East 85th Street, about four blocks from the town house.

The iron rail apparently gave way when they leaned against it and they plunged to the roof of a street-level Great Way Foods supermarket at the corner of 84th Street and First Avenue.

Miss Corey, who had attended Philadelphia's Moore College of Arts and whose family lived in Cherry Hill, New Jersey, was killed instantly. But Shepard survived the fall because he landed on top of Cheryl. He suffered severe internal injuries and two shattered legs.

Melanie Cain was distressed to learn that Cheryl Corey had been killed and returned to the seventh floor to encounter even greater anxiety when she discovered that Jack Tupper still had not returned.

After reentering Tupper's apartment, calling his name, and being greeted by utter silence, Melanie went next door and rang the bell. Jacobson opened the door.

"Get out of here!" he bellowed.

Before he slammed the door shut, Melanie got a terrifying eyeful of disarray in the normally neat apartment.

Glass was broken on the floor, tables were overturned, a wall mirror was shattered, and blood was spattered on the floor.

Melanie fled back to Tupper's penthouse in panic. She began mulling over the thought of calling the police. But meanwhile . . .

A yellow late-model Cadillac had stopped beside an empty, weed-grown lot used to receive rubbish and garbage dumped by people who live in the area. The site was near Bartow Avenue, in the Bronx, close by the huge Co-Op City housing development.

A family of four — a husband, wife, and two children — were driving by that site at the very instant the late-model Cadillac had stopped beside the lot.

They saw two men pouring liquid on a crate and setting it afire. The men then disappeared over a mound of rubbish. Seconds later, the witnesses saw a yellow Caddy pull away.

The man behind the wheel of the family sedan noted the license plate of the Caddy and jotted it down on a piece of paper: 777-GHI, a New York State plate.

Then the family drove to the nearest firehouse, that of Ladder Company 61 in the Co-Op City section. There they encountered Fireman Dennis Smith, the author of best-selling book, *Report From Engine Company 82*, a story about the epidemic of fires that had reduced the South Bronx to America's most arson-ridden community.

Smith was told that the men started the fire and he was given the paper with the plate number of the Caddy.

As two fire engines headed for the fire, the family also returned to the scene. There a uniformed police officer questioned them and got a description of the car, as well as its plate number.

Why all that extraordinary interest in the yellow Caddy and the two men who dumped a crate and set it afire?

Because when the fire in the crate was extinguished, the firemen and police found the charred remains of a man inside!

The description of the yellow Caddy and its license plate was on the police air-waves for only a few minutes before a sector car from the 45th Precinct spotted the Caddy in heavy traffic on Bruckner Expressway and flashed a report on the radio.

Another cruiser from the 41st Precinct, a bit farther south in the Bronx, also sent a message that the patrolmen in that car had caught sight of the yellow Caddy, but congestion on the road thwarted pursuit.

Then another flash on the air alerted other units further down in the South Bronx that the car hadn't eluded the NYPD.

At precisely 5:05 p.m., the Caddy turned off the expressway at 138th Street and a blue-white police car bore down on the fugitive vehicle. That police car was but one of eight NYPD cruisers that surrounded the yellow Caddy at that critical moment.

The two men in the front seat were ordered out and made to spreadeagle against the car. As they stood, feet apart, hands on roof, they were frisked. No weapons were found.

They were asked for identifications. The diminutive, mustached man who had been driving the car identified himself as Howard Jacobson — the former famed horse trainer now turned real estate entrepreneur.

The man who was a passenger in the car said he was

Salvatore Giamo, a 22-year-old laborer from the Astoria section of Queens. Police were to learn later that he was an illegal Italian immigrant who had been working at odd jobs—including most recently at the former Park East Hospital which Jacobson was in the process of converting to apartments.

A police officer asked Jacobson where he'd been and where he was going with the Caddy.

"I was just trying out the car," he responded. "I was seeing if I liked the way the car drove. I was thinking of buying it . . ."

Giamo confirmed Jacobson's story. But when the cops checked license and registration, they found the car was owned by a Salvatore Prainito, 23, of Whitestone, also in Queens. As they were to learn shortly, Prainito was Giamo's cousin and also a laborer employed by Jacobson on the hospital conversion project.

Most significant about Giamo and Prainito, the authorities were to determine subsequently, is that they were both Italian nationals who had come to the United States several years ago and had overstayed their visas.

Jacobson and Giamo were taken to the Eighth Homicide Zone Detective Squad in the Bronx, where sleuths under the command of Lieutenant John J. Power, chief of the unit, attempted to question the suspects who were reported to have driven away from the scene of the burning crate containing a human corpse.

Jacobson protested during the questioning: "I've got nothing to hide . . . but I'm not going to answer any of your questions. I want to phone my lawyer. . . ."

He was allowed to make that call.

Giamo had nothing of any significance to add.

Detective William Sullivan, to whom Jacobson said he

had nothing to hide, ask him to sit tight.

"We'd like to look over your place," the detective said.

"Be my guest," Jacobson responded, handing the key to his penthouse to the detective.

Sullivan and other detectives drove to the town house on East 84th. They arrived to find four imposing-looking men standing in the doorway of John Tupper's seventh-floor penthouse, talking to a frantic, choked-up Melanie Cain. She was reciting her fears about Tupper's fate.

"He's disappeared!" she was saying. "That's not like him at all. I'm very concerned. All I know is that when I looked in Buddy Jacobson's apartment earlier this afternoon, I saw things in there that made me wonder . . ."

Before Melanie could finish that sentence, Detective Sullivan intruded: "That name you just mentioned, Jacobson — is that Howard Jacobson?"

"Yes, Howard Jacobson," Miss Cain replied, looking somewhat puzzled. She stared at Sullivan for a moment, then cast an eye at the other sleuths alongside him.

"Are you detectives, too?" she wanted to know.

Sullivan whipped out his gold shield and identified himself. "We're from the Eighth Homicide Zone in the Bronx," he said.

The men who'd been talking with Melanie broke into wide grins. One of them said, "Hey, Bill, we're from the Fourth Homicide Zone. We responded to this young woman's report that her friend was missing and that she suspects he might have been murdered . . ."

In what has to be one of the most unique coincidences in NYPD annals, the detectives from the Fourth Homicide Zone in Manhattan, headquartered on 82nd Street, were headed by Lieutenant John J. Power.

John and James Power just happen to be brothers.

And, as Detective Sullivan was to tell me later: "We bumped into each other . . . the detectives from the Bronx and the ones from Manhattan, and we sort of solved each other's cases in the hall."

Well, not exactly. The crime was apparently solved only after the detectives, opening the lock with the key Jacobson gave Detective Sullivan, entered the adjoining penthouse and had a look around Buddy's digs.

Some mysterious holes in the woodwork and walls of the apartment prompted the sleuths to ask the Scientific Research Division to send Ballistics Unit and Crime Scene Services Section detectives to the scene.

Those holes turned out to have been caused by .38-caliber bullets — the same slugs that were removed from the burned corpse found in the Bronx. Dr. Michael Baden, the city's chief medical examiner, who supervised the autopsy on the remains in the morgue in Manhattan, not only established the identity of the victim as John Tupper, but also determined the contributing causes of death.

The findings showed that Tupper had been the victim of a "brutal killing." The report said: "His skull was fractured and his face badly slashed by a knife. He was also shot seven times in the head and torso."

In the autopsy, three bullets were extracted from the charred remains — one from the skull and two from the chest. The other four bullets passed through the body and were later gouged out of the depths to which they had plowed in Jacobson's penthouse walls.

In addition to the bullets in the apartment, detectives turned up other critical evidence . . .

On the roof, the investigators found a throw rug that was said to belong to Melanie. She had taken it from its place in the center of Jacobson's living room when she moved in with Tupper, but he had not allowed her to install it in his apartment. He was a wood-lover and had no tolerance for any form of floor covering. So the rug was rolled up, tied, and placed against the wall on the seventh-floor landing.

But this rug was not where Melanie said she had stored it. Instead, it was on the roof. Although still rolled up, it was no longer tied. And when the police opened it — it was bloodstained.

At first blush, the cops theorized that after Tupper was slain in Jacobson's apartment, the body was wrapped in the rug and carried downstairs to the yellow Cadillac, deposited in the trunk, and driven to the Bronx, where it was dumped and set afire.

But there was only one flaw in that surprise. The body dumped in the Bronx lot happened to be in a wooden crate.

Only after the detectives entered John Tupper's apartment next door to Jacobson's, to check the place for clues, did they conclude on what role the tug had played. It apparently had been used only to haul the murdered man's body from Jacobson's flat into Tupper's. But it had not even served that function unflawed.

The body apparently had slipped out, police concluded, and fallen on the floor in front of the elevator. Thus, when Melanie Cain exited from the elevator shortly after noon after returning from her apartment-renting jaunt, the carpeting which Jacobson was removing was not stained by a painter's spilled white paint.

It had been soiled by the red blood of John Tupper's mortal remains after they fell out of the rug, the probers believed; and the white paint which Jacobson was cursing when Melanie stepped out of the elevator was only a cover-up. Something very red — presumably the blood of John

64

Tupper's body—had stained the rug. Something was needed to cover it over to make excuses for removing it. And the spilled paint served that function.

That piece of telltale evidence was disposed of, according to Jacobson at a much later time, at the steel trash bin in the street in front of the hospital Buddy was remodeling into apartments.

As police finally pieced together the sequence of events following John Tupper's torture slaying, the body was being carried in the rug only down the hall to Tupper's penthouse to be placed in one of several wooden gun crates that were in one of the rooms and being used for storage. The crates had been left behind by the previous occupant, a former Green Beret officer and veteran of the Vietnam war. He was a demolition expert and had brought the crates with him when he left the Army and moved into Jacobson's town house.

From the very start of tracing the progress of Tupper's body from Jacobson's apartment to the Bronx dumping ground, both the Eighth and the Fourth Homicide Squad detectives were in complete agreement that Howard had help, at least in disposing of the body—if not in the homicide itself.

And here is the role ascribed to those whom the sleuths believe participated in the crime:

After the murder, which police said occurred at about noon, Salvatore Prainito and Salvatore Giamo helped put Tupper's body into the crate, then hauled the crate down the stairs to the street. There they put the box into a van and drove away with it, with the understanding that Prainito would return to the hospital at 4:30 p.m. and pick up Jacobson so he could guide them to the dumping ground.

Meanwhile, detectives determined that Jacobson's 17-year-old son, Douglas, who had been living with his father since Melanie moved out, was left behind in the apartment to clean up the place.

The divorced Jacobson also had another son, David, who assumed the role his father abandoned at Aqueduct racetrack as a horse trainer.

The 4:30 p.m. rendezvous was established, authorities related, because that was quitting time at the hospital and Jacobson didn't want the other workers to suspect anything amiss by his absence.

Downstairs, Jacobson assertedly found Prainito waiting for his cousin Giamo's yellow Caddy. Prainito was in the passenger seat, the engine was running. Parked behind the Caddy with motor on was the van bearing the crate with Tupper's corpse. Giamo, police said, was in the driver's seat.

In his account of his activities that Sunday afternoon, Jacobson told police that when he left the hospital at 4:30 p.m., he met both Prainito and Giamo at First Avenue and 76th Street, a short walk from the hospital, and was given the ignition key by Giamo, whom Buddy quoted, "You take the car for a drive and when you get back, if I'm not here, give the keys to my brother-in-law. He's going along with you."

Buddy, who hadn't owned a car in five years, said he drove uptown to 96th Street, turned east to the Franklin Roosevelt Drive, then headed north, crossing the Willis Avenue Bridge into the Bronx. He then proceeded along Bruckner Expressway and followed it into the New England Thruway extension to the vicinity of Co-Op City.

Police didn't dispute the route he took, but they did not agree that this was just a leisurely drive to try out the car.

Jacobson, they said, had urgent business — to get rid of the body in the van.

It was raining when the Caddy and van reached the destination beside the empty, weed-grown lot used by people in the area as an illegal dump for garbage and rubbish.

The time was 4:55 p.m. when that family of four out on a Sunday drive spotted the two men pouring liquid on a crate and setting it afire. Then, after seeing the men drive off in the yellow Caddy, the husband drove to the nearby firehouse, reported the fire, and turned in the license number.

The question came up in Lieutenant John Power's mind about why the family had not also noticed the van. But as Detective Sullivan and the other sleuths deduced, the crate had already been dumped and the van driven away.

Thus, when the family spotted the two men — closing the trunk of the car before driving off — the early belief was that the crate had been hauled to the dump in the back of the Caddy. But after examining the trunk, police concluded there was no way the six-foot-long gun crate could have been hauled in there. Thus the conclusion that a van was used for that mission.

Let's get back to the town house and two other key discoveries of evidence that homicide sleuths had made in their search of Tupper's penthouse.

They turned up a telegram and a tape recording, both highly incriminating, in light of the train of events of that Sunday, August 6th . . .

The telegram found in Tupper's apartment had been sent on July 29th from Alexandria, Virginia, where Buddy Jacobson had been visiting, and it said:

"Sorry for the past week and for the abuse I must have put you through for the past five years. You always hurt the

67

one you love. Jack [John Tupper] is a good guy and will love you and be honest with you. You're right, I would always be a bum. Believe me when I tell you that I had no idea, in spite of all the hints you gave me that we would ever part, but it is best. Excuse me if I slip and think of old times once in a while, but if I didn't care would I feel this way? 'Sounds like a song.' "

The message was signed, "Your best pal, Fred."

Tupper's brother, Kevin, who found the telegram as he and other family members removed personal belongings from the apartment said: "Fred was another nickname for Jacobson . . ."

The tape recording was a revelation. It was a desperate plea to John Tupper, who had apparently taped his conversation with Jacobson, unaware of what was happening.

"Listen, Jack," the voice said, "you forget Melanie . . . you give her up . . . and I'll set you up in business. You want to go back in the restaurant business? Well, I'll set you up. I'll give you a hundred thou . . . How does that sound?"

"No way," the response came. "You take that money and you know what you can do with it. No deal, no way . . ."

With that evidence, Lieutenant John Power, the Bronx homicide chief, decided it was enough to book Howard Jacobson for murder.

Next day at his arraignment, Jacobson was held in $200,000 bail. And although he had the resources to post as security against the bond, he was not released until many weeks later. The reason: Bronx District Attorney Mario Merolla repeatedly opposed Jacobson's freedom on grounds that his freedom would invite his assassination. Merolla gave no specifics on why anyone would want to do away with Buddy, yet he insisted Jacobson would be unsafe if released. I visited Buddy Jacobson during this period of his incarceration in the Bronx County Jail in the shadows of Yankee Stadium where the Bronx Bombers were battling their way to a second successive American League pennant and the championship in the world Series.

"All I want is to have a chance to speak to Melanie Cain," Buddy told me. "If I can only talk to her, I'll get her to tell me who really killed Jack Tupper . . ."

Bronx lawyer Otto Fusco finally obtained Jacobson's release on bail after fortifying the bond with the security of Buddy's real estate holdings.

In the meantime, Buddy Jacobson was indicted by a grand jury for Tupper's killing. The indictment came after both Salvatores, Prainito and Giamo, had refused to answer questions before the grand jury.

No sooner had he been released from his Bronx County Jail confinement, Jacobson went into hiding. He did not return to his penthouse because, as he told me in a telephone interview: I'm terrified. They're out to get me and I'm not going to let them. So, until the trial, you will neither see nor hear from me."

Meanwhile, Prainito and Giamo have been charged by the Immigration and Naturalization Service with overstaying their visas, but deportation was out of the question because of their purported roles in the murder case.

Authorities were still weighing further action against the cousins as *True Detective* went to press. Some time later in the year, Howard Jacobson's murder trial will be held in Bronx County Court. And I'll be there to cover the proceedings for TD readers . . .

Rolling Stones
Rock Festival
Murder Case

by Bryan Williams

It took a fantastic amount of incredible detective work to crack.

Can a man be callously knifed to death in front of at least 300,000 witnesses and his slayer get away without being caught?

The answer is "no," a California grand jury decided in March, 1970. But for slightly more than two months, it appeared the impossible had happened — a murder before the largest public gathering in the area in a decade and no solution by law enforcement agencies.

The credit for not letting the impossible happen must be given to the Alameda County Sheriff's Department and its chief, Sheriff Frank Madigan. And for a sheriff's department to emerge with top billing in a drama that featured such internationally acclaimed rock music groups as England's Rolling Stones, Santana, Jefferson Airplane, Crosby, Stills, and Nash, it took quite a performance. But the sheriff's men were capable of such a performance. As the turned-on group would have expressed it, they were "right on, man — right on!"

This most improbable of homicides and investigations began with just the slightest confusing vibration in November, 1969, in New York City, a continent away from where murder was to occur a month later.

In New York, the nine Rolling Stones announced that they planned to hold a free concert on the West Coast, probably in San Francisco's lush Golden Gate Park, as a reward for fans who had made their most recent American tour a smashing success. The announcement reached San Francisco via the press wire services, but it did not create much of a stir.

The Stones, however, never really firmed up any arrangements with San Francisco. A group purporting to represent the rock group held exploratory talks with officials of the city's Recreation and Park Commission, but no request was ever made to hold one of the biggest balls in history in Golden Gate Park. Not that the park could not have handled the job, it once accommodated half a million people in a religious festival.

November passed into December, with announcements continuing that the Stones planned to hold a minor Woodstock West in Golden Gate Park. The date was to be Sunday, December 7th, the 28th anniversary of the bombing attack on Pearl Harbor and America's entry into World War II.

Confusion was more evident four days before the event. The Stones advance arrangements group then announced the concert would not be in the park after all. Instead, it would be held 50 miles away, across San Francisco Bay at the Sears Point Raceway. And it would not be held on Sunday; it would be pushed up to a day earlier.

In many ways, the new scene was ideal for the holding of a rock festival. The raceway was in the flat marshland of Sonoma County, near the merging point of the wide Sacramento and San Joaquin Rivers. In a sense it was an isolated, off-the-beaten-path setting and the race track with

71

its parking lot and uncluttered surroundings could easily have accommodated Woodstock's audience plus 100,000 more.

The festival was still supposed to be free to the public, with the Rolling Stones picking up the tab for raceway leasing and even the salaries of the other rock groups scheduled to appear on the program. There was even talk of a contribution to war victims of Vietnam.

Slightly more than 72 hours before curtain time, the rock festival again was homeless. The Stones and the race track management announced that Sears Point was out as a setting. Reasons for the abrupt cancelation remain cloudy, but the Stones since have filed an $11,000,000 damage suit against the raceway.

Advance men for the festival again went scene hunting. The search took them to Alameda County, 25 miles south of the raceway and in the law enforcement domain of Sheriff Madigan. Again an auto race track caught the fancy of the advance men. This was the Altamont Speedway.

Unless one had been a fan of stock car racing, destruction derbies, and midget auto racing, Altamont Speedway would not have been a household word. Prior to the rock festival its largest crowd had been 6,500 patrons.

The speedway sits in a bowl formed by the rolling hills at the end of Altamont Pass, a four-lane freeway leading up and over 1,000-foot mountains to the interior valleys of California.

With its adjoining 80 acres of hillside and grassland, it is undeniable that the speedway was capable of accommodating a rock festival crowd of 300,000. It did just that, and one person in that crowd was a killer.

The agreement between the wandering festival and the

Altamont Speedway management was reached early Friday, one day before the festival was to be held.

The logistics were formidable. An elaborate stage for the performing groups had been almost completed at the Sears Point race track, 65 miles to the north of Altamont. It was dismantled and trucked to the new scene. Helicopters were chartered to transport the delicate amplifying equipment.

As chill dusk set in with concert time less than 14 hours away, all was confusion at Altamont. But order was emerging from the confusion. The steel towers to carry the vibes from the big amplifiers had been bolted together and raised. The stage of plywood floorboards on steel scaffolding was almost complete. The generator to supply the lighting was whirring away. And trucks bearing portable toilet booths were arriving.

The first of the crowd, which would swell the following day to the largest ever assembled in California for a rock music performance, was already arriving on the hillsides. They were the young and they came in campers mounted on pickup trucks, gaily painted Volkswagen buses, some on motorcycles, and the majority in automobiles.

They parked on the hillsides and spread bedrolls on the ground. Campfires glowed. Some slept in battered auto hulks left from past disaster derbys at the speedway. And there was much more going on, the men from Sheriff Madigan's Department were to find out later.

The peregrinations of the festival certainly were enough to complicate a law enforcement official's life, if not drive him to madness. They gave him no time to make any reasonable crowd control plans. And, with the festival being held on private property, Sheriff Madigan was denied the opportunity to send officers there except by invitation, which was not being extended by the festival promoters.

The promoters had announced via the newspapers, that they planned to have adequate security forces and there was one report that they planned to jet 100 off-duty New York City policemen to Altamont for the day.

At a disadvantage from the start, the sheriff's department took all the precautions possible. Leaves were cancelled, roadways to the speedway were hastily posted in an attempt to keep illegal parkers off private property, and the machinery for the mutual assistance pact by which other police agencies could be called to help, was readied for action. Then the sheriff's department waited out the few grim hours until the start of the festival.

Even as the deputies waited, the violence of death was beginning at Altamont, where at least 10,000 camped on the hillsides.

Two young men from New Jersey, Mark Seiger and Richard Salov, both 22, were in a group ringing a campfire near a road. There was another young man and a pretty young woman in the campfire group. The young woman had brought her infant child to the festival. None of them saw the auto as it sped from the roadway through the campfire, knocking down all in its path. Salov and Seiger were killed. The young man and young woman were near death from injuries. Somehow, the infant had not been harmed.

The driver never slowed as he lurched through a swaying turn and sped back to the roadway. The few campers who had seen the death auto could describe it as possibly a 1964 Plymouth sedan. No one had gotten the license number. But everyone seemed certain the driver was on a "bad trip," LSD variety.

The thin sun came up on a scene of movement never before equalled in the western United States. Like fabled lemmings moving inexorably to the sea, the young rock music buffs surged through Altamont Pass to the speedway. To say it caused the greatest traffic jam in the state's history is to understate a truth. Frustrated rock fans began parking on the forbidden shoulders of the freeway and even usurped the middle dividing strip. Under construction and almost completed was a quarter-mile of multi-lane turnoff that would connect with the interior valley freeway system leading to Los Angeles. This was converted in desperation by the Highway Patrol into a bumper-to-bumper parking lot. But it couldn't handle the flood that spilled over to all adjacent highways.

One car caravan of fans took a back road supposedly delivering them to the speedway. They stopped where the road ended and walked eight miles to their destination.

A helicopter pilot was later to describe the 300,000 on the hillside as "a great brown moving mass—so many it was unbelievable."

Death occurred again at the beginning of the festival. But it was self-destruction rather than murder. The speedway site was skirted by the wide, concrete-lined canal of the California Water Project, which takes water the length of a state for irrigating the southern area.

As a deputy sheriff pleaded with a youth to climb back over the protecting chain link fence, the youth slid down the steep concrete lining wall of the swift-flowing canal and sank beneath the water. There was no chance for rescue and almost a week passed before the canal surrendered the body.

The Altamont score for death stood at three when Santana, first of the performing groups, grooved into the loud vibes of the first melody of their "set" of a dozen melodies.

The day passed with Jefferson Airplane belting out its set, the Flying Burrito Brothers doing their musical thing, followed by a half score more famed groups. Darkness was setting in as the Rolling Stones, wealthiest and most famed of the groups, prepared for their finale number.

It had been a nightmarish day for officers trying to bring some sort of order to the freeway. Rubber-necking motorists slowed to almost complete halts to view the vast crowd visible on the hillsides. That caused a chain reaction of slowing. The Highway Patrol called in tow cars, which began moving hundreds of illegally parked cars off the highway. It was futile, because there weren't enough tow cars in all California to clear that jam.

In the dusk, in the glare of floodlights, the Rolling Stones began their throbbing set of melodies. Their reward was an ovation and the Altamont free rock concert was finished and became a part of history. It was immediately followed by the most monumental of traffic jams. But then came the murderous footnote to Altamont.

At 10:50 p.m. a corpse was delivered by deputy sheriffs to the Alameda County Coroner's office in Oakland, 27 miles to the north of the speedway.

The dead man — he really was a boy rather than man — had been brought from Altamont. He had literally been punched to death with an extremely sharp instrument. There was a deep gash in the left temple. He had been stabbed in the right neck. In addition, there were, according to Senior Coroner's Investigator Roland W. Prahl, "numerous stab wounds in the back."

One wound was near the spine. It had penetrated the rib cage and terminated in an area where several large arteries criss-crossed. The severance of any one artery could cause death within but a very few minutes. It was apparent the dead youth had little or no chance for life after that wound.

The young man was black. He had been slim and of medium height. His clothes were those of modern youth. Especially rock-oriented youth. The slacks were bell bottom and wide. The shirt was a splash of many colors.

The sheriff's deputies who brought the body to the coroner's office had taken delivery of it from one of the many doctors who had volunteered to man first aid stations at the rock festival.

There was no great mystery to the youth's identity. Papers in a wallet indicated his name was Meredith Hunter, his age 18, and home address in a residential section of Berkeley not too many blocks distant from the University of California.

But there was the mystery of who and why a knife had been plunged into the youth. And the call from the morgue was to the Eden Township Station of the sheriff's department and Detectives James Chisholm and James Donovan.

The detectives were members of the Sheriff's Crimes Against People Detail, the bureau charged with keeping its jurisdiction free of the deadly acts ranging from mugging to murder. The detail was stationed, not in the crowded metropolitan Oakland headquarters of the sheriff's department, but in the sub-station in the community of San Leandro, eight miles to the south of Oakland. But although the sub-station bore the rustic sounding name of Eden Township, it was not a rustic detail.

The offices are modern, the men experienced. Detective Chisholm was a veteran of 12 years investigative experience. Detective Donovan had served 19 years in the sheriff's department, 11 years spent in the uniform patrol division. Before the investigation into the murder at Altamont was complete, Detective Chisholm was promoted to lieutenant.

At the moment of beginning the investigation, it would be fair to believe that neither detective would have wagered on a chance for future promotion. They were faced with a homicide, hours old, and committed in the presence of hundreds of thousands of witnesses who had scattered to the four compass points. Even the Rolling Stones were, at the moment jet-borne to their homeland across the Atlantic.

Meredith Hunter's teenage sister had made her way to the Oakland morgue in the post midnight hours. There she had positively identified the dead youth as her brother. It had been a terrifying experience for the young girl. Her brother had attended the rock festival with a group of friends, including his teenage girl friend.

One of the friends had called the apartment Hunter shared with his mother and sister and had informed the family that young Meredith had been injured. The friend didn't have too many details — something about a brawl and Hunter had been carried away on a stretcher.

The worried sister began checking the numerous hospitals in the vicinity of the festival. Not one had a patient remotely resembling the youth. Then the sister had made her call to the morgue.

Meredith Hunter seemed a most unlikely candidate for homicide. He had never had a brush with police, and as a schoolboy in Berkeley, he had been a credit to his family and school. His sister confided to investigators that he had owned a pistol, but this was not a surprising circumstance when one considers that Berkeley has become known as the riot and violence center of a nation. Also, the sister said that to her knowledge, the brother had never carried the gun from the home.

Like millions of teenagers, he had become a rock music fan and had attended the earlier, well organized and perfectly policed festival at Monterey, 80 miles away on the California coastline. On the Saturday of the Altamont festival, Hunter had awakened early and had joined his friends for the bumper-to-bumper ride in an automobile to the speedway.

The information led Detectives Chisholm and Donovan inevitably to the girl friend of the slain youth and to the half dozen in the party. There was not too much information available about the fatal assault—the festival fans had become separated in the throng. But there was a great deal of information proving that Altamont had been no universal love feast.

It was, in fact, the bummiest of bummers.

The dope dealing, according to the festival fans, had begun in the evening before the festival. First it had been free offerings—pot, LSD, reds, bennies, speed crystals and even a smattering of brown smack heroin. If pushers were afraid this generosity would put them out of business for the next day their fears were groundless. They were able to peddle bennies at $1 a pill, the same for reds, and speed fetched $3 and $5, depending on whether the customer wanted a "three cent" or "nickel" bag.

From helicopter height, the pall from marijuana looked like the smoggiest day ever in Los Angeles. As one freakout put it, "Man! smell that good merchandise!"

The biggest surprise to that unbelievably large crowd was the security force which was to make all safe for the performers and listeners. It was not the promised detail of

100 off-duty policemen from New York. It was a band of at least 50 Hells Angels, who rode their snarling motorcycles through the crowd, running down any who stood in the way.

The Angels rode double, with their "old ladies" clinging behind them on the motorcycles. When a young chick in the crowd expressed her resentment at being clipped by a cyclist, the rider said to the woman in the rear: "You gonna let her talk about an Angel that way?"

The "old lady" dismounted and cuffed the chick squarely in the mouth. She remounted and sped away with her beefy, soiled consort.

With apologies to none, the Angels buzzed their bikes right up to the stage and parked in a line in front.

Bearded, unkempt, muscular, the Angels were wearing their "colors," a winged death head insigne on the backs of their sleeveless jackets and an array of lettering declaring the wearer as a "HELLS ANGEL," plus more lettering announcing his home community or state.

There was a moment of shock when one of the musicians of Jefferson Airplane took the microphone and said grandly:

"Will the Hells Angels please take the stage."

The Angels did just that brandishing their security weapons, which were sawed-off, lead-weighted billiard cues. A grizzled news photographer, a veteran of all the Berkeley street and campus riots, observed:

"It was like appointing the wolves to guard the sheep."

And who appointed the band of motorcycle misfits to act as policemen? Detectives Chisholm and Donovan were later to establish that one of the managers of the Rolling Stones had agreed to supply the Angels with $500 worth of beer if they would provide security.

80

The use of Angels in that capacity was not unknown to the Rolling Stones. They had used the Angels as police in a rock festival in England. But those were English Angels and as different from American Angels as kippers and hot dogs.

What happened afterward was strictly a bad trip. Some of the Berkeley street people had strewn yellow bennies, LSD tabs, and red downers across the stage ramp. The Angels helped themselves, washing them down with liberal swigs of cheap red wine.

Wine at the festival was bigger than drugs. After the combos and their fans departed Altamont, a cleanup crew estimated there were half a million empty gallon jugs on the hillsides.

The young and disenchanted rock fans told the sheriff's detectives how, as the electric guitars throbbed, the Hells Angels had systematically turned what had been billed as a love festival into a carnival of violence.

Anyone approaching the stage, said the young witnesses, was struck, preferably on the head, with a sawed-off pool cue. Sneering Angels were indiscriminate. A chick as well as a stud suffered a bloody head. Someone set an Angel's motorcycle afire. That called for mass head-knocking by Angels of those within range near the stage.

As the Jefferson Airplane swung into mid-part of its melodic set, Angels surged across the stage, pool cues on high. One musician protested the beating of a young black man, whose only crime was enjoying the music. The musician reeled away from the pool cues aimed his way. Angel boots were used on victims. They even turned their violence inward, pouncing on a neophyte member hoping to become a full-fledged Angel. The neophyte was beaten solidly for several minutes but almost miraculously he regained his feet and protested to all that he held no grudge against his tormentors and only wished to win full membership in the outlaw band.

When one questions how such a small band of thugs cowed such a huge throng, the answer is easily supplied by the detectives. The Angels were organized. The crowd was not. From vast experience, the men of Sheriff Madigan's department were aware that the lone Hells Angel is a negligible force. He has never been noted for bravery. But in the mass, Angels display a bullying bravado. And with an absence of police to curb their predatory ways, they were bully boys indeed.

The respect of Hells Angels for police in the San Francisco and Alameda County areas is not a feigned thing. Past encounters have put the fear, if not of God, at least of police uniforms in the Angels. They usually mute their motorcycles and doff their colors when traveling through the areas.

And from the sickening account of the bad day at Altamont emerged a nugget of very usable information. That was the repeated reference to the moving picture crews that seemed to be photographing everything that happened.

Checking with the management of the speedway, Detectives Chisholm and Donovan learned that the free festival had been less charitable than first supposed. The Rolling Stones had commissioned a movie of the rock festival. They were to be the stars. Thus the Altamont scene was a huge movie set, with the 300,000 fans cast as unpaid extras.

A New York movie film company had accepted the assignment at Altamont. The detectives learned that 17 crews had been assigned to the festival. The crews had been easily identifiable by the cameramen's khaki hats with yellow stripes painted in the center. Ironically, each crew had a small squad of Hells Angels assigned as a protective force.

Long distance contact with the movie company established that there had been three crews zooming in on stage during the Stones' performance. The company's manager said he would be glad to screen the thousands of feet of film, a project that might take many days, and forward to the officers any footage that appeared to have a bearing on the stabbing of Meredith Hunter.

Less than a week had elapsed before the detectives experienced the second "break" of importance. It was the statement of a young man who said he had been a witness to the killing. The youth had come to the officers but he was not an altogether willing witness. He believed the fate of Meredith Hunter might be awaiting him if the slayer learned about his cooperation with the sheriff's department.

As a guarantee of protection Detectives Donovan and Chisholm have kept his identity secret.

The youth, however, told the officers he was but three feet away from Hunter as both stood in front of the stage just left of center in the early evening. The youth said he did not know Hunter but had noticed him as both he and the murder victim gazed up at Mick Jagger, most famed of the Rolling Stones, as he sang and cavorted in a wild-colored antic costume before the microphone.

The youth told officers he recalled seeing a Hells Angel, fat, long-haired and wearing Angel colors, reach down from the stage and give Hunter's hair and ear a lusty tug, laughing as he did it. The youth said there was no apparent reason for the Angel's acts.

The black youth, said the witness, broke away from the Angel's grip. The fat Angel, according to the youth, smashed Hunter in the mouth. Hunter reeled backward into the mass of humanity clustered in front of the stage. The Angel, said the youth, was right after Hunter. More Angels then began piling into the growing melee.

Hunter, according to the youth, tried to run through the crowd. He had uttered not a word to his tormentors. As the mass in front of the stage watched, said the youth, one of the Angels in the pack flashed a knife aloft and buried it in young Hunter's back.

Although wounded, Hunter suddenly produced a pistol, a long-barreled, shiny affair, and waved it aloft. The youth told the officers the act seemed more a showing-off of the weapon than a threat.

But the fans, said the youth, screamed at Hunter "not to shoot." An Angel wrested the pistol from the black youth. Hunter tried to bolt back in the direction of the stage but he fell on his knees. An Angel kicked him in the face. He was stabbed repeatedly and Meredith Hunter slumped to the ground. He then uttered his first and last statement to his tormentors:

"I wasn't going to shoot you."

The witness remembered that the Rolling Stones had stopped their wild melodies and the musicians peered apprehensively in the direction of the bloody scuffle. The youth said he and another young man had used their own hands to wipe away some of the blood from Hunter's wounds and then had tried to lift him up to stage level so the gravely wounded youth could be taken quickly to the first aid station tent in the rear of the stage.

The Hells Angels barred the way saying, "Take him around some other way." Someone added: "He's going to die anyway."

It had taken 15 minutes for those carrying Hunter to make their way through the jam of humanity to the aid station. By that time there was nothing the doctor who had volunteered his services could do. He didn't have the proper equipment, and there had been too much loss of blood. Meredith Hunter died minutes later.

Mick Jagger, at the microphone, had signaled for a halt to the music. Ironically the Stones were playing "Sympathy."

Jagger pleaded with the vast crowd to be "cool." He had seen the bloody hands of those who had wiped the gore from Hunter's wounds and had called for a doctor to tend someone who was "hurt." Rolling Stone Keith Richard stepped to the microphone. Indicating the rampaging Angels, Richard said:

"Either those cats cool it, man, or we don't play!"

An Angel lurched to the microphone and bellowed, "you!"

The Stones deemed it cool enough to continue their set. Finally they ended with one of their best selections, which had the most unfortunate title for the occasion. It was "Street Fighting Man."

The young witness to the killing was asked to describe the Angel wielding the knife. He was not the fat one who started the scuffle, replied the youth. He was well built, but smaller. He was young, probably in his early 20s. The witness remembered the most striking thing about the killer was his hair. It had been dark and long, but the man also had been balding. In fact, said the witness, the hair had hung from the beginning fringe of baldness at the back of his head.

The witness said he would never forget the killer. He

would know him if he ever saw him again. But, unfortunately, he had no idea of the slayer's identity at the moment.

Christmas, 1969, passed without the slayer of Meredith Hunter in custody. The new year came. But it was not idle time for Detectives Donovan and Chisholm. For one thing, they were suffering eye strain from gazing at movies of Altamont on the murder day.

Most interesting to the officers was a nearly four-minute sequence. It had been taken by a camera stationed 50 feet in front of the stage. But a zoom-in lens had made things as plain as three feet away.

The film sequence was, as the rock fans would say, "right on" what the detectives had been told by the young witness to the slaying. It showed the beginning of the brawl started by the fat Angel. It showed Hunter trying to flee and it showed a smaller, jacket-wearing Angel plunging a knife in the back of the retreating black youth. The film showed the victim's mouth open in what undeniably was a shriek of anguish. It showed Hunter drawing his gun and waving it ineffectually. It ended showing Hunter and his attackers struggling and sinking out of sight of the camera below the level of the stage, a stage on which the Rolling Stones were gazing in the direction of violence in baffled hesitation.

The film presented the detectives with their murder, but not their murderer. Identification would still be the problem. Moving picture frames have none of the clarity of still pictures. What flickers on screen with perfection is grainy, flawed, and indistinct when converted into a blown-up black and white photograph.

It happened that way in many of the frames of the killing sequence. But not in all. From one in particular there emerged the face of a Hells Angel, young, with dark hair receding but still trailing to almost shoulder length from the balding spot at the back of his head. The face was distorted in a grimace of the man exerting himself committing murder.

The only remaining problem was to identify the man in the photograph. And what a problem that turned out to be!

Detectives Chisholm and Donovan cannot give exact details of the solution. There is a murder trial in preparation and there are many prohibitions in today's law against peace officers talking about their profession.

But the officers have been able to give a peek at what effort goes into naming a criminal. They spent days tracing and questioning Hells Angels. It was frustrating, for Angels were not and are not the most cooperative witnesses. To listen to a Hells Angel, one would be asked to believe the Altamont festival was the best and most gentle of times. And the Angels were near unanimous in their avowals that their conduct had been firm but humanitarian. If murder had been committed, it certainly was not the fault of the Angels said the Angels.

There were other avenues open to the detectives. There were the illegal parking citations placed on the hundreds of autos towed away from the festival. They were a source of names and addresses of those present at the festival. And the car owners were spread all over California and in many other states of the union. The detectives decided to concentrate on the California registrations.

It brought them into contact with more than 1,000 of the 300,000 rock fans at the festival. It wasn't all personal contact. The detectives had to rely on the cooperation of more than two dozen police departments in communities as far south as San Diego on the Mexican border and Crescent City to the north on the Oregon border. It was willing cooperation but still the detectives spent many hours on the road driving to personal follow-ups of contacts made by others.

At some point in the marathon questioning the name of "Al" began to emerge as the possible slayer. Then the surname "Pisaro" or "Pasaro" or even "Passaro" was added to the Al.

There was a grudging admission from the Angels that the club membership included an Al Passaro in the Angels' San Jose "choir."

San Jose is a sprawling community of 100,000 residents 33 miles to the south of Altamont. The address given for Passaro did not prove helpful to the detectives. It was a vacant lot in San Jose.

But the records of the San Jose Police Department were more enlightening. According to the record, the suspect's full name was Alan David Passaro. He was 21, weighed 150 pounds, and stood 5 feet 10 inches. His hair was dark brown and his skin swarthy.

Passaro had first been arrested as a teenager for auto theft. He had been sent to Juvenile Hall. Five years later he was arrested for the same crime and fined $250 and placed on two years probation.

That same year he was arrested for assaulting a San Jose police officer and resisting arrest. He was acquitted of those charges.

The following year Passaro was arrested on suspicion of possessing explosives but again, the charges were dropped. One month later he posted bail after being charged with possession of marijuana and dangerous drugs. While still on bail, he was arrested again in San

Jose on charges of receiving stolen property, grand theft, and conspiracy. Again bail was posted. Passaro was free on double bail at the time of the slaying at Altamont.

Twenty days after the rock festival slaying, and while Detectives Chisholm and Donovan were in the first stages of the mostly frustrating investigation, Alan David Passaro had been brought into court and sentenced to state prison on a variety of charges stemming from his last series of arrests. California law specifies indeterminate sentences and Passaro's prison term could run 20 years.

But it was a sentence which provided the detectives with an exact address where Passaro could be found. That was, the Hells Angel's cell in Soledad State Prison, where the majority of California's rough young criminals are kept in conditions of rigid security.

Detectives Donovan and Chisholm went to the Soledad Prison and brought Alan Passaro to Alameda County Jail. The Hells Angel suspect no longer was the black-jacketed, swaggering man of the motorcycles. Passaro looked awfully square, the result of prison barbering and tailoring.

Nevertheless, the enforced return to Squaresville was not enough disguise to stop him from being identified as the man in the movies of the killing. The young witness, who said he would never forget the face of the slayer, identified Passaro as the man he had seen scuffling with Meredith Hunter in the front of the Altamont stage.

On March 24, 1970, Detective Donovan and, by then, Lieutenant Chisholm, took the results of their investigation to the Alameda County Grand Jury. The jurors peered at the film of the slaying, heard testimony from nine selected witnesses, and voted to indict Alan David Passaro on one count of murder, a crime which can carry the death penalty upon conviction in California.

It had been 110 days since Meredith Hunter had been butchered to death at Altamont. It had been 110 days since Detectives Donovan and Chisholm had begun their investigation.

Arnold Rothstein:
The Gambler Who Was
Too Smart To Live

by Peter Mathews

Rothstein's first mistake was trying to welsh on $361,000 worth of markers. His second mistake was bragging that he'd never pay off.

In the waning years of the 1920s the older generation, from one end of the country to the other, was convinced that America had become Sodom and Gomorrah reborn. It was the decade of Prohibition, when everyone broke the law with impunity, fattening the coffers of bootleg booze barons who became multimillionaire warlords dealing in violence and death and official corruption. It was the era of short skirts, the flapper, the Charleston and rah-rah college boys in raccoon coats who flouted the moral conventions of generations past. It was a boom period for Wall Street, when speculators became millionaires overnight. It was a glad-handing, free-wheeling, high-spending ten years when the national motto might have been changed from "E Pluribus Unum" to "Easy Come, Easy Go."

On the night of November 4, 1928, a dapper, tallish man in his middle 40s was summoned to the telephone from his table in a Broadway restaurant, a well known rendezvous for the sporting and theatrical crowd. When he returned to the table he slipped a .38 revolver to a friend and said, "That was McManus. I'm going over to see him. If anybody asks for me, I'll be back in half an hour."

The speaker was Arnold Rothstein, known to Broadway and the underworld as "The Brain," gambler extraordinary, loan shark to big time hoodlums, evil mastermind of the infamous "Black Sox" World Series fix, head of a narcotics syndicate, a man with his fingers in many pies, none of them legal. Only a few weeks before Rothstein had written markers, or IOUs, totaling $361,000 for losses he suffered one night in a card game. The men to whom he had lost this money were unsentimental citizens who did not take kindly to any delay in being paid.

Yet Arnold Rothstein, supremely arrogant and a law unto himself, had announced he would never pay off. A lesser man would have been quaking like a bowl of jelly in fear of the special forms of retribution designed for welshers, but as Rothstein walked the few blocks from the restaurant to the Park Central Hotel that night, unescorted, the matter of his 361 Gs in markers was the farthest thing from his mind.

His concern, rather, was for the one and a half million dollars he had bet on Herbert Hoover to defeat New York Governor Al Smith for the Presidency in the election the next day. This was one of the few times Rothstein had ever bet substantial money on the outcome of an event he could not personally control, but even in this case, he had not left matters entirely to chance. On the contrary, he had ordered his henchmen to canvass every state in the Union, sounding out public opinion and weighing the trend of political feeling as carefully as any modern day pollster. When the results of this survey were in, Rothstein decided Smith didn't have a ghost of a chance to move into the white mansion on Washington's Pennsylvania Avenue, and he backed his opinion with a million and a half clams.

As even the most casual student of American history knows, Herbert Hoover defeated Al Smith; Rothstein won his bet. By one of those quirks of chance which all heavy losers dream about, he never collected his winnings.

For, about 10 minutes after leaving the Broadway restaurant to keep his appointment in Room 349 of the Park Central, someone blasted a slug from a .38 into Arnold Rothstein and 12 hours later he was dead.

And as all Broadway hipsters know, nobody—but nobody—has to pay off to a dead man.

New York City's police department in recent years has become known as one of the finest in the world, but it was not always so, through no fault of the great majority of the men who filled its ranks. In 1928 it was next to impossible for honest cops to do their jobs; Jimmy Walker was mayor and he would serve for four more graft-ridden years before the corruption of his administration caught up with him and he was forced to resign and flee the country. The police department, during his regime, was politically infested and controlled; and many of the politicians, as later investigations proved, had been on Arnold Rothstein's payroll.

It came as no surprise to anyone, therefore, that the investigation of the gambler's death got absolutely nowhere. After he was shot, Rothstein managed to make his way out of the hotel, clutching the wound in his abdomen. Bystanders, seeing his condition, called police, who reached him just as he collapsed on the sidewalk on the 56th Street side of the hotel. He was rushed to Polyclinic Hospital, only a few blocks away, and detectives maintained a vigil at his bedside until he died.

But it was fully 10 hours after the shooting before police headquarters was even notified of the gunplay! And when it finally was reported, the conduct of the investigation was a marvel of ineptitude. For example, no one thought of taking Rothstein's fingerprints at any time, either while he was gasping out his life in Polyclinic, when his body went to the morgue, or while he lay in a funeral parlor before he was interred.

His fingerprints were not on file anywhere, and without them, it was next to impossible even to prove he had been in Room 349 where the shooting took place. In later years, when the facts became known, there were wholesale firings and resignations from the police force, but at the time, as newspapers of the day pointed out, it was painfully apparent that there was a strange official reluctance to probe too deeply into the facts behind Arnold Rothstein's murder.

The answer, if ever it was to be found, would have to come from somewhere along the twisted trail of Rothstein's astonishing career.

The son of an honest and well-to-do cotton manufacturer, Arnold Rothstein was born in New, York City on January 24, 1882, which made him almost 47 when he died. Boyhood chums remembered him as the best crapshooter in the neighborhood, and later as a talented pool player. The only legitimate job he ever held was a brief tenure as a salesman in his father's employ. This ended in Chicago, on his first road trip, when he gambled away not only his expense money but his sample cases and their contents as well.

"There are some things you can't explain," A.R. said of this incident, "and knowing my father, I never tried. I managed to get back to New York and got a job selling cigars. Since this took me into the poolrooms, I began laying my salary on the horses. That taught me a lesson in how not to make money."

He wound up eventually as a member of a political club which was a hangout for New York's biggest gamblers, and from such fellow members as Bald Jack Rose, Dago Frank, Bridgie Weber and Gyp the Blood, young Rothstein received a liberal education that enabled him to give full expression to his larcenous instincts in any direction.

Extremely vain, he dressed like a fashion plate. Socially ambitious, he tried to cultivate celebrities, such as playwright and wit Wilson Mizner, actor John Barrymore, and well-known newspapermen. A name-dropper, he was fond of referring to such people as his close friends.

In truth, they tolerated his attempts at friendship because he was "a colorful character." It was often said of him that he'd bet "which way your grandmother would fall."

To this comment, Mizner once remarked, "If true, you can bet Rothstein has an inside track with the guy picked to push her."

A.R. invented "Bankroll poker," the game in which two or more players select five numbers from the serial numbers on greenbacks to make the best poker hand. He was an inveterate winner, too, aided no little by a bank teller he paid to save for him bills whose numbers provided practically unbeatable poker combinations.

He was also famous for sitting in speakeasies in the summertime and betting large sums on how long it would take a certain fly to jump. A one-time associate explained his uncanny success with this dodge:

"I hope I croak if A.R. didn't have a guy clocking flies for days to get the form on their habits. So when he bet on flies jumping, he was betting the percentages. They figured out that the average fly will stay put about nine seconds. They also figured out that in a joint that's filled with smoke and very hot, the flies get groggy and then they'll hold still for 20 seconds, give or take a couple."

The horses, too, came in for their share of attention from

Rothstein. For several years the colors of his Redstone Stables, black cross-stripes on an oxblood ground, were well known at Eastern tracks. For the same period of time rumor was rife that he was doping his own and other horses, bribing handicappers and fixing jockeys. His stable was finally ruled off the turf when he pulled off a betting coup with a horse that was rated as little more than gluebait. In one race with this nag, he clipped the bookmakers for a cool $800,000!

Though Arnold Rothstein was most widely known, and is still remembered, as a gambler, the term was never more inappropriately used. A.R. made his bets up in the big numbers, certainly; but when he did so it was seldom a wager, in the accepted sense. It was a sure thing.

Never was this more clearly demonstrated in his infamous career than in the 1919 World Series between the Cincinnati Reds and the Chicago White Sox. Rothstein, the wisenheimers said, had finally gone off his rocker: the White Sox, heavy favorites in the betting, were a cinch to win, but A.R. was laying a bundle on Cincinnati. The possibility of a fix in the World Series, even with a guy like Rothstein, "The Brain," involved, was not even considered. Yet it happened. The White Sox, incredibly, bumbled their way out of the pennant. Rothstein won $1,500,000.

Even before the full truth was finally aired, American League president Ban Johnson publicly stated: "Arnold Rothstein is the man behind the fix."

Rothstein indignantly threatened to sue for libel. He never did. He issued numerous ambiguous statements, but significantly, he never actually denied the charge.

The players who had thrown the Series were exposed and punished. Nothing happened to Rothstein.

Nor did anything happen to him in the exposure of a Wall

Street "bucket shop" operation in which canceled checks proved that he had received $331,000 of the money milked from unsuspecting investors.

He was also named as the brains behind a $5 million bond robbery for which Nicky Arnstein, husband of Fanny Brice, went to prison in Atlanta. A.R., in his usual mysterious way, escaped prosecution, although $4 million worth of the stolen bonds were never recovered.

In 1928 Arnold Rothstein was a millionaire many times over. At the peak of his nefarious career, he had carefully cultivated the underground legend that he could do no wrong. His credit was unlimited and his gambling methods, when he stood at a crap table or sat down to play cards, were known and accepted: He doubled all losing bets until he won. If he left a game losing, he never paid off in cash. He gave markers, and they were always honored.

But despite his eminent standing in the underworld, A.R. was unloved by his associates. Some years before he had married an actress featured in a Broadway hit show and she had retired from the theater to devote her life to him. She was, apart from his heartbroken parents, undoubtedly the most loyal person in his existence. Even when, shortly before the bark of a .38 put a period to his career, he told her he had fallen in love with a younger and more shapely showgirl, she was still loyal; she offered to step aside if it would make him happy she would have done it, even if he did not offer a generous settlement.

Apart from these women, however, Rothstein commanded respect and loyalty only with money, or with the blackjack of fear. Many men had reason to fear him, because of knowledge he held which he could have turned against them whenever he chose, or if they gave him reason to do so. Otherwise he was a man hated and despised for his

97

arrogance of manner, for his sneering contempt blatantly displayed toward anyone and everyone from whom he was not seeking a favor, for his acid tongue with which he delighted in humiliating any and all who could not fight back.

The woods were full of people who would have been happy to see Arnold Rothstein dead—gamblers on whom he had welshed, hoods who had done his dirty jobs and then been deserted by him when the law caught up with them, innumerable "business" associates who ended up on the short end of their deals with A.R., even a procession of Broadway ladies to whom he promised the moon and then discarded when the spirit moved him, without even a piece of green cheese.

A former bodyguard, Jack "Legs" Diamond, might have gunned him down if someone hadn't beaten him to it. Legs knew that A.R. had sent a couple of gunsels to Denver to knock off his brother Eddie, suffering from tuberculosis and confined to a sanitarium in the mountain city. The plot was foiled, but after Rothstein's death, Diamond's boys blasted three of A.R.'s torpedoes in reprisal.

Bearing all this in mind, no one can argue that Arnold Rothstein had not long been ripe for killing, but that event itself was not actually set in motion until the night of September 7, 1928.

This was the night of the now legendary poker game at the West 54th Street apartment of Jimmy Meehan, little more than a block away from the Park Central Hotel. Among those present at the green baize table for this game were Meehan, the host; George McManus, a respected gambler whose aversion to violence or any kind of rough stuff was well known; "Titanic" Thompson, a Toledo gambler whose nickname derived from his miraculous survival of the *S.S. Titanic* sinking; and "Nigger Nate" Raymond, a gambler of considerable experience in a minor league sort of way, but making his debut appearance in such fast company.

Rothstein began to play in typical fashion, with a worried frown on his pudgy face which, to those who knew him, was a tipoff to his supreme confidence. Intimates have disclosed that his was a poker face in reverse. He showed concern when he was winning and the worse the cards, the more he smiled. Occasionally he displayed yet another telltale symptom; when he became extremely excited, blotches of color appeared in his pale cheeks, but men who played with him have admitted this was of little help for his opponents, since the blotches might appear either when he held a very powerful hand or a very bad hand.

It has been established that Rothstein was set for a crooked killing when he went into this game, that at least one man at the table was his confederate and ready to do his boss' bidding with a full set of intricately contrived signals. He had arranged for 12 sets of detection-proof marked cards to be rung into the game during the course of the evening. This could be accomplished quite naturally because in a big game the decks are changed frequently, since it is easy for a sharpie to mark a deck in just a few rounds of play.

The game got under way according to plan and in two hours A.R. had won 38Gs. The frown that creased his brow looked like a set of permanent wrinkles. No chips were used, and as he raked in the piles of 20s, 50s and $100 bills, Arnold Rothstein knew he had it made.

But his confidence soon evaporated and the frown gave way to a broad smile that became more sickly and forced with each passing hour.

Something had gone wrong, and the reason for Rothstein's distress — aside from the money he was losing — was that he didn't know what had happened. He was unable to determine whether his partner, or partners, were crossing him; whether another group at the table were pulling their own swindle and more successfully than his was working; whether his cold decks had been replaced by strange sets of marked pasteboards or, perish the thought, honest decks or whether he had forgotten or become confused in reading the almost invisible markings.

There was no way of pinpointing the cause while the game was in progress and it was unthinkable that he could walk out on the game. His reputation was at stake, and Arnold Rothstein was very jealous of his reputation as America's foremost gambler. The result was that when daylight began seeping about the edges of the drawn shades and poke streaks of sunlight through the billows of heavy blue smoke from countless cigarettes and cigars, Mr. Rothstein, "The Brain," had dropped $210,000.

And A.R. was showing the strain. His face looked like a splotchy blob of baker's dough. His smile was a painful grimace. His tailored silk shirt looked as if had slept in it. He kept his fingers from trembling only with the greatest effort as he dealt.

He hadn't put any cash into the pots for hours, only his markers. At one point during the morning he tried to change his luck by cutting the deck with Titanic Thompson, betting $40,000 on every card. It was a seesaw struggle. A.R. won, lost, won, lost, and ended up another 40 Gs in the hole.

The game ended 4 o'clock on the afternoon of September 8th. Titanic Thompson had won $30,000. Several other players were winners in varying, smaller amounts. Nigger Nate had made a score of just under a quarter of a million dollars. George McManus lost $51,000. Arnold Rothstein was in the bag for $361,000.

Then a curious thing happened, as the gamblers settled their accounts before leaving the table. Nigger Nate, who had gone into the game with $17,500 in cash and won $246,000, realized that he was holding $280,000 in markers; he had for his night's work only 38 Gs in cash, and over 200 Gs in IOUs.

Rothstein had taken the cash from his winning pots and given markers for his losing hands. As a result, the heavy loser was about to walk out with $40,000 in cash!

Rothstein then tallied up the IOU's he had given each player, wrote the total for each on a pad he carried in his pocket, and took back his markers from each man. Nigger Nate, a stranger to this company and unimpressed by his fellow players' trust in the great A.R., opined that he felt he had a right to keep the IOU's.

"I'll treat you exactly the same as I treat any other player," Rothstein snapped at him contemptuously.

Nigger Nate was ready to tangle right then and there, but McManus hastily pacified him, explained that this was customary, that A.R. was temporarily short of ready cash because he had over a million laid on the election, and that there was no question whatsoever about his paying off.

Raymond grudgingly accepted the explanation and gave Rothstein his IOU's. A.R. added them up and entered the total in his little book.

But as the weeks passed, Nigger Nate Raymond saw no sign of any payments from Rothstein. To aggravate the situation, word got back to him that A.R. had told McManus he had more than a passing suspicion the game was crooked, and he'd be damned if he'd pay a dime on his markers.

Understandably, Nate was becoming madder by the minute, but friends calmed him down by suggesting Rothstein might be giving him "the treatment." They said A.R. was purposely needling him, hoping to get him so impatient for his money that he'd be willing to settle for half, or possibly two-thirds of the full amount he had coming.

That was how matters stood on the night that Arnold Rothstein left the Broadway restaurant to meet George McManus at the Park Sheraton. That was how matters stood within minutes of his arrival at Room 349, when a .38 pistol roared and a bullet tore into his body.

A.R. lived for another 12 hours, but true to the code of his breed, he refused to name the man who shot him.

Detectives found that McManus had registered into the hotel suite under the name of George A. Richards, Newark, New Jersey. The spacious living room of the suite was littered with butts and empty bottles, and dirty highball glasses. A ragged hole, freshly made, was found in one of the window screens, and it was later discovered that the pistol had been tossed through this hole, to the street below, where it was found shattered. There were no bloodstains, but it was pointed out that Rothstein's wound was not of a type which bleeds profusely, and he had staggered from the room within seconds of being shot.

It seems incredible that no one in the investigation did anything about taking fingerprints in the room where the shooting took place. Consequently, when various suspects were eventually questioned, it was impossible to determine conclusively whether they had been in the murder suite.

Since George McManus was the only one who could positively be connected with Room 349, he became the Number One suspect, and three weeks later he was indicted for first-degree murder.

To the denizens of Broadway, the aroused New York press was quick to point out, this was a preposterous charge, since McManus' reputation for abhorrence of violence was well established. The state's charge that McManus had shot Rothstein because of his anger at losing $51,000 was also denounced as absurd, since witnesses had pointed out that none of McManus' losses had been won by Rothstein.

The result of McManus' trial was a foregone conclusion, under the circumstances. After 10 days of testimony, the judge, on December 5th, directed the jury to bring in a verdict of not guilty, and McManus was cleared of the charge of murdering Arnold Rothstein.

The repercussions of the Rothstein affair, however, were to rumble on for years, with investigation after investigation of the matter which resulted in wholesale resignations from the police department and other branches of the city government. The conclusion of one official report stated, in no uncertain terms:

"The whole spirit of the investigation which took place after Rothstein's death reflected the attitude of total indifference on the part of the commanding officers of the detective division to the ordinary routine which should have been followed in a case of this kind."

But though the official investigation of Arnold Rothstein's murder bogged down in a hopeless muddle, Broadway and its denizens came up with a version which is probably as close to what actually happened as anyone will ever get.

White Way oracles insist that A.R. went to the Park Central to discuss some ordinary business with George McManus. McManus was a harmless character and the business must have been harmless too, else Rothstein never would have left his gun with his friend in the restaurant.

At McManus' suite, A.R. found a number of men, some of them drunk, to judge by the number of empty bottles counted by police. One or more of the men present, it is theorized, had played in the fabulous poker game in which Rothstein dropped his big boodle, and with them A.R. now became embroiled in a heated argument. Basing their theory on Rothstein's known tendency toward sneering sarcasm, Broadwayites reason that he so enraged at least one man that he pulled a gun, but that someone else attempted to deflect the gun just as it was fired. that would explain the medical report of the bullet entering Rothstein's abdomen and angling downward into his groin.

George McManus undoubtedly witnessed the shooting, but he died in 1941 without ever naming the killer.

A belated investigation of Rothstein's effects, months after his death, turned up evidence which enabled G-Men to break up successfully a $7 million dope wholesaling operation.

And when Rothstein's estate was finally inventoried, his assets totaled $2,512,993.07. Which made Broadway's smartest gambler the richest man in the cemetery.

The fact is, he was just too smart to live.

America's No. 1 Murder Mystery

by W. T. Brannon

Who Killed Senator Percy's Beautiful Daughter?

"We have checked out 1,153 leads. In all, we have personally talked to about 8,000 persons in 48 states and five foreign countries — France, India, England, Africa and Canada. We have taken 439 finger and palm prints and given voluntary polygraph tests to 41 subjects. As long as leads continue to come in, we're going to check them. We haven't solved the case yet, but we're sure going to keep trying."

Edward Eggert
Chief of Police
Kenilworth, Illinois

Outside the pages of an English mystery novel, it was an unlikely place for murder.

Kenilworth, Illinois, a mile-square suburban community about eight miles north of Chicago, nestles on Lake Michigan between Wilmette and Winnetka, two larger suburbs. The little city's population remains virtually constant at about 4,000 because the 850 homes occupy just about all the space available.

Sheridan Road, snaking northward along the lake-front from Chicago, is the suburb's principal public street. The majority of the other streets are private roads on which large estates are situated.

Such is Devonshire Lane, a quiet street shaded by tall elms and poplars its entire length of 200 feet eastward from Sheridan Road. At the end of Devonshire Lane is Windward, a three-acre estate shielded from Sheridan Road traffic by honeysuckle bushes and high stone walls.

The main house is a rambling, three-story, Tudor style structure of English graystone, with a total of 17 rooms, seven of them bedrooms. In a recently built addition to the first floor, there is an indoor swimming pool.

Just inside the entry gate is a two-story guest house and south of it a four-car garage with servants quarters above it. There is an outdoor pool and near it a tennis court, both for use when the weather is mild. To the east is a private beach on Lake Michigan.

Windward had been the home for some years of Charles H. Percy and his family. At the time the family moved into the mansion, Percy was chairman of the board of Bell & Howell. He since has become the junior United States Senator from Illinois and there has been a lot of discussion about his being a dark horse candidate for the Republican presidential nomination this year.

At five o'clock Sunday morning, September 18, 1966, Charles Percy, whose friends call him Chuck, was asleep in his bedroom on the second floor of his home. At that time, he was in the last stages of his campaign for the senate seat, opposing then-Senator Paul H. Douglas. Paradoxically, Douglas had been one of Percy's instructors when he attended the University of Chicago.

At that hour on that mild Sunday morning, the future senator was sleeping soundly, but his wife wasn't. She had heard a noise from somewhere down the hall and had gone to investigate. Now, she ran screaming back toward the bedroom, pausing momentarily to press a button that set off a siren on top of the house, the only burglar alarm in the house at that time.

Mr. Percy had been awakened by the siren and by his wife's cries. "It's Valerie!" she screamed, and there was terror in her voice. "She's been stabbed! Call the police!"

Thoroughly awake now, Percy sprang out of bed as his wife explained there had been a man in the room, bending over 21-year-old Valerie's bed and that he had blinded her by shining the beam of a flashlight in her eyes.

The siren had stopped for a few moments, but Mr. Percy switched it on again, then dialed the telephone operator, identified himself, and asked her to get the police. "There's an emergency here."

Then he ran to his daughter's room, his wife close behind. He saw the girl lying on the bed and she was still; he noted that one side of her body was bathed in blood. While Mrs. Percy went to where the girl lay, Mr. Percy turned and ran downstairs, thinking he might be able to head off the assailant. The front door was locked.

As he came out the back door of the music room opening onto a stone terrace, he heard the family dog barking. Had the killer managed to escape through the back toward the beach?

Then Percy remembered the eight nurses who had been slain on Chicago's South Side only three months before and he had a horrible thought: "He is upstairs."

He wheeled and ran back upstairs, determined to protect his family.

But the attacker was not there. Mrs. Percy came out of the girl's bedroom and said she thought she had detected a pulse; maybe there was a chance. Percy checked all the bedrooms on the second floor, then ran back downstairs. But he didn't find the assailant.

Then he made two more phone calls. One was to Dr. Robert Hohf, a next-door neighbor who is a surgeon at Evanston Hospital.

"Doctor, this is Chuck Percy," he said. "Could you come over to our house immediately, please? Valerie has been injured."

"I'll be right over," Dr. Hohf replied.

"Thank you, Doctor," Percy said.

About two minutes before that, Mrs. Hohf had been awakened by the siren, which the doctor had not heard. She had gone to the windows that look out over the private beach and Lake Michigan. As her husband dressed hurriedly, she told him she had seen nothing on the beach. At that time, they assumed there had been some sort of accident.

At Windward, Mr. Percy made a third phone call. It was to Orlando W. Wilson, then Superintendent of the Chicago police, at his home. Wilson promised help.

In the orderly manner and with the self-restraint that had distinguished Chuck Percy during his meteoric rise from a $12-a-week clerk to a millionaire industrialist at 40, he got together the members of the family who were in the house — Valerie's attractive blonde twin, Sharon, 21; her half sister, Gail, 13; and Mrs. Percy — and led them to a sofa in the family room on the first floor. An older son, Roger, 19, was at college in Menlo Park, Cali-

108

fornia, and Mark, 11, was spending the night with a friend.

By this time, Kenilworth police had arrived. Mr. Percy showed them to Valerie's room, told them of calling Dr. Hohf. One of them went next door and escorted the doctor to the Percy home and led them up the circular stairway to the girl's room on the second floor.

It was a scene of horror he had not been prepared for. The girl he had known as a blonde beauty now was sprawled on the bed, the bloodsoaked covers crumpled on the floor between the bed and another twin-size bed that had not been used. The bed itself was bathed in blood. The girl's skull had been crushed and there were vicious stab wounds in her throat, chest and abdomen.

Dr. Hohf went downstairs, where he found the family waiting in silence. He knew they had been a very close family and this refusal to yield to emotions was an exercise in discipline. Chuck Percy stood up and they clasped hands.

There was no outburst, no wailing, just grim acceptance of the morbid fact.

"They were marvelously controlled," Dr. Hohf said later. "They accepted. Then they tried to organize themselves for doing the many things that must be done. They withheld their great grief. They did not, through that long day, impose their grief on others."

Dr. Hohf stayed around an hour or so, doing whatever he could to help. Dr. Andrew J. Toman, Cook County coroner, arrived soon and Dr. Hohf accompanied him to the girl's room. Within a few minutes there were many others who came as a result of the call to Police Superintendent Wilson.

In the forefront of these was Director Dan Dragel of

the Chicago police crime lab, himself one of the country's leading forensic scientists. In his wake were a dozen selected technicians who had come in mobile crime labs and brought portable scientific equipment.

Meanwhile, a brief resumé of the crime had been telephoned to Kenilworth headquarters and had gone out on the police radio, a band that is received by six North Shore suburbs — Evanston, Wilmette, Winnetka, Skokie and Lincolnwood in addition to Kenilworth. Within minutes, roadblocks had been thrown up in every direction and motorists were being stopped and questioned.

Kenilworth Police Chief Robert Daley, who had been notified at home, brought his top investigators, Sergeants Edward Eggert and William Sumner. For the Kenilworth officers, it was their first homicide investigation; never before had a murder been reported in Kenilworth.

While Dr. Toman and Dr. Hohf made a preliminary examination of the slain girl and Dragel's scientists (some of them with doctor's degrees) began searching for evidence, the Kenilworth officers questioned members of the Percy family. From their accounts, the police pieced together a chronology of events:

The day before, Chuck Percy had spent in campaigning. His most faithful helper had been his beautiful blonde daughter, Valerie Jeanne. In the evening, Percy had a speech scheduled at the Germania Club on the north side of Chicago and Valerie went home.

She had planned to entertain two of her young male friends, both of whom had been active in her father's campaign. Also at the dinner were Mrs. Percy, Sharon, Gail and Mark. Sharon left early because she had a date. Mark left to spend the night with a friend. The two

110

young men said goodbye to Valerie and left about nine o'clock.

Sharon returned about 11. Gail was in her bedroom and so was Valerie. Sharon had borrowed a raincoat from her twin and went to Valerie's room to return it. Valerie was watching television and Sharon stayed only a few minutes to chat and then returned to her own room.

Mr. Percy returned home about midnight. He and his wife watched television in their bedroom for an hour or so, then went to sleep. Mrs. Percy was awakened by a moaning sound and she thought it came from Sharon's room. She got up to investigate and discovered the sounds had come from Valerie Jeanne's room.

She opened the door of Valerie's bedroom and saw a figure bending over Valerie's bed about 12 feet across the room. She saw that Valerie had been stabbed and that her body was bloody in the moments before the person in the room shone a flashlight in her face, blinding her.

She ran screaming down the hall, and it must have been then that the killer made his escape. She said she was unable to say for sure whether the person in the room was a man or a woman.

However, Mrs. Percy said that Valerie's nightgown was pulled up above her waist and the stepmother pulled it down. This suggested a man and a sex crime. But officers at the time discounted the possibility of a sex crime because of the viciousness of the assault.

It seemed more likely that this was an act of vengeance by somebody who wanted to kill a member of the Percy family, perhaps only Valerie. Mrs. Percy said the person in the room had not spoken and had made no move to harm her. This strongly suggested that the killer had gone deliberately to Valerie's room and that she was the intended victim.

This theory was given credence by the fact that there were others on the second floor, that other rooms could have been entered before the intruder reached Valerie's if he had been seeking just any member of the family. There was the implication, too, that the killer was someone who knew the layout of the house well and knew exactly how to reach Valerie's room.

But how had he gained entrance in the first place?

Director Dragel's men found the apparent answer. There were two doors leading from the back of the music room to the stone terrace. A rectangular section, about 12 by 18 inches had been cut from the screen door and a similar slab had been cut from the glass panel of the other door.

The glass had been pushed inside and it had been shattered on the floor. The intruder apparently had reached through the openings to unlock the doors from the inside. The technicians immediately began dusting likely surfaces, including some pieces of the broken glass, for prints.

Outside, footprints were discovered in the sand of the private beach and, for a short time, it was believed that the killer had entered and perhaps left from the beach. However, Mrs. Hohf said she had looked out at the beach and had not seen anyone or anything moving. On the chance that the killer had entered from the beach, the technicians made a thorough search of the path the intruder would have taken from the music room, through the living room and up the circular stairway to the second floor. But no traces of beach sand could be found. Moreover, when the beach was examined more closely, the detectives found no one trail, but a welter of footprints. They discounted the possibility of the killer having come in from the beach.

After Dr. Toman had completed the preliminary examination, the body was removed to the Cook County morgue in Chicago, where Dr. James Henry, the coroner's pathologist, was waiting to perform the autopsy.

When this was completed, Dr. Toman said Valerie had died of a fractured skull. He said her head had been literally crushed by repeated blows by some sort of blunt instrument. This had made triangular marks of the sort that would have been made with an angle iron or a fireplace poker. He said also that she had been stabbed a dozen times, *after* she had been beaten. It appeared that the killer, not content merely to take a life, was bent on destroying all vestiges of the girl's beauty.

The family obviously was in a state of shock despite their courageous efforts not to inflict their grief on others, and all but necessary police questioning was postponed to allow for the passage of time, with its healing effect.

Meanwhile, the technicians methodically went through the rooms of the Percy mansion checking everything that might have any bearing on the investigation. Vacuum cleaners were used to gather up material in the slain girl's room and along the route believed to have been taken by the killer.

Technicians with fingerprint powder brought out 20 good finger and palm prints. Four of the palm prints were on the wrought-iron railing of the patio outside the music room. One was on the door-jamb of Valerie's room. About 15 fingerprints were found on tables in the music room and on the banisters of the circular stairway.

This meant a procedure that would be painful but not new to the police: All members of the family as well as servants and any others who regularly had access to the house, would have to be fingerprinted. It was only through this tedious process that finger and palm prints could be eliminated. If any were left over they would be suspected as those belonging to the killer.

In addition, the technicians picked up 17 plastic bags of material with the use of vacuum cleaners, any of which might bear some clue to the killer. The bags were sent to the crime lab in Chicago and Director Dragel said each bit would be studied under the microscope. He said weeks might be required to go through it all.

After it became clear that the killer had not tried to escape in a car—or had managed to get through in the few minutes before the barricades were thrown up—the suburban police lifted the roadblocks.

However, cruising squads watched for suspicious persons, particularly for a young man with bloodstained clothing. Dragel said it was almost certain from the amount of blood in Valerie's room, that the killer's clothing was badly stained—so badly, he speculated, that he had been compelled to dispose of it soon after leaving the girl's room.

Chief Daley, a veteran of 32 years—his first and only job had been as a Kenilworth policeman—readily admitted he did not have enough help and accepted the offers that came from Chicago. Commander Francis Flanagan, Chicago's homicide chief, sent as many detectives as he could spare; Captain Maurice Higgins, chief investigator for the state's attorney, sent Lieutenant Nick Juric and a dozen detectives; other men came from the Cook County sheriff's department and from the various north shore suburbs.

Lieutenant Juric and his men set up roadblocks along Sheridan Road and questioned motorists going in both directions: Had any of them been along that way at any time during the night or early morning? If so, had they seen anybody on foot? Had they seen anything else unusual?

In an effort to find the bludgeon and the knife used by the slayer, his discarded clothing, or anything else that might be considered a clue, Kenilworth Boy Scouts were enlisted to crawl over the estate on their hands and knees and search every inch.

They turned up the broken blades of a pair of scissors, a pocket knife and a single moccasin. These were examined by the technicians, who found that all three items appeared to have been exposed to the elements for a long time. Director Dragel said they had no apparent connection with Valerie's killing.

With so many law enforcement agencies entering the investigation, Chief Daley went to the rather cramped Kenilworth police station, where he coordinated the manhunt by radio and telephone. All Kenilworth officers were contacted and leaves were canceled. Additional telephone lines were installed and several of the Kenilworth policemen were detailed to record phone calls, record interviews with people who came to the station and interrogate witnesses.

As soon as the news was generally known, mostly by radio and television but also by word of mouth, telephone tips began to come in at the rate of one each minute. Numerous persons came to the station to offer suggestions and information; none of these was brushed aside, though little of value came from what they said.

115

The tips were relayed to teams of investigators and each was carefully checked out.

Since Mrs. Loraine Percy was the closest link to the killer and the only person known to have seen him besides his victim, she was questioned again. However, she was in too great a state of shock to add anything substantial to what she already had told.

One aspect that puzzled investigators was the failure of the dog, Li Poo, (which is Chinese for guardian) to bark at the intruder and awaken the family. An English butler, who had arrived only about ten days before and was in his quarters over the garage, said he heard no sound from the dog. Yet the dog barked fiercely at the first policeman to arrive.

Did this mean that the intruder was someone known to the dog, somebody who regularly visited in the Percy home? How else account for the dog's failure to raise a clamor?

News of the tragedy had reached most of the world and brought immediate reactions. One of the first was from Senator Paul Douglas, Percy's opponent in the senatorial race, who sent a telegram to Mr. and Mrs. Percy:

"My heart goes out to you over your cruel and terrible loss. My deep sympathy and condolences to you both. I am calling off my campaigning. May God bless and keep you both."

Mayor Richard J. Daley of Chicago sent a message in which he said:

"Our deepest sympathy and condolences to you and your wife in this hour of tragedy and sorrow. The full resources of the Chicago Police Department are available to the authorities to apprehend the perpetrator of this terrible crime."

There were many others from prominent men, both in political and business life. Peter G. Peterson, who had succeeded Chuck Percy as chairman of Bell & Howell, came with his wife, as did many other noted industrialists and socialites. There was a steady stream of neighbors, bringing food for the family and their visitors.

The detectives, meanwhile, had searched Valerie's room and in a dresser drawer, which the intruder could have found with little trouble, was a large sum of money. Members of the family said they believed this was all that Valerie had in the room, that none of it had been taken.

The family members also were asked to check the house to determine whether anything had been stolen. They complied and reported that nothing was missing. This apparently ruled out robbery as a motive for the crime.

Then what was it?

Hoping that a motive might be discovered in the life of the girl or some member of the family, the police quietly began checking the background of each family member, starting with Chuck Percy.

A native of Pensacola, Florida, Chuck Percy had lived in the Chicago area from the time he was a small boy. At the age of five, the ambition and energy that were to make him one of America's outstanding men were apparent. He sold magazine subscriptions and by the time he was eight, the YMCA gave him an award for selling more subscriptions than any other boy in a metropolitan area.

He had almost limitless energy when he attended New Trier High School in the north shore section of

Chicago. During this time, he held four jobs at the same time — as an office boy, a janitor, a car hiker and a newspaper carrier.

One reason for this was necessity. There had been a Depression and his father had lost one job after another. Finally, at the time Chuck entered the University of Chicago, the father had gone to work for Bell & Howell as office manager.

From his extracurricular activities in high school, Chuck had saved enough money to go into business when he entered the university. He sold food, coal, linens and furniture to university residences and fraternity houses — and grossed several thousand dollars a year.

Robert Maynard Hutchins, who had been called a boy wonder because of his youth when he became president of the University of Chicago, said of Percy: "He was the richest kid who ever worked his way through college."

Despite this, Chuck Percy wasn't satisfied. He had his eye on the company where his father worked, Bell & Howell. While he was still attending the university, he went to work part time for the company.

When he was graduated from college, he obtained an appointment with Joe H. McNab, then president of Bell & Howell. According to the story, Percy asked McNab: "Can I be an officer in this company in three years?"

McNab was impressed and gave Percy a job. He took a special interest in the young man and moved him from one department to another, at the same time allowing him to buy company stock.

Prior to America's entry in World War II, Chuck

Percy had worked his way up to manager of the company's war coordinating department. After Pearl Harbor, Percy enlisted in the Navy as an apprentice seaman, but later won a commission as a lieutenant.

After the war, Percy returned to Bell & Howell and steadily worked his way upward, studying in his spare time at the Chicago Kent College of Law. On January 12, 1949, when he was 29, Chuck Percy was elected president of Bell & Howell. He became chairman of the board in 1961, but resigned from the company May 5, 1966, to campaign for the U.S. Senate.

In one previous political campaign, in 1964, he had been the Republican nominee for governor of Illinois, but was defeated by the present governor, Otto Kerner.

That was the business side of Chuck Percy's life and as the detectives knew, any man who makes rapid advances incurs some enemies along the way, regardless of how hard he might try not to. As far as the detectives could find out from early inquiries, Charles H. Percy had no known enemies in his business life.

But his political life was another matter, and that was something that would require careful investigation.

Then the detectives looked into Percy's private life. He had been married to Jeanne Valerie Dickerson in 1943 and from this union, three children had been born—the twins, Valerie Jeanne and Sharon, and Roger. They still were quite small when their mother died during an operation in 1947.

On a vacation, Chuck Percy went to Sun Valley, Idaho, where he met Loraine Diane Guyer. She was a native of Altadena, California, near Los Angeles, and her father was an investment banker. After attending public schools and some boarding schools, she had studied at the University of California at Los Angeles and at Mexico City College.

The year after she met Charles Percy, she went abroad to study, but she kept in touch. He went to Europe to visit her and they became engaged.

"I think I said I enjoyed Europe so much that he should bring me home," she said later.

They were married in 1950. "The children were so young when we married they were like my own children," she said. "I told Chuck it should be up to them what to call me. I walked in the door and they said Mother not once, but twenty times."

Two children were born of the second marriage — Gail, 13, and Mark, 11. "Now there are two age levels, but everyone gets along marvelously," Mrs. Percy said.

The Percy family soon gained a reputation for being very close. Whenever possible, Chuck Percy took the family with him. They often went on outings such as picnics.

When the twins were ten, Valerie and Sharon decided they would have their own lives. They stopped dressing in identical clothes and each had her own interests. There was no enmity in this, just a desire on the part of each girl to be an independent individual. Valerie attended Cornell University, while Sharon went to Stanford. Both studied in Europe during their junior years, but Valerie was in Paris and Sharon in Lausanne, Switzerland. Both were graduated in June, 1966.

After graduation, Valerie began traveling with her father on the campaign trail. Sharon, whose closest friend was John D. Rockefeller IV of West Virginia, went to Africa, where she worked as a volunteer for the Central African Republic, teaching English and helping in a youth center.

It was an endeavor similar to that of the more widely publicized Peace Corps. Sharon had returned from Africa only a few weeks before the tragedy.

Roger, then 19, also had helped his father in the senatorial campaign during the summer, but had to quit after Labor Day when he went to Menlo Park College in Menlo Park, California. He had been notified of the death of Valerie and returned to Chicago by plane the same day.

In all they could learn about the family, the police investigators could find no motive for murder. Yet, it seemed certain that the intruder had entered the house and gone to Valerie's room for no other purpose than to kill her.

Police speculated that the intended victim had been Chuck Percy rather than his daughter. They reasoned that Mr. Percy was the last person to go in the house and that he might have been followed. The killer might have looked up from the stone terrace in the rear and noted the light still on in Valerie's room, which was directly over the terrace; but he might have thought it was Mr. Percy's.

Proponents of this theory believed that the killer was in Valerie's room before he discovered his mistake and that it was too late then to turn back.

But, if this was the case, why had he made no move to harm Mrs. Percy when she entered the room?

Because the intruder seemed to know his way about the house, some detectives had another theory. They speculated that the killer was someone who had a key to the house and that he actually had entered by unlocking a door. They theorized that the breaking of the glass had

121

been done to lead the police on a false trail.

However, when some of the shock had worn off, memory returned to Mrs. Percy and details of that fatal morning were recalled a bit at a time. She told the detectives she had been awakened by the tinkling sound of breaking glass. But she was drowsy, only half awake and her thought at the time was that one of the girls had, in her sleep, knocked a glass off a bedside table.

Thinking it was no more important than that, she went back to sleep, she told the detectives. Next, she remembered hearing a sound as of footsteps on the tile floor of the music room. But in a house where there always were a lot of people engaged in a political campaign, the sounds didn't register enough to awaken her fully.

She had no idea how much time elapsed between these sounds and the moaning from Valerie's room that eventually aroused her to the extent that she got up to investigate. She said she was sure now that the killer was a man because she remembered that he was wearing slacks.

She gave a vague description and Chief Daley said he had a mental picture of an ordinary man, five feet eight inches tall, weighing about 160 to 165 pounds. However, Mrs. Percy said she would not be able to identify the killer.

Mr. Percy was questioned about possible political enemies. He said a few crank letters had been received at his headquarters, but none had threatened Valerie, or even mentioned her. Percy was asked to prepare a list of persons who in his opinion should be questioned about the murder. These included people who possessed house keys. There were about 40 people altogether who regularly visited the Percy home in connection with one phase or another of the campaign.

Lieutenant Juric set up a command post in a room at Kenilworth headquarters and his 12 detectives began running down leads, including questioning of persons on Mr. Percy's list. These people were asked where they had been at the time of Valerie's death, whether they knew anything that might help in the investigation — such as a motive — and if they were willing to submit voluntarily to lie detector tests.

Every person who was asked to take the test agreed. In all, 41 people agreed to take lie tests and arrangements were made to start giving them.

Meanwhile, in Chicago, Dr. Edward J. Kelliher, widely known psychiatrist for the Chicago municipal court, studied the known facts and expressed some opinions.

"The facts so far revealed indicate that the murderer knew Valerie and that he went to her home for the purpose of murdering her," Dr. Kelliher said. He added that she was killed by a person in a fit of rage and that the motivation could have been vengeance or jealousy.

Dr. Kelliher said there were four points that indicated the assailant did not intend to harm anyone else and enumerated them:

1. Valerie was singled out from other women in the house, including her twin sister, her half sister, Gail, and her step-mother.

2. The bludgeoning and stabbing were concentrated about her head, "indicating that the murderer wanted to attack her personally."

3. When he made no move to attack Mrs. Percy, this indicated he harbored no animosity against any other

member of the family.

4. The killer apparently was familiar with the layout of the house and where each family member slept.

It was unusual that the killer did not attack Mrs. Percy when she discovered him, the psychiatrist added.

"When he encountered Mrs. Percy, he may have been taken off guard and did not strike out at her because he had gotten to his intended victim and did not have any plans for harming anyone else," said Dr. Kelliher.

"The act of shining the light in Mrs. Percy's face is more in keeping with someone who knew the mother and feared she might recognize him but at the same time didn't want to harm her."

The psychiatrist said that the stabbing in the face and head might mean that the killer resented something about Valerie that led to an uncontrollable rage.

"She was a well known, personable young lady but to a person who was mentally off balance, a harmless act might be interpreted as the gravest of all insults," he said.

Another Chicagoan, Dr. Eric Oldberg, president of the Board of Health, had this acid comment:

"When we have sanctimonious clergymen getting headlines and popular adulation for 'civil disobedience' and a personal choice of just and unjust laws; and when we have the highest judicature of our land concerned solely with the protection of the criminal accused, then the fringe is bound to feel sanctioned and to creep out of the woodwork and do the job of the assassin."

Leads in the case came from other sources. One was from nearby Evanston, whose chief of detectives, Lieutenant Robert Bennett, told of an assault on an Evanston girl under circumstances somewhat similar to those in the murder of Valerie Percy.

At about 3:30 a.m. on June 30th, the 19-year-old girl was awakened in her second-floor bedroom when she was struck on the head. A young man was standing over her and he warned: "Be quiet and you won't get hurt."

He struck her again and when she screamed, he fled. He had managed to get into the room by placing a ladder under the window and removing the screen. He left by scurrying down the ladder. He had stolen some of her clothing which, with a ball peen hammer apparently used to hit her on the head, were found a short distance away by the police.

A light in the bedroom closet had been on and the victim said she had a good look at the intruder. She described him as 15 to 17 years of age, about five feet ten inches tall, wearing glasses with large lenses, a green plaid shirt and light slacks.

From the girl's description, a drawing had been made and published at the time. But the attacker was still at large. Now, copies of the sketch were sent to Chief Daley in Kenilworth and other copies were distributed to the newspapers and television stations.

Meanwhile, there were other developments. Seymour Simon, then president of the Cook County Board of Commissioners (now an alderman), had five anonymous phone calls to his office and home and asked Chicago police for protection.

Though Mr. Simon characterized them as crank calls, his wife obviously was frightened and policemen were posted at the front and rear of the Simon home.

Two calls were received by two different secretaries in

his office. They were the same: "Simon's cars will be wired. We'll bomb them."

Later, there were three calls at the Simon home. The first said "Simon's house will be bombed." The next one was to Simon's 23-year-old son, and it threatened violence to his mother, and said she "would get the same thing the Percy girl got."

Other calls to the Simon home voiced similar threats. Then a friend phoned Simons' office and left a message: He had been in a Loop hotel when he heard two men he didn't know say they planned to bomb the Simon home.

Chicago police began looking for the men and trying to run down the calls. But the persons responsible were not found and as far as the police could determine, the threat was the only actual connection with the Percy crime.

After Valerie's funeral on Tuesday, the Percy family quietly slipped away to go into seclusion at an undisclosed location. They kept in touch with Chief Daley through a friend.

Then Senator Russell Arrington of Evanston, a friend of Percy, disclosed to investigators that there had been a threat to harm Chuck Percy, Richard Nixon, Barry Goldwater, Senator Everett Dirksen and Representative Gerald Ford of Michigan.

The letter was addressed to Mr. Percy and postmarked in Chicago. It had been received in May and Arrington had a copy because his name had been mentioned.

"We hope we won't have to take you on a one-way ride," the letter said. "Be careful of what you are saying. . . . Just watch what you say from now until June."

Referring to Goldwater and Dirksen the letter read: "We've been ordered to watch such men when they come to town. Arrington already is in town . . . It won't be long before we go to Washington for Mr. Ford."

Senator Arrington said: "I consider it a crank letter." However, it already was in the hands of Chicago postal inspectors and Director Dragel's handwriting analysts at the police crime lab. They had had no luck in tracing the person who wrote it.

On Wednesday morning, shortly after he had seen the published sketch of the Evanston attack suspect, a cab driver reported to Sergeant Daniel Barrett of the Area 2 homicide unit in Chicago that he had taken a man resembling the portrait to an address in Glencoe, about three miles north of the Percy home, about 4:30 Sunday morning. He didn't recall the address, but told police he could show them the house where his fare, who was about 20, got out of the cab.

Kenilworth police thought it possible that the same man had been responsible for both the Evanston attack and the killing of Valerie Percy for several reasons:

Both girls were quite attractive; both were attacked in the pre-dawn hours by a man described as a "sexual psychopath;" yet neither had been molested sexually.

However, when the Glencoe man reported by the cab driver was located, he was able to establish that he could not have been the killer.

In a continuing effort to locate the murder weapons, skin divers searched Lake Michigan near the Percy private beach. One of them found a bayonet that could have been the weapon used to stab Valerie. Dr. Toman said the knife used had two edges and after he had looked at the bayonet, he said it could have been the

127

knife.

The bayonet was turned over to Director Dragel whose technicians examined it for bloodstains and other evidence. It was not ruled out and police have not revealed whether stains or extraneous material were found. They do say they are not sure whether the bayonet was one of the weapons.

When the bludgeon was not found, cutters from Coast Guard base in Chicago dragged the lake with powerful magnets designed to attract metal. But they found nothing that was considered the bludgeon.

Two possible clues were developed on Tuesday, September 27th. Sharon Percy, through a friend, had relayed a message to Chief Daley: She and Valerie had been to the shopping section of Evanston a couple of days before the murder and returned on a Chicago Transit Authority L train to Kenilworth.

In the same car had been a young man with whom Valerie was acquainted. She had introduced him to Sharon, who couldn't remember his name and who couldn't describe him. The three had left the train at the Linden Station in Wilmette, the closest point to the Percy home.

Checking in the neighborhood, detectives found a drug store near the L station. The employees recalled a "rough-looking" young man who had come into the store about the time the Percy girls started home that day, September 17th. But they didn't know if the man followed the Percy girl.

Continuing their investigation, the detectives found a neighbor, a woman, who had been on the same train. She remembered Valerie introducing him to Sharon but she said only a first name had been given. She said the man was between 18 and 25.

Police searched for him but failed to find him. They checked at other stores near the L station but could find nobody else who had seen him. However, since the Percy girls were striking beauties and would be noticed anywhere, it seemed likely that any man following them would have been noticed, too.

The next day, Chief Daley assigned 20 detectives to make a third search of the Percy grounds. During the original search, a glove of black wool with a leather palm was found. At first, it was believed the glove was a child's. But the glove could have been used to make some of the smudges found on the screen door when technicians examined it for prints.

The search was made and the matching glove was not found. Detectives do not know whether it has a bearing on the case or not.

About two weeks after the tragedy, the Percys returned to Kenilworth and Mr. Percy resumed his campaign for the Senate seat, spending some time on that while trying to help the police in their continuing investigation. Senator Douglas resumed his own campaign at the same time, but was careful not to make any personal attacks on Chuck Percy who, in turn, avoided any such tactics against the incumbent senator.

At Kenilworth police headquarters, much of the outside help had been withdrawn, but the tips continued to come in. There was more than the 12-man force could handle and Chief Daley asked for help. William Morris, Superintendent of the Illinois State Police, assigned a team to help run down the tips and any other leads.

As some of the horror faded, it was like a curtain being lifted from the memory of Mrs. Loraine Percy. She now recalled more about the man she had surprised in Valerie's room:

This came about at a reenactment of the events of that tragic morning, in an effort by the police to jog dormant memories. The only one who remembered more, however, was Mrs. Percy. She said the man who shone the flash-light in her face had bushy hair, especially full at the temples. She said he wore a bold-striped sport shirt, maybe a check or a plaid. She estimated his age at between 18 and 25.

Another thing that was brought to the attention of the police — it already had been related by Mrs. Percy — was the possibility of a sex crime. When Mrs. Percy entered the room the second time, Valerie's nightgown was up around her shoulders. She said she pulled it down to the girl's knees, drew a sheet over the lower part of her body and wiped some of the blood from her face with a pillow case.

This had been overlooked by many investigators because in the initial phases of the case, little consideration was given to the possibility of a sex crime, especially after the post mortem revealed that Valerie had not been raped.

But now, Sergeant Sumner remembered other cases where there had been no sexual molestation, yet the motive had been sexual. In the Heirens case, for example, it had been said that he derived sexual excitement from stepping over the threshold of a woman's room. None of the women and girls he murdered or attacked had been sexually molested, yet it was generally agreed that his crimes, including the dismemberment of little Suzanne Degnan, had been sexually motivated.

In the weeks and months that followed Valerie Percy's

murder, numerous young men charged with sex crimes, especially stabbing murders, were investigated, but none could be connected with the Percy case.

Because of the lack of space in Kenilworth, headquarters for the investigation was moved to the more modern building of the Winnetka police. A filing system was set up for the more than 10,000 persons who have been interviewed up to now. In addition to the folders on each person questioned, subjects they discussed were entered on file cards to form a cross-file for ready reference.

The 41 persons who volunteered to take lie detector tests were cleared of suspicion. These included all the people known to have been close to the Percy family, to have been in the house in the hours prior to the murder, and those young men who had had dates with Valerie.

In the November, 1966 election Charles Percy defeated Senator Douglas and now is the junior United States senator from Illinois. For about a year and a half he has been in Washington with his family [In April, 1967, daughter Sharon married John D. Rockefeller IV] and he has become prominent in the affairs of the country and of the Republican party. He often is mentioned as a possible presidential or vice presidential nominee.

But Senator Percy has continued to give full cooperation to the police in their investigation, which sometimes has been necessarily repetitious. On March 1, 1967, Chief Daley retired to become village manager of Kenilworth and he was succeeded as chief by Sergeant Edward Eggert, who has been one of the principal investigators from the beginning.

Chief Eggert continued to run down every conceivable lead. There are eight confessions by young men who had varying motives. One in the West apparently wanted a free trip to Chicago. In each of these cases, the confession was proved to be false.

Numerous persons were fingerprinted, everybody known to have been in the Percy home — and most of the prints were eliminated. However, there still is one clear, though partial fingerprint, found on the French door to the music room, and five palm prints that have not been identified. Chief Eggert and Director Dragel of the Chicago police crime laboratory hope they'll find a suspect with a matching fingerprint or palm print.

In December, 1967, the Percy mansion was sold. By that time, the police had been over it dozens of times and apparently had squeezed from it every available clue.

The full time investigation, coordinated by Lieutenant Richard Robb of the state police, ended on March 19, 1968, when there were no more live leads.

However, Chief Eggert says that every new lead will be followed up and he still hopes for a solution. The finger and palm prints, the glove, and the bayonet remain as possible clues.

Even though he no longer is actively assigned to the case, Lieutenant Robb said: "You don't close the books on a homicide case, any homicide case."

Chief Eggert and Sergeant Sumner still are in Kenilworth. Both are intimately familiar with the case, and both are ready to move at the first sign of a break.

On Tuesday, May 7, 1968 almost 18 months after Valerie's murder a press conference was called in the State of Illinois Building in Chicago. It was attended by Governor Otto Kerner, State Safety Director Ross V. Randolph and Senator Percy.

Governor Kerner announced that jurisdiction in the

investigation had been relinquished by the Kenilworth police because all leads had been exhausted. Safety Director Randolph said that a special squad of Illinois State Police investigators to be known as the Percy Homicide Detail would take over investigation of the case.

At the suggestion of the state police, Randolph said, Senator Percy had offered a reward of $50,000 for information leading to the arrest and conviction of the killer. It was expected that this would produce many additional tips from the public, one of which might lead to the killer. The reward money has been deposited in the Harris Trust and Savings Bank in Chicago by Senator Percy.

It was announced that Governor Kerner, who has announced his resignation to take an appointment as a federal judge, will head a committee to determine who shall receive the reward money in the event of a solution. Others are Robert Galvin, chairman of the Motorola Corporation, and Gaylord Freeman, vice chairman of the First National Bank of Chicago, both close personal friends of Senator Percy.

"Speaking as an individual, I have taken a deep personal interest in this case from the outset," said Governor Kerner. "I believe that this case must be solved."

It had not, however, as this was written.

Day of Reckoning for Sal Mineo's Murderer

by Chris Edwards

Behind-the-scenes details from Los Angeles court records . . .

No matter what the fan magazines or the Chamber of Commerce says to the contrary, Hollywood is a jungle at night. Even the boulevards — Hollywood and Sunset — are seamy in the glare of their bright lights, garish neon and their sidewalks studded with the names of the stars who are the trademarks of show business. It is the home turf of the acne-faced runaways, teenage hustlers both male and female, heavy-lidded pimps checking on their ladies, perverted chicken hawks in voracious quest of young boys, the usual assortment of ferret-faced junkies willing to do anything for a score.

But generally the average Square John is safe. The most he'll get is a proposition — hetero, homo, dead center transvestite.

The real trouble comes when he strays off the main drags and onto the dimly lighted side streets, the dark alleys and the gloomy, silent apartment house garages and carport areas. You don't have to be looking for trouble. It will find you there soon enough.

That side of Hollywood is the dangerous side, as film actor Sal Mineo found out on the night of February 12,

1976 when he returned to his apartment house after rehearsing a play and parked in his carport on Holloway Drive—just a few blocks below the Strip.

In daylight it is a quiet residential neighborhood peopled by comfortably retired senior citizens, young working couples and families whose children walk to neighborhood schools unafraid.

But at night the safest place is behind locked doors.

The dark-haired, 37-year-old actor was returning from the Westwood Playhouse, where he had been rehearsing for the play, "P.S.: Your Cat is Dead," and pulled into the carport area at the rear of the apartment house. It was only 9:15 pm.

Suddenly other residents of the building began hearing the chilling screams of a man begging for his life. "Oh, no! Oh, my God, no! Help me, please!"

A tenant in the building ran from his apartment, down the stairs and to the alley driveway at the rear of the building. He said later, "I saw a man in the fetal position, lying on his side. Because of an incline the blood seemed to be coming from his head.

"I turned him over and said, 'Sal, my God!' And I saw his whole chest covered with blood on one side."

By then other tenants began arriving and caught sight of someone driving off in what appeared to be a yellow Toyota. The tenant said he lifted Mineo's head in an attempt to talk to him but he appeared to be in a semi-conscious state.

He continued: "I saw he was going into an ashen color and I immediately started to give him mouth-to-mouth resuscitation. I was getting a response, then all of a sudden he gave it (a breath) back—and that was it. Everyone was yelling, 'Get the police! Get an ambulance.' But

135

it was too late for an ambulance."

It was determined later that a single thrust of a heavy-bladed knife had pierced Mineo's heart and his death was attributed to massive hemorrhages. He had died on the cold pavement like a character in one of his 1950s films.

His car keys lay beside the actor and his wallet remained untouched in his pocket, indicating that if the motive was robbery, the killer got scared off before he could go through his victim's pockets.

The neighborhood was being plagued by strongarm robberies. From February 7th to March 7th at least 10 persons were held up. Mineo was the only one slain, but most of the others had been in mortal danger, whether they realized it or not.

The murder occurred in an unincorporated area of Los Angeles County and sheriff's homicide detectives took over the investigation. In several of the other robberies in the area a knife and a gun had been used and, as it eventually turned out, one man was involved in most of them.

Lieutenant Phil Bullington of the sheriff's homicide detail, along with several other detectives, quizzed neighbors and other tenants of the building.

The only thing they seemed to agree on was that the crime took place about 9:15 p.m.

Some reported seeing a young man with blond hair and dark clothing run from the carport area after the stabbing. Others said they thought the suspect was a Negro with a bushy Afro hairdo. Still others thought it was a Mexican.

Several witnesses agreed that they had seen the suspect flee in a yellow Toyota. But except for these conflicting descriptions, the detectives had little to go on.

The killer struck in the dark and fled into the dark as empty handed as he had come. But Sal Mineo paid with his life.

Atty. Marvin Mitchelson, the owner of the apartment house, said Mineo had kept an apartment in the building for three years and used it whenever he was in Los Angeles. He lived there alone.

Mineo was born on January 10, 1939 and made his acting debut on Broadway at the age of 11 in "The Rose Tattoo." He went on to appear in more than 20 feature films and dozens of TV shows. As Plato, a switchblade-wielding juvenile delinquent, he became a teenage idol in 1956 in the James Dean movie, "Rebel Without a Cause." The role brought the 17-year-old Mineo a nomination for an Academy Award.

He won his second nomination for best supporting actor for his role as a concentration camp survivor in "Exodus."

His last stage appearance before his death was in "P.S. Your Cat is Dead" in San Francisco, the same role he was rehearsing in Los Angeles at the time he was murdered.

The role he played was that of a comic bisexual burglar.

Mineo's background as a kid growing up in the Bronx fitted him for the roles he was most identified with in the 1950s — a street fighter.

At the height of his success in the '50s, he bought his family a $200,000 home in Mamaroneck, N.Y.

He was survived by his mother, sister and two brothers. Funeral services for the slain actor were held in New York five days after his murder and the church was

137

jammed with mourners.

Mineo's brother-in-law, Chip Meyers, said in the eulogy, "He lived his life with courage, abandon, humor, style and grace. His art, what he created, will always stand. Nothing can take it away from him."

Three years before, Mineo had eulogized his father from the same lectern.

The detectives were extremely careful about disclosing the route of the investigation. But this much is known. Several weeks after the killing, Sheriff's detectives went to the home of a black woman living in South Central Los Angeles.

According to the woman, the detectives talked to her son, Lionel R. Williams, 21, about Mineo's death. She said she told the officers that to the best of her recollection her son was home with her the night of February 12th watching television.

In the weeks that followed, she said, the detectives checked on her son from time to time. They knew he was not a fugitive but made no move to take him into custody and filed no charges against him in connection with the Mineo case.

Some time later a girl friend of Williams told the detectives this story:

She said that when Williams returned to their apartment on the night of February 12th his clothing appeared to be bloodstained. She said he told her he had just stabbed someone. When the television news reported the death of Mineo later that night, she quoted him as saying to her, "That's the dude I killed."

However, the detectives had to admit that in spite of what the young woman told them, they could find no corroboration of her story or direct evidence to link the young black man to the stabbing death of the actor. They learned that Williams had apparently mistreated the girl and that she lived in fear of him, reason enough for a vindictive woman to try to get him out of her life and into jail.

And without hard evidence to support her statement, a district attorney wouldn't touch the case with a 10-foot pole.

Williams was certainly a suspect worth watching, but at this point there was little that could be done about taking him into custody. He would be back on the street in five minutes.

Because of the murder of Mineo, sheriff's detectives focused their attention on an unusual number of similar strongarm robberies that had taken place in the west side area of the city, including Beverly Hills.

On February 7th, a young couple were entering an apartment house to visit friends when they were braced by three young thugs, one of whom put a gun to the man's head and threatened to kill him. The victim watched helplessly as one of the men manhandled his wife and he vowed he would never forget that man's face. The couple was robbed and the thugs fled.

Five days later Sal Mineo was killed in the same neighborhood.

A half-hour after Mineo was killed, a man was driving into his underground garage. When he got out of his car, two men approached him, knocked him down to the floor, punched him and robbed him. The crime was almost a carbon copy of the Sal Mineo murder except that in the case of Roy his life was spared.

On February 19th, a young woman was walking on the street to her car when a man grabbed her, snatched her purse, punched her so hard that she is now deaf in one ear. She screamed, he fled and she said she was positive she would recognize him if ever she saw him again.

Then on February 26th, about two weeks after Mineo's killing, a motorist was driving on the street when two men in a Buick blocked his way. One of the pair, armed with a ball peen hammer, smashed his windshield and demanded his money.

The two men fled, but police caught them about 20 minutes later. In the car the officers found several of the victim's credit cards, and the ball peen hammer.

One of the two men in that car was Lionel Raymond Williams. Both men were taken into custody, but eventually they were released. But before he was sprung, Williams told a sheriff's deputy, "I want to talk to someone about the Mineo case."

He told the officer that he had been at a dope "shooting gallery" and heard some "blood dudes" talking about killing Mineo for a contract of $1,500 for a "dope burn"—a report the police did not believe.

It was about that time when the officers spoke to Williams' mother about Lionel and kept a loose surveillance on the robbery suspect.

Still another robbery—this one in Beverly Hills—took place on swanky Rodeo Drive in front of the exclusive Gucci's. Two couples on an evening window shopping tour were robbed at gunpoint. Among the things taken was a probation officer's badge from one of the women victims.

Somehow the robberies were never linked to one another, or to the killing of Mineo. No one seemed to conclude that a general description of one of the suspects cropped up from time to time. And as valuable hindsight was to reveal, that man looked suspiciously like Lionel Raymond Williams. It would be some time, however, before he was nailed to the crime wave.

Sheriff Peter Pitchess said the investigation of the Sal Mineo slaying ranged from California to Nevada, Arizona, Michigan, Washington, New York and Florida in the months that followed the killing. But he never would say what his men were looking for, or whom they were trailing.

But always in the background lurked the shadowy figure of Lionel Williams.

One major problem with the Williams angle was that witnesses at the scene of the crime could not agree whether the suspect was black or white, and Williams was a light-skinned black.

The short, stocky Williams was eventually arrested in Inglewood, Calif. in April, 1977 on traffic warrants and turned over to authorities in Michigan, where he was being sought on a bad check charge. No link to the Sal Mineo murder was involved.

Now the Los Angeles detectives knew that Williams would be behind bars for some time to come, and they advised Michigan prison authorities to be on the lookout for any reports that Williams was shooting his mouth off to other prisoners — a common practice among new "fish" — trying to establish themselves as tough guys in the eyes of other inmates.

So far, the detectives had indications that Williams had blabbed to his pals and girl friends about the Mineo murder in Los Angeles. Now he might have some incriminating statements to make to his fellow prisoners.

Williams had been sentenced to 10 months in March, 1977 in Michigan. He was scheduled to be released in mid-January.

In October 1977, Deputy Sheriff Ronald Peek of Calhoun County, Michigan, told a Los Angeles detective that he heard a conversation between Williams and an inmate. He said he heard Williams say, "I killed a dude a while back," and when the other inmate asked him who it was, Williams replied, "Actor by the name of Sal Mineo."

The deputy first regarded the conversation as "jailhouse talk" and thought no more of it, until he learned that Williams was a prime suspect in the case. Then he passed the conversation along to the Los Angeles officer, and things happened.

Armed with a court order, officials were given permission to bug Williams' cell to record any conversation he might have in connection with the Mineo murder.

Williams was due to be released from the Michigan jail on January 8,1978, but on January 5th he got the bad news. Los Angeles County was seeking to extradite him to California on charges of killing Sal Mineo. Declarations filed to support the arrest warrant for Williams included statements made by his girl friend, by Deputy Peek, and at least one fellow inmate in whom he had confided.

The information filed by the Los Angeles County Sheriff's Office stated that Williams lay in wait for Sal Mineo and with a single thrust of a hunting knife pierced his heart, causing him to bleed to death in a few minutes. Because of the lying-in-wait element of the case, the conviction would carry with it the death penalty for first degree murder.

Another point of the investigation was the small yellow car seen leaving the scene of the murder, its lights out. It was identified by witnesses as probably a Toyota.

But the Los Angeles investigators learned that on February 12, 1976, the day Mineo was killed, Williams had borrowed a 1971 Dodge Colt from a Lincoln Mercury dealer and they had a loan agreement signed by Williams to prove it.

According to the declaration against Williams, the investigators determined that the appearance of the Dodge Colt is very similar to that of a Toyota. It was simply another bit of circumstantial evidence that was piling up against Williams.

Little by little the case was being constructed against Lionel Williams. At best it was a circumstantial one, and plainly lacking in cold hard evidence that could put Williams at the scene of the crime or place the murder weapon in his hand.

At a January 4, 1978, hearing in Calhoun County Circuit Court, Williams waived extradition and agreed to return to Los Angeles and face up to the first degree murder charge that had been filed against him. He was handcuffed and dressed in jailhouse fatigues and slippers when he appeared in court. On the way he confided to newsmen that he had nothing to do with the murder of Mineo. No one appeared to notice the freshly tattooed dagger on his left arm.

Asked whether he felt he would be found not guilty, he turned to a newsman and replied, "Yeah, man! I'm cool."

And as he was led from the courtroom after the hearing, he grinned and said to one of the deputies, "This is a big deal, ain't it?"

It was indeed.

It had been nearly two years since the murder of the talented actor and a prime suspect was finally in custody for the slaying, albeit with very little evidence to go on. However, lawyers are quick to point out that many a man has gone to prison on circumstantial evidence of the kind that was building up against Williams. It remained for the prosecutor to convince a jury that the defendant was guilty beyond a reasonable doubt.

Williams was booked into the Los Angeles County jail and bail was set at $200,000. His arraignment was set for January 16th in Beverly Hills Municipal Court. At the arraignment he made a formal denial of guilt to the robbery and pleaded innocent to the homicide charge.

His bail was upped to $500,000.

At this point Sheriff Pitchess called a press conference and exclaimed, "The sheriff's bulldogs have done it again!" He was wasting no time in taking credit for the arrest of Williams. However, he did not disclose how his men put the case together, although it was generally believed that it was Williams' own big mouth that brought him most of this grief.

Pitchess did say, however, that his investigators felt the motive for the killing was robbery, even though the killer had fled before he could take the actor's wallet.

Pitchess said the death weapon was a hunting knife, but that it had not been recovered. He said Williams became a top suspect shortly after he was arrested in Los Angeles and returned to Michigan on a charge of passing a worthless check for $174. From that time the evidence against Williams began funneling into the sheriff's office.

All Deputy District Attorney Burton Katz would say

144

about the apprehension of Williams was, "I've spent a lot of time in some of those places (Washington, Michigan, New York, Nevada and Arizona) trying to piece things together."

Pitchess said, "Our belief is that it was premeditated murder, because as you will recall, Mineo was returning from the rehearsal of a play and came directly there to his place of residence and had just left his car when he was attacked."

Asked about the statement of one witness who described the fleeing killer as a white man, Pitchess said the witness had only "a fleeting glimpse" of the suspect and could well have mistaken Williams, a light-complexioned Negro, for a Caucasian.

Toward the end of January, 1978, the district attorney's office took the case before the grand jury, over the objections of Williams' attorney, Robert Harris. Harris charged DA made that move only because the evidence was extremely weak and would not have survived an adversary proceeding such as a preliminary hearing.

Harris also charged that when Katz presented his case to the grand jury he did not present "exculpatory" evidence that might point to the innocence of Williams.

Said Harris, "One thing I know for sure is that Mr. Williams' mother who says Williams was with her on the night of the murder was not even subpoenaed to appear before the grand jury."

Prosecutor Katz responded that he went the grand jury route to keep the forum from turning into a circus as would a preliminary hearing open to the public.

He said he also went to the grand jury for the protection of the witnesses—several of them convicts—who were in fear of their lives. Katz said, "We've already lost one of our witnesses," but he declined to say whether this was the result of foul play or because of threats.

The defense attorney also complained that Katz had not turned over to him all the evidence against Williams, as required by the rule of discovery, particularly the tape recording made in the Michigan jail.

Katz replied that investigators had been working around the clock to transcribe 82 hours of tape and would turn them over to the defense when they were completed.

The grand jury returned indictments charging Williams with a series of strongarm robberies in a period of time before and after the Mineo slaying. Williams pleaded not guilty to 10 counts of robbery and one count of armed robbery when he appeared before Superior Judge Paul Breckenridge in May of 1978. He was also re-indicted on the murder charge so that all charges could be consolidated for a single trial.

A former schoolmate of Williams was named as a co-defendant in one robbery count. This man later testified against Williams and linked him to the murder of Mineo.

The murder and robbery trial of Lionel Williams finally got under way in January, 1979, nearly three years after the murder of Mineo. The strong point of the case against Williams, a pizza delivery man, was the suspect's own big mouth and the testimony of those who reportedly listened to Williams bragging about murdering Mineo. The testimony of his partners in crime linked him to the robberies, along with the testimony of the victims of the crimes.

The prosecutor, Deputy District Attorney Michael Genelin, relied heavily on bugged testimony and on statements from witnesses to whom Williams allegedly spoke of the crimes.

One of these was a young Marine who admittedly participated in one of the robberies with Williams and to whom Williams spoke of the Mineo murder.

The Marine, Allwyn Price Williams, 26 (no relation to the defendant), testified that Lionel Williams told him about the killing while they were just talking "in general" and reminiscing about their gang-fighting days one day in January, 1977, about a year after the killing.

"We came to the discussion that he had killed someone famous" said the Marine. When asked who it was, the Marine said, the defendant told him, "Sal Mineo."

The Marine testified, "He (the defendant) said he was in Hollywood driving around below Sunset, somewhere in there. He was going to rob someone for some money and then he stabbed someone. He told how he done it, and demonstrated."

In response to a request from the prosecutor, Allwyn Williams demonstrated how the defendant indicated the manner in which he murdered Sal Mineo. The court reporter recorded the action as "the right hand downward thrust kind of motion."

The Marine said the defendant told him that Mineo "grabbed his chest and yelled, 'Ah' or 'Oh.' "

According to the witness, Lionel Williams told him the purpose of the stabbing was robbery, but no money was taken and the suspect ran from the scene and returned to his car.

The young Marine said he was on leave from his duty station in Hawaii and was testifying under a grant of immunity from prosecution.

The Marine witness also described a robbery in which he participated with Lionel Williams and a third man. This was the March 7, 1976 stickup near the Gucci shop on Rodeo Drive in Beverly Hills—about a month after the murder.

Said the Marine, "We were looking for someone to rob who we felt would have money. And we saw four potential victims—two males and two females."

He said they parked the car around the corner and he and Lionel Williams walked toward the couples. "Williams had a gun on one of the men and we demanded some money. We were given what we wanted," the Marine said.

He said among the things they took from the two couples was a probation officer's badge.

Another prosecution witness was Ronald Peek, the former deputy in the Calhoun County jail in Michigan. He testified he was making his rounds in the jail in October, 1977 when he heard Williams tell of killing Mineo. Peek said he told another deputy what had been said, but they discounted the statement as jail talk and didn't report it to higher authority for two months, after they learned Williams was linked to Mineo's murder.

A woman deputy in the same jail told the six-man, six-woman jury that she had heard Williams say it was easy to kill someone, but she heard nothing further before she ordered him from the jail kitchen.

The one big gap in the case for the prosecution was the absence of a murder weapon. There was no doubt that a hunting knife style of weapon was used. The size of the wound indicated that.

After the killing it could have been disposed of in any one of a number of ways. It was steeped in the blood of Sal Mineo, and chances are the killer would not want to be found in possession of the weapon.

But after the arrest of Williams in Michigan, the big-mouthed suspect couldn't resist telling detectives that he had purchased a hunting knife about the time of the killing but that neither he nor the weapon had anything to do with Mineo's death. Nor did he know what had become of the knife — probably lost it somewhere.

So it was long after Williams' arrest for murder that the detectives were directed to an outdoor type store in Hollywood where they asked about a certain type hunting knife, and if the management could determine from a check of its records whether such a knife had been sold on or about February 16, 1976.

Out came the records, and up came a receipt indicating that such a knife had been sold in the store on February 12, 1976, the day of Mineo's death. Williams was not named in the store records.

The management furnished the detectives with a knife similar to that sold on February 12, 1976. The weapon was turned over to the coroner's office where it would be matched against the measurement and markings of Mineo's wounds.

The conclusions of the coroner were that such a knife could without a doubt inflict the wounds that killed Sal Mineo.

Williams seemed to be playing a game with the detectives, telling them where he had bought a knife, a description of it, knowing all along it would be matched against the wounds and also knowing it would be of little use as evidence.

But the tale of the knife did not end here. There was a picture of it tattooed on Williams' left arm, and it matched exactly the weapon that had been purchased by the authorities.

Almost proudly, Williams had told the officers that he had the tattoo imprinted on his arm after he left Los Angeles and went to Michigan.

He told the officer, "I had it done while I was back in Michigan after the Mineo killing." But he never admitted he had anything to do with the killing himself.

Prosecutor Genelin described the tattoo as Williams' "Mark of Cain." He called Williams "a strange breed of cat, totally unconcerned with any human being. He doesn't give a damn who he hurts. He told his girlfriend that when he felt bad he had to go out and hurt someone."

When Marine Williams and Lionel Williams were in the Los Angeles jail, the murder defendant flashed a note to a visitor—a note that was intercepted—which read:

"I want Big Perry down here right away. It is important. The Rock is trying to kill me. I want to do something to Rock right away. He can kill me. So do something about him. He is against me all the way. Important. He is in high power."

According to the prosecutor, "Rock is a nickname for Marine Allwyn Williams. Lionel Williams knew that the Marine had finked on him and could send him to the gas chamber, so he apparently was soliciting his murder—or at least bodily harm—in the county jail."

The Williams trial went on for nearly four weeks and not a single eyewitness to the murder of Sal Mineo was called—because there was none. Several persons had witnessed elements of the crime but none could positively identify Williams as the killer.

Williams had boasted to several persons that he had stabbed Mineo to death, and he even directed the investigators to the type of knife that had killed the actor. But not once could anyone put the death weapon in Williams' hand.

But there were people who could identify him as one of the men who robbed them on the streets of the Wilshire and Hollywood districts—robberies similar to the Mineo case—as well as the testimony of those who took part in some of the robberies with him.

And there was the knife—the one he directed the officers to, the copy of which he had indelibly tattooed on his left arm. And although he never explained why he had it drawn there for everyone to see, the reason appeared obvious—Lionel Williams was a braggart. Without saying so, he wanted people to know—or at least speculate—that he had killed Sal Mineo.

In his closing argument, defense atty. Herbert told the six-man, six-woman jury, "I want somebody to play the murderer. I want him to have large curls. I want him to look like an Italian. And I want him to have large cheekbones. I want him to have along thin nose. I want him to be about five feet ten inches tall. And I want him to be white.

"Look around the room and point out who is the last person in the world that you would cast for this part. And I submit to you that he is sitting at the end of the counsel table (Williams.)"

And he concluded, "Whether Lionel Raymond Williams is a saint or scum or some place in between, you are to judge him only by the standards of reasonable doubt and your own conscience — and nothing else."

Prosecutor Genelin told the jury that if they numbered the "coincidences" linking Williams to the Mineo murder and they draw lines from number to number, a face will start emerging — "and that face is the face of the defendant."

He concluded, "I am convinced from the evidence that we have that you will find this defendant guilty of everything he is charged with. All I ask aside from that is that you enforce the law."

The jury deliberated the fate of Lionel Williams for seven days and then convicted him of second degree murder in the fatal stabbing of Sal Mineo. He was found innocent of a companion armed robbery count involving Mineo as a victim. However, he was found guilty on the 10 other counts of robbery.

When the verdict in the murder count was pronounced, Williams slowly and deliberately turned around and looked scornfully at the courtroom audience. Then he unwrapped a stick of gum, popped it into his mouth and turned toward the bench.

Judge Ronnie Lee Martin set March 15th for sentencing. On that date he sentenced Lionel Williams to serve at least 50 years in prison. In imposing consecutive sentences of five years to life for the murder of Sal Mineo and the series of robberies, the judge said, "The defendant should be committed to state prison for as long as the law allows."

Murder At Madison Square Garden

by Terrence Flint

More than 70 years have passed since Harry Kendall Thaw killed Stanford White at the Madison Square Garden Roof in New York, yet, while time has dimmed the recollection of affairs of national and international importance, seven decades have not obliterated the memory of this famous murder case.

Let us go back to the warm summer night of June 25th, 1906, at the Madison Square Garden Roof, where *Mam'zelle Champagne* was having its premiere with Viola de Costa in the title role.

It wasn't a successful opening. The first night audience was openly bored by the ineptness of the actors and the dullness of the script. So much so, that many of them walked out on the show. Those who lingered saw the curtain ring up on a real life tragedy — a stirring and intense drama.

In the audience, with several friends, were Harry Thaw and the beautiful young woman he had married a little more than a year previously, Evelyn Nesbit Thaw. With their party they were making their way to the elevator which gave to the street. The lift was slow in arriving. Thaw detached himself from his group and, while the actors on the stage were still striving to enliven an obvious flop, he walked over to the table where Stanford White sat alone.

He took a gun from his pocket, fired one shot at White and, as the stricken man fell forward, pumped two more into him. Then he turned and walked away.

A dead silence fell over the audience and actors alike as the three sharp reports rang out. Groups dispersed. Some ran toward White's table. A number of women fainted, others screamed — and some, more cynical, booed what they believed was a stage trick. The actors and the girls in their scanty costumes stood frozen on the stage. Here and there many men, Broadway-wise, shouted: "It's Thaw; Thaw did it!"

Who was this Harry Kendall Thaw with the grand manner and the calm mien, who so unconcernedly turned on his heel and walked toward the elevator as though nothing had happened?

It was recorded in statistics some years ago that the two most publicized persons in the world were former President Theodore Roosevelt and Harry K. Thaw with Thaw holding the lead.

Thaw had for years been known as one of Broadway's most prodigal playboys. His lavish contributions to what was then known affectionately as the Gay White Way had made him a singular figure. He had, for instance, once staged, for a hundred of the loveliest girls in New York's musical productions, a dinner party that was reputed to have cost him $60,000. He had been embroiled in numerous fights in the gaudier and sportier of the many restaurants.

His father was dead, but before his decease he had accumulated a fortune of more than $40,000,000 in Pittsburgh steel. This vast wealth was left to his wife, with certain restraining clauses which forbade his son Harry from having any disposition of the income. He had reason for this.

In his adolescence, Harry had journeyed several times to Europe, and, despite his years, he had made these tours memorable, sometimes unfragrantly. He had prepped in a school in Ohio and had entered what is now known as the University of Pittsburgh. He then transferred, without being graduated, to Harvard.

With other gilded youths, he had his rooms on the Gold Coast of Cambridge. The wealthy young man was little inclined toward the cultivation of his mind; so little indeed, that one day President Charles W. Eliot — that flame of intellect — summoned the young millionaire to his office and gave him three hours in which to pack and depart the university. Thaw said it was because of high-stake poker, but it was rumored there were other reasons. Whatever the cause, diploma-less he went hence, schooling a thing of the past.

New York was his destination. The hostelries and restaurants were in for boom years while Thaw romped up and down Broadway and in and out of stage doors. It was thus he met Evelyn Nesbit.

She, like Harry, was fatherless. Her dad had been a Pennsylvania lawyer, but he had gathered nothing from his profession; there were no legacies for the widow or the children, Evelyn and Howard. Like Harry, Evelyn had been born on a holiday, December 25th, 1884. When she was little more than fifteen years old, her mother brought her to New York to place her on the stage.

With every respect for the much-abused term, she was a raving beauty. Her features were classic and, with all her immaturity, she had a figure to inspire sonnets, intrigue artists and captivate sculptors. Her mother ap-

155

plied with her to George Lederer for an engagement. Lederer at that time held the place as a producer which Florenz Ziegfeld later was to occupy.

Lederer wanted no trouble with the Gerry Society — guardians of those who wish to grace the stage before the age of sixteen — but finally he succumbed to the girl's pleas and made her one of the chorus.

From the moment of her first appearance she exercised a spell over all beholders. It was not long before she was posing for the town's foremost artists. It was not long, either, before she was in *Floradora,* and then later in *The Wild Rose,* with plenty of stage offers.

It was while she was with the *Floradora* company — not as a member of the Sextette, by the way — that Thaw met her and laid siege to her heart. She had another admirer, too: John Barrymore, then a struggling young actor who aspired to be a cartoonist. And still another: Stanford White. He, the oldest, was the most assiduous of the suitors and, for many reasons, the most important.

At the time Stanford White was attracted to Evelyn he was the greatest architect in this country. It has been said since, that his death retarded the progress of American architecture for, at least, ten years — the march of national beauty was halted because he had surrendered to an irresistible infatuation.

White was born in New York City on November 9th, 1853, so that when a bullet ended his life, he was more than fifty-two years old. His family traced back three hundred years on American soil. He was one of the elect socially; in his work he stood without a peer, and his acquaintance numbered every person of note on both sides of the Atlantic. Every exclusive club was proud to have him on its roster.

He had studied his profession under Henry Hobson Richardson of Boston. A senior fellow-student was Charles Follen McKim, with whom he subsequently formed the firm of McKim, Mead and White. The combination was destined to take New York from the ugliness of the late McKinley period, and give it form and dignity.

Among the triumphs of White's genius were Madison Square Garden, where he met his death; Sherry's where his slayer fortified himself with liquor hours before *Mam'zelle Champagne* rang up its curtain; the Herald Building, whose owner, James Gordon Bennett, issued orders to "give White hell" when his name was being dragged in the gutter; the Hall of Fame at New York University, where he inevitably would have been honored with a niche had not an assassin's bullet opened up the inglorious side of his life; the church of Dr. Charles W. Parkhurst, who thundered, from the pulpit White had designed, against the iniquities he represented.

His other works include the Washington Arch, the Tiffany Building, Gorham Building, the Metropolitan Club, and the Colony Club. He even had a commission from Richard Canfield, the noted gambler, who in a later day was driven out of business by District Attorney Jerome — the same Jerome who, in a still later day, was to be the relentless prosecutor of Thaw. Throughout the country there are other splendid structures, still significant because they sprang from Stanford White's mind.

White, when he fell under the spell of Evelyn Nesbit, was married. He had married into a family descended from the original patrons of New Amsterdam. Bessie Springs Smith was his wife's name. At a bachelor dinner to him before the wedding in 1884 — the year of Evelyn's birth—every man of note in New York was present! Richard Watson Gilder, Sargent, LaFarge, Weir, Abbey, Saint Gaudens and some forty others. An impromptu verse was born in the brain of one of the well-wishers present, important only for its subsequent inapplicability:

> Who builds well
> Escapes Hell;
> Stanford White
> Builds aright.
> Honor his art,
> His head, his heart.

White, as has been said, had passed the half-century mark when Evelyn—her friends, to her delight, afterward corrupted this to "Evil Un"—reached into his heart. He had a son at Harvard—a boy older than the chorus girl he, the father, plied with attentions.

Thus, we have the principal actors in the tragedy. Now to the conflict, the steps which impelled the profligate to shoot down the satyr.

Thaw, it has been related, was not actually an heir to his father's estate. That fortune of $40,000,000 had been left in its entirety to the mother, Mary Copley Thaw. She had two other sons, Josiah and Edward; the Countess of Yarmouth was one of her daughters, and Mrs. George Lauder Carnegie the other. Harry, however, for all his waywardness, was her favorite child; she was to him a doting and indulgent mother, so he never lacked for money to burn a lurid trail along Broadway.

He, like many another youth of his time, was entranced by Evelyn. It was not in his character to worship from afar; his was the direct approach. He recommended himself to the chorus girl while she was in *Floradora* by sending her a backbreaking box of roses with a note, and within the note a $50 bill. The note itself craved the opportunity of dining with her. Such generosity and ardor were not to be unnoticed. She dined with him the next evening and then raced to her dressing room to get ready for the performance. Seemingly they were attracted to each other at once, for this was the first of many delightful tete-a-tetes.

All this time the handsome John Barrymore was devotedly hovering near Evelyn. Not many years ago the Barrymores were identified as the Royal Family of the American stage, but, when John knew Evelyn, the mantle of royalty was far from his shoulders. Nevertheless, with his admitted poverty and his lack of prospects, he held an important place in the girl's heart.

White's approach was more delicate, more insidious and subtle. He knew every beautiful woman on the stage, and he induced one of them to bring Evelyn to him for luncheon. It is not to be expected that the girl, then less than seventeen, could fail to be impressed by this man of distinguished appearance, position, charm of personality and thoughtfulness.

This last quality, thoughtfulness, made the deepest impression. White had Evelyn's mother take her to a dentist, to expensive modiste shops, to beauty parlors. He expended every consideration which might add to the girl's beauty and happiness.

He knew of Thaw, of course — who didn't? — but he brushed thoughts of him aside. He refused to believe that this wastrel, for all his youth and wealth, could cast his influence over Evelyn. Her mother, too, as an ally of

159

White, strove desperately to break any grip Thaw might have on her daughter's affections.

All of them reckoned without Barrymore. Evelyn was bewildered and flattered by the knowledge that she had three men at her feet; one with social place, one with limitless money, and one with nothing but his art. The one with none of the world's goods, Barrymore, had the strongest appeal for her—the appeal of physical attraction, brilliant personality and good looks. She refused to give him up for either of the others.

White, more readily than Thaw, recognized the strength of the Barrymore competition. With the mother's help he sought to dissuade her from Barrymore's society. A stormy scene followed between the girl and her mother—one at which Barrymore was present.

John wanted to marry Evelyn and she was willing. In a panic, Mrs. Nesbit flew to White. He took control of the situation. In his wisdom he recognized that the deepest impression on the girl was made by the person last with her. His kindness, his consideration, his wide knowledge of the world, were brought into play. Without scorning the actor—this merely would have brought Evelyn to his defense—White made her see what a mistake marriage to a penniless player would be. His solution was a simple one; to send the girl away to a young ladies' finishing school in New Jersey.

With fatherly patience, White told Evelyn that if, after she completed school, Barrymore still was in her thoughts, he would offer every assistance to their union. He knew Evelyn's malleability, he knew of her fickleness, he had the consciousness that her desire for a new experience would tear her away from Barrymore. He won. Evelyn went to the school.

It is to be deplored that she wished much less to be a lady than she did to demoralize the school. She brought to the young misses who were being educated for an exalted station in life, the sophistication of Broadway, the slang of the stage and a worldliness altogether alien to her academic surroundings. She didn't last long, and thus, perhaps, the innocence of her schoolmates suffered no real injury.

She went back to Broadway again, joyously and recklessly. Thaw then had his innings — now that Barrymore was about out of the picture and White momentarily interested elsewhere. He had Evelyn and her mother go to Europe and he traveled in another boat to meet them in Paris.

Mrs. Nesbit was completely unhappy. She cabled frantically to her confederate, White. The young people escaped from her, and together — and intimately — toured the Continent. As man and wife they visited various countries. Thaw asked Evelyn to marry him. She refused. Then as precipitately as she had departed, she returned. White greeted her warmly on her arrival.

She had been unhappy, she told him. She recounted some of her experiences and White had her make an affidavit to a lawyer, Abe Hummel — a redoubtable counsel in criminal cases. The architect meant to have this document as a weapon over Thaw, whom he now acknowledged as a formidable rival.

The gilded youth, on returning, faced this animosity and started a counter-attack, when he learned of the affidavit. From every available source he dug up scandal against White. He went to Anthony Comstock, then head of the Society for the Suppression of Vice, to enlist his aid.

Thaw put such facts as he had before the district attorney, but won little encouragement. He asked the assistance of the police, but they demanded proof before they would act. This, even when he charged that White had hired Monk Eastman — the most notorious gangster of the city — to do him in.

In the midst of the excitement he had stirred up, he whisked Evelyn to Pittsburgh and there, on April 5th, 1905, they were married. Upon their return to New York they took a suite in the Hotel Lorraine, Fifty-fifth Street and Fifth Avenue, later a sacrifice to the office building craze which grew up in the Coolidge administration.

Rightly or wrongly, Thaw still felt that White was trying to win Evelyn away from him. He still believed that the menace of Monk Eastman's gunmen dogged his steps and — on the advice of Roger O'Meara, chief of police in Pittsburgh — he armed himself. He continued, with private detectives and with the bewhiskered Comstock, to seek proof that White had ravished hundreds of young girls. The name of White uttered in his presence was sufficient to throw him into a frenzy of rage.

We come now to the night of the killing:

Harry and Evelyn were living in the Lorraine. They had made their plans see the opening of the new show at the Madison Square Roof Garden. Evelyn's dressing was tardy, so Thaw told her he would wait for her at Sherry's where they were to have dinner. At the bar he had a number of drinks with Tommy McCaleb and Truxton Beale. He invited them to dine with Evelyn and him, but, as Beale was not in evening dress, they changed their destination to Martin's — then one of the famous eating places in New York.

162

This sudden decision proved contributory to White's killing a few hours later. White came into the restaurant a few minutes after the arrival of Thaw's party, with his son and another Harvard student.

At all times Evelyn was conspicuous, but that night, in shimmering white satin, she easily was the most beautiful woman in the place. If White saw her when he entered, he gave no sign. Nor did Thaw notice White's arrival until Evelyn passed him a note.

"The B. just walked in," it said. Defense counsel, some months afterward said "B" meant blackguard.

White tried to induce his son and his friend to go with him to the new show, but they already had tickets for a different show.

As dinner at the Thaw table progressed merrily, Harry said:

"We are having such a good time here, why not stay?"

"No," said Evelyn. "I don't want to. I want excitement. I want something better to do than sit here and drink."

And so — still another step — they went to the theater. Captain Wharton had been invited impromptu by Thaw, so, when they reached their seats on the roof, there were only four places for five people — Wharton, McCaleb, Beale, Evelyn and Harry. The latter solved the difficulty by walking around the back of the roof.

White was seated alone at a table close to the stage. He had gone behind the curtain, but the company was in such a state of nervous excitement that the stage manager had pleaded with him to delay his visit until after the show. That is why he was out front — another step in the direction of his death.

As Thaw roved restlessly, the party he had deserted became more and more fed up with the performance.

Finally Evelyn, who wanted excitement, gave the signal for departure—a welcome one to all of them. Two things happened then, two trivial, accidental things which induced the party to pause, and these brief interruptions brought about the extinguishment of one of the great minds of America.

One pause came, strangely enough, through the compelling beauty of White's own achievement. In the soft night, silhouetted against a lambent moon, the Giralda Tower of the Garden rose majestically, and the group stopped to admire the picture it made. The nude Diana, poised upon its pinnacle, was a great sight. These—the products of White's genius—halted the departure. The elevator dropped away without them. The Thaw party had to wait for its return.

Harry, who had been oddly agitated ever since they arrived on the roof, excused himself as they paused beside the elevator shaft. They gave his absence no further thought until a shot rang out, and then two more.

Describing the scene, after the killing; Thaw said:

"I saw White and I said to Tommy McCaleb, 'Excuse me.' There I saw White thirty feet in front of me and, as he watched the stage, he saw me.

"I walked straight toward him and about fifteen feet away, I took out my revolver. He knew me and he was rising and held his right hand toward, I think, his gun and I wanted to let him try; but a man, a dozen men, might have maimed me, cut off the light, allowing him to escape and rape, more American girls as he had; too many, too many, as he had ruined Evelyn.

"Half rising, he gazed at me malignantly. I shot him twelve feet away. I felt sure he was dead. But I wanted to take no chances; I walked toward him and fired two

164

more shots. He dropped. Evelyn uttered a cry, 'My God, Harry, what have you done?' I held her close and told her, 'It is all right, dearie. I have probably saved your life,' then I kissed her."

The first shot, as the coroner disclosed, had gone to White's brain after entering his left eye; the second hit him in the mouth and, as he toppled forward, the third struck him in the shoulder.

As Thaw rode down in the elevator, Evelyn clung to him. "Harry," she said, "I'll stick to you, but you're in an awful mess."

And she did stick.

When he was placed in a cell in the Tombs, he demanded champagne. Of course, it was denied him, but a physician was found who prescribed this as a sedative to his nerves; accordingly, Thaw enjoyed a pint of vintage wine each day.

His mother was on the ocean, on her way to visit her Countess daughter in England when her son took the law into his own hands. Her vessel was not equipped with radio, so the dire news did not reach her until her boat touched Liverpool. She turned right around and came back on the next ship to be with her boy.

As one would expect, eminent counsel was immediately retained. Thaw's lawyers realized the seriousness of his plight much more than he did—he had no fear whatever of the outcome. The first plan was to prove insanity—a fairly logical premise in the circumstances. They reckoned without their client, however; he instantly discharged them and engaged new attorneys. He scented a plot by Stanford White's friends.

In this move he had his mother's support when she arrived; she would suffer no blight to be attached to the family name. The strategy of the new counsel was to demonstrate that Thaw was rendered temporarily insane — that he had suffered a brainstorm — because his wife had been debauched.

To prove this, it was necessary to turn popular opinion against White. For this purpose a well-known author was engaged to put on a campaign and the Thaw money financed a play based on the "unwritten law."

Thaw had seven lawyers on his staff, among whom was Delphin M. Delmas, the brilliant San Francisco criminal attorney. For the State the district attorney, William Travers Jerome, had one assistant, Francis P. Garvan. Justice Fitzgerald sat on the bench when the trial was opened on January 23rd, 1907.

Eight days were required to fill the jury box — which gives an idea of the fixity of opinion which prevailed among the talesmen, but finally the taking of testimony got under way. The presentation of the prosecutor's case was not difficult. There was no question of the crime, its perpetrator or its victim.

When the defense opened, the first innings were given to alienists, called to prove that the defendant had suffered temporary lapse of reason because of the story his wife had told him of her seduction by White. Day after day was consumed in long descriptions of how an interval of insanity could have been induced, without damage to the essential theory that the slayer had been sane before the deed and, after the brainstorm, regained possession of his original sanity.

Jerome, fighting practically single-handed, combated the theory and kept the score at least even until Evelyn was called to the stand.

Marriage with Thaw and the murder of White seemingly should have eliminated Barrymore as a factor in Evelyn's life, particularly after the years which had intervened since their attachment. District Attorney Jerome, however, would not have it so. Day after day, he compelled the actor—under the duress of a constant subpoena—to sit within the rail in the sight of the defendant and his wife. If the spectacle of his erstwhile rival was intended to unnerve Thaw, the plan failed; if it was hoped to disconcert Evelyn, its purpose was unachieved. The only person unnerved was the unhappy actor; the only one disconcerted was Jerome.

Evelyn had just reached the age of twenty-three, and despite the vicissitudes of the seven years she had been in New York, her beauty had ripened into more than a fulfillment of its earlier promise.

For three days, she was examined by the defense counsel. Delmas conducted the questioning. Which brings up the fact that the array of counsel had undergone a severe disruption. The earlier spokesman for Thaw was compelled to abdicate and Delmas, under threat of abandoning the case, took command. His first move was one of great adroitness. He was compelled to prove that Thaw suffered derangement because of the wrong done to Evelyn by White. Delmas did this, not by proving what had happened, but by making Evelyn disclose what she had told to Thaw of her seduction. Thus, he avoided bringing facts to bear and solved the difficulty by having her testify what she had related to Thaw—a move which practically tied Jerome's hands, when he came to cross-examine.

Her story was an amazing one. She said that when Thaw offered her marriage in Europe, she refused him because she had been ruined by White.

167

She had met White first in 1901 through another chorus girl. Eventually, the two girls joined him and another man for luncheon in his rooms in the Madison Square Tower. The room was entirely draped in dark velvet.

The other man left, and White conducted the girls to a room higher in the tower, a room which had a red velvet swing. Their host had the girls take turns on the swing. It was, as she related it, a jolly occasion, one to which she in her juvenile innocence attached no significance.

White insinuated himself into her friendship by doing innumerable favors for her and her mother. She was thereby so inclined to him that she felt no misgivings when, one evening after the theatre, he invited her to supper in his tower rooms. She believed, she said, that others would be present. Still she felt no fear, not even when White ushered her into another room and persuaded her to have some champagne to ease her fatigue.

"Then everything got very black," she testified.

She awoke to find herself in a room of mirrors, all around the bed, on the walls and over the bed. White was in the room with her.

On cross-examination, she told Jerome that was the story she had related to Thaw when he was importuning her to be his bride. He persuaded her, she testified, to go over the harrowing narrative again and again. Notwithstanding, he married her, but only, she said, when his mother pleaded his case.

With all his skill, Jerome could not break down her story in any major particular. He did win from her the admission that, like the Yukon maid who was betrayed and "re-betrayed," she associated with White after her seduction. He did hear from her lips a voluntary tribute to the man who had violated her:

"Outside of this one terrible thing about Stanford White, he was a very grand man. He was kind and considerate and extremely thoughtful—much more thoughtful than most people. He had a very peculiar personality. People liked him very much. He made a great many friends and kept them."

Jerome pounded on the fact that when Evelyn took flight to Europe, with Thaw, she had White's letter of credit for $500 with her. She explained she had spent the money on her mother.

The Hummel affidavit she repudiated in its entirety. She said that she had been coerced into signing it, and she never knew its contents. This affidavit, in brief, dwelt upon the fact that Thaw was a moral pervert given to sadistic habits, and cited a series of degenerate instances.

The defense got into the record the fact that Thaw had made a will in which he set aside $50,000 in the event he came to his death from other than natural causes. This fund was to be used for discovery of the circumstances and the agents contributing to his demise.

Anthony Comstock was called to the stand to corroborate the Thaw contention that White had violated innumerable young girls, but the vice-hunter was unable to testify to anything of his own knowledge.

Much was made of the fact that at a stag dinner, attended by group of wealthy men, a huge pie had been brought into the dining room and out of it, when opened, stepped a young girl. In the modern point of view, the event as it was told on the stand would be just a little off the line of decorum, but as it was blazoned forth

169

at that time, it was made to appear as a gathering of libertines. And, when the news of it broke before the trial, many of the distinguished company who had been at the Pie Dinner found it necessary to depart immediately for Europe.

After Evelyn's testimony, Delmas again shifted ground. He discarded the temporary insanity idea almost wholly, and placed his main reliance on the "unwritten law." Jerome countered with an application for a sanity commission. The Court granted the request. After prolonged hearings, the commission brought in a finding to the effect that Thaw was sane.

Thaw did not testify in his own defense.

He did, however, enjoy the role in which he appeared. He relished the letters of encouragement which came to him from the public, as witness this note which he tossed across to Delmas on March 1st:

Dear Mr. Delmas:

You may be pleased to hear that today besides over 60 American letters I rec'd 26 from abroad, most appreciative. Many also spoke of you. Most of the foreign letters were from England; Sat. I assume more will follow.

Yours Very Truly,
H. T.

Jerome in his summation made a masterly array of the facts as brought out in the testimony, dwelling frequently on the fact that between the time of the alleged confession by Evelyn of her seduction and the commission of the crime, a long interval had ensued. It was a straightforward demand for a conviction; an insistence

170

that Thaw pay with his life for the life he had taken.

The summing-up of Delmas, several days in duration, was a direct appeal to the emotions of the jury, a frank offering of the unwritten law as sufficient justification for the act. Lingeringly, he dilated on the state of Thaw's mind as he heard Evelyn's revelations.

"What was the condition of his mind," he asked, "when he saw the form, the hideous form of the man who had caused so much suffering to him and his wife? If you have been in danger, if there have ever been moments when your life was hanging on a thread, you know men under those circumstances take life lightly and that their minds go back over the past like forks of lightning.

"Harry Thaw saw in a panorama the whole picture of the past. He saw this man in the form of a friend and protector insidiously laying his plan to get into the confidence of the mother and daughter. He saw him paying money to the mother in order that she might absent herself from the city so that he might perpetrate the ruin he had in mind.

"He saw him plying this child with wine, inflaming her youthful imagination with the luxury of surroundings. He saw her losing her mind and senses under the power of the drug. He next saw her in a bed of pollution and he saw her in the hideousness of it all. He saw him next morning kiss the hem of her garment. He saw her stretched out on the bed in sickness.

"He saw her in Paris, as he lifted her as a mother carries her first born. He remembered his offer of marriage, her refusal and the agonized accents of her story. He saw the renewal of the pledges of love and his vows that he would marry her. He saw the man poisoning her mind with infamous stories. Then he saw her rescued and restored to him once more. He saw her when he led her to the altar and made her his bride. He saw the man saying, 'I'll get her back again.' Then his mind reeled, and the tower where reason stood enthroned, tottered.

"He struck as a tigress strikes to protect her young. He struck for the purity of the American home. He struck — and who shall say that if he believed on that occasion he was an instrument of God and an agent of Providence, he was in error?"

The jurors, after forty-seven hours' deliberation, were unable to agree. It was disclosed afterward that seven were for conviction as charged, and five were for acquittal.

The second trial was begun on January 6th, 1908, almost a year from the time Thaw first faced a jury. The late Victor J. Dowling presided. In this trial the forensic Delmas was superseded by the logical Martin W. Littleton. His first step was a startling one to the Thaw family: he insisted on attempting to prove that Thaw was insane, not only at the time of his act, but before; that, in fact, he suffered from hereditary taint. Even Mrs. Mary Thaw had to accept this fiat.

It is of little use going into the testimony of this new hearing; it followed along the lines of the first, and Justice Dowling insisted on expedition. Evelyn again told her sorrowful tale, and it was obvious to the onlookers that she had succeeded even better than she had with the twelve men who heard the case before.

Within a month the case was closed and the jury brought in its verdict:

"We find the defendant not guilty on the ground of insanity at the time of the crime."

172

It is significant to observe that this was the verdict for which the defense had striven in the first trial.

Evelyn shook each of the jurors by the hand and then stood beside her husband while he awaited discharge from the Court. Justice Dowling, however, dropped a bombshell into the Thaw camp.

He adjudged Thaw insane and committed him to Matteawan, an asylum for the criminally insane. Thaw, who was waiting to deliver himself to the throng of his admirers as a free man, almost fainted at the verdict.

Within a few hours he was on his way to Matteawan, there to lodge for seven years. His was not the fate of the other prisoners, however. It presently became noised about that he not only had the freedom of the place but that his liberty extended beyond the walls. He was seen with Evelyn at various times in some of the roadhouses close to the asylum.

As a reporter, I first met Evelyn on the day the second jury brought in its verdict. She still was garbed in the schoolgirl frock which was such a pleasing ensemble to the men in the box: a simple dark blue dress with a broad white collar and a black hat trimmed with a spray of violets.

If a digression may be permitted at this point, I became much better acquainted with her in later years. Totally aside from her beauty, which was flaming at all times, day or night, she had an unusual mind. She had memorized, for instance, every ballad Kipling ever wrote, and she knew every one of his stories from *Stalky* to *The Night Mail*. She had a talent for art; she sketched well and for a year she studied sculpture, with every promise of success in that difficult field. For another year she became a student nurse.

Her sense of humor was delightful; her gift for telling stories was a rare one; her sense of observation was keen and her interpretation of events was broad and understanding. In a time when dancing was a vogue, she was exceptional. With these marked attributes, she lacked mental stamina, her inclinations were many but her persistence to carry through was deficient.

Evelyn Thaw was not immoral, in the ordinary acceptance of that term; she was unmoral. Without any seeming consciousness of her beauty, she refused to ape the ways of the professional beauty. Nevertheless, she was fully aware of her power over men and she exerted it to the utmost. She would not, for example, tolerate the presence of another woman at her table and she made it practically a duty to bring every man within her orbit to an expressed admiration of her.

Without fear, she had a peculiar fascination for snakes. Frequently she would visit the Bronx Zoo and, with the permission of Dr. Raymond Ditmars, drape herself with some of the most dangerous of reptiles. She never suffered an injury in the indulgence of this odd whim.

After Thaw's incarceration—such as it was—in the insane asylum, his lawyers redoubled their efforts to free him. They resorted to the process of *habeas corpus,* and it became almost an annual event for Thaw to be brought down to White Plains for an inquiry into his sanity.

One after another, these efforts were defeated and each time Evelyn was called to the stand. Finally she tired of this—as she tired of everything else—because the Thaw family had done little for her support during the years. In the last hearing she turned on him:

"I want it understood here," she exclaimed in court,

174

"that Harry Thaw hid behind my skirts through two dirty trials and I will not stand for it again. I won't let Thaw throw any more mud at me."

Immediately after this, she announced her determination to earn her own living by returning to the stage, and with Jack Clifford as a partner, she opened at Hammerstein's Roof Garden—then at Forty-second Street and Seventh Avenue, where the Rialto Theatre now stands.

Almost simultaneously with this announcement, Thaw escaped from Matteawan. How he accomplished this had best be left unsaid. He and his abductors fled by the way of Coaticook into Canada.

If the Canadian courts were unflattered by this visit, the populace of Sherbrooke, where he halted his flight, took him to their hearts. They threatened to storm the jail and liberate their hero. A commission was appointed by the court and, when the fugitive's seventeen lawyers had presented their case, found him sane. It looked again as if Thaw's troubles with the law were over, but a new shock awaited him. The immigration authorities branded him as an undesirable alien and before counsel could fend off the blow, Thaw was dumped back on American soil, finally bringing up at Colebrook in Coos County, New Hampshire.

It was there I became acquainted with Thaw. His room in the hotel was opposite mine and we became quite neighborly. The first I received of him was that he was inordinately proud of his conspicuousness. He regarded himself with an extraordinary affection, and this included a warm esteem for his literary talents. Each day, in the manner of a potentate, he would issue statements. He took to himself a censorship of the news and

175

would chide severely any reporter who failed to give him better than an even break.

The same public fervor which had greeted him in Canada was evident among the woodsmen of Coos County. We got wind of a plot to spirit him away, and because he had eluded the reporters when he was flung back to the States, we were vigilant to be in on it. It was this preparedness which defeated the plan, much to the chagrin of Thaw and his followers.

The prisoner's following included a host of lawyers, King's Counsellors, attorneys of New Hampshire, personal attorneys and others skilled in the processes of New York law. Also he had bodyguards, secretaries and flunkies. On the other side there were Jerome, as special deputy attorney general, Franklin Kennedy, also from the state attorney general's office; New Hampshire prosecutors, county solicitors and guards. About twenty-five newspaper reporters dogged his steps too, so that all-in-all Thaw had quite an entourage.

The scene shifted to Concord, with a stopover in Manchester. In Concord the usual *habeas corpus* was invoked and, as the legal operations promised to be prolonged, Thaw took a house on the edge of town.

In our various stops, we found that a burlesque troupe was playing simultaneous engagements. The enterprising manager saw the possibilities of a press story, so one night between shows, he marshaled his company for a visit to Thaw. Standing in the snow they serenaded him, a tribute which so touched Thaw that he invited them within the house. It was interesting to watch the girls pampering the Thaw vanity.

Because of the delay in the proceedings, my paper called me back to New York. I was at breakfast before departing when Thaw came into the dining room of my hotel.

"Why are they recalling you?" he asked. "There cannot be any story bigger than this."

"I imagine it is for the Sulzer trial," I told him.

"Then you'll see Martin Glynn, the acting governor," he said. "I have a message to him which I wish you would deliver. Will you tell him that he has the opportunity to become the biggest man in the country if he will issue orders to the attorney general to call off his forces. It is within his power to issue a pardon for me and it will make him the best-loved man in the state."

The message was never delivered, though not for lack of opportunity.

When the New Hampshire Courts finally decided that Thaw, although sane, should be extradited for his escape from New York, I rejoined his barnstorming aggregation. Our next stop was in Boston, and the crowd which met us at the South Station was enormous. A band blared, *See the Conquering Hero Comes!*

We put up at Young's Hotel while the crowd outside clamored for Thaw. Suddenly we of the newspaper group, and the throng outside heard the public being addressed from the balcony by someone who looked like Thaw and who was paying florid compliments to his public. It must have bewildered and gratified the auditors that the speech was delivered in a warm, rich Irish brogue. It wasn't Thaw, of course, although the words and gestures were his. It was Tom Thorp of the Evening Journal, who since has been many times in Boston to officiate at the football games in the Harvard Stadium.

Arrived in New York, the flight was made subsidiary to the sanity issue, Thaw's lawyers contending that, as a

177

sane man, he had a right to make his escape. John B. Stanchfield represented him in the hearings before Justice Peter A. Hendrick. It was in this trial that an alienist testifying against Thaw suddenly demanded of the court that he be released from the influence of the defendant's hypnotic eyes. He was hastily dismissed as a witness. Another instance of the Thaw blight.

When Justice Hendrick gave Thaw a clear bill of sanity in July, 1915, all of us believed he had staged his last court appearance. It was not to be.

In a little more than a year, there came the startling news that he had beaten a boy in one of New York's hotels. The boy appealed to the police and Thaw again took refuge in flight. He went to Philadelphia and in a rooming house there attempted suicide. This is the one time on record that the man's self-esteem failed him.

Those of us who had been on Thaw cases before, wearily betook ourselves to Philadelphia to be faced with the fact that his lawyers were engaged in the work of proving him insane. They did, too, and he was put away in a sanatorium. It wasn't long, however, before the Pennsylvania courts reversed this verdict and Thaw was free again.

The charges of the boy he had assaulted failed because of the youngster's disappearance. The case could not be proved without him, so the matter was dropped and Thaw again had the freedom of the city. I met him again some years later as he was being driven down Sixth Avenue, New York, and he was exuberant in his greeting. Nothing about his appearance or his manner indicated a derangement temporary or permanent.

It was not like Thaw to keep out of the newspapers, even after the action of the Pennsylvania court. He popped into print now and again after affrays in night clubs. He even visited that in which his former wife — they had been divorced a number of years by this time — was a hostess in Atlantic City, but he became involved in a row there.

Evelyn's decline was more pitiful. After she and Thaw were divorced, she married her dancing partner Clifford — but later they were divorced. What she lacked in artistic ability, she made up in notoriety, but after a few years, even that resource failed her.

The last time I saw her was in the Atlantic City night club, just off the Boardwalk. Despite her rouge and forced gaiety, she was merely a shadow of her former self. Her glamour had disappeared.

With friends and money gone, she attempted suicide in Chicago. A year or so later, she tried again, but was saved in time for a worse fate. The last heard, of her, she had been arrested for possession of narcotics.

So closes the history of this famous case.

On March 4th, 1931, the editor of this magazine was invited to dinner by Thaw at his favorite hotel on Park Avenue. Later that evening in his apartment, Thaw handed him a book he had written and published in 1926, entitled *The Traitor* — White being the traitor. As he did so, he remarked, "This is the whole story," then added as an afterthought, "that b----'s death saved hundreds of other innocent girls."

As Mark Twain would perhaps have put it, "That last remark seems slightly exaggerated."

A Rage To Destroy
The Pristine Screen Beauty?

by Gary C. King

Shrinks ask: Why was his warm passion twisted.

The beautiful young screen actress Rebecca Scheaffer must've been excited, even over-whelmed, by the challenges awaiting her. In less than an hour — at 11:00 a.m. on Tuesday, July 18, 1989 — she would be meeting famed director Francis Ford Coppola to read for a part in his upcoming film, *The Godfather, Part III.*

At the age of 21, she was already an experienced and accomplished actress, but she had been rehearsing for the audition for days. Naturally, she wanted to be at her best. It wasn't every day that one got a chance to read for Coppola.

A comer in Hollywood, she had already co-starred with Pam Dawber in the TV series, *My Sister Sam,* in which she played Patti Russell, Sam's ditsy younger sister. She had also appeared on two television soap operas, *One Life to Live* and *Guiding Light,* and had a role in an episode of *Amazing Stories* on NBC.

She had fared well on the big screen, too. Early in her career she had nabbed a walk-on role in Woody Allen's *Radio Days.* Only recently, she'd co-starred in *One Point of View,* directed by Dyan Cannon, and *Scenes From the Class Struggle in Beverly Hills.*

With those credits already behind her, Rebecca's star was on the rise. Those in the motion picture industry knew that the part in the Coppola film, if she obtained it, would be the vehicle to push her over the top.

Tragically, Rebecca's time ran out that fateful morning before she would keep her appointment with Coppola . . .

Rebecca's doorbell rang at 10:15 a.m. Her apartment's intercom system was broken and it was impossible to know who was calling without going to — and perhaps opening — the outer security door in the hallway.

Rebecca walked to the door and opened it. A shot rang out and she slumped to the floor in a heap.

Violent crime is rampant in many areas of Los Angeles, but not in the city's quiet, ritzy Fairfax district, located near Beverly Hills and West Hollywood.

Rebecca's neighbor, Dave Casey, was startled by the deafening commotion. He'd been sitting in his living room when he heard the gunshot, followed by two blood-curdling streams. He could tell the noises came from next door.

Unhesitatingly, he ran outside to see what was amiss. He found the young actress lying on her back in the building's entrance. There was a patch of blood at the center of her chest, growing larger with each passing second.

Quickly, Casey returned to his apartment and called 911. In an excited and agitated state, he briefly described what he'd heard and found, and gave the dispatcher an address in the 100 block of Sweetzer Avenue.

He was assured that police cruisers and a team of paramedics would be along within minutes.

Even though help was on the way, Casey knew he had

to begin administering first aid if Rebecca was to have even a slim chance of survival. He took several towels to the fallen actress and pressed them to the wound in her chest to try to stop the bleeding. But it was no use. The blood continued to flow from her body, completely soaking the towel compresses almost as quickly as he could press them in place.

Even as he feverishly worked to stem the blood flow, all color drained from her face.

As this was going on, Homicide Detective Dan Andrews was going over some active case files when his telephone rang.

Somehow, he knew, intuitively, even before he picked the phone up, that he was being summoned outdoors and would soon be confronting the sweltering smog-filled jungle of concrete, steel, glass, and wide boulevards that made up most of L.A. Still, he had to answer the call.

He was hastily informed of the shooting in the Fairfax district. According to departmental procedure, it was his turn to head an investigation, and this was going to be his case.

Uniformed officers and paramedics, the dispatcher told him, were already on the scene. So were curious onlookers and neighbors. Detective Andrews surmised that crowd control could prove to be a problem. He knew he would be facing chaos over there.

As Detective Andrews hurried to his patrolcar and sped to the scene, he must've recalled the chilling murder of *Poltergeist* actress Dominique Dunne in 1981, and the near-fatal stabbing of *Raging Bull* actress Theresa Saldana a year later. Both of these incidents had remarkable parallels to this slaying.

Detective Andrews arrived shortly, accompanied by

fellow Detectives Frank Bolan and Paul Coulter, and he briefly conferred with the officers who responded to the original call. He was informed that the wound Rebecca had sustained had caused considerable damage.

There were witnesses, he was told, but it was going to be difficult to sort them from the curious onlookers.

Andrews instructed the uniformed officers to round up the witnesses and traverse Sweetzer Avenue and the adjoining side streets in search of the shooter and any evidence that might prove pertinent to the case.

Although they doubted that Rebecca would survive, the paramedics worked frantically and did what they could for her at the scene, then whisked her off to Cedars-Sinai Medical Center by ambulance. Her condition grew worse en route and she was pronounced dead on arrival at 10:45 a.m.

By this time news-hungry reporters, who are often at the scene of a crime before police, were wandering through the district's well-manicured lawns and elegant, tree-lined streets. They were asking questions of the inhabitants, which consist of both young and old, middle class and wealthy, prominent and unknown.

Most were clearly disturbed by what had occurred, shocked by the savage brutality and senselessness of the crime. Some had important information about a suspicious stranger seen lurking in the area that morning.

"This is a quiet neighborhood," said one resident, who had a business nearby. "Things like this aren't supposed to happen here. We have a lot of notables around here and there has never been any real trouble. I didn't hear the shot, but there were a lot of people gathered around outside when I came out. It was madness."

Another resident told a policeman and a reporter that

she had observed a bookish-looking man with curly brown hair flashing a photo of Rebecca Scheaffer several hours before the shooting.

Another witness confirmed this description and said that the stranger been in the area for several hours showing Scheaffer's photo and asking questions about the young actress, including her whereabouts.

He had been particularly concerned about verifying precisely where she lived, said the witness.

As the canvass widened, Investigators Andrews, Bolan and Coulter interviewed witnesses closest to the crime scene who heard — or perhaps even saw — the shooting. They worked quickly and methodically, their desire, naturally, being to retrieve as many details as possible while the events were still fresh in the witnesses' minds.

Among those interviewed was Dave Casey, who, although still visibly upset, was able to tell the probers about the gunshot and the victim's screams.

"There were two screams," he said. "Not the kind of screams when you're surprised. They were the screams of a woman who was extremely hurt. I knew something was wrong then."

He explained how he'd found the young, gravely injured woman, called authorities, then returned to the scene to try and stop her bleeding.

Another witness, also an actress, informed the probers of Scheaffer's inoperable intercom, and explained that the only way she could see who was summoning her was to go to the front door.

She said she heard Scheaffer walk past her apartment only seconds before hearing a loud blast and Scheaffer's screams. When she opened her own door and peered into the hall, she said, she saw Scheaffer lying in the foyer, moaning.

But why would Rebecca have opened the door to someone she didn't know?

"There is some speculation that the (shooter) may have stood to either side of the window in the door," said Officer Roger Mora. "She could have opened the door without knowing who was there, but that's only speculation."

Yet another witness told police of a man he saw jogging from the area right after the shooting. The man, according to the witness, fit the same general description of the man seen by other witnesses flashing Rebecca's photo.

The suspect fled north on Sweetzer Avenue and then east down an alley. In the alley behind the building, he said, "was a man with a yellow shirt and short kinky hair, trotting up the block."

Andrews and his colleagues now knew the approximate time of the shooting, and they had eyewitnesses who they hoped could place a suspect at or near the scene of the crime.

But who was this mystery man? And what could possibly have been his motive for shooting the young actress?

Working under the simple premise that the sooner he identified a suspect, the sooner his questions would likely be answered, Andrews brought in a police artist to work up a composite of the suspect from the witnesses' descriptions.

When completed, it was to be distributed to the print and broadcast media and to other law enforcement agencies in the region.

Andrews also requested a forensics wagon. When it arrived, specialists began searching the area where Rebecca was shot, concentrating their efforts on the porch, the outer entrance to the apartment building, and the foyer.

185

Experts meticulously searched for latent fingerprints in the doorway and on the intercom panel.

Believing that the gunman was still in the area police promptly set up a dragnet operation in an attempt to locate and apprehend him. Witnesses reported seeing the suspect discard items as he fled up the alley. Police hoped he'd also tossed aside his weapon.

They launched an extensive search of the area near Scheaffer's apartment in an effort to recover the items.

Their search took them well into Tuesday night. By now, they knew that the suspect had successfully eluded their dragnet and, in all likelihood, taken the gun with him.

According to Detective Bolan, the investigators had developed no motive as yet for Scheaffer's killing. They were looking into the possibility that the attacker was one of her fans. Police had not found any records of fan harassment, and there was nothing to indicate that she had known her killer.

In an attempt to better understand her life and, perhaps, to uncover someone who might've wanted to do her harm, the detectives began interviewing those closest to her, including friends, relatives, and professional associates. At every turn, background information revealed that the young victim was well-liked, just as they had expected.

"She didn't have an enemy in the world," said her agent. "She was one of the nicest people I've ever known — sincere, honest and kind. She was a very successful young actress, on the ascent, getting job after job. I can't believe this has happened."

"Words cannot express the grief and rage that I feel," said actress Pam Dawber. "My question is, Why? My heart and sorrow go to her mother and father for losing such a beautiful child."

Probing deeper into her personal history, the detectives learned that Rebecca was born on November 6, 1967, in Eugene, Oregon. She moved to Portland with her family in 1980. She went to Lincoln High School until her junior year when, at age 16, she moved to New York City to embark on a modeling career and to complete her education at the Children's Professional School.

She subsequently appeared in *Seventeen Magazine,* then traveled to Japan, where she modeled for one year.

"From my standpoint, it seemed very natural," Rebecca had said in an interview about her decision to leave home for a modeling career. "But I know my parents went through hell."

Scheaffer's hopes of a career as a fashion model were soon thwarted. Because she stood at 5 feet 7 inches tall, two inches short of the minimum standard for fashion models in the United States, the career she had eagerly gone after didn't take off.

Rebecca hadn't despaired. She moved to Los Angeles, where she pursued acting, paying her high rent and bills through temporary roles in soap operas and walk-on parts in movies.

But the money wasn't enough, and soon her telephone was disconnected and her bank cards were cancelled. Still, she didn't give up.

When things looked bleakest, Rebecca began searching for waitress jobs at cafes, coffee houses and bars, with no luck. Finally, a break came in 1986 when she returned home to her meager apartment after a day of job-hunting and found a note taped to her door.

It was from Warner Brothers, requesting that she audition for a co-starring role on *My Sister Sam*. She got the part, and from that time on her future was made.

At 2:00 a.m. the next morning, in an unusual development that occurred even as investigators continued running down leads, LAPD detectives received a telephone call from a woman in Knoxville, Tennessee. It turned out to be their first real break in the case.

The woman, who identified herself as a relative of 19-year-old John Bardo of Tucson, Arizona, told detectives that Bardo had called her only minutes before Scheaffer was killed.

She said that Bardo had described traveling to California to see the actress. He said he planned to harm Rebecca, but he hadn't told the relative enough to prompt her to notify the authorities earlier.

She said that Bardo had written to her previously and said that if he "couldn't have Scheaffer, no one could."

She explained that she hadn't realized the seriousness of Bardo's call until she heard that Scheaffer had been killed.

"She told us that Bardo had a fixation for Miss Scheaffer and had expressed the intent to harm her," said Detective Andrews. "He was an obsessive fan, and there were indications that he had written affectionate letters to her and had tried to contact her a number of times in the past."

The relative, according to Andrews, also told investigators that Bardo kept several video cassettes of the *My Sister Sam* series, and had obtained an autographed picture of Scheaffer.

A short time later, anticipating that Bardo might return to his home in Arizona, LAPD contacted Tucson police to inform them of the tip they had received. Tucson police assured their colleagues in Los Angeles that they would be on the lookout for the young man and would immediately begin checking things out at their end.

Some eight hours later, in what initially seemed unrelated to the Scheaffer case, a young male pedestrian walked onto the Interstate 10 freeway near downtown Tucson and began "playing tag" with fast-moving cars, zigzagging on foot near a freeway exit.

The responding officers reported that he appeared to be disoriented and dirty, and was possibly attempting to commit suicide by running toward oncoming cars, and hurling himself at them.

His suicidal behavior wreaked havoc with the traffic, and there were several instances in which he nearly succeeded in getting himself killed. Fortunately, the police arrived quickly and arrested the young man for jaywalking.

It wasn't until approximately 10:00 a.m. that a connection was made between the Tucson jaywalker case and the Los Angeles slaying of Rebecca Scheaffer.

Suspecting that Bardo had just gotten off a Greyhound bus from Los Angeles shortly before walking onto the freeway, Tucson authorities began to query him about the Scheaffer case. They advised him of his Miranda rights, but, according to the Tucson police spokesman, Sergeant Paul Hallums, Bardo was willing to talk.

"The guy's real passive with everybody," said Hallums. "He's being passive and polite with everybody."

According to Detective Andrews, "Bardo made statements (to Tucson police) that led us to believe he was connected to the murder."

Andrews sent Detectives Coulter and Bolan to Tucson to question the suspect.

Although Arizona officials were unwilling to disclose all that was said during their interviews with Bardo, they did release some of the details.

Among the things they said Bardo had told them was that he had discarded a yellow shirt, a gun holster, and a book near Scheaffer's apartment. The book, it turned out, was a classic novel about an alienated, depressed youth, J.D. Salinger's *The Catcher in the Rye.*

The book, reflected detectives, had been the choice of John Lennon's assassin, Mark David Chapman, which he placidly read after shooting the former Beatle on December 8, 1980, in New York City.

Over the next several hours, Los Angeles police searched the yards and buildings adjacent to the alley near Scheaffer's apartment where the man with the yellow shirt had been seen trotting up the block after the shooting.

It took a while, but police found a yellow shirt above a dry-cleaning shop and the red paperback book on the roof of a rehabilitation center. The holster was also found nearby.

Unfortunately it held no handgun.

"It could have been picked up by a passerby, or if it was discarded in a trash can, it might have been picked up and disposed of by now," said Detective Andrews.

Andrews said the gun was believed to have been a .357-caliber Magnum, purchased legally in Tucson. Although there is no background check to purchase a gun in Arizona, one must be 21 — Bardo was 19 — and an Arizona resident.

"We know where, when and how the gun was purchased," said Andrews. Although he revealed few details about the purchase of the gun, Andrews said that the gun may have been originally purchased by someone else and given to Bardo at a later time.

Meanwhile, a search of Bardo's home in Tucson where he lived with his family turned up videotapes of *My Sister Sam*. A relative told detectives that Bardo knew who Scheaffer was, but insisted that Bardo's interest in the actress wasn't out of the ordinary.

"He watched her on TV, and he was a fan of hers," said a relative. "But he watched a lot of shows. It wasn't as if he was an obsessive fan. He didn't have any photos of her on his walls."

Bardo had attended Pueblo High School in Tucson during his freshman and sophomore years, but despite grades of all A's and one B, he dropped out. School officials barely remembered him when called on by authorities, and they said they assumed he'd transferred to another school or moved when he failed to return for his junior year.

"He was just a face in the crowd," said an assistant principal at the school. "The only mention of him is in the freshman class picture. From what we know, he didn't participate in any activities."

Investigators learned that until a week before Scheaffer's slaying Bardo had been employed as a custodian at a fast-food restaurant near his home. Employees said he'd been unable to cope with the pressures of working in a fast-food environment.

Neighbors painted an unfavorable picture of the suspect in their descriptions to police and members of the press, saying that Bardo often exhibited bizarre, sometimes destructive behavior. He was often seen hanging from the eaves of his parents' single-story house, swinging himself in through the windows, and was often seen charging into a concrete wall in his back yard.

"He was always out acting funny," said a kid from Bardo's middle-class subdivision. "He used to jump out of the windows a lot and (would) often get down on his knees and scratch at the side of the house."

Other neighbors said it wasn't unusual for him to play hide-and-seek with imaginary friends in his front yard. Many said they had initially been concerned about Bardo's bizarre behavior, but had become accustomed to it over time. Some said he was prone to wide mood swings, and others portrayed him as potentially violent.

A few days before Scheaffer's slaying, police learned, Bardo had become upset because of a neighbor's party and threatened to quiet things down with a .357-caliber Magnum.

"If you don't shut up, I'm going to get my .357 Magnum and shoot you," a guest of the party quoted Bardo as saying.

"He said he would come back and bring his .357 Magnum," said the neighbor responsible for throwing the party. "But he never came back. The next day he said, 'I'm sorry it happened. I didn't feel very good.' "

"He was a real 'Psycho' guy," said yet another neighbor in his characterization of the slaying suspect.

Investigators learned that Bardo had been sending Scheaffer letters through her agents in New York and Los Angeles for about two years.

"I wouldn't call it a threatening letter," said Andrews. "I would call it an affectionate letter, but a bit rambling. There is no indication she ever saw it."

Police also learned that Bardo left Tucson on a Greyhound bus bound for Los Angeles on Monday, July 7th, the day before Rebecca was shot to death. No one, it seems, had been concerned that he was missing.

"(His relatives) knew he was out of town," said Sergeant Hallums. "He does that periodically." He had traveled to Los Angeles several times in the past, including a trip about a month before the July 17th trip following an argument with relatives.

"There have been indications that he has visited California a number of times, and there were ongoing attempts to contact (Scheaffer)," said Andrews.

On one such occasion, on June 2, 1987, Bardo made several telephone calls to Scheaffer's production office, asking to speak to the actress. After his efforts failed, he showed up at the lot known as "The Ranch" at the Burbank Studios where Scheaffer was taping a segment of *My Sister Sam*. He was carrying a teddy bear and a bouquet.

He insisted on seeing the actress to give her the flowers and the bear, but security guards refused to allow him entry. When he refused to leave, they escorted him to the office of the chief of security.

"I thought he was just lovesick, which I think he was," the security chief told the investigators. "He was terribly insistent on being let in. 'Rebecca Scheaffer' was every other word. 'I gotta see her. I love her. If I could just see her for a minute.' "

The security chief said he told Bardo that he could not interrupt the taping of a television show, and he finally persuaded Bardo to just go home. He told investigators that he drove Bardo to a run-down motel in Hollywood, after Bardo promised he would return to Tucson.

"He seemed to be an intelligent kid," said the security chief. "He was no raving lunatic, no dumbbell, but something was definitely wrong, mentally. There was something haywire going on, but I didn't perceive it as potentially violent."

Security has since been tightened at the studio lot.

In the uneasy aftermath of Scheaffer's violent death, many wondered how Bardo had been able to discover her home address so easily.

"If a person is inquisitive enough, a trail can be found," said Detective Andrews. Bardo, Andrews explained, found the trail six weeks before Scheaffer's death when he walked into the offices of a Tucson detective agency that advertises its ability to find missing persons. He showed the private investigators a studio publicity photo of the actress and explained that he was an old friend. He said he wanted her current address so he could mail her a gift. He paid the firm $250 for their services. The agency in turn easily located Scheaffer's home address through the California Department of Motor Vehicles' public records.

As investigators probed deeper into Bardo's background, they learned that Rebecca Scheaffer had not been the only celebrity he had been fascinated by. And they learned that his travels to satisfy such fascinations had not been limited to California.

In 1984, Bardo, at age 14, hitchhiked from his home in Tucson to Manchester, Maine, in an attempt to meet schoolgirl Samantha Smith, according to Tucson Police Captain Michael Ulichny.

(It should be recalled that Smith gained international recognition in 1983 when, at age of 10, she became a pen-pal of then-Soviet Premier Yuri Andropov. Later that same year, she visited the Soviet Union and became an international peace symbol. She died tragically on August 25, 1985, along with her father in a plane crash.)

In following up, LAPD detectives learned that Bardo had made at least a dozen telephone calls to Smith over a period of several months and had spoken with Samantha at least once in what was described as a long, rambling conversation.

"He was just a troubled kid," said one of Smith's relatives, who noted that she began screening Samantha's calls after she became well-known.

She described Bardo as persistent but never rude. "I finally asked him not to call anymore. He was difficult to get off the phone. He'd keep talking and talking. You almost had to be rude to get him off the phone."

The relative said that she never sensed Bardo was a threat to Samantha.

Bardo was picked up by the Kennebec County Sheriff's Office only a few blocks from Samantha's house. He had no weapons on him, and there was no indication that he planned to harm Samantha. He was held as a runaway.

Before his plans went awry in Maine, police learned, Bardo had also planned to travel to New York to seek out pop music stars Tiffany and Debbie Gibson.

Why did he have such a strong desire to meet famous females? Was he simply bored with his own life? Was he trying to make his life more meaningful? Or did he suffer from delusions, somehow believing that he could win the affections of the celebrities he admired if he could only meet them?

"It looks like he felt a compulsion to meet the people he became obsessed with," said Sergeant Hallums. Whatever caused his seemingly uncontrollable obsessions, no one yet knows for certain.

After reviewing the facts of the case, the Los Angeles County District Attorney's office issued a felony arrest warrant for Bardo accusing him of one count of murder. He was held without bail in the Pima County Jail in Tucson under a 24-hour suicide watch.

At his arraignment before Pima County Justice Pro Tem Walter Weber, Bardo's bail was set at $1 million. Public Defender Lori Lefferts was assigned to represent Bardo, who decided to fight extradition.

Meanwhile, Rebecca Scheaffer's family brought her body back to Portland, Oregon, for burial. More than 300 people gathered at the Ahavai Sholom Cemetery chapel to mourn Rebecca's death, including several of her celebrity friends. Pam Dawber and her husband, actor Mark Harmon, were among those in attendance.

"We are shocked by the senselessness of what happened to Rebecca," the rabbi told the tearful mourners who were gathered around Rebecca's light wood casket, graced with a spray of white, blue and mauve flowers.

"The truth of the matter is that her life will ultimately be a source of comfort to her parents. She had succeeded at an age where most others are still finding themselves. Perhaps what was known best about her was that she evoked admiration rather than jealousy."

"She brought more in her short life to other human beings than most of us bring in a lifetime," said another rabbi. "Rebecca was a precious gift to her parents, to her friends and to the entire land. She has been snatched back to the earth, but she will never cease to touch our lives."

In the meantime, on Thursday, August 10, 1989, in a move reminiscent of the drama and intensity of the old Perry Mason TV mysteries, two LAPD detectives arrived in Tucson after a red-eye flight, took Bardo from the Pima County Jail and spirited him back to Los Angeles with the full approval of Los Angeles County District Attorney Ira Reiner.

The highly unusual—if not questionable—move was made possible after Los Angeles County Deputy District Attorney Marcia Clark, assigned to prosecute Bardo, discovered a momentary lapse in Arizona's ability to hold the suspect after Bardo's attorney, Lori Lefferts, filed the wrong motion in the wrong court to fight her client's extradition. Lefferts, said Clark, failed to immediately take corrective action.

"I didn't act until I was certain it was the legally proper thing and the right thing to do," said Clark of her actions.

"I'm not saying Ira Reiner did anything wrong," said Deputy Public Defender Stephen Galindo, appointed to represent Bardo in Los Angeles. "But all the facts surrounding the transfer are suspicious."

Lefferts said that she'd planned to argue that Bardo was mentally incompetent and should not be extradited.

"There's nothing I can do," Lefferts conceded. "Arizona law does not allow me to get him back."

A month later, despite all the defense protests, Los Angeles Municipal Court Judge David M. Horwitz ruled that Bardo was returned to California from Arizona legally. Bardo's rights had not been violated.

On Tuesday, December 6, 1989, a preliminary hearing was held in Los Angeles Municipal Court. Following the presentation of testimony and evidence, Robert John Bardo was ordered to stand trial for murder in the shooting death of Rebecca Scheaffer. He was ordered held without bail. According to Deputy District Attorney Marcia Clark, Bardo could face the death penalty or life in prison without parole if convicted. However, under protection of the U.S. Constitution, Bardo must be presumed innocent until and unless proven otherwise in a court of law.

In the wake of Rebecca Scheaffer's violent death, legislation has been introduced restricting access to driving records in California. The bill, signed into law by Governor George Deukmejian, allows Californians to request that the Department of Motor Vehicles keep their home addresses confidential. The law took effect on January 1, 1990.

Editor's Note:

Dave Casey is not the real name of the person so named in the foregoing story. A fictitious name has been used because there is no reason for public interest in the identity of this person.

How Success Killed the Lennon Sisters' Dad

by Chris Edwards

The tragic irony behind the wanton murder of "the
man without an enemy in the world" is that if his
talented daughters had remained nobodies, he'd
probably be alive today . . .

The big surprise was that William Lennon, 53, devoted father of the singing Lennon sisters, had even a
single enemy the world. He was a man who was well
liked by all who knew him. But obviously he had at least
one enemy—the one who murdered him at high noon
on a warm August 12, 1969, in broad daylight, shooting
him in the back and then delivering a coup de grace with
a second shot in the temple.

Bill Lennon was an ex-milkman who gave up his
route to manage the singing careers of his pretty daughters in 1955 when they made their debut on the Lawrence Welk Show.

At that time Diane was 16, Peggy, 14, Kathy 12, and
Janet 9. For the next 11 years they appeared with Welk
every week and millions of TV viewers loved not only
their simple presentations of sentimental ballads, but
also their devotion to their family and the wholesome-
ness of their personal lives which were carefully watched
over by their parents.

When the singing sisters branched out on their own in 1966, Bill Lennon turned to working as a golf pro, although he still kept close tabs on the careers of his daughters as well as on the lives of his wife and seven other children at home. They ranged in age from nine to 19.

On Tuesday, August 12, 1969, he went to work as usual about 9:30 a.m. at the new Marina del Rey golf course beside the sea at the western edge of Los Angeles. He worked through the morning under a warm sun in the cool of the ocean breeze. A few minutes before noon he decided to knock off for lunch and head for his car in the golf course parking lot. There a man was waiting for him.

What took place in the next few minutes was hard to believe even for the mesmerized witnesses who watched with disbelief the tableau that developed. As Lennon approached his car, a rather disheveled looking man approached him and appeared to engage in a brief conversation — perhaps more like an argument. One witness said he saw the man open a gunny sack he was carrying, reach into it and pull out what appeared to be a rifle. A split second later Lennon and the stranger appeared to be struggling for possession of the gun.

In less than a minute, Lennon broke away from the heavyset man and sprinted for the open gate leading from the parking lot to heavily-traveled Lincoln Boulevard, desperately seeking someone to help him, to protect him from the evil that pursued him.

Just as Bill Lennon reached the gate — and when safety seemed only a few feet away — the stranger stopped, leveled the rifle and fired one shot. Lennon staggered as the .303 caliber slug ripped into his upper torso. He slumped against a telephone pole, clutching it for support but gradually slipping to the pavement.

Calmly the rifleman walked up to the wounded man, placed the muzzle of the gun against his temple, and fired the second shot. This eliminated all doubt that the rifleman was determined to murder Bill Lennon.

The shots galvanized the witnesses into action. Someone ran for a phone and called the police while others ran to the assistance of Lennon as his killer sprinted across the busy street, opened the trunk of an old Oldsmobile or Buick, threw the rifle inside, climbed behind the wheel and drove off.

Police officers who arrived at the scene in the first patrol car caught a glimpse of the car pointed out to them by witnesses, as it slid into the traffic flow. The officers took off in hot pursuit, but a few minutes later they had to admit that the killer had given them the slip.

Mr. Lennon was rushed to a nearby hospital, but he was pronounced dead on arrival. Doctors said he might have survived the bullet wound in the torso, but the second shot into his temple put Bill Lennon beyond medical help, killing him instantly.

Hollywood reeled under the impact of the slaying of Bill Lennon. Just three days before his killing, actress Sharon Tate, 26, heiress Abigail Folger, 26, Jay Sebring, 35, a Hollywood hair stylist; Voityck Frokawski, 37, a Hollywood hanger-on, and Steven Parent, 18, were found murdered and their bodies scattered about a Benedict Canyon estate just a few miles from where Lennon was murdered.

And on the following day an equally bizarre double murder was uncovered in the Silverlake District of Los Angeles when the bodies of a wealthy market owner and his attractive wife were found by relatives. The head of Leno La Bianca, 44, had been covered with a white hood and his chest pierced with a meat carving fork which had been used to etch a row of Xs and the word "war" into his chest. The back of his wife, Rosemary, 38, had been ripped to pieces by what police said could have been a knife or a whip. The La Bianca slayings had weird and ritualistic overtones, as did the Tate killings of the day before.

Then, a mere two days later, Bill Lennon, the man without an enemy in the world, was shot to death in broad daylight, apparently without reason.

Eight murders in four days—murders which seemed to be connected by one slender thread: All appeared to be the work of madman.

But one thing was clear—Bill Lennon was about as far removed as a man can get from the freaky world in which Sharon Tate and her associates moved.

Sharon and her companions in death were Hollywood jet-setters, the speed clique that orbited in a galaxy of junkies, pushers, speed freaks, hustlers, sex nuts, fags, and the usual fringe characters, the hangers-on, the baskers in reflected glory who are so prevalent in Hollywood.

If there was one man on the Hollywood scene who was as far removed from that world as anyone can get, it was Bill Lennon, a religious, clean-living, hardworking, devoted family man whose reputation was as unblemished as that of Sharon and her ilk was tarnished.

The murders of Mr. and Mrs. La Bianca was another puzzler. Although they were wealthy—their estate was valued at more than $500,000—they lived quietly in one of the older sections of Los Angeles. So far as anyone could determine they had no enemies. Their home was not robbed, but whoever killed them mutilated their bodies in sheer hatred.

The Homicide Bureau of the Los Angeles Police Department suddenly found themselves involved in a series of strange murders — all unrelated, but all connected by a single thread . . . there was no doubt that all eight persons were slain by deranged or depraved madmen. And these madmen were still loose.

The first thought that came to the minds of the police was that the gallery of murder victims could have been the chance victims of a single madman like those who fell under the rifle fire of a deranged young man sniping from a high tower of a Texas university or the homicidal maniac in Chicago who broke into nurses' quarters and killed eight nurses one by one while the prospective victims waited in an adjoining room like sheep waiting for the slaughter.

In any case, Los Angeles was scared out of its wits. A number of show business stars openly admitted they were carrying guns. People were paying premium prices for watch dogs. Private security patrols were short of men to fill the demands made on them. The reasoning of the terrified went something like this — Sharon Tate and her weirdo friends had probably left themselves wide open for a vengeance killer. But why would anyone want to kill the La Biancas and mutilate their bodies without taking a single thing from their home? And why in the world would anyone want to kill friendly, sincere Bill Lennon, whose only claim to fame in the eyes of the public was that he was the father of the Lennon sisters. His private life was an open book. It revolved around his family.

But the fact remained that someone killed him, and not by accident but with a deliberately administered coup de grace, as if to make sure that Bill Lennon died. Whoever killed him obviously hated him.

The question that nagged all who knew him was, "Why?"

The suspect in the Lennon killing was described as a white male about 30, six feet tall and weighing about 220 pounds. Witnesses said he was wearing a dirty green sweater, blue trousers and had a goatee. Police Sergeant Art Hansbrough told newsmen that the man was "sloppily dressed" and wore a crumpled hat.

Lennon lived with his wife, Isabelle, in a modest two-story frame house in the nearby beach community of Venice. Bill Roberts, another pro at the golf course, described Bill Lennon as a "very fine man," and added the words that were to be sounded by millions throughout the world: "I didn't think he had an enemy in the world."

Homicide investigators hear this statement all the time, but rarely is it as true as it was in the case of Bill Lennon. In light of his murder, however, it was clear he did have an enemy, and investigation would show that his enemy was a fantasy locked in the twisted brain of a war hero.

In a manner of speaking, the father of the Lennon sisters was killed by a phantom, a hallucination which became confused with reality.

Police questioning members of the Lennon family learned that several years before the murder, a man had been arrested by the U.S. Secret Service after he threatened to kill President Lyndon B. Johnson. Incredible as it seemed, the man had accused the president of preventing him from marrying Peggy Lennon, a member

204

of the singing sisters.

The man was identified at the time as Chet Young and very little information was released to the press about him. However, approximately three weeks after the murder of Lennon, police disclosed that a car believed to have been used as the getaway car by the killer of Bill Lennon had been found abandoned in Berkeley, California, some 400 miles north of Los Angeles.

Police also disclosed that Young was a man who had long harassed the Lennon family.

Jimmy Lennon, brother of the slain man, said a Chet Young had been hounding the Lennon family for years with threatening letters and telephone calls. He had demanded that he be permitted to marry one of the sisters — any one. Shortly before the slaying, Young reportedly wrote to the family saying he was "stepping in to sever the umbilical cord between the Lennon Sisters and their parents."

Police said Young had been committed to a state mental hospital at Atascadero, California in 1965 as dangerously insane, but for some reason no record was found that explained why he was released from custody. The police hesitated to say flatly that the man known to have been harassing the Lennons was the same man being sought for the murder of Bill Lennon, but nevertheless, a murder warrant was issued for the arrest of Chet Young. He was described as being armed and extremely dangerous.

Additional questioning and search of these records revealed that Young had been harassing the Lennon family since 1962, when he began writing love letters to Peggy Lennon, and that he had also been confined in a federal mental institution for threatening the life of Lyndon Johnson because the president would not arrange his marriage to Peggy Lennon.

The thought of a homicidal maniac on the loose led police to take extra precautions for the safety of the Lennon family. When the sisters made their first television appearance after the murder of their father, the studio audience was composed mainly of off-duty police officers and their families. Chet Young had been known to attend such shows and had often been seen by the sisters in the past, lurking in the background of such audiences, although he never approached any one of them.

The Lennons were virtually certain that Chet Young had killed their father. After the murder, the singing sisters — with the exception of Peggy — moved into their mother's home. Peggy had just moved with her husband and children to a new home in the San Fernando Valley and police were certain Young would not be able to find her.

At one time there were 22 Lennon children and grandchildren living in the modest two-story frame home of Bill Lennon in the Venice area of Los Angeles. And all were heavily guarded by the police until homicide officers were convinced that Young was no longer in the Los Angeles area. But the police continued to guard the singing sisters.

Detective Sergeants Don Ham and Jerry Moon were assigned full time to tracking down Chet Young. They dug up every scrap of information they could find on him, hoping it would give them some clue to where he might seek refuge, with friends, members of his family, or possibly in some part of the country where he might have lived or traveled.

It was learned that Young was a graduate of Colorado

State College in Golden, Colorado and served two years as an Air Force officer, including a tour of duty in Korea. After he left the Air Force in 1955 he worked infrequently, dabbled in Communism and slipped slowly into a state that was later defined as schizophrenic paranoia. Air Force records showed that his real name was Marvin Major, but somewhere along the line—it was not clear when or why—he changed his name to Chet Young.

Police were told that in 1962 he began writing to the Lennon family. Sometimes he would write four or five abusive, rambling letters a month. Then months might pass before he would write again. The theme of the letters was always the same. He was seeking the hand of Peggy Lennon in marriage and was certain that her parents were keeping him and Peggy apart. It was when he charged the cause of the separation to President Johnson that he was arrested and placed in the mental institution, only to be released several months later.

Chet Young was the best and only suspect the police had for the killing of Bill Lennon, so an all-points bulletin was circulated throughout the United States for his arrest. But the weeks went by without a trace of the murder suspect. From time to time there were reports that he had been seen at various points along the Canadian border, but they never materialized. Young vanished from sight.

The letters to the Lennon family stopped, but the family continued to live in fear that he might return at any time to claim another victim.

Dealing with a deranged man such as Chet Young, it was hard to figure out what he would do next. But this much was known: He had a fixation about the Lennon family, a fixation that had burned in his twisted mind for years. He had killed one member of the family. He had nothing to lose. And it was possible he would kill again in a desperate attempt at vengeance against a family who would not admit him to their tight circle.

Days stretched into weeks and police agencies heard not a word about the whereabouts of Chet Young. They had expected that he might tip his hand and give away his location by writing another letter to the Lennon family. And each day the postman came to the homes of the Lennon sisters, he was greeted with some apprehension and some hope that Young might write and give the police something to go on.

But there was only silence.

Then on about October 3rd or 5th, nearly two months after the slaying of Bill Lennon, Chet Young drove a black 1962 Oldsmobile Cutlass into the Mother Lode country of Northern California on the western slopes of the Sierras. No one noticed the car as it pulled off a main highway onto a tree-shrouded dirt logging road where Young headed for a confrontation with destiny.

There he wrote two letters. One dated October 3rd was addressed to Peggy Lennon, the other, dated October 5th was addressed, "To Whom it May Concern." The first letter began with the salutation: "My Darling Wife" and read:

"In spite of all the obstacles and troubles caused by the capitalistic leeches I did manage a trip to town and back. [This would indicate that he had been hiding out somewhere in the High Sierras, probably in one of the many abandoned mining cabins that dot the area.]

"I bought four magazines [containing articles and

photographs of the Lennon sisters] and have been reading them. Thank you for not crying in the pictures [apparently referring to photographs taken at the funeral of Bill Lennon].

"I, too, have trouble reconciling that life in a capitalistic society can be so completely insane and senseless and that the stupidity never ends."

Then he made a reference to Peggy and her children, which in his twisted mind he believed to be his, and continued, "I know you will explain to them that what I did was for the benefit of all concerned. Please explain to them that taking my own life was not my wish but the lesser of two evils . . . that it's better to be dead than let 200 million capitalistic freaks turn me into a zombie. [One of the things which bugged Young apparently was that if he were captured by the police he would be declared insane and that a lobotomy would be performed by surgeons to alter his brain functions.]

"I would like to be buried deep at sea but I despise the American people so much that I can't stand the thought of asking them for anything. The idea is to get me as far from the detestable insane capitalisms as possible and end their exploitation of our lives and names and I want them to leave us completely alone.

"I have no friends. If anybody tells you they are my friends after I die, tell them to go to hell.

"I should know soon whether or not there is an afterlife. I shall try to let you know. In fact, I will tell you everything I can and do everything I can to make your life peaceful and happy until you can join me.

"I know that if there is an afterlife I shall be with you.

"Of course, I would like very much to eliminate Dick Cathart [Peggy's husband]. He had a wife and children

[I believe this man was married before] what does he want with mine?

"If I had only known what I know now I would have killed him long ago. Now, of course, there is no chance. I had to give up on him in favor of Bill and as the magazines say, he's heavily guarded. I don't need the magazines to tell me this.

"How I would like to get Cathart . . ." [He then added the names of other members of the Lawrence Welk show with whom the sisters had been associated for eleven years.]

"I cried today and I haven't cried since I was in grade school. We went for a walk today (make believe). You and I and Julie and Chris and Jose and Michael. We threw rocks in the river and I carried the boys on my shoulders and we had such a good time.

"I can't stand the thought of leaving you. Yet I know I better think about what they will do to me if they ever catch me. And I have it easy compared to you. For me it will soon be over. I can't anticipate what will happen after I am gone but if you can I would like a wedding band.

"It is now Sunday night, Oct. 5, 1969. Until we meet again, God bless you. Your husband, Chet."

The second letter, addressed "To Whom it May Concern," read:

"Mrs. Peggy Lennon is my wife and closest living relative. Capitalistic insanity cannot change this. They couldn't destroy our love. They only destroyed our God given right to be together. Consult only with Peggy Lennon concerning the disposition of my remains.

"It was easy to wait three hours until "High Noon" to kill Bill Lennon who instigated so many of the crimes. It

210

was certainly justifiable and the least I could do as a husband and father for my wife and children.

"I know what the American people have planned for me — torture until I am deprived of my sanity or a lobotomy. I obviously have no alternative. Death is better than torture or a lobotomy. A Zombie, a living trophy to the incredible evils of Yankee capitalism."

This brief letter was not signed.

Police authorities later theorized that it was shortly after he wrote these letters that Chet Young carefully blocked the wheels of his car with rocks and set out to destroy himself. He placed a garden hose in the exhaust pipe and thrust the other end of the hose into the trunk of the car.

With the same careful preparation, he removed the spare tire from the trunk to make more room in his death chamber and put it on one of the seats. He started the engine, and placed a heavy bottle on the accelerator to keep the engine roaring.

Then he climbed into the trunk with a rifle and curled his 6 foot 2 inch frame among stacks of fan magazines which contained stories and photographs of the Lennon sisters, and waited for death. But apparently because the garden hose fit so loosely into the tail pipe, death did not come as he had expected.

It was then he decided to use his rifle . . . the same weapon which had taken the innocent life of Bill Lennon . . . and fired a single fatal bullet into his chest.

On October 11th four hunters trudging down the lonely logging road in Tuolumne County 24 miles from Sonora spotted the car and the hose leading into the trunk from the exhaust pipe. They notified Sheriff Miller Sardella in Sonora, the only city in the rural county.

When Sheriff Sardella found the body he notified the Los Angeles Police Department and the two Los Angeles detectives who had been in northern California seeking leads on Young were sent to the scene. Sergeants Ham and Moon were assisted in their investigation of Young's death and the identification of his body by Sardella, Deputy Coroner Ray Antonini of Tuolumne County and Stephen A. Byrne of the U.S. Secret Service.

They studied the letters, verified the identification, and sent the rifle to Los Angeles for ballistics tests.

Tests of the .303 Caliber English made rifle found clutched in Young's hands proved beyond doubt that it was the same weapon which had killed Bill Lennon a month before.

The contents of the trunk of Young's car revealed the extent of his mad infatuation with the singing sisters and their family. He had collected scores of fan magazines containing articles about the singing group and pasted them on long pieces of paper and in a makeshift scrapbook. Some of the pasteups indicated Young suffered from sexual aberrations.

He had begun writing to Peggy in 1962, asking her to marry him. His intentions were ignored and the infatuation obviously developed into a love fantasy.

It was not until after the case of Chet Young was finally declared closed by the Police Department that two of the Lennon sisters permitted themselves to be interviewed about the strange man who had intruded into their lives and killed their father. They talked of the terror that gripped the family after Bill Lennon's murder and of pity for the gunman who eventually killed him-

212

self.

It was Janet and Diane Lennon who recalled the long, tragic history that led to their father's death. The oldest and youngest members of the singing sisters, they generally speak for the family. Here is the text of the interview as reported by a Hollywood correspondent for the Associated Press:

Janet: "He (Young) started writing to Peggy back in 1962, when he was in an institution in Colorado. Right from the start he seemed to believe that he was Peggy's husband, and he would ask questions like, 'How's our baby?' At first we weren't alarmed. They were cuckoo letters, but we got others of that kind, too."

Diane: "Then, in 1964 or 1965, he started appearing here at ABC when we were doing the Welk show. He never bothered us; he just stayed in the background. But you couldn't miss him — he was a very tall man, with strange eyes. We'd see him at the back of the stage or hanging around the parking lot."

Janet: "We still didn't connect him with the letters. That didn't happen until the FBI came to our house about that time. It seems he had been writing some threatening letters to the President. He somehow blamed the President for standing in the way of him and Peggy. The FBI told Mom to look at pictures of Chet Young and watch out for him because he might be dangerous.

Diane: "We didn't have to look at the pictures. We knew he had to be the man who had been hanging around the studio."

Janet: "Then one day he came up to the door of Mom and Dad's house. He knocked on the door, but no one answered it. We called the police, but he was gone by the

213

time they arrived."

Diane: "In Lent of 1965, one of our brothers came home from Mass and said, 'I think I saw that man in church; he was sitting close to me.' So we called the police and this time they picked him up. He was taken to Atascadero state mental hospital."

Janet: "He was picked up once more, but we weren't given any details. We still didn't consider him harmful. As far as we could tell, he wasn't violent. Just sick."

Diane: "About a year ago, we started getting copies of fan magazine stories. These were stories they do about us, saying that Daddy was forcing us to work and that made us unhappy, that our husbands were leeches, all a sort of thing. Apparently his car was stacked high with those magazines."

Janet: "He sent copies of the stories to us, to our friends, our aunts and uncles, members of the Welk organization. How he managed to acquire the addresses of all of them, nobody knows."

Diane: "One day last April he followed me home. I was panicky, and I ran in the house and called Daddy. I told him that I had been followed by a white car. Daddy knew. He had seen the white car, too. Yet still, I wasn't afraid. I thought he was simply mentally sick. I thought he was just a big, dumb man who would never really be violent."

Janet: "The letters started coming every two weeks. After a while, we didn't open them. They just contained movie magazine stuff, and it depressed us to read them.

Diane: "When the murder happened, we knew immediately who had done it. The mere fact that he had argued with Dad was enough. Dad would never have argued that way with anyone he knew. He was the sweet-

214

est, gentlest, most understanding man. He never had an enemy in the world."

Janet: "After it happened, we all moved into Mom's house. All except Peggy, who had just moved to a new house in the San Fernando Valley where he wouldn't have known the address."

Diane: "There were 22 of us in that house, as well as two policemen 24 hours a day. It was difficult, especially for the children, because they couldn't even go out to play. After a while the police checked a few places where Chet Young might have been, and they figured he had to be out of the city. So we were allowed to go to our own homes. But for two months we had guards with us everywhere. And the police were simply wonderful — so warm and sympathetic."

Janet: "So was everyone. The letters were fantastic. Every morning at 7 we had a special mail delivery with huge boxes of letters. People sent cards and flowers and food. I don't know when we'll be able to answer them all."

Diane: "When we heard that Chet Young had killed himself, we all felt so bad for him. It must be terrible to be mentally ill; you can imagine what torture he went through."

Janet: "We felt relieved, too, that we wouldn't have to go through a trial. That would have been so hard on Mom. Now she's getting along fine; she's terribly busy with the family."

The body of Chet Young was shipped to Denver, where he was buried at Logan National Cemetery since he had served with honor in the Air Force during the Korean War.

The murder of Bill Lennon had been solved and Los Angeles police officially closed the case. But they could

215

not help but speculate that had Chet Young been kept in the mental institutions in which he had been confined for short periods of time, the father of the singing sisters would be alive today.

And that Young's suicide may have saved the lives of other members of one of America's most beloved families.

How I Would Have Handled The Taylor Case

by George C. Craft,
Well-Known Private Investigator

Blackmailer, thief, dope pedler, jealous admirer, thwarted lover—whose hand pulled the trigger that snuffed out the life of the brilliant motion picture director?

In fiction the murderer invariably leaves one or more clues which ultimately lead to his capture. In real life the killer frequently leaves no clue—or at least none which the police can follow through—and escapes detection.

But there was one capital case, the shooting of William Desmond Taylor, chief director of the Famous Players-Lasky Studios, in his home in Hollywood, in 1922, in which there was such a multiplicity of clues that the authorities simply ran around in circles without getting anywhere. And today the killing of this man, made famous because of his clever direction of Mary Pickford and other noted screen stars, is as much of a riddle as in the hour when his body was discovered. Among America's great unsolved murder mysteries, the Taylor case holds a leading place.

"He hadn't an enemy in the world," was the announcement acclaimed by his friends immediately following the discovery of the crime. And, for a time, there appeared to be good ground for the assertion, for Taylor, a witty, intelligent, traveled *bon vivant,* was not only an authority on art, books, music and the stage, a dabbler in sociology, an all-around athlete, a crack shot, a competent civil engineer with a host of friends, but also was respected and liked as an actor and director. Incidentally, his intimate friends included men as well as women, though the latter fluttered about him like moths, fascinated by his polish, good nature, generosity and always immaculate dress.

In Taylor's case, as in others, crime brought to the surface the other side of his personality, uncovered skeletons he had tried to bury, made the police and public acquainted with things which suggested many reasons why someone might have desired his death. His story, a tale of adventure in many lands and among all classes of persons, is as interesting, as bizarre, as that of any figures created by the writers of detective fiction.

A few minutes after seven in the evening of February 1, 1922, Mabel Normand, beautiful screen comedienne, appeared at his bungalow home, in Hollywood, to keep an appointment made earlier in the day. While they discussed a dancing lesson he had taken in the afternoon and a book by Freud, which he had purchased for her, Henry Peavey, Taylor's man-of-all-work, entered and arranged glasses, a shaker, etc., for the mixing of drinks. Then he left, after the actress had stated that she would not remain for dinner. Miss Normand's chauffeur was cleaning her car in the street fronting the court in which were the homes of Taylor and a few others.

At twenty minutes to eight the director escorted the

actress to her automobile, wished her a laughing good night, and returned to his home. A few minutes later persons living in the court heard a loud report, which most of them took for an automobile backfire. But Mrs. Douglas MacLean, wife of an actor, whose home was not far from that of Taylor, looked out and saw a man roughly dressed, with his cap pulled low, come out of the director's place, close the front door, and walk away through the rear entrance to the court.

Ten minutes thereafter Howard Fellows, Taylor's chauffeur, appeared at the house for orders but, receiving no response to his rings, returned home. Edna Purviance, another screen star, who lives next to the Taylor bungalow, returning home at midnight, noted lights in her neighbor's house.

The following morning, when Henry Peavey opened the place, he found Taylor, shot through the heart, lying dead near an overturned chair in front of his desk. On this were some cheques returned by the bank that day, which the director had been examining, and his purse, containing about $75.00. Taylor's revolver, of thirty-two calibre, was found clean and fully loaded in a drawer on the floor above. He had been killed instantly with a thirty-eight calibre bullet, fired at close range, but at such an angle that it disproved any suggestion of suicide. Nothing was stolen from the Taylor place, and the murder weapon never was found.

For several months the authorities worked night and day to uncover the killer, bringing into the open every person they could locate who had been on intimate terms with the director. Miss Normand was grilled repeatedly. She protested that the director was nothing more to her than a dear friend, though Peavey and others stated that she had been engaged to him. Miss Normand suggested no lead which indicated the murderer's identity.

Then a silly love letter, with X's for kisses, from Mary Miles Minter, was found in Taylor's effects. From the girl's statements it appeared that her infatuation had been that of a young actress for a clever, elderly man who had directed some of her pictures. Other actresses, with whom Taylor had been associated, and to whom he had given cheques and valuable presents, were questioned to no purpose.

The principal suspect was Edward F. Sands, former secretary to Taylor. While the latter was in England in 1921, Sands disappeared with an automobile, jewelry, money and clothing belonging to his employer, and later, it was charged, returned to Los Angeles and stole more jewelry from the house. In December, 1921, Taylor received a letter from him, enclosing pawn tickets for some of the plunder, and apologizing for the "inconvenience" he had caused. At the time of the killing there were two warrants for his arrest, and Claire Windsor, an actress, told the police that the director had said that he would kill Sands if he ever laid hands upon him.

Reports that Sands had been seen in Hollywood just previous to the murder proved to be without foundation, and Mrs. MacLean, who knew the man well, said he was not the person she had seen in Taylor's doorway. She also was certain that the man was not Fellows, who admitted that he was at the house and thought she might have mistaken him for a stranger.

A countrywide call for Sands' arrest was sent out, but

he was not located, though persons in many places were arrested on suspicion of being the man, and many cranks asserted each was the missing secretary. Dope peddlers whom Taylor had driven from the neighborhood of the picture lots, including some he had thrashed, and many others whom rumor said had been in the neighborhood of the Taylor home on the fatal night, were picked up and questioned. Nothing definite against any of them was uncovered.

The story of Taylor's past, a life spent partly in wild places and partly among the social elect of large cities, most of which came to the authorities after the slaying, proved the director to have been a most unusual man. Somewhere in that past, many years of which remain shrouded in mystery, I believe lies the key to the killing. I am convinced that somebody who had a greater incentive for murder than a passing fancy for some screen actress, kept after Taylor until able to strike him down at the height of his greatest success.

The slain director, whose correct name was William Cunningham Deane-Tanner, was born in Ireland in 1877, the son of a retired major. He had a brother Dennis. Taylor, though a splendid athlete and a fine scholar, was a wild boy and, after being graduated from Dublin University, quarreled with his father and left home. He traveled all over the world as a soldier of fortune, occasionally acting, sometimes engaged in civil engineering.

The first record of Taylor in this country was in the late 90's, when he appeared in the company of Fannie Davenport. In 1900, still using his correct name, he was manager of a shop in Fifth Avenue, New York, owned by Arthur Taylor, where art works and rare antiques were sold. Owner and manager were close friends, and it was the former's name which Taylor took when he discarded his own. Taylor was a master in his line, making $25,000 a year, but he was a free spender and not an infrequent drinker. However, he never neglected business.

Among the prettiest women in Manhattan in those days was Ethel May Harrison, a member of the original "Floradora" company, daughter of a wealthy family. She and Taylor were married in the famous Little Church Around the Corner in December, 1901. The couple maintained a fine establishment, and were members of many organizations, including the Larchmont Yacht Club. Something more than a year after the wedding a daughter, Ethel Daisy Deane-Tanner, was born.

Though the man lived at a rapid pace, it was not until 1908 that his friends learned that all was not well at home. When, on October 23rd of that year, he disappeared suddenly, they were stunned. After attending a Vanderbilt Cup Race, he went to a hotel, sent for his clothing, drew $500 from money owed him, kept $100, and mailed the rest to his family—then vanished. His books were in perfect order and, as he had suffered with neuralgia, it was suggested that he was the victim of aphasia. A search was made for him by private detectives, but the police never were notified.

However, his wife did not accept the aphasia theory, and his friends soon learned the nature of the skeleton in his closet. This was that, almost throughout his married life, he had kept up an intimacy with a beautiful woman he had known before his marriage and she had refused to be entirely discarded.

Then came a further disclosure. Three months before his disappearance Taylor and a pretty blonde, not the woman previously mentioned, spent some time at an Adirondack resort under assumed names. His identity became known to the clerks at the hotel through the markings on his linen and cheques he cashed. When he departed, he left a valuable ring as security for part of his bill. This woman was married, and it was believed that, later, he paid blackmail to protect her name. Finally, when he learned that his escapade had become known to several persons, it is believed that he fled to protect the woman and prevent divorce proceedings.

In 1910, obviously in good financial circumstances and using the name of Taylor, he called upon friends in Los Angeles. Though he would not explain why he had changed his name, he discussed his absence, stating that he had been shanghaied from New York, taken around the Horn, and landed at a north Pacific port. He added that he had done well in Canada and the Klondike and, after some weeks of looking over the budding motion-picture industry in Southern California, returned to Prince Rupert, British Columbia, where he was in business. In 1912 his wife divorced him for "misconduct and desertion," and two years later married a New York business man.

Returning to Los Angeles in 1913, he obtained a position with a motion-picture company, advanced rapidly, and soon was a featured performer. As a star in a film entitled "The Soul of Youth" he was recognized by his Eastern friends, and they informed his daughter and former wife where he was and the name he had assumed. His daughter wrote him a letter, and he replied, later returning East to see her.

Early in 1918 he enlisted in a Canadian regiment and, after seeing service overseas, was retired with the rank of captain. He promptly returned to pictures and soon became a director of note, and a favorite with many beautiful screen stars. To all queries put to him concerning a possibility that he would marry one of these, he replied that he would not, as he never really had loved but one woman, a former theatrical partner. He never stated whether this woman was dead or what had prevented them marrying. But, some time later, he was openly engaged to one star, but she broke the engagement, saying there was too great a difference in their ages. However, they remained friends to the day of his death. It was in the last year of his life that he led in the fight against the Hollywood dope peddlers.

I have kept in close touch with developments in the case through many dependable agencies. Frankly, I am at sea concerning the murderer and his or her motive. I know that essential facts never came to light; possibly these were suppressed by persons who, for selfish motives, would not help.

I don't believe that Sands, with two warrants hanging over him for serious offenses, came back, faced Taylor in the open, and killed him. He didn't do things that way.

Possibly the dope handlers had Taylor killed, but I doubt it. He was but one of many fighting them, and the addicts were so crafty that the police and others striving to suppress that traffic learned little from them.

Personally, I believe the slayer was a man who had an old grudge to satisfy. Maybe he was a disgruntled soldier who had served under Taylor, perhaps someone he had crossed in the Klondike, possibly the one who tried to blackmail him when he disappeared in 1908, or a person come back from his years of wandering in Europe and Asia. The theory of a blackmailer is a likely one, for Taylor always was outspoken against that class of crooks and repeatedly said they should be shot down like dogs.

And, mark this: The day before the director was killed, he drew $2,500 from a bank and redeposited it a few hours previous to the murder. Did he draw it out to pay a blackmailer and then change his mind? Was he killed because he finally determined to stand his ground and fight?

On the basis of investigation of such leads I would shape my case.

The Sharon Tate
Sex Cult Massacre

by Chris Edwards

"The most bizarre murder case in American History . . ."

Clad in black and moving with the stealth of night people, the little band moved through the inky darkness toward the big house at the dead end of the Benedict Canyon Road high in the Hollywood Hills. But before they could approach the sprawling ranch type home of sexpot movie actress Sharon Tate, there were a number of chores to be done.

One of the raiders climbed a telephone pole and severed the wires with a pair of bolt cutters. Another one of the group pressed a secret silver buzzer that allowed the big double gate leading to the estate to swing open.

Then they shot and killed a teenage boy with five bullets in the head as he tried to start up his car outside the big house. Fortunately for the little band, the small caliber gun made little sound. Only one of the raiders was armed with a long-barreled revolver.

The rest carried gleaming bayonets.

One of the group climbed into the house through a window and quietly opened a door for the others. There had been a small party in the house earlier, but as midnight neared on that fateful August 9th, all was quiet. Beautiful Sharon Tate, eight months pregnant with her first child, was in her bedroom. Her house guest, Abigail Folger, 26, the coffee heiress, was in another bedroom.

Miss Folger's boy friend, Voyteck Frykowski, 37, was stretched out on the living room couch and Jay Sebring, 35, the well known Hollywood hair stylist, was sitting on Sharon's bed, talking quietly to her.

The black-clad gang first awakened Frykowski. With a bayonet at his throat, he was warned to keep quiet. Bewilderment and terror was evident in his eyes. He scanned the faces of the group, seeking recognition, looking for assurance that it was all a bad dream or a poor joke. But he found none.

When Frykowski demanded to know who the intruders were and what they wanted, one raider replied in a sepulchral tone:

"I am the devil and I'm here to kill!"

At the point of gun and bayonet, Frykowski was tied up. It was at that moment that Jay Sebring walked in on the bizarre scene. When he screamed in fear and surprise, he was shot, then run through with a bayonet.

He died in a pool of his own blood on the floor beside the living room couch.

Disturbed by the commotion and the sound of the shot, Miss Folger ran into the room and one of the gang plunged the bayonet into her body.

It was at this time that Sharon Tate, one of Hollywood's most beautiful and successful actresses, walked in on the blood-drenched scene. Puzzlement first, then sheer horror, twisted her face. Her mind reeled as she struggled to identify these blackclad creatures, some holding bayonets dripping with blood. Not one had she seen before, and they were threatening not only her life, but that of her unborn child.

Suddenly, Frykowski broke loose from his bonds and ran for the door. The butt of the long-barreled revolver crashed down on his head, shattering the plastic grips. But when he kept running he was shot in the back. The handsome Polish playboy made it through the door, but he collapsed and died on the neatly trimmed lawn outside.

Miss Folger, despite her first stab wound, tried to escape out the door and headed for the caretaker's house at the rear of the property, where a number of large watchdogs were penned, but it was a futile flight. One of the black-clad killers caught her and plunged the bayonet into her body several more times.

Only beautiful Sharon Tate remained. In desperation she pleaded with the killer band, *"Please let me have my baby!"*

But there was little mercy to be shown in that midnight blood-letting orgy. Not one but several members of the gang plunged their bayonets into her body until she had been stabbed a total of 18 times! But strangely enough, they showed her one final act of consideration. Not once did one of the razor-sharp weapons violate her abdomen.

Nevertheless, when she died, the perfectly formed infant boy in her womb died with her on the living room floor.

The frenzy of the blood bath over, the silence of death settled over the canyon mansion. It was broken only by the excited chatter of the killers, and the occasional howling of the watchdog out back, who seemed to sense death in the midnight air.

The killers wiped their hands on a towel. One of the group wadded it into a swab, dipped it in one of the pools of blood on the floor and then wrote the single word "Pig", on the front door. The bloody towel was then draped over the head of Jay Sebring like a grotesque hood. Someone looped a length of nylon cord around Miss Tate's neck, threw it over a rafter on the open beam ceiling, and looped the other end around the neck of the hair stylist in a final grisly touch that linked the beautiful actress and the handsome playboy—who had once been her boy friend—together in death.

Overlooked in the orgy of murder was William Garretson, 19, the caretaker who lay sprawled on his bed in a small house at the rear of the property listening to rock records, completely oblivious of how closely death had passed him by. It was his friend, Steve Parent, 19, who had been the first to die. Parent had just left Garretson's quarters and was headed for home when he was murdered. A double twist of fate killed him. Had he left sooner—or later—he might be alive today. As it was, he had the misfortune and bad timing to cross the path of the killer band.

Finally, the black-clad killers stepped over the bloody bodies of their victims, climbed into their car, and vanished down the canyon road as silently and unnoticed as they had come.

The motive? There appeared to be none. All they got was $73 in cash which Miss Folger, the millionaire heiress, forced upon them in a desperate but futile attempt to buy her life.

At 12:30 a.m. on the morning of August 9, 1969, the canyon mansion was again cloaked in silence, just as it had been when the killers arrived. The only difference was that the $200,000 rustic estate had become a blood-soaked killing ground.

In their wake the savage night people left behind what was to become one of the most baffling mass murders in the history of violent crime. And the blood-letting was not yet over. There would be more to come.

At 8:30 that Saturday morning, Mrs. Winifred Chapman, a maid, drove up to the sprawling house at the end of Cielo Drive to begin her day's work, but she never entered the mansion that day. As she entered the gate and pulled into the parking area, the sight she saw made her blood run cold. In horror and terror, she fled to the home of a neighbor, roused a 15-

229

year-old boy, pointed toward the Tate home and gasped:

"There's bodies and blood all over the place!"

The teenage boy kept his cool, got on the phone and called the West Los Angeles station of the Los Angeles Police Department. In no time at all the canyon road was swarming with police officials, coroner's deputies, crime lab technicians and hordes of press representatives. The police entered the estate with guns drawn, not knowing what they would find.

The silence was broken by the sound of a dog baying behind a guest house facing the driveway. Then the officers heard the voice of a man yelling at the dog to be quiet. Amidst the carnage in and around the Tate mansion, they realized, someone was alive. The question in the minds of the officers was, simply: Could it possibly be the killer?

The officers kicked in the door of the guest house and, at gunpoint, took William Garretson under arrest. He was clad only in pin-striped bell bottom trousers. After several hours of questioning he was booked on suspicion of murder.

Explained Lieutenant Robert Madlock, "He was taken into custody because he was on the premises where five persons were murdered."

The body of Steve Parent was found slumped down behind the wheel of the white Rambler registered to his father. The youth lived with his parents in El Monte, some 25 miles east of the Benedict Canyon mansion, in a different city, a different world.

On the lawn in front of the sprawling ranch-style home was the body of Miss Folger, wearing only a night gown.

In the living room, clad only in a bra and bikini panties, was Sharon Tate. A few feet away, and connected to her by the nylon cord which had been slung over the rafter, lay the body of Jay Sebring.

Police gave out few details. They said the phone lines to the home had been cut by someone who would have had to climb a pole near the gate. They said no weapon was found at the house, nothing of value appeared to have been taken, and there was no indication that the place had been ransacked.

The midnight foray appeared to have murder and only murder in mind.

But why?

That was the big question, and the one on which police concentrated all their efforts. When — and if — they found the motive, the resulting investigation could be given some direction.

Four of the victims were members of what has been called the "rich-hippies" set that flourishes in the environs of Hollywood. But young Steve Parent was a complete outsider. And it appeared that the murderers killed him under the impression that he was the caretaker, since they appeared bent on destroying everyone at the estate. Parent's broken-hearted parents said he had gone to work in Beverly Hills that fateful Friday and apparently went to visit Garretson, a recently made friend, after work.

The handsome youth, who had nothing in common with the jet-setters who lived and played in the rustic red and yellow home, appeared to have died simply because he happened to be in the wrong place at precisely the wrong time.

The question that plagued the police was: Why was this massive murder committed?

In their investigation of the tragic drama the detectives compiled this cast of victims:

Sharon Tate — She was the daughter of a career Army officer, reared as an "Army brat," the 26-year-old wife of Roman Polanski, maker of sensational horror movies such as "Rosemary's Baby." Sharon was one of the most beautiful girls in Hollywood. She moved among the "beautiful people" of the jet set, sometimes called "rich hippies." She was eight months pregnant with her first child. Her husband was in England and some gossip columnists had hinted their marriage was heading for the rocks. Among movie fans she was best known for her role in "Valley of the Dolls." She had once described herself as a "mad irrational character who simply loved men. I love them because they are men." Before her marriage to Polanski, Miss Tate said she had been in love with Sebring. Alternately gay and sad, friends described her as an insecure and lonely person.

Jay Sebring — at 35, he was handsome, slightly built and had made a half million dollars, it was said, in the men's hair styling craze that swept the country in recent years. He sought to prove his masculinity by becoming one of Hollywood's best karate experts. But in his sleek sports car parked outside the Tate home, police said, they found his crutch — a quantity of marijuana and pills.

Wosciech (Voyteck) Frykowski — He was a Polish emigré who at 37 was a tall, handsome and powerful man. He had once been an assistant on Polanski's films but had apparently squandered inherited wealth and became a hanger-on in the Tate-Polanski circle. Police said he also smoked marijuana and they had been told he also used cocaine. He had been Abigail Folger's boy friend for more than a year. He was described by a friend as a sophisticate. And in Poland, where it is not easy to be a playboy, the friend said, "he had style." He had been married and divorced twice, fled from Poland, lived in Paris and reportedly "chippied with underworld characters, and moved in what was described as a pot oriented world."

Abigail Folger — She was heiress to the Folger coffee fortune. At 26 she was pretty, but far less attractive than the starlets who moved in the Tate-Polanski group. She had been graduated from Radcliffe with honors and had come to Los Angeles to do social work. But according to a police informant, she became Frykowski's girl friend and became increasingly fascinated with the study of black magic.

Steven Parent — He was the only "straight" person among the murder victims and in all probability hadn't seen, much less known, any one of those who were to die with him. Two weeks before the murders he had given a ride to Garretson, caretaker at the Tate estate, and Garretson had invited him to drop by sometime and listen to records with him. Parent did this on the night of August 9th. And on his first visit to the mansion in the canyon, he met his death.

That, then, was the cast of doomed characters in this incredible, bloody charade. From simply scanning the backgrounds of the victims, police quickly realized, the investigation of the murders was apt to take off in almost any direction; a motive might be found anywhere — dope, black magic, sex cults, seances, witchcraft or simply a wild, orgiastic party that got out of hand. Now detectives had to determine who, if anyone, had been in the house that night for the small party and left before — or after — the mass murder.

One thing appeared clear. The crime had been carefully planned by someone who appeared to know there would be five persons at the estate, who knew how to open the gate by pressing the silver button, and who had enough foresight to cut the telephone wires to keep anyone from locking himself into a room and calling police. To cut the wires the killer would have had to climb a tilting pole, a feat that would require considerable physical agility.

The macabre symbolism in the rope that had been thrown across the roof beam and looped around the necks of Sebring and Miss Tate appeared to have some meaning. The loops around the necks of these two victims were far too loose to have caused their deaths by strangling, and there appeared to be some reason deliberately to link this couple together in death.

233

A careful search of the house uncovered no narcotics on the premises, save for the contraband reportedly found in Sebring's black Porsche.

The coroner set the time of the mass murder at about midnight and a nearby resident in the canyon told police, "I thought I heard some shots about midnight. About three or four. They weren't too loud. More of a 'Clap! Clap!' sort of thing." The neighbor also thought she heard a scream, but that was not unusual at parties at homes in the area.

Garretson, the young caretaker, said he heard nothing in the guest house but conceded he was playing his rock records, which could have drowned out the shots and screams. What surprised police was that the killers didn't hear the phonograph and go looking for Garretson. A possible explanation was that they thought Parent was the caretaker and had accidentally left his record player on.

The police probers began compiling a list of persons who knew or who reportedly knew the jet set murder victims. They had by this time assumed that the object of the midnight raid on the mansion was not Steve Parent, the young man from El Monte. And as nearly a score of detectives made their rounds, questioning these friends and acquaintances, they met with a wall of silence in many instances.

Not even the most avid of Hollywood's publicity seekers wanted to be tarred with the Sharon Tate murder brush. All kinds of closets could be opened and all kinds of skeletons and ghosts could be released. Few were willing to be tainted by such a scandal. Sex or booze is one thing. Witchcraft, dope and reports of unusual orgies are quite another.

Police questioning of young Garretson proved most unrewarding. Two days after his arrest he was released from custody. Police simply explained that there was no evidence to link him to the murders which had occurred only a few feet away from where he lay listening to records.

He gave this account of his actions on the night of August 8-9. He said he left his quarters about 9 p.m. to buy groceries on the Sunset Strip, returning about 10 p.m. He said he noticed Abigail Folger's Firebird parked at the estate but he was not quite sure whether he had seen Sebring's black Porsche.

About 11:45 p.m., he said, Steve Parent arrived at the cottage and brought along a clock radio for him. And around midnight Parent called a friend and said he was coming over to spend the night. (This indicated the phone wires had not been cut at that time.)

About 15 minutes later, Garretson said, Parent left, but the caretaker insisted he never heard the shots that killed his friend minutes later. Garretson said he listened to rock music on his stereo and wrote letters until early morning. He said he tried to make a phone call about 5:30 a.m. to learn the time and found the telephone dead.

"I didn't know what to think," he said. "I was a little bit frightened."

He said he dozed off and was awakened by the barking of Christopher, a Weimaraner, one of the three dogs he was being paid $35 a week to care for.

And finally, he said, the police rushed him and placed him under arrest.

Police did learn that a different type of person sometimes visited the guest house on the property in addition to the jet setters who visited the main ranch house. These included the Hollywood Boulevard types, the hitchhikers, the midnight cowboys and other youths who had been invited there by young Garretson or his friends.

This opened the possibility that one of them might have returned to rob the occupants of the main house.

Cleared by the police, Garretson announced through his

attorney that he would file a million dollar false arrest suit against the City of Los Angeles. And with that he returned to his home in Ohio to rejoin his family and return to college. He had seen all he wanted of the Hollywood jet set.

In the days that immediately followed the massacre, a score of detectives assigned to the case settled down to the nitty-gritty police work of doorbell ringing and questioning anyone and everyone who might have some knowledge of what might have gone on in the Tate-Polanski home since the couple had rented it in February, 1969. In the course of that investigation they were to talk to a total of 625 persons. Detectives listened to all sorts of gossip and sensational rumors, some true, some false, and some that lay in the gray area between the two extremes.

That investigation indicated that if any one of the victims had been the primary target for the killer, it could well have been Frykowski, and the others might have been killed simply to keep them from identifying the murderer. For there was more than one report that the handsome Polish playboy was involved with drugs; police were told he trafficked in LSD, heroin, marijuana and cocaine.

If true, this opened up all kinds of possibilities.

The detectives were also told that Frykowski had two partners in his dealings, that he quarreled violently with them for some unknown reason, and that the pair had been seen in Hollywood as recently as two days before the murders. An all-points bulletin was issued for their apprehension.

But 24 hours later the investigation of the Tate murders took another unexpected tack. Another macabre blood bath spilled into the laps of the Los Angeles police, and it was so similar to the Tate murders that it was promptly dubbed by newspaper headline writers as "The Copy Cat Murders."

Shortly after midnight on August 9th—just 24 hours after

Bob Crane

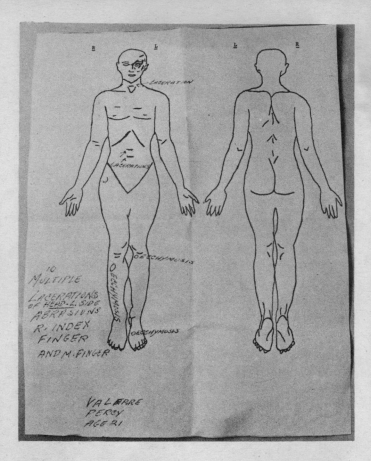

Cook County Coroner's sketch showing
the wounds that killed Valerie Percy.

George Rose in costume for his role in
The Mystery of Edwin Drood.

Vicki Morgan at the time of her $5 million "palimony" suit against Alfred Bloomingdale.

Ramon Novarro

Sharon Tate

Sal Mineo

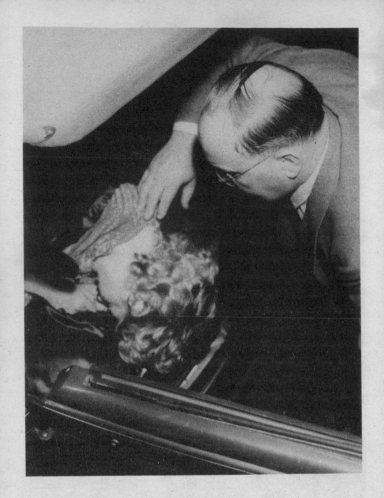

Thelma Todd's body in the front seat of her car.

the slaying of Sharon Tate and her friends, Leon·La Bianca, 44, and his wife, Rosemary, 38, returned to their $50,000 hilltop home in the Los Feliz district of Los Angeles after a water skiing outing at Lake Isabella. They were accompanied by Susan Struthers, 21, Mrs. La Bianca's daughter by a previous marriage.

La Bianca parked his Thunderbird in the driveway, still hitched to the trailer that carried their sleek speedboat.

The La Biancas dropped Miss Struthers off at her apartment and went on home alone. At 8:30 the following Sunday morning, Frank Struthers, 14, who had been water skiing with friends, came home to find the front door locked and the lights burning inside, but no one answered his persistent door bell ring. He phoned his sister from the home of a neighbor and, with her boy friend, the young woman came over to her parents' home.

The young man and the boy looked in a window and found themselves gazing upon a scene of horror. Mr. La Bianca, in his pajamas, lay on the living room floor. He had been stabbed repeatedly and the word "War" and a series of "X's" had been carved into his chest with a knife. A carving fork protruded from his abdomen.

Over his head was draped a white hood.

In the master bedroom was the body of Mrs. La Bianca, clad in a negligee. An electric cord was wound around her neck and it appeared that most of the flesh had been flayed or skinned off her back.

On the refrigerator, written in blood, was the inscription, "Death to Pigs" in letters eight inches high.

Police Sergeant Terry Pierce said, "The bedroom was in a turmoil, like she gave quite a struggle. But there was nothing out of place in the living room. Evidently La Bianca was surprised."

Here again the police were to grope aimlessly for a motive. La Bianca was wealthy. He and his wife owned a small chain of four prosperous supermarkets, but nothing of value appeared to have been taken from the home.

The similarity of the La Bianca and Tate murders stunned detectives, however. There was no indication that either home had been forcibly entered. Both crimes had a ritualistic air to them — the hooded corpses, the almost orgiastic use of knives, the inscriptions in blood that contained the same word, "PIG", the shockingly excessive 'overkill' tactics. And the complete absence of a motive.

La Bianca had lived in the hilltop house since he moved there as a boy 30 years before. It was in an upper middle class district, but far removed from the fast way of life linked to the Tate-Polanski circle 15 miles away. However, the presence of the gleaming Thunderbird and sleek speedboat in the driveway might have given the house a look of affluence that could have attracted the killers.

So far as police could determine, there was no social connection between the La Biancas and the Tates; they were worlds apart and apparently had no mutual friends. But the slayings were too similar to be a coincidence. There was some speculation that the La Bianca murders might have been committed by someone who was inspired by the Tate murders. However, this was only a theory, without facts or even rumors to support it.

Said Sgt. Bryce Houchin, "There a similarity in the slayings. But whether it is the same suspect or a copy cat, we just don't know." However, one police officer told newsmen that in his opinion the inscriptions written in blood in the Tate home and in the La Bianca home appeared to have been done by the same person.

It was the 'overkill' in both the Tate murders and the La

Bianca murders that gripped the imagination of the police officers investigating both cases. So much of the violence was unnecessary. And the question that plagued them in the Tate killings returned to plague them in the La Bianca killings — WHY?

Why had these people been singled out for such cruel and inhuman deaths? But in the days that followed, the press continued to play up the Tate story and eventually the La Bianca murders slipped into the shadows. Tate, Sebring, and Folger were household words; there was more news value in them. And there was more to speculate about than in the case of the La Biancas, quiet people who lived only for their family.

In the Tate case there was a new rumor or report nearly every day. The Los Angeles Times reported that a Polish friend of Frykowski told police the playboy had been in the midst of a mescaline experiment when he was murdered. The friend said that Frykowski had planned to take dosages of the drug for eight or ten days and added that Jay Sebring might have been involved in the experiment with him.

The friend also said he went to the Tate home on August 7th, two days before the murders, and found Frykowski "wobbly and uncoordinated." He said, "Sebring was sitting in a chair, his head tilted to one side as though he were watching a movie only he could see. Sharon was in a bedroom. Through an open door I could see her combing her hair.

"But she wasn't high. She did not use drugs. She was perfectly straight. She was a warm, sweet person."

Another friend told police that Frykowski's use of mescaline had changed his personality in recent weeks before his death, and added, "I had a feeling something terrible was going to happen."

The police investigation of the macabre murders centered in a large part around the handsome Pole, apparently because, it was thought, he was involved with people who might have had a reason to kill him as a result of their connections in the narcotics traffic.

The two men sought by police as possible suspects and friends of the slain Pole surrendered and were cleared after questioning by detectives. Both men had air-tight alibis for their movements at the time of the slayings and police said there was no reason to hold them.

During the days that followed, police continued their questioning of friends, relatives and acquaintances of the murder victims, but admittedly little progress was made. Gossips had a field day with rumors. Even a respectable news magazine fell for one and put it in print, only to have it emphatically denied by the police and coroner.

The magazine reported that the bodies of some of the victims had been sexually mutilated. Police said without qualification, "None of the bodies had wounds involving sex organs." But it was a good story while it lasted and was never retracted by the magazine.

Police did admit, however, that "narcotics aspects in connection with the crime are under investigation" and newsmen learned that a quantity of marijuana, pills resembling "speed" and possibly some LSD had been found in Sebring's racy sports car. Police also revealed that there had been no evidence of excessive drinking in the Tate home on the night of the murders.

The probe of the "narcotics aspects" of the case led police into two lines of investigation:

1. That the killer or killers might have "freaked out" on drugs and killed in a paranoid frenzy.

2. That one or more of the victims had been involved in the narcotics trade; involved in the sale or theft of drugs, cheated a narcotics dealer or customer and been ordered killed. It was

quite possible that the others were killed simply to keep them from identifying the killer. The only thing that clouded this theory was the weird, ritualistic symbolism connected with the murders and, again, the "overkill." It was not a gangland type rubout.

There was no doubt the crimes were premeditated. The cut phone lines were proof of that, and this would tend to scratch the "freak out" theory as well. The question that continued to come up day after day was simply: What was the motive both in the Tate killings and in the La Bianca killings? There was no tangible connection between the two cases, but some detectives felt certain it would be found eventually.

A week after the murders, Roman Polanski, Sharon Tate's husband, appeared on the scene and invited newsmen to accompany him on a tour of what he sarcastically called, "The orgy place." "You will see how innocent it is", he said.

Dried patches of blood could still be seen where the bodies had fallen. The word "Pig" in blood was still visible on the front door, and dark patches of blood on the living room rug indicated where Sebring and Miss Tate had died.

The whitish powder liberally sprinkled throughout the entire house by crime lab technicians in their quest for fingerprints was clearly visible. However, police had made no mention of what the fingerprint search had turned up. The prints were of little use to police until they came up with a suspect with whom they could match them. There is only a small chance that latent prints can ever lead the police to a suspect. They usually have to have the suspect before the prints are of any use, unless they are lucky enough to get a complete set left by a person whose fingerprints are on file, and that is rare.

In the master bedroom that had been occupied by Miss Tate, striped sheets covered the bed. On top of a Spanish-type dresser were a Turkish water pipe and a number of books on natural childbirth, baby care, and one entitled, "Name Your Baby"—something Sharon Tate never got to do.

The house itself looked like anything but a setting for sexual orgies or the black arts practices hinted at by Hollywood gossips and columnists. The house had been rented by Miss Tate and Polanski for $1,000 a month. She had planned to live there and await the arrival of her baby while her husband was making a film in Europe. Rather than occupy the big house by herself, Miss Tate had invited Miss Folger and Frykowski to share the house with her as her guests.

The mansion, situated on a ridge overlooking the canyon, had once been occupied by Cary Grant and Dyan Cannon before their marriage broke up, and by Terry Melcher, son of actress Doris Day; Melcher had occupied it about six months before the Polanskis. Although the place had an estimated value of $200,000, it was in more than a little need of paint and general repair.

There were two bedrooms in the main building and the most notable feature of the residence was its huge living room and massive fireplace. At one end of the living room is a loft, accessible by ladder, from which guests at parties could gaze down on the merry-making below.

In a press conference, Polanski refused to tie the rap to Frykowski despite the rampant rumors that the handsome Polish playboy might have been responsible for the killers focusing their attention on the Benedict Canyon home. Polanski prefaced his remarks by stating emphatically:

"Sharon didn't use drugs. She didn't touch alcohol. And she didn't even smoke cigarettes."

Of Frykowski he said, "He was a man I knew from Poland for a very long time. He was a very kind human being who wanted success but who had very little talent. I saw him in Paris after he defected from Poland and he was struggling

242

along. The only help I could give him was money and encouragement."

Polanski, as well as the police, was admittedly puzzled. However, there were many who — rightly or otherwise — were not, and they gave proof of this by circulating all kinds of rumors and stories, none of which ever imparted much direction to the search for the murderers.

But among the reports assiduously checked out by police who had vowed to leave no stone unturned were these:

Sebring and Frykowski had recently beaten up a dope pusher and that he came back to kill them.

. . . Sebring was in debt to gamblers and a rubout followed.

. . . Members of the jet-set circle had picked up some male hustlers — called "rough trade" in Hollywood circles — and brought them to the house for fun and games. And it was these games that might have gotten out of hand on the night of the murders.

. . . Then there was the theory that one of the caretaker's guests who got a look at the big house might have returned with robbery in mind.

. . . There were also reports that narcotics had been delivered to the house by tough underworld-looking types. But police checked all these possibilities and eliminated them all. Not one produced a single good suspect.

Steve Brandt, a Hollywood writer and friend of the Polanskis, said he firmly believed that someone who had been invited to the Tate home that night went berserk under the influence of some kind of drug and committed the crimes. He told a reporter, "It couldn't have been a big party. Sharon would have wanted to retire early. The only thing she was interested in was that baby. Her personality changed after she became pregnant. She was unbelievably happy. All that talk of an orgy — nothing could have been farther from her mind.

"But Miss Folger and Frykowski were involved with strange people. She was interested in witchcraft, black masses, that sort of thing. She and Frykowski would go to weird, kinky places. I think it was someone they brought in who turned homicidal under something like LSD.

"A person who is suicidal tries to commit suicide under LSD. A person who is homicidal may turn to homicide. I believe that is what happened."

Brandt said that about five days before the murders he met the handsome Pole and Miss Folger in a Hollywood after-hours place. "His eyes were unfocusing, staring," Brandt said. "He looked like something from the movie, 'Village of the Damned.' I said to him, 'Are you on something?' and he said, 'Yes, it is the greatest. Mescaline. Want to buy some?' "

Brandt said the Pole spoke of a new drug he was getting— something he called Fairy Dust.

Depressed over the mass killing in Benedict Canyon, Steve Brandt took his own life three months later.

The inability of the police to come up with suspects in the mass murder struck terror into the hearts of residents of the canyon areas. The poor have to live with their fears; the wealthy can afford to share them with guard dogs, for which they now paid as high as $2,500, or with private guards posted around their homes.

A police task force of 20 detectives—the largest assembled on a single case since the Los Angeles slaying of Senator Robert Kennedy—checked out every rumor, every name found in any victim's black book, and listened to anyone with a story to tell regarding the Benedict Canyon slayings. A pair of eye glasses found near the Tate home shortly after the killings indicated that the person who owned them had a head shaped like a volley ball. There was an immediate search for such a person and opticians were asked to check their files for lens prescriptions similar to those of the mysterious eyeglasses.

But weeks and months after the crime there still were no "prime suspects" in the case. There was a barrel of rumors but no substantial leads.

By virtue of his best seller on a multiple murder in rural Kansas, Truman Capote got more than his share of air time on NBC's Tonight Show. He suggested that a "very young, enraged paranoid" was responsible for the mass murder. He theorized that the killer had known the victims, that he had been in the house earlier in the evening and left abruptly after someone said something which triggered his deep strain of paranoia.

He theorized that the killer went home, got a knife and a gun and returned to the house, and at gunpoint forced Miss Tate and Sebring to tie themselves together. Capote said he thought the killer shot Frykowski and Miss Folger as they tried to escape, and then shot young Parent as he saw him leaving the estate.

He said the killer probably experienced a sexual release after completing the crimes, was drowsy, and probably slept for two days.

Truman Capote may be one hell of a writer, but he'd make a lousy detective. His theory eventually proved to be dead wrong.

F. Lee Bailey, renowned criminal attorney, concluded that the murders were committed by one man whose dignity was affronted and ignited "an explosion in his brain."

There were many who took advantage of the murders. A writer friend of Miss Tate banged out a quick sex and drug exposé for a national magazine. A friend of Sebring did the same for a movie magazine. Some said Sharon Tate used pot. Her husband denied it. As if in reply, a magazine reported that Sharon had once boasted of taking 67 LSD trips and never made a salad without sprinkling it with marijuana. MGM released Polanski's "Fearless Vampire Killers" and 20th Century Fox released "Valley of the Dolls," making sure to mention prominently that Sharon Tate was staring in it.

But more than three months after the slaying in Benedict Canyon, the case appeared to be no nearer solution than ever. At least, there were no suspects in custody, and the story which had been such big news was now all but forgotten by newspaper readers. It had slipped into Limbo with the long forgotten La Bianca murders.

But it was far from forgotten by the police.

The actual turning point in the investigation of the puzzling mass murder of the wealthy Los Angeles jet setters came from a source as far removed from the setting of the crime as anyone could imagine. In order to understand it, it is necessary to take up the strange odyssey that began in the Haight-Ashbury district of San Francisco on April 12, 1968, when 14 young hippies heeded the call of their leader, whom they called by different names — Jesus — God — Satan, climbed aboard an old green and white school bus and headed south.

The drug scene in the Haight-Ashbury had gotten out of hand. The love and flower children were being assailed on all sides by drug pushers, pimps, hustlers of every stripe and police. The 14 who climbed into that bus that was to become their home longed for the Southern California sun and a break with a past which had soured.

Their leader was Charles Manson, a strange little man, full-bearded and long-haired, who carried a guitar and who likened himself to a wandering minstrel. At 34, Manson had a "rap sheet" as long as his arm, but he had a strange and eerie power over those who followed him. One beautiful teenage girl described it this way:

246

"We belong to him, not to ourselves. If Charles says it is right, it is right. He is a very beautiful man."

All this despite the fact that he had spent 18 of his 34 years in reform schools, jails and prisons.

On the way south, a baby was born on the bus and Manson was reputed to be its father. And Ventura County deputies got an eyeful when they rolled out on U.S. 101 to investigate a report that a school bus was in a ditch near Oxnard, just north of Los Angeles. The passengers, none of them injured, were sprawled out, nude, on the grass beside the busy highway, soaking up the Southern California sun they had long been seeking.

The names of most of the people on that bus will never be remembered, but some are worth keeping in mind. They are Charles Manson, Patricia Krenwinkel, and Susan Denise Atkins. Both girls were members of Manson's harem. Miss Atkins, a former resident of San Jose, had been with Manson and had borne him a child since she met him in the Haight-Ashbury in 1966. Miss Krenwinkel had been with Manson since 1967 when she first saw him in Manhattan Beach near Los Angeles.

One look was enough to make her leave her car in a parking lot, walk off her job, leaving her paycheck behind, and climb aboard his bus-harem. This is but a minor indication of the strange powers this man exercised over people, particularly young women.

Until 1969, Manson and his "family" lived off people. One of their benefactors was Dennis Wilson, a member of the Beach Boys musical group. Another was Gary Hinman, a graduate student from UCLA who lived in Topanga Canyon and shared his home with Manson and his "family." In July, 1969, the group established a commune at a rundown movie ranch in Chatsworth, in the San Fernando Valley. The personnel of the family changed as hippies came and drifted on, but the band that was to become known as The Manson Family usually numbered about 25 — most of them young and pretty women and girls. The word was that as a lover, Charles Manson was "the greatest."

In August, 1969, a week after the Tate murders, Los Angeles police swooped down on the Chatsworth ranch, rounded up a number of Manson's people and booked them on charges of auto theft. The suspicion was that the Manson Family financed their way of life by stealing Volkswagens and converting them into dune buggies, one of Southern California's most popular recreational vehicles.

Most of those arrested were freed because of insufficient evidence. Others were released on bail. Most heeded the call of Charles Manson and once again boarded the school bus for a new haven. This time their destination was Death Valley, a forbidding, inhospitable land of bare mountains, salt lakes, and barren flatlands. With the permission of the owners they set up a camp at the Barker Ranch in Golder Wash, an almost inaccessible area 20 miles northeast of the nearest town, Trona. They used an abandoned stone house as their headquarters.

In early October, Inyo County sheriff's deputies began hearing reports that the hippie band had driven a group of prospectors out of their cabins and had taken over the place, setting up a base of operations for converting VWs into dune buggies.

The raid on the desert commune was led by James Purcell, a California Highway Patrolman, whose "beat" covers some 3,000 square miles of Death Valley and who was more familiar with it than other lawmen in the area. The raid took place at dusk and with pistol in hand, the young patrolman shoved open the door of an old mining cabin.

There was a single candle burning in the room. When his eyes became accustomed to the semi-darkness officer Purcell could see a dozen hippies seated around a rough table at their evening meal of sugared rice puffs, caramel popcorn and candy bars. He ordered them outside, their hands in the air. There other officers took them into custody.

The raid had been carried out at dusk to avoid detection from lookouts, stationed in a number of watchtowers and equipped with walkie-talkies. One such lookout, found asleep at his post with a shotgun cradled in his arms, was a young man by the name of Charles Watson, officers said.

Alter the hippies were taken under arrest, Purcell went back into the cabin to make a more thorough search. He went into the bathroom and shined his flashlight around until his eye caught what seemed to be a dirty mop hanging out of a tiny cupboard under a wash basin stand. Purcell opened the door and in that tiny 36 by 18 by 20 inch space was a small man with his knees buckled up against his chest. The shoulder-length mane of dark hair which Purcell thought to be a mop had given Charles Manson away. He was taken along to the county jail in Independence, California, along with the rest of his followers.

The journeys of the Manson family were over.

Twenty-six members of the family were taken in that raid. A few were released, but most were held on charges ranging from arson to auto theft and possession of dangerous weapons. The girls among them were pretty. Some had babies. Most of them were nude when they were arrested; a few wore only bikini bottoms. The girls carried sheath knives and all appeared to be reasonably clean for having lived in the desert where water could ill afford to be wasted for bathing. Inyo County deputies decided there might be more than local interest in the hippies, so the names of all arrested were placed on inter-city teletypes and dispatched to all law enforcement agencies throughout the West.

One name caught the attention of Los Angeles law enforcement authorities—Susan Atkins. A witness had identified her as being present during what was described as a torture murder in July, 1969, in Topanga Canyon. The name of the victim was Gary Hinman, the musician who had befriended the Manson Family and allowed them to stay at his home about that time. The murder had attracted little press attention, but police recalled that one of the strange things about it was that the killer or killers had scrawled on the wall of one room in blood: "Political Piggy."

A man by the name of Robert Beausoiel had been tried for the murder, but the trial resulted in a hung jury—8 to 4 for conviction. Beausoiel was currently awaiting a retrial. And according to the testimony of a witness at that trial, Daniel De Carlo, Miss Atkins had been present when the murder was committed. As a result, she was transported from the small jail in Independence and confined in the huge Sybil Brand Institute for Women in Los Angeles.

From that cell, in early November, 1969, she opened a Pandora's box of trouble for the Manson Family.

One of her cell mates was Shelly Nadell, 34, awaiting trial for forging prescriptions for narcotics. It was in this woman that Miss Atkins confided. Why she did is not known, but for the first time since 1966, Miss Atkins had been cast adrift from Charles Manson. He was no longer around to impose his will on her, and when her pent-up secret burst forth, Miss Nadell listened. Cautiously, without appearing to pump her pretty, darkhaired cellmate, Miss Nadell gathered names, dates, places, details and nicknames, and turned them over to the police.

Detectives from Los Angeles appeared at the Independence

jail and took away nine members of the Manson Family. The local officers didn't know much about what was going on, but one of them did hear mentioned a single word, "Tate," and noted the penal code section under which the hippies were removed to Los Angeles: "187 P.C. — Murder."

At this point, detectives were convinced of this much: The information Susan Atkins had related to Miss Nadell contained details that could only have been known by a person who was present at the scene of the Tate killings. The officers appeared to be nearing the end of the "who" in the Tate murders, but as yet unanswered was the question "why."

Miss Atkins also reportedly told her cellmate that members of the Manson family also took part in the La Bianca killings. The use of the word "Pig" found at the scene of all three crimes — Hinman, Tate and La Bianca — seemed to lend credence to this.

At the completion of two weeks of intense investigation by scores of police probers, Los Angeles Police Chief Edward Davis was ready to make his play. On December 1st, he called a very important press conference in the auditorium of the Los Angeles Police Building. There, behind a battery of 15 microphones and under a battery of bright hot lights, he announced that 8,750 hours of police work had ended in a solution to the Tate and La Bianca murders. He told newsmen that three murder warrants had been issued for the arrest of two men and a woman, charging them with murder.

The chief identified one of the suspects as Charles Watson, 24, the lookout who had been asleep when Inyo County Sheriffs deputies raided the Death Valley commune of the Manson Family. Watson, he said, was being held in a Texas jail on an unrelated charge.

The women charged with five counts of murder in connection with the Tate case were Patricia Krenwinkel, the 21-year-old girl who ran off to the Haight-Ashbury district in 1968, and a girl identified only as Linda Kasabian, 19. A short time after the announcement in Los Angeles, Miss Krenwinkel was arrested in Mobile, Alabama, and Mrs. Kasabian, pregnant with her second child, surrendered to police in her former home town of Concord, New Hampshire.

On the night of November 19th, Deputy District Attorney Vincent Bugliosi and six homicide detectives from Los Angeles obtained a search warrant and hurried off to the hippie encampment in Death Valley. What they obtained there, if anything, has not been disclosed.

The press conference by Chief Davis revealed only the bare bones of an incredibly bizarre story. Aware that most details would have to wait until later, newspaper reporters began digging into the backgrounds of the principals connected with the mass slaying, Charles Manson, Charles Watson, Pat Krenwinkel, Linda Kasabian and Sue Atkins.

Manson was born a bastard in Cincinnati, Ohio on November 11, 1934. His mother, who was 16 at the time, later went to prison along with her brother for beating up and robbing dates she had hustled in waterfront bars.

This was the tragic beginning for Charles Manson, who was identified as the mastermind of a renegade hippie band suspected of killing at least 7 persons — perhaps more — according to police.

When his mother went to prison, Manson went to live with a succession of relatives, none of whom, apparently, wanted him. In 1945, Manson was made a ward of the court and sent to a school for boys in Terre Haute, Indiana.

Alter 10 months he ran away and later was sent to a correctional institution in Plainfield, Indiana. By the time he was 25, he had spent 13 years in reformatories or jails. In 1951 he stole a car in Indiana, was arrested in Utah and sent to the

National Training School for boys in Washington, D.C. He was shuffled along to other reform schools, an unbending adolescent, hiding his loneliness, resentment and hostility behind an oddly ingratiating facade.

Reformatory tutors who tried to train him could only report him as being "totally unreceptive." By the time he was paroled from the federal reformatory in Chillicothe, Ohio in 1955 at the age of 21, he had developed the capability for doing exactly nothing.

He moved back to relatives in McMechen, West Virginia, and married a waitress in a hospital dining room. But by the time she gave birth to her first child, Charles Manson was back in jail, this time at Terminal Island in California, for transporting stolen cars across state lines. He later did time for transporting women across state lines for prostitution, as well as for escape and parole violation. He was finally released from prison in 1958. By 1960, he was back in stir for cashing two stolen government checks.

At McNeil Island Prison in Washington, Manson developed an interest in the occult and began experimenting with off-beat religions. He also developed an interest in Scientology, the mystical, pseudo-scientific philosophy which had captured the imagination of thousands of young people.

In prison he learned to play the guitar, discovered he had a rather pleasing voice, and even wrote a few songs. Thus did mysticism and music become his dominant interests. He would use them later to influence others when he was free.

When he was finally released from prison in the mid-1960s, Manson found that a whole new world had opened up to him—the world of the hippie. He headed for Berkeley and fancied himself as a wandering minstrel and a walking musician. And thus did he begin his nomadic roaming in earnest.

Someone gave him a piano, which he traded for a camper

truck, which he eventually traded for the green and white school bus in which he and 13 of his followers headed south to Los Angeles in 1968 to escape the deterioration of the Haight-Ashbury district. During that 10-day journey one of the young women gave birth to Manson's child.

Sometime after Manson's arrival in Los Angeles he reportedly met Dennis Wilson of the Beach Boys group and ingratiated himself with the popular musician. Wilson apparently thought he sensed talent in Manson, wanted to help him, and permitted Manson and his "family" to move into his palatial Palisades home.

Manson reveled in the adulation of the young women in his "harem" and the young women apparently found what they were looking for in the strange little man who told them he was God, or Jesus, or Satan. He played the part of the guru and made them believe he possessed the gift of prophecy. But he also played on their fears, predicted terrible things would happen to them if they failed to obey him, and sometimes threatened them with bodily harm. Whatever the magnetism was that surrounded Manson, it exerted a powerful hold on the impressionable young people who surrounded the ex-con.

The persons charged in connection with the Tate murders were typical of Manson's followers.

Charles Watson was the last of three children born to a couple who operate a service station and general store in Copeville, a town of 150 population, 25 miles northeast of Dallas. His cousin is sheriff of Collin County, Texas, where Watson was being held awaiting extradition to Los Angeles.

His parents were proud of their youngest son. He was a good boy and never made below a B during high school. Standing 6 feet 2 inches tall, he was a halfback on the high school football team, played baseball and set track records that still stand in Class A high schools in Texas. He was sports editor of the school yearbook and went to North Texas State University, where he majored in business management.

After three years at the university he became restless and headed for California in the spring of 1967. He enrolled at California State College in Los Angeles. He also had a good job, made good money and had more than $1,000 worth of clothes. Then, according to friends, he became involved with people on the drug scene and he dropped out of sight for six months. The friend said that when he saw him again:

"This nice guy who came out here from Texas had become someone else. He was a completely different personality. He was almost incoherent at times. He had very little communication with anyone he had previously known in the straight world."

Friends said Watson spent a lot of time with some type of guru and talked of him constantly. Somewhere along the line he joined Manson's roving band of hippies. And when he returned home to Texas in October, people commented how different he was from the handsome clean-cut boy who had left home two years before.

Now he stood accused of taking part in one of the most brutal murders in criminal history. What had happened, everyone who had known him asked, to that nice Charles Watson?

Little was known about Linda Darlene Kasabian, the 20-year-old girl who was five months pregnant with her second child when she surrendered to police in Concord, New Hampshire, and willingly waived extradition to California to face the music. She snapped at newsmen who tried to question her:

"I don't care if the whole world comes down. I'm not talking."

She had spent the week before her arrest in Milford, a small mill town near Concord, with her mother and step-father.

Said her mother: "I know my daughter, she was never violent. She loved children. There was no hate in her at all. She was searching, searching for love."

Linda had quit high school at 16 and married a fellow student. They lived together for three months and she was a divorcee at 17. After the divorce she moved to Boston and married a boy named Kasabian, moved to California and lived in hippie pads up and down the state. Eventually she and Kasabian split up and went their own ways.

Her father, a bartender in Miami, Florida, said his daughter showed up there about November 1st and left shortly after Thanksgiving. A newspaper reporter quoted him: "What can I say? She was not a bad girl and she was not a good girl. I wouldn't say she was depressed while she was here. She was happy as hell. In fact I kept looking through her luggage to see if she had any drugs. I wondered if she was high."

Her father reportedly said he had seen his daughter only twice in the 15 years he was separated from her mother. "I remember the first time she came to Miami. She stole a lot of things from my apartment. She was buying dope with the money she got."

He said he saw his daughter for the last time when he put her on a plane for Boston. No one seemed to know when she first met Manson, and a large block of her life remains a mystery. What part she allegedly played in the Tate-La Bianca killings has not been revealed.

Patricia Krenwinkel was a stable and conservative girl until she met Manson. When that meeting took place she abandoned her car in a Manhattan Beach, California parking lot. She quit her job without even bothering to pick up her pay check, climbed into a VW bus with Manson and some others and left town.

Her father, an insurance agent, says, "I am convinced he

was some kind of hypnotist. It was all so spontaneous."

His daughter was graduated from University High School in Los Angeles and went to live with her mother in Mobile, Alabama. The Krenwinkels are divorced. The girl attended Spring Hill College, a small Catholic school in Mobile, but left after one semester. She returned to California and got a job as a file clerk.

Two weeks after she left Manhattan Beach, her father received a letter from his daughter, then in Seattle, saying she was "trying to find myself." He next heard from her in Sacramento, where she asked him to send her some money. In October, 1969, he heard from his daughter again and gave her an airline ticket to return to her mother in Mobile. It was there that she was arrested in connection with the Tate murders. But she refused to waive extradition and remained in jail in Alabama, pending an extradition hearing.

Susan Atkins apparently had been with Manson longer than any of his other followers. Certainly, she was among his most devoted "slaves." Not much is known about her background except that she is from San Jose and met Manson in the Haight-Ashbury district of San Francisco in 1966. At the time of her arrest in Death Valley, Sue Atkins was 21.

Her father, who asked that his name not be revealed, had a long talk with newsmen in San Jose. He reportedly blamed himself and lenient courts for his daughter's predicament. "I should have been more firm,", he was quoted, "I should have demanded more. I loved her and I still do.

"But we don't have a correctional system. We punish, we don't correct. I tried for three years to have various courts keep my daughter off the streets." He said that so far as he knew, his daughter came into contact with drugs in San Jose. He said, "She should have been put away somewhere, where help could be given, not turned back out on the streets to go through it all

257

again.

"My gripe is not with the police, but with the way they have been restricted by the courts. All we ever hear about is the rights of individuals, but they should not have the right to keep on committing crimes when the evidence is right there in front of the law."

The most puzzling part about the case at this juncture was that although Manson was called the mastermind of the hippie family, the evil genius who controlled the minds of his followers, he was not named in any of the warrants issued by the district attorney's office. To reporters, this seemed to indicate that the police had no physical evidence to connect him with the crimes. However, he was being held in Independence on charges strong enough to keep him in jail until the Los Angeles police should need him.

What was the spell that bound his followers to Charles Manson which reputedly and repeatedly made them willing to do whatever he asked? Three men who had lived in the Death Valley commune tried to explain it for newspaper reporters when Manson was being held on the arson and grand theft auto charges.

Tom Orr, 19, and Ed Reedy, 21, said they met Manson in the Haight-Ashbury district in 1967, when the hippie movement was in full bloom. They followed him to Los Angeles, lived with him on the movie ranch during August of 1969. And they migrated with him to Death Valley the following month.

Said Orr, "The whole thing was held together with black magic. You don't believe it? Well, it really exists and it is powerful."

Added Reedy, "Manson believes that he — and all human beings — are God and the devil at the same time. He believes that all human beings are parts of each other."

258

Another follower, Mitch Krebs, explained, "You see what that means? It means that human life has no value. If you kill a human being, you are just killing part of yourself. So it is all right." The others nodded in agreement.

Krebs continued, "But you couldn't kill an animal. Not a bug, not a snake. Nothing. You couldn't eat meat because it would mean killing an animal. It was crazy."

The three men said Manson had a hypnotic power over his "family," particularly over the women, who would do his sexual bidding with him or with others. They said he had a fabulous reputation as a lover, and the women adored him.

Orr said, "The women around the place were his property. You were welcome to share them, but then *you* became his property, too. He needed to have some men around — there was a limit to what one man could do. But then his women held power over the other men."

He said the family raised money by sending the women out to panhandle. Krebs said, "They could beg more in two hours than I could earn in a week. They were so good at panhandling that they didn't have to hustle and become prostitutes." Orr and Reedy said it took them months to realize that Manson was exerting more and more control over their lives and they split from the family shortly before the arrests were made in Death Valley on October 10th.

According to Orr, "Manson was always saying that ours was a democratic setup and that everyone had an equal voice, but that he was the receptacle who was receiving instructions from God.

"No one moved unless Charlie knew about it. You woke up in the morning at the ranch and you didn't know whether you should get out of bed or go outdoors or anything until he told you what to do. He would tell us stories and there were key words he would implant. He was always talking about love, and we were all caught. The girls particularly. They still are."

Reedy added, "The first time I ever saw Charlie he came into a room where Herb Mars was sitting and went over and kissed his feet. Literally kissed his feet. He was an insane genius. He was insane — but he was a genius. Somehow he could keep planting thoughts with you and the next thing you knew, you were stealing a car and you thought that was the very thing you should be doing."

Some of the girls in his "family" felt much the same way.

Mrs. Ellen Day, 26, a member of the "family" and old enough to know better, gave this appraisal of Charles Manson: "He was magnetic! His motions were like magic, it seemed like. The first time I saw him he was petting a cat. I don't know why that struck me, but it seemed so kind.

"The first time I heard him sing it was like an angel. He wrote songs, made them up as he went along. Some were beautiful happy songs, others would be sad and moving.

"It was all very peaceful at the Chatsworth ranch. Everyone in San Francisco where I had been had been having abortions. At the ranch they loved children. I had a shack of my own. We took care of each other. We sunbathed, cooked, and kept the place clean." Mrs. Day gave birth to a child while she was a member of the "family" at the ranch.

Another girl, Sherry Muller, 21, said, "He (Manson) gave out a lot of magic. Everyone was always so happy around him. But he was sort of a changeling. He seemed to change every time I saw him. He seemed ageless. The main way we all got together so much was to sing. It was a spontaneous feeling. That's what made everybody happy. I guess."

The 21-year-old girl with the close-cropped red hair described her other companions in the commune which was raided in Death Valley as "peaceful, beautiful people."

Mrs. Day, who was taken in the Death Valley raid and

charged with possession of a stolen pistol, told her story as she sat in a second-rate motel room where she lives on welfare while awaiting a trial date. She said: "there was no dope either at Chatsworth or in Death Valley," and she was once admonished for drinking beer. Sunbathing in the nude was a common practice for both men and women, she added, and she insisted that sex played a small role in commune life.

Miss Muller told reporters, "The nights in the commune reveal the whole universe in motion before your eyes — the magic of infinite pictures in multi-colored dots — pin-prickly, tickly visual sensations that set you to laughing to image-making and then to drifting — to sleep with your mind projected, afloat in full emptiness.

"All of us came flocking to the desert at various times, stopping by a stone house set in a valley, up a wash. We used it as a get-together for singing. It was a warm place for babies and had a water hole."

However, other hippies who knew and associated with Manson during his sojourn in the Los Angeles area, had other things to say, some not so flattering about the man who wanted to be called Jesus. They said he talked of triggering a war between the blacks and white by killing the whites and blaming it on the blacks.

One youth said, "He said he was building a bunch of dune buggies. He said he was going to mount machine guns on them. He said he would take his army of dune buggies and kill every white mother — every white pig — between here and the desert.

"Then he was going to make an exodus — take his people to a big hole up in Death Valley and hide there. From there he would just sit back and watch the revolution. He hated the Establishment. It was not that he felt it owed him anything. He just didn't belong.

261

"He had strong anti-black feelings, too. They came from those years he spent in the pen, I think. He didn't talk about it much, but it was just one of those feelings you get."

In describing Manson, another youth said, "He simply overpowered you. It was the way he looked at you. His eyes did strange things. When Charlie talked, people listened. Some people listened too close, I guess."

The same youth said that Susie Atkins praised Manson constantly to anyone who would listen and spent much of her time tempting to recruit new members into the family.

"Susie said the only way to join was to agree to give up your life for all the members of the group," the youth said, adding, "She once handed me an ax and put her head down. She said, 'Go ahead and kill me,' and that kind of shook me up."

Commenting on Manson's reputation with the girls in the commune, the long-haired youth said, "The word was that he was one hell of a good lover. That was part of it, I guess. It was those eyes, too. He was a real powerful man."

Another man in his mid-20s said he never got along well with Manson "because I wouldn't go on Manson's trip," adding, "But he was real heavy. He could do just about anything he wanted. He said only the most down, the most wasted came to him and he makes them what they are. He changed a lot of people, and he did it without drugs. He did it with his head."

A 30-year old writer who lived in one of the Los Angeles area communes said of Manson, "I first met him about three years ago when he came down here from San Francisco in that bus. He was the only cat I had ever seen with a harem. He had total control over them. They did what he told them. He also had his own creative style of singing and playing the guitar. He was an artist."

But the hippies who spurned him had this to say, "He was

never really one of us. We're against guns and against killing. Apparently he wasn't part of the Establishment, either. He just didn't fit anyplace."

The national and international press flocked to Independence, California and swamped the facilities of that small town on the fringe of Death Valley when Manson was scheduled to make his first public appearance since the Tate case had broken. The occasion was a preliminary hearing on arson and theft charges in connection with the alleged dune buggy theft ring.

His stature surprised most of the spectators. Manson is a short, small-boned man whose dark hair reaches down to his shoulders. His full beard was well trimmed and he managed a smile on several occasions when he recognized a member of his "family" in the courtroom or on the short walk from the jail to the courthouse.

One glassy-eyed young woman who watched as he disappeared back into the jail sighed, "Man — they sure got a lot of love locked up in there!"

Manson had been ordered held for trial and was remanded to jail in Independence until a Los Angeles County grand jury decided whether or not to indict him in the Tate-La Bianca murders.

The grand jury was scheduled to hear the case on December 5th and December 8th, and there was no doubt that Sue Atkins would be the chief witness.

Her attorney spelled that out even before the grand jury convened. Richard Caballero, 39, was appointed by the court to defend Miss Atkins. He had been a top prosecutor in the district attorney's office for eight years and during that time had sent at least five murderers to the San Quentin Death House. It was this experience in death penalty cases which prompted him to have Miss Atkins testify before the grand jury.

He said he wanted to put her role in the slayings in its proper perspective. "I feel that by taking this approach and having her present her story now, it will help show her state of mind to the grand jury — and especially to the prosecution in its later determination of whether to seek the death penalty." He said that if Miss Atkins waited until later to reveal the power that Manson exercises over her, it would be open to the suggestion that it was fabricated simply to save herself from the gas chamber.

Cabellero said that when the grand jury convened, Miss Atkins would tell all she knew about the Tate-La Bianca cases, including her own role.

Deputy District Attorneys Vincent Bugliosi and Aaron Stovitz were expected to seek murder indictments against:

Manson who was being held in Independence; Miss Atkins, under indictment for the murder of Hinman; Charles Watson, being held on a fugitive warrant in Texas, Patricia Krenwinkel, 21, under arrest in Mobile, Alabama; Linda Kasabian, 20, under arrest in New Hampshire; and another person mentioned in connection with the slayings for the first time, Leslie Sanktson, 19. She was identified as a member of the Manson family, and had been arrested in the Death Valley raid. Later, for the record, her name was entered as Leslie Van Houten.

Stovitz, 45, a deputy district attorney for 18 years, has vast trial experience and is well known in legal circles for his expert cross-examination technique. Bugliosi, 35, has the reputation of being one of the most tenacious prosecutors in the office of District Attorney Evelle Younger.

Among those listed as witnesses to be called before the grand jury appeared the name of Terry Melcher, son of actress Doris Day. He was expected to testify that Manson knew the location of the Tate home and other details about it because he (Manson) had once been there when Melcher rented the house some six months before Sharon Tate and her husband began renting it in February, 1969.

Police investigators had learned that Manson had dreams of becoming a professional musician and had been led to feel that Melcher, a TV producer and record company executive with good business connections, might be able to help him. On one occasion at least, Manson went to the Melcher-Tate home to discuss a business deal, but eventually Melcher refused to help further Manson's career.

It appeared that it was this that eventually resulted in the Tate and La Bianca murders.

Miss Atkins reportedly told her attorney that in revenge for Melcher's rejection, Manson told a number of his followers to kill "the pigs" in the Benedict Canyon home, which had become a symbol of rejection to him, a symbol of protest. But what Manson apparently didn't know was that by this time Melcher had moved out and Roman Polanski and Miss Tate had moved in and thus became the unwitting targets of Manson's bitterness. Miss Atkins said she went there under "an insane, almost hypnotic influence" from Manson.

On December 5th, scores of newsmen jammed the corridors of the Hall of Justice as Miss Atkins, demure in a rose-colored velveteen dress with puff sleeves and miniskirt, walked down the hall to the grand jury hearing room. The cool, detached composure of the leggy brunette, her thin face framed in her shoulder-length brown hair, struck members of the press. And apparently she retained that almost ethereal composure for the two-and-a-half hours in which she testified before the grand jury.

When she emerged from the jury hearing and was returning to her jail cell, she was asked how she felt, now that she had

265

unburdened herself.

She replied in a word: "Dead!"

Attorney Caballero explained, "She doesn't feel that way because of any fear of getting the death penalty, but she thinks that she has died within herself—in a spiritual way. Her whole world revolved around Manson. Now that world no longer exists. It is difficult to fathom how this girl's mind works but she really regards herself as dead."

"How does she feel about Manson now? She regards him with a mixture of love, fear and hatred," Caballero said. "She said she feels Manson could still harm her by conjuring up a vision."

Miss Atkins reportedly told the grand jury substantially the same story she had related previously to informants and to the police. Among other things she had revealed was that Charles Manson, leader of the hippie family, was responsible for the Tate slayings and that he had reproved his "slaves" for the messiness of the Tate slaughter. However, according to Miss Atkins, Manson himself was not present when the murders took place.

Miss Atkins said Manson accom-nerve because of the Tate murders.

Miss Atkins' reconstruction of the seven murders—Tate and La Bianca—has been along these lines:

She, Charles Watson, Pat Krenwinkel, and Linda Kasabian went to the Tate estate on the night of August 8th upon Manson's instructions. She said Manson ordered them to kill everyone in the house and steal what money they could find. The four, clad in black—which Miss Atkins referred to as their "creepy crawler" clothes—entered through the gate at the estate after Watson climbed a pole and cut the telephone lines with a bolt cutter.

Manson had told them where to find the switch to open the

266

gate. They immediately encountered young Steven Parent as he entered his car to leave the estate after a visit with the caretaker, Bill Garretson. Miss Atkins said Watson shot Parent with a .22 caliber pistol, the only gun the raiders carried.

Her story went on: Watson climbed through a window and unlocked the front door, admitting Miss Atkins and Miss Krenwinkel to the home. The Kasabian girl never entered the house and remained outside during the slaughter.

Frykowski, who had been sleeping on the couch, was awakened by the intruders and, in fear and disbelief, asked, "Who are you?" Then he heard a terrifying reply from Watson:

"I am the devil and I'm here to kill."

At gunpoint, Frykowski was tied up and Watson ordered that the bedrooms be searched. In one, Miss Tate was in bed, her former boy friend was sitting on the bed talking to her. In another bedroom, Abigail Folger was in bed reading. At knifepoint, the three were forced from the bedrooms into the living room. There, the story continued, Miss Tate, Sebring and Miss Folger were tied together with a nylon rope later found draped over a beam and around the necks of Miss Tate and Sebring.

Watson told all four that they were going to die, Miss Atkins said, and when Sebring screamed in terror, Watson shot him. Later Sebring was also stabbed. Upon Watson's orders, Miss Atkins said, she slashed with her knife at Frykowski, who was trying to loosen his hands. The Polish playboy reportedly ran for the front door where Watson slugged him with the gun, shot him and then stabbed him, Miss Atkins reportedly testified. Frykowski's body was later found on the front lawn.

According to Miss Atkins, Miss Folger also loosened her bonds, struggled with Miss Krenwinkel and was stabbed. Miss Atkins said Watson told her to stab Miss Tate, but she refused. However, Miss Atkins said, she did hold the scantily clad actress while Watson stabbed her a total of 18 times. During the course of the brutal assault, Miss Atkins said, she experienced a sexual orgasm.

Then, Miss Atkins reportedly testified, she, Watson and Miss Krenwinkel ran out the front door; outside, Watson stabbed Miss Folger, who had staggered out onto the lawn.

According to Miss Atkins, Watson then walked over to Frykowski who was dead or dying, and kicked him in the head. She said Watson then ordered her to write an insulting message on the front door in blood with a towel on which the black-clad raiders had wiped their hands. She said she chose the word "Pig," which was found on the front door by the police.

Miss Atkins said the three raiders rejoined Miss Kasabian and returned to the Spahn Ranch in Chatsworth, where they were living in a commune at that time. She said that when Manson was told what happened, he admonished them for being sloppy and agreed to accompany them the next night on another murderous raid designed to keep the hippie band from losing their nerve.

The following night, Miss Atkins said, six persons left the ranch in a single car; these included Manson himself, Miss Atkins, Miss Krenwinkel, Watson, Mrs. Kasabian, and Miss Leslie Sankston (later identified as Leslie Van Houten).

Miss Atkins said the La Bianca home was the third choice of the raiders on the night of August 10th. She said they stopped outside a home in another neighborhood but when Manson looked in a window and saw photographs of children on a table he decided to go to another house. Miss Atkins said he didn't want to take victims in a residence occupied by children.

Miss Atkins said she was sleeping in the car when it stopped outside a second house and she did not know why Manson decided not to enter it.

Her story continued: "Outside the La Bianca home, Miss Atkins, Mrs. Kasabian, Watson, Miss Sankston and Miss Krenwinkel remained in the car while Manson entered the house alone, confronted the couple at gunpoint and tied them up." She said Manson came out and sent Watson, Miss Krenwinkel and Miss Sankston in to kill and rob them.

Because Miss Atkins was not inside the house, she could not detail the part each person allegedly played in the triple slaying. However, Miss Atkins said she was told that a girl stabbed La Bianca with a carving fork and left it in his stomach. She also said Watson returned to the car with a wallet containing credit cards and handed it to Manson. Then she said the car drove away, leaving behind Watson, Miss Krenwinkel and Miss Sankston. According to Miss Atkins, the trio hitchhiked back to the Chatsworth ranch.

The grand jury was reportedly told that after the murder of La Bianca and his wife, the killers took showers at the death scene and then leisurely dined on food they took from the family's refrigerator before they left to return to the ranch.

Some details of the killing of Gary Hinman were also revealed at this time by a young motorcycle club member who had testified at the previous trial of Robert Beausoleil for Hinman's murder and who testified before the grand jury on December 8th.

Daniel De Carlo, as disclosed in the transcript of the Hinman trial, testified that Manson not only had directed the Hinman slaying but, before it was committed, slashed the victim's ear with a sword, then left before Hinman was stabbed to death.

The witness said Manson had sent Beausoleil and other members of the "family" to the Hinman home to force the musician to hand over $20,000 he was thought to have hidden. According to the testimony of De Carlo, Beausoleil tortured Hinman for six or seven hours and then telephoned Manson, and said, "Gary isn't cooperating."

"You know what to do," De Carlo said Manson replied. Then, according to De Carlo, Beausoliel killed Hinman.

Informants have told the police that Miss Atkins has definitely placed Manson at the scene of both the La Bianca and Hinman slayings but insists he was not at the Tate home.

Attorney Caballero also testified before the grand jury and reportedly explained to them that he had advised Miss Atkins that by telling her story she was waiving immunity to indictment herself.

Previously, Caballero said that at no time did his client kill, although she was under the spell of Manson and would go anywhere he told her to go. The attorney said, "Susan is still under his control. This is the most bizarre, most nonsensical case I have encountered in my twelve years as a criminal lawyer. It is the most motiveless case, the most unusual." He insisted that his client was under the spell of Manson, and thus was not responsible for her actions.

On the other hand, Mrs. Kasabian's lawyer told reporters that his client lives not only in fear of Manson but of other members of the Manson family as well.

Other witnesses who testified before the grand jury were Terry Melcher, who was believed to have told the jurors of his acquaintance with Manson and how it could have mistakenly led the hippie killers to the Sharon Tate home.

Another key grand jury witness was Daniel De Carlo, 23, onetime leader of a motorcycle gang who lived briefly with Manson's group at the Chatsworth ranch. It was reported that De Carlo told the jurors that he heard members of the "family" talking about the murders at the Tate and La Bianca homes.

He also had been a witness at the trial of Robert Beausoleil for the stabbing death of Gary Hinman. And one report had it that he had been invited to go along on the Tate murders, but refused. Prosecutor Stovitz said later that De Carlo had no part whatsoever in any of the murders.

Besides the testimony of the witnesses, the jury was also told that a fingerprint found at the Tate home matched the prints of Watson and that a knife found at the Tate home had the fingerprints of Miss Atkins.

Police officers who testified at the grand jury hearing included M. F. McGann, Danny Galindo, Harold Dolan, Frank Escalante, Manuel Granado, Jerome Boen, Bill Lee, R. M. Lucarelli, Frank Patchett and R. L. Calkins.

The jury deliberated 22 minutes on the testimony given by 22 witnesses over a two-day period before they returned the indictments sought by the office of the Los Angeles District Attorney Younger.

Manson, Watson, Miss Atkins, Miss Krenwinkel and Mrs. Kasabian were indicted on seven counts of murder and one count each of conspiracy. Each of the murder counts represents a separate victim — Miss Tate and the four slain along with her, Frykowski, Sebring, Parent and Miss Folger; and Mr. La Bianca and his wife.

Miss Sankston was also indicted on the conspiracy charge as well as on two counts of murder involving the La Biancas.

Miss Atkins, Mrs. Kasabian, and Miss Sankston, in custody in Los Angeles, were arraigned on December 10th in Superior Court. The district attorney's office began extradition proceedings against Miss Krenwinkel in Alabama and Watson in Texas.

On December 9th, Los Angeles detectives went to Independence to return Manson to Los Angeles for the December 10th arraignment.

Grand jury foreman Joseph Bishop said the 21-member jury found the testimony on the two murder cases "shocking" and commented that the jurors were particularly appalled by the viciousness of the killings as described by County Coroner Thomas Noguchi, one of the witnesses.

Bishop described the crimes as "probably the most infamous in California history." He said the testimony of Miss Atkins was the key factor in the decision of the jury to return the indictments against the half-dozen members of the Manson family.

Meanwhile the police are still investigating the possibility that the "family" might have been involved in a number of other murders, and at this writing, the probe into the activities of the "family" is still continuing. A number of unsolved murders which occurred in the Los Angeles area during the time that the "family" was there have been brought under close scrutiny.

It must be remembered that the indictments returned by a grand jury are simply accusations and that those indicted do not stand convicted of a crime. Any conviction must come from a jury of their peers and, until such a judgment is rendered, those accused must be considered innocent.

On the basis of matters as they now stand, everyone connected with the investigation that led to the arrest of the "Manson family" agrees that the reported solution of the Tate-La Bianca murders is even more bizarre than the crimes themselves.

It must be proved in a court of law after due process, to be sure, but if the charges lodged by the State of California are believed by the jury or juries who will pass judgment, one man exercised such control over the wills of five persons that they slaughtered seven people they not only did not know, but of whom they had never heard.

273

Show Business Beauty
Hammered To Death

by Joseph McNamara

The blonde, blue-eyed singer was found in her bed, the back of her head battered in by a heavy weapon. Baffled New York authorities checked and rechecked her private life till they picked up the first stirrings of the rumors that led to an arrest.

New Rochelle, N.Y.,
Nov. 14, 1978

The police patrol cars seemed a bit incongruous on the long sweeping driveway of the $200,000 Tudor-style home. "Mansion" would be more like it. The imposing 14-room house was laid out amid tall conifers and expensive shrubs on two acres of rolling land in the fashionable Beechmont section of northern New Rochelle—a Westchester County community just north of New York City.

Two officers strode swiftly past a child's tricycle into the two-story home, glancing just casually at the in-ground swimming pool, now covered over for the approaching winter. They were there on business, a grisly business. The business of murder.

The 28-year-old mistress of the house, Linda Scott, a rising Country and Western singer who went by the professional name of "Charlee," had been discovered brutally beaten to death in her upstairs bedroom.

The body of the blonde, blue-eyed singer had been found lying face down on her large blood-spattered bed. There were several ugly wounds, the blood congealed, on the back of her head. The blood on the coverlet was dry. Linda Scott's body was fully clothed, as though she had been up before and had lain down for another nap.

Beside the bed were several of her suitcases, partially unpacked, but carefully, not ransacked. It was about 4 p.m. on Friday, November 10, 1978, that the tragic discovery was made by the victim's two shocked daughters, Tamara, 10 years old, and Carmen, 7.

The youngsters had danced up the huge lawn, still green under its dusting of fallen leaves, and swept joyously into the house after finishing classes in the neighborhood's Roosevelt School. The children eagerly awaited the warm greeting of their mother, who had just returned home the previous night at 11:30 from a six-week singing road tour.

"Mom! Mom!" they called excitedly.

When Mom wasn't on a singing tour, they well knew, she made it a habit of spending as much time as she could with them and lavishing affection on the two children of her broken marriage. She was by all accounts an excellent mother, not unduly permissive with her children, but generous with her warmth and love and time, the investigators were to learn during a questioning of all those who knew her.

Inside the home as the children rushed in a maid went about her duties and a chauffeur and other domestics flitted but the place. But there was no Mom to be seen anywhere. The two girls romped noisily throughout the sprawling house in pursuit of her. And then, in her bedroom on the second floor, they made their ghastly find.

It was just minutes later, after a hurried telephone call, that the New Rochelle officers of the law brushed past the two Lincoln Continentals that were parked in the stone driveway and went into the house.

In the bedroom a quick but expert check of the woman convinced the policemen that she was dead — and had been for several hours. They radioed back to headquarters for detectives and other backup men, including forensic people and a coroner. An intern from a Westchester hospital pronounced Linda Scott dead for the record.

While photos were being made and fingerprint men were dusting their way around the house, the detectives examined the room and other areas. They found that the place had not been ransacked and nothing of value appeared to have been taken. Nor did they find any means of forced entry to the posh residence.

From the congealed blood and condition of the body, the sleuths assumed the young woman had been dead for some hours, but it would be up to the medical examiner to determine this. A talk with the maid turned up the information that the domestic had last spoken to Linda Scott about 10 o'clock that morning. The maid assumed the singer had been sleeping since.

A careful search of the premises failed to turn up any sign of an apparent death weapon, assumed to be some kind of heavy bludgeon.

News of the murder quickly spread through the neighborhood and a small clump of people gathered in front of the house. The area is bathed in woods, dotted by older homes on the north side of New Rochelle, near the campus of Iona College.

Miss Scott had moved into the house the previous June

with her two children, but no one in the neighborhood seemed to know her very well. She was on the road pursuing her singing career much of the time, they pointed out.

With the name Linda Scott, the detectives began to probe her background, but some confusion arose. Linda Scott, it turned out, was a singing sensation of the 1960s who had earned more than half a million dollars on a series of hit songs before she reached the age of 17. Among them was a popular single called "I Told Every Little Star."

That, however, was not the Linda Scott who was savagely bludgeoned to death in her Westchester bed. There were two Linda Scotts singing, it seemed. And the ill-starred one who met her untimely death at the hands of a murderer was less well known, and often used the name Charlee. This slowed down the investigation for several hours.

Having straightened out the confusion, the probers learned that the victim had been born in Sunflower, Kansas, and had performed since she was six years old. Despite her early start, she had achieved only a small measure of modest success until about two years ago. Then she recorded three singles, including "Keep Them Pillows Soft and Warm," which sold about 100,000 copies. And more recently she had cut an album "Standing in Your Shoes," in Nashville, Tennessee.

"She had no real hits, though her singles were reviewed very favorably in the trade," one recording executive told the detectives. "She was a real exciting lady who we thought was going to be a big star soon."

In fact, the shapely young singer was contracted to open a weeklong engagement in a nightclub, the Grand Finale II, on West 70th Street, in Manhattan, on December 4.

"She was a sweet, wonderful girl," said a spokesman for the night spot. "She had just returned from a gig in California. There was no indication of any problems."

In pursuing her identity, detectives had questioned executives of WHN, New York City's top Country and Western radio station. They said they had never heard of the slaying victim and had never aired any of her recordings.

"She only worked locally," said one radio station staffer.

An executive for a small label known as Amerama Records told the police Linda had been on tour during the previous summer and that she had done a television special that was shown in six cities, including Atlanta and San Diego.

Those who did know her in the recording industry described Charlee as a "loveable person," "a lot of fun to be with." No one was uncovered during the police interrogations who would be inclined to bash her head in during a murderous fit of fury.

This was true also of the small bar-night clubs in New Rochelle, Yonkers and other small cities in the New York suburbs where Charlee had worked her act. Officials of the clubs and workers alike praised the winsome young singer who had come out of the West to seek her fortune in New York.

The detectives were intensely interested in questioning Linda Scott's ex-husband and her current fiance. The husband, whose name the authorities withheld from the press (Scott was Linda's maiden name), was living in California.

An investigator was dispatched to the West Coast and he talked with the former hubby, who was divorced from Linda about four years. After some questioning, the authorities were convinced that the ex-husband had, indeed, been in California at the time of the bludgeon slaying.

Also, they were assured that the relationship between the blonde thrush and her former husband since their divorce had been an amiable one and neither appeared to have borne any ill feelings toward the other.

It had been an early marriage for Linda and the pair of ill-starred lovers just appeared to have drifted off in different directions in life, the authorities learned.

Linda's fiance also came under intense probing. He was an attorney name Harry Green, who was also the singer's business manager. Green owned the luxurious home that Linda and her two children lived in, though he lived elsewhere, and also was owner of the two Lincoln Continentals that were at the singer's disposal.

Just the day before she was slain, Linda and Harry had announced their engagement. But they had been linked romantically for about two years, and the previous June the singer and her children had moved into Green's posh digs.

"Mr. Green, we'd like to ask you a few questions," one of the investigators from the Westchester County District Attorney's office began.

"Oh, yes, I'll cooperate in any way to get to the bottom of this terrible crime."

Green was then asked about his whereabouts on the morning and afternoon of Friday, November 10. And he readily supplied a schedule of his day's activities. These were promptly checked out by the detectives, and they proved okay. Green was quite a well-known attorney about town and in nearby New York City. And, it turned out, part of his activity was pushing the career of his beloved.

At the time of her death, Green was working hard to get Charlee booked into the Lone Star Cafe, a nightclub in Manhattan that specializes in Country and Western music.

Further questioning into the relationship of the attorney with the shapely singer continued.

"Well, what do you think?" one investigator asked another after the quizzing.

"Looks clean to me . . . I think he really loved the girl and his grief seems on the up and up."

By now, the results of the autopsy came in from the Westchester Medical Examiner's office. But they offered no new clue to the vicious killing. Cause of death was officially listed as savage beating of the head with a blunt object. There were no other wounds on the body. Nor were there any indications that the pretty singer had been raped. Time of death: several hours before being found.

"Back to square one," mumbled a dejected detective.

The maid was requestioned. Her name was Peggy Reed.

"Miss Reed, when was the last time you saw Miss Scott?" she was asked.

"As near as I can tell, it was about 10 o'clock in the morning," the maid said.

"I was about to leave on a trip to do the shopping . . . I just wanted to see if there was anything special she wanted."

"Did you see her at anytime after that?"

"No, when I returned from shopping she was nowhere about," the domestic replied. "I just assumed that she was in her room sleeping. She had gotten in late the night before from a long tour; I figured she was exhausted."

The detectives questioned her further, but the distraught woman could not provide any further information to help them in the puzzling investigation.

Now, the probers turned to the chauffeur and began questioning him. He was 21-year-old Michael D. Spearman, who lived in the murder house. Spearman drove the two Continentals that were at Linda's disposal. He also acted as a handyman around the posh home in the affluent area of New Rochelle.

Further, the young man performed as a stagehand for Miss Scott while she was on her singing tours, often handling the lights and doing other technical chores to help out her short-handed retinue.

Spearman was married, but in August of 1978 he left his wife and child in Kansas City and moved to New Rochelle, where he took on the multi-faceted chores in the Linda Scott household. He was now asked by the investigators what he had been doing on the ill-fated morning of the murder.

The young chauffeur said he had been in and out of the house most of the morning, and even later in the day. But he could not spell out specifically the exact times of his comings and goings.

After questioning him at some length, the authorities were no nearer a solution of the crime. They were not able to learn of any suspicious person who might have prowled the grounds of the home. They questioned others who might have had any connection with the home, delivery persons who may have made stops there, the mailman on his rounds.

Neighbors were interrogated, some for the second time. Although Miss Scott and her children had moved in some five months before, she was not well known to any of the neighbors.

"I guess her singing trips kept her away some, and we never got to really know her," one neighbor told the detectives.

The neighbors were asked if they had seen any strange cars parked in the long winding driveway. Or the pleasant treelined street outside. None had.

On the next day a spokesman for the New Rochelle Police Department told eager newspaper reporters that they had made no arrests in the murder nor had they any strong leads in the baffling case.

By this time, the investigation had turned up the identities of several former boyfriends of the slain singer. And these were questioned about her murder. An extremely attractive woman, Linda had had no trouble getting the attention of the opposite sex. The probers spent some time with each of the ex-swains, but all of them were able to account for their time at the hour that police believe Linda Scott met her death.

Despite the fact that the neighbors had not seen any suspicious automobile parked near the murder scene, the detectives had appealed in the local newspapers to anyone who might have seen anything unusual on the day of the slaying to contact them.

And now they struck luck. A driver reported to the local authorities that he had seen a light blue van parked just off the road at a wooded spot not far from the home of the murdered singer.

The driver, whose name was withheld by police, said he thought nothing of it at the time. But when he saw the appeal in the newspaper, he came forward. The van, this driver said, had no driver in it at the time, a fact which he could ascertain since he approached the parked vehicle head on.

Detectives went to the scene and examined the area off the roadway. Sure enough, there were tire tracks in the soft earth. Crime lab technicians were called and they made a plaster cast of the tire tracks, believed to have been caused by a vehicle approximating the weight of a van.

While the spot was down the road from the Linda Scott home, the authorities realized that because of the wooded nature of the terrain, someone could have easily slipped up to the house without having been seen by neighbors of the slain woman.

"This looks like our best lead so far," one detective declared.

The informant driver was sought out again.

"I know you told us you could not give the license plate registration of the parked car," one DA's man said. "But could you remember any number on the plate, any letter?"

"No," the motorist said. "I didn't pay that much attention to the van. I believe it had New York plates . . . I think I would have noticed if it had out of state plates."

It wasn't much to go on. Detectives asked the State Motor Vehicle authorities in Albany to run them a computer readout of all light blue vans registered in Westchester in preparation of what promised to be a mammoth job.

"We don't even know the year of the car," one detective groused.

While awaiting for state action, however, other detectives began checking local gas stations to see if anyone had come in for a container of gasoline during the critical hours of that Friday. One service station operator a mile away did have such a customer.

"Fella said he ran out of gas down the road," the owner

said. "Don't know what kind of car he had, but I've seen the guy — a young kid, works in the supermarket on Main Street."

Further investigation turned up the sought after "young kid." A 19-year-old youth, he was a stock clerk on a 3-to-11 p.m. shift. He had run out of gas on his way to work and had left the car to seek fuel.

The plaster cast matched his tire. But a check with his home, the gas station and the store where he worked proved that he had not tarried along the way, and he was absolved from any connection with the murder.

The standard practice in investigation of puzzling murders is to try to link them to others in the community. But New Rochelle, the home of several colleges, while a bustling little community, is not a crime-ridden one. The area is far above middle income, which does not eliminate crime, but it does hold down certain types of violence.

As a matter of fact, there had been another case in the recent past of a pretty young woman beaten to death in her bed. But the husband, in that case, had been implicated and was in stir. Obviously, he had no possible connection with the savage bludgeon killing of Linda Scott.

About this time, the investigators began to hear rumblings of a bit of abrasion between the mistress of the house and some of the help. Requestioning of the domestics revealed that several of them felt that Linda Scott was a bit condescending toward them. In short, she had a knack of annoying them with her attitude.

Spearman, the chauffeur, was one of them, the detectives learned. Of late, the were told, the chauffeur and his lovely boss had argued over just what his duties were. Since they spread from the realm of the domestic into the professional life of the shapely singer, it was easy for the sleuths to see that some confusion might result.

What the investigators also saw was that some resentment might also result, that the man who lent some professional expertise toward advancement of the career of the singer might not want to switch to the lowly cap of a chauffeur, with its inference of inferiority.

Further questioning revealed that among people connected with the house, it was known that Spearman had a crush on the beauteous "Charlee."

"Hey, this fatal beating occurred the day after Linda announced her engagement to Harry Green," one prober noted. "We better talk to Spearman again."

They did, on the weekend after the slaying. And after about an hour, Spearman, a short, pudgy man with a medium-length afro hairstyle, admitted the bludgeon-murder of Linda Scott, according to New Rochelle Police Commissioner William Hegarty.

Spearman, a native of Olathe, Kansas, assertedly battered the head of Miss Scott with a baseball bat while she was asleep in her bed.

"This killing was planned," Hegarty said at a news conference on Monday, November 14. "We believe the slaying was a result of apparent difficulties between employer and employee."

Asked if there had been a romance between the blonde singer and her strapping young chauffeur, the police commissioner declined to comment.

After questioning Spearman, investigators returned to the Scott home and on the property found the baseball bat that assertedly had been used to club the life from Linda Scott. The authorities refused to say exactly where the bat was found.

Spearman was booked on a charge of second degree

murder in New Rochelle police headquarters and held for arraignment in the local municipal court. Brought before New Rochelle Court City Judge Ben Mermelstein, Spearman was denied bail and was ordered to the Westchester County Jail in Valhalla, where he awaits trial.

While the legal niceties were being carried out, funeral services for Linda Scott were being held at the Campbell Funeral Home in Manhattan. Burial took place in Texas, where her parents still live.

One detective noted, with some irony, that the dedication on the cover of her album, "Standing in Your Shoes," noted "a very special thanks to Harry Green for his inspiration and support and to Tamara and Carmen for giving me something to sing about."

For Charlee, or Linda Scott, if you wish, the song had ended.

It must be assumed that Michael D. Spearman is innocent of the charge against him until he is proved guilty in a court of law.

Editor's Note:

The names Harry Green and Peggy Reed are fictitious and were used because there is no public interest in their true identities.

Riddle of The Bludgeoned Gay's Double Life

by Andrew Lowen

The forensic team found a trail of blood everywhere in the victim's apartment. Then detectives spotted another dried substance, not blood, which told them the actor lived a unique lifestyle and if they pursued what it was, they'd nab their killer.

London, England
August 12, 1983

British character actor Peter Arne left the television studio in a buoyant mood. He had good reason to be happy. He had a starring role in one of the episodes of the popular science fiction series, "Dr. Who." Rehearsals had been an "unqualified success."

The producer had slapped his back and given the thumbs up sign. Arne, always the professional, had turned in yet another cracking performance.

On the morning of August 1, 1983 — a Monday — Arne, aged 61, had been to the studio primarily for a costume fitting appointment, which had lasted until midday.

This had been followed by a brief chat with the show's producer, and then Arne set off for home in his impressive white Rolls Royce limousine.

Despite the heavy London traffic, the drive from the

BBC studios to his luxurious apartment in stylish Knightsbridge—just behind the world-famous Harrods department store—would have taken him no more than 30 minutes.

Neighbors in Hans Close recalled seeing the Rolls Royce outside the apartment block at around 1:00 p.m. when they heard shouts coming from inside the actor's home on the ground floor.

The status symbol car was still in the street when the cops arrived the following morning a little after eight o'clock—after a maid had found the actor's body in the hallway of his apartment, his dog whimpering beside its dead master.

The police quickly sealed off Hans Close. Neighbors were rounded up for questioning as Detective Chief Inspector Jock Hudson, of Scotland Yard's Murder Squad, took charge of the investigation. Fingerprint experts went to work on the car and inside the apartment, while a doctor began a preliminary medical examination on the battered body.

Alongside the body, the cops recovered a bloodstained log of wood.

"Obviously the murder weapon," Hudson told his partner, Detective Sergeant John Graham. The log was dropped into a transparent plastic bag, which was then sealed and whisked off to Scotland Yard's science laboratory.

As the police photographers snapped away from every conceivable angle, immortalizing the ugly scene, Hudson outlined the body in white chalk on the black, short-cropped hall carpet.

Arne, who had also just finished filming a guest role in the ABC-TV series "Hart to Hart," was naked. His hair

288

was matted with his own dried blood. Much of his head had been crushed, and there were also massive bruises on his shoulders, back, chest, stomach and legs.

After the body had been removed, neighbors spoke to the cops about the argument that had been heard the previous day, the Monday afternoon.

One woman told Hudson: "It wasn't loud enough for me to hear actual words. There was just a lot of shouting and banging. It must have lasted about ten to fifteen minutes. Then there was silence. It seemed to be all over. I didn't think any more about it."

When she was asked "How many people were arguing?" she replied, "Seemed just like two. There was definitely no woman involved. The voices were male. I'm sure of that."

This was backed up by the other witnesses.

The forensic boys had found a trail of blood leading from the bedroom into the living room and then into the bathroom and hallway. There were smeared bloodstains on the bathroom mirror and on walls and doors.

One forensic officer, who took Hudson on a guided tour of the apartment, pointing to the trail, explained: "He staggered along here, groping with his hands, probably blinded by his own blood, trying to grip the walls, stumbling and slithering as he went along.

"All the time he was being further battered, until finally, he collapsed and died just a few inches short of the front door," the forensic officers said.

The sheets on the gigantic water bed were also saturated in blood and other stains. These sheets, along with all clothing in the apartment, were removed for forensic analysis.

A pile of casual clothes had been found at the bottom of

the bed — black sweater, brown corduroy trousers, underpants, socks and sneakers. These were also taken into "custody."

Two empty wine glasses were on a table beside the bed. Tiny remains in each glass revealed that two people had been drinking white wine at some time in the bedroom. An officer, wearing gloves, placed both glasses in another transparent bag.

"Could be useful fingerprints," commented the cop in charge of the forensic team.

Two stubbed-out cigarettes were also extracted from a bedside ashtray. "With a bit of luck, we should be able to determine the blood group of the smokers from their saliva," the forensic chief explained to Hudson.

Neighbors told the cops that Arne was something of "a mystery man." He lived alone, but had lots of "strange visitors."

As one woman put it: "Very weird people have been going to that apartment. I assume they were actors. You know what actors can be like. Different from the rest of us, aren't they? We — that's my husband and I — just shrugged our shoulders and let them get on with it. You know, live and let live."

This was typical of the comments the cops were getting from everyone in the neighborhood they spoke to, without there being anything specific and tangible.

Next call was on Arne's London agent, in the throbbing West End — showbizland of the capital.

The agent was shattered when the news was broken to him. He just couldn't believe it, and it was almost an hour before he could bring himself to discuss the slain actor.

The agent revealed that Arne had been a close friend of Noel Coward and appeared in more than 50 movies.

Among his movie credits were "Return of the Pink Panther," "Straw Dogs" and "The Moonraker." He had also stared in "Arrangement in Tangier," a thriller movie that was due for release shortly after the murder.

He told the cops that Arne was "a wonderful man, very gentle," who had "fans all over the world." He added: "Everybody loved him, but he was a very private person. His private life was his own affair."

When asked if Arne had any known enemies or kept "strange company," the agent replied: "Not that I know of. I can't imagine that Peter could possibly have had enemies. He was such a likeable person.

"As for his friends, I knew virtually nothing about his private life. He was a very shy person. He wasn't the sort of guy who would go around back-slapping in bars. You could say he was very much an introvert, like so many people with talent in the arts."

Hudson then asked: "What about women friends? Was he much of a ladies man?"

"He wasn't a womanizer, if that's what you mean. I don't believe he had a regular woman who he was dating. He never mentioned anyone to me. To be honest, I never really gave it much thought."

The autopsy produced no surprises. Time of death was narrowed to a two-hour period between 1:00 p.m. and 3:00 p.m. on Monday, August 1st.

The cause of death was multiple fractures to the skull, caused by a blunt instrument, namely the log of wood found beside the body.

Several good latent fingerprints had been lifted from the two wine glasses taken from Arne's bedroom. More than half of the prints belonged to the actor, but the cops were convinced that most of the others were the fingerprints of the killer. Copies of those prints were stored away in the master computer at Scotland Yard.

Medical scientists at the Yard were also able to establish that the two cigarette butts found in an ashtray in the bedroom of Arne's apartment had been smoked by people with very different blood groups.

One of the smokers had been a member of the very common "O" positive blood. But the other had very rare, "B" negative blood coursing through his or her veins.

A check with the victim's personal physician established that the actor's blood group was "O" positive.

"Good," was Hudson's comment to his partner. This meant that the killer could well be a man or woman with a very rare blood group, which could prove his or her downfall.

The cops were puzzled by the contents of Arne's wardrobe. Half the wardrobe was filled with glossy silk suits, each one costing in the region of $1,000. But the other half was full of smelly, threadbare, tattered clothes—the kind of items you would expect to see only on the body of a panhandler.

There were trousers with patches on them. Jackets with the arms coming away at the seams. Shoes without soles. Socks with gigantic holes. And three or four filthy raincoats infested with lice.

Under the bed, Inspector Hudson's men found a stock of sadistic magazines directed at homosexuals, extolling the delights of humiliation, degradation and subjugation.

"Nothing appears to have been stolen," the head of the forensic unit reported to Hudson. "Neither is there any sign of a forced entry.

"Robbery couldn't have been the motive for murder. I should say it's certain that the victim knew his killer.

Knew him or her well. Someone he trusted . . . implicitly. We're looking for a Judas."

The science laboratory also had some interesting information, gleaned from tests on the sheets which had been removed from Arne's water bed.

The analysis of the bloodstains had proved nothing more than Arne's blood group was "O" positive, which the cops already knew from the actor's doctor.

But there had been other stains . . . large amounts of dried semen. The semen had not come from one man, however. From the semen, it was possible for the medical scientists to determine the blood group of the men who had ejaculated on that bed.

The scientists were satisfied that the semen had come from two men — one with "O" positive blood and the other with the rare "B" negative.

Now the cops were beginning to get a vivid picture of what had taken place in the victim's apartment on that fateful afternoon of August 1st, even though they did not have one eyewitness.

Hudson was later to tell pressmen: "Although this was a very private and intimate murder, it was as if we had planted a fly on the wall in that bedroom and that fly was able to speak and make a statement.

"That's what the scientific boys can do for you these days. We are living in the age of Science Fiction detection. Soon people like me will be obsolete and redundant. It'll all be done by robots and remote-controlled mechanical men on wheels."

The investigation was scarcely 24 hours old when the cops got the kind of breakthrough they were praying for.

Scotland Yard has under cover cops who specialized in mixing in homosexual circles. This is a very important area of criminal intelligence. A great amount of crime generates from this area because people, especially the rich, famous, and powerful — like aristocrats, show-business personalities and politicians — are susceptible to blackmail.

One drop-out homosexual — the son of an English peer — admitted that he had been one of Arne's lovers.

"I enjoy doing what Peter did," he told detectives. "I am very rich, loaded, but every night I join the tramps, pan-handlers) of London, sit on the pavements drinking cheap wine with them and then choose one to take back to my beautiful home with me for the night.

"There's something so exciting about being between spotless white, crispy, freshly laundered sheets with an ab-solutely flea-infested derelict of a human being. That is so sexually exciting. Peter felt the same way too.

"All day he would be mixing with celebrities in the world of showbusiness and the turn-on for him was de-scending to the other end of the scale at night for his sex-ual pleasures.

"Although he appeared with some of the most famous actresses in the world in movies and TV series, he was never at ease with the opposite sex.

"The truth is that he enjoyed being dominated. The only relationships he had with women was when he found someone who was prepared to indulge in sadism and hu-miliation.

"He warmed to a woman if she was prepared to ill-treat him. He relished being spat upon, kicked and abused. During his life he encountered only a handful of women who were capable of responding to his sexual needs.

"All of those women, needless to say, were in the theatre, a couple of them very famous — legendary names, you might say.

"One of them would make him strip and then would loop a dog's metal choke-chain around his neck, attached to a leather leash. She would talk to him as a dog, and treat him as such, as he pranced around the bedroom on all fours.

"If he tarried, she would belt him with the leash and kick him if he yelped. He couldn't get enough of that, but she tired of him. It was just a piece of experimentation for her, not a way of life.

"Peter was always afraid that one of these women might reveal his dark secret in her memoirs or in the newspapers.

"One of them did have the opportunity to blacken his name. Her life story was published recently and Peter was terrified that he was going to be named and portrayed as a pervert.

"But he was safe. He wasn't mentioned. The actress no doubt knew that by telling the details of her relationship with Peter she would also be crucifying herself."

The detectives learned that Arne rarely missed a night on the streets. He would have his main meal of the day at lunchtime, eating in the ritzy atmosphere of one of London's most fashionable restaurants.

After dark, he would go to his bedroom and dress *down*, blackening his face with boot polish and using all the tricks of the theatrical make-up department to turn himself into a convincing panhandler, a veteran streetwise beggar.

Around midnight, he would join the ranks of the penniless, pathetic drop-outs in the dimly lit alleys and derelict buildings of the city, where he would scrounge for filthy scraps of contaminated food among the garbage cans.

And it was in this environment that he would also search for a bed companion for the night.

The peer's son further explained to Hudson: "It was a real turn-on for him to see the face of the real tramp when they arrived at his beautiful house.

"No one would believe he owned the place. It was beyond their comprehension. They would think that the owners were away on holiday and Peter had found a key to the place.

"He would enjoy watching them soak in the bath, sip champagne and then slip between spotless sheets, tasting for a night a way of life that was way beyond their wildest dreams."

He was then asked: "When did you last see Mr. Arne?"

"Two or three nights before he was killed," was the reply.

"Where?"

"In Soho."

Soho is a square-mile of the neon-lit, glowing West End of London which is alive with prostitutes, pimps, drug pushers, clip-joints and every kind of gangster.

"What was he doing?"

"He was about to initiate a make."

"What does that mean?"

"You know . . . He was picking up a guy. A dead-beat. A tramp."

"Do you know his name?"

"Tramps don't have names. They're just tramps. They don't even have numbers."

"Did they go off together?"

"I can't say. I assume so. But I didn't see them. I was too concerned with my own business."

"Would you recognize him if you saw him again? The

tramp Mr. Arne was talking to?"

"You must be joking!"

Hudson then asked the suspect to account for his movements on the day of the homicide.

The answer was: "That's easy. I was in the hospital all day. I was undergoing tests because I'd been in contact with a hepatitis case. I was cleared and allowed to go, but not until the evening of August 1st."

Before releasing this suspect, the cops checked out his alibi. It was unbreakable. No way could he have slain his old "Friend of the Streets."

One final question was asked of him, however, by Hudson.

"Why did your affair with Mr. Arne end?"

"Just ran out of steam," he replied. "There wasn't much fun in it for either of us, really. I mean, we were too much alike. By that, I mean we were both wealthy.

"The attraction for people like me is to have a relationship with someone from the other end of the social and economic spectrum. You know, it's a walk on the wild side."

Hudson didn't understand, but he'd seen enough of life not to be amazed. He was past being shocked or surprised by people.

On the second day of the investigation, the cops came up with a witness who, at first, hadn't realized she'd seen anything of significance.

The witness was a midwife who had been visiting the home of a pregnant woman in Hans Place around the time of the homicide.

She recalled seeing a scruffily-dressed, bearded man loitering near Arne's apartment around 1:00 p.m. on August 1st.

She was able to provide the cops with a pretty good description. "Aged about thirty, Six feet tall. Dark face. Frizzy black hair with streaks. Bearded. Looked like a tramp. Seemed to be behaving furtively and as if looking for someone. Kept looking inside Arne's Rolls-Royce."

By this time, a thorough check had been made of all fingerprints on file at Scotland Yard.

Nothing came from the file on past or present criminals. But sleuths got lucky when checking the aliens' list. A set of prints lifted from one of the glasses in Arne's bedroom was a perfect match with those of Giuseppe Perusi, a 32-year-old teacher of Italian.

Perusi, a bachelor, had a work permit allowing him to reside and carry on his business as a private tutor in Italian in Britain. The permit had to be renewed every year and one of the conditions stipulated that the police had to be informed of any change of address.

The cops, led by Hudson, promptly raided Perusi's last known address, a cut-price, rather shabby apartment in Earls Court, a district of London known as the 'Transit Camp.' The whole area is full of one and two-roomed apartments, most of them occupied by foreign students and itinerants, the majority of them living on a tight budget.

Earls Court is one of London's most cosmopolitan districts, but it lacks the color and verve of a Greenwich Village. It's very drab and downbeat, a reflection of the economic status of most of its unhappy inhabitants.

"He hasn't been here for three months or more," said a startled girl, opening up the gate and almost being trampled into the floor by a posse of cops.

The girl, from Boston, U.S.A., who was in London to study art at one of the many specialist colleges, found herself in the hot seat for an hour or so until she'd successfully convinced Inspector Hudson that she was in no way implicated.

Hudson soon realized that the suspect had vacated the apartment about three months earlier, without reporting his movements to the police.

"I didn't really known the man," the girl explained, naturally rather shaken. "The place was vacant when I moved in. He came back about a day or so later to collect a small suitcase which he'd left.

"He'd left the place in a terrible state. He was very dirty-looking. It seems hard to believe that he was a teacher."

The owner of the house was questioned, and he said he hoped the cops found Perusi quickly because he had left owing a month's rent.

Undercover cops working the streets were briefed personally by Hudson. He was certain that their man would be found among the "twilight people" of the city, the drifters and derelicts.

It did not take the "street cops" long to build up a vivid picture of the prime suspect. For months he had been living rough, having given up teaching in preference for a life among the city's panhandlers.

But recently he had been bragging about "having a rich boyfriend." Not just rich, but "famous" and the owner of a Rolls Royce.

The cops began applying the pressure and a few minutes before 10:00 p.m. on August 7th, they got the final breakthrough for which they'd been waiting.

An informant tipped off Hudson that Perusi was trying to pick up a new male lover in Denmark Street, Soho.

Hudson and his team swooped, but Perusi was no fool and must have "smelled" their presence, because quite suddenly—and without warning—he took off in a gallop, using the crowds of pedestrians as a camouflage to help him escape.

He was seen dashing down an alley, notorious for its non-stop line of massage parlors and clip joints, leaping over several garbage cans and heading in the general direction of the River Thames.

Cops were literally coming out of the capital's stonework. They were everywhere. On foot. In cars. Leaping on buses. Grabbing taxis. Blockading the subways and underground railway stations. They had Perusi in the net and they had no intention of letting him go. It was just a question of time.

An hour later, he was spotted running along the embankment. The cops were quickly on his heels, but he was certainly fit considering the dismal life he led.

He passed the House of Commons and Big Ben, but the end came for him on Lambeth Bridge. The cops were closing in from both ends. There was only one way of escape left open to him.

Still not ready to give himself up, he climbed on the metal structure of the bridge, hesitated for a couple of seconds as the police rushed him, and then jumped.

It was along way down and it seemed several seconds before the splash was heard that very dark night.

The River Police immediately joined the chase, searching the water for several miles, but there was no sign of Perusi.

Hudson was devastated. He was sure that his quarry had made it to either the north or south bank and had escaped.

The manhunt continued, even more intensively than ever, and came to a sudden halt on August 10th, when the

300

body of Giuseppe Perusi was washed up at Wandsworth Reach, about three miles from where he dived into the Thames.

He hadn't made it to safety after all.

Hudson had failed to get his man, but he had solved — and closed — the case.

At a press conference, he announced: "The case is now closed. There is no doubt that Perusi was our man. I would have liked him alive, but it's too late to think about that. In this life, you rarely get what you would like. You have to make the best of what you get."

When you're a cop, it pays to be philosophical. It saves a lot of heartache and frustration.

Hudson would be the first to testify to that.

The Truth About Ramon Novarro's Murder

by Chris Edwards

The slaying of Ramon Novarro on October 30, 1968, was an exercise in complete futility, senseless brutality, utter stupidity, and base perversion. None of the 22 injuries inflicted on the 69-year-old actor by his killers were severe enough to have caused his death, and a minimum of pity could have saved his life.

His death netted his killers less than $50 in cash and it brought to an abrupt end a career which had spanned nearly 50 years on the stage, screen, and in television.

The vicious crime was committed by two brothers — perverted, immoral, worthless young men — who had no appreciation whatsoever of the artistic talents or the glory that once belonged to him. They had never even heard of Ramon Novarro. To them he was simply "a soft touch."

But perhaps even more than destroying Ramon Novarro, his killers destroyed the good name he had established over the long years he spent in Hollywood, respected by untold thousands of fans.

Even a public figure such as Ramon Novarro is entitled to some privacy, the right to shield his secret propensities from pubic view so long as they don't become matters of public scandal. And his violent death revealed his shame as well as that of his killers, one of whom was so disturbed by what would be revealed at his trial that he tried to kill himself in his jail cell.

302

Asked during the trial why he had tried to kill himself, one of the killers of Ramon Novarro sobbed in agony, "You think it is fun to sit up here and say, 'Yes. I slept with men' or 'Yes, I did this and I did that!' And I could see it happening. This trial has been hard on me," he added, "But now I want to live."

Despite his advanced age, so did Ramon Novarro.

The body of Ramon Novarro was found on the morning October 31, 1968 by his secretary when he entered the actor's mansion to begin his daily task of helping the actor compile his autobiography. It was to contain all the glamorous episodes in the life of the Mexican-born actor from his days of swashbuckling glory in "Ben Hur" and "Prisoner of Zenda," his memories of the days when he and Rudolph Valentino were the nation's leading matinee idols, to his roles in modern television shows.

The nude body of the actor was found on his bed, his hands tied behind him with an extension cord. His body was a mass of bruises that began at the top of his head and covered his face, torso, genitals and legs. And the Spanish-type hilltop home, where the actor lived alone, looked as though it had been ransacked.

There were an abundance of clues. In fact, there were too many for Los Angeles detectives to put much trust in any one. Scrawled on the bedroom mirror with a grease pencil were the words, "Us girls are better than faggots!" In Novarro's right hand was a rubber contraceptive.

In his left had was a pen and under his body, written on the bedsheet a foot long, was the word, "Larry," on a pad on the nightstand the word "Larry" was scribbled four more times. There were what appeared to be four fingernail scratches on the actor's throat.

Elsewhere in the house detectives found a collection of

empty beer cans and liquor bottles. In the kitchen were the remains of a dinner which had been served for three. Chairs were overturned, drawers pulled out and emptied, and the rest of the house was in a general state of confusion. It was obvious that whoever had killed Novarro did so for the purpose of robbery — or at least tried to make it look that way. However, the sexual overtones of the robbery were plain to see.

A number of things put homicide detectives on the trail of Paul Ferguson, 23, and his brother, Tom, 17. A check of Novarro's telephone bill revealed that about 8:30 p.m. on October 30th, a 48-minute phone call had been made from the house in the Hollywood Hills to a Chicago number. It was a relatively simple matter for the police to trace that call, locate the person who had received it, and find out who had placed the the call.

The call had been made to a pretty 20-year-old Chicago girl who not only told the police that Tom Ferguson had called her, but vividly recalled what he had said; also, that he had called her again on November 2nd and begged her to mention that October 30th call to no one.

Among the things he told her on the night of October 30th was that he and his brother were in the home of Ramon Novarro and she quoted him as saying:

"My brother Paul told me there is $5,000 in the house and we are going to tie him up to make him tell us where it is."

During this conversation, the girl disclosed, she could hear in the background the pitiful and chilling screams of a tortured human being.

On November 6, 1968, the brothers were taken into custody in Bell Gardens, a suburb of Los Angeles. They were booked on suspicion of murder and held without bail. One thing was clear from the start—Tom Ferguson was only 17 and, under the law, he could not be condemned to death in the event he was found guilty of first-degree murder.

And there was no doubt in the minds of officials of the district attorney's office that the murder of Ramon Novarro was first-degree. A death that occurs during the commission of a robbery is automatically first-degree. And so is a death that occurs as the result of torture. Premeditation is not a required factor because in most torture cases there is no intent to murder—just to torture the victim enough to make him tell what his assailants want to know.

Fingerprints found in various places in the Novarro mansion left no doubt that Paul and Tom Ferguson had been in the house.

The case was presented to the Los Angeles County grand jury on December 17 and 18, 1968 by Deputy District Attorney James Ideman and after the evidence was heard, the brothers were indicted for murder and ordered to stand trial.

The trial of the brothers began on July 28, 1969 in the court of Superior Judge Mark Brandler. Deputy District Attorney Ideman would handle the prosecution. Cletus Hanifin, a veteran criminal attorney, represented Paul Ferguson and the court appointed Richard Walton, a capable young criminal attorney, to represent Tom Ferguson. A jury of seven men and five women were selected and Ideman made it unmistakably clear to them that he would seek death in the gas chamber for Paul Ferguson and that only Tom Ferguson's age should spare him from the same fate.

In his opening statement on August 5th, he told the jury what he expected to prove:

"The victim in this case, Mr. Ramon Novarro, at the

time of his death was a month short of being seventy. He lived by himself in a large Spanish-type house and it seemed obvious that he was a man of some wealth."

Continued Ideman, "We will show that the Ferguson brothers were living in Gardena. They were in need of money. Paul Ferguson was what is known as a hustler — a male prostitute. He would earn money by having sex with older men. Now they (the brothers) were in need of a great deal more money than would be obtained by any one sexual act. So Paul Ferguson obtained the name of Ramon Novarro and called him.

"Now Mr. Novarro was a homosexual and probably had been one for many years. But he was a discreet homosexual. He did not go out into the streets and try to pick up people. The young male prostitutes would come to his home and he was usually careful about who came to his home.

"Paul Ferguson called Novarro to try to get an appointment to see him and gave the name of his brother-in-law as having referred him. . . .

"The Fergusons obtained a ride to Novarro's home from a friend on the afternoon of October 30th.

"They told him (the friend) they were going to see a man and get some money from him. . . . The Fergusons were received by Mr. Novarro and at first things went in a congenial manner. They drank together and had some supper. Later on apparently Paul Ferguson and Mr. Novarro went into the bedroom. Sometime between 8:30 and 9 p.m. Paul began demanding money from Mr. Novarro.

"But Mr. Novarro's practice — possibly because of his propensities — although he was a wealthy man — worth between a half million and one million dollars, mostly in real estate — he had hardly any items of value around the house.

306

I'm speaking primarily of cash.

"He had very little cash and transacted nearly all of his business by check. He had approximately $45 in his possession. Novarro usually kept his wallet in a dresser drawer and when his valet checked it the day before his death it contained $45."

Said Ideman, "Somehow the Fergusons picked up the idea or had the idea that there was a large amount of money concealed in the house. Somewhere between 8:30 and 9 p.m Mr. Novarro attempted to pay Paul Ferguson for the sex act he had with him. He attempted to pay him by check and it was at this time that Paul Ferguson began demanding money from Mr. Novarro.

"There wasn't any money to give and then he began to beat him. In a period of time he was joined by his brother who for a while had been in another room.

"Mr. Novarro was beaten . . . There were something like 22 different injuries to his body. The wounds, I think, can be fairly described as torture."

Then Ideman ticked off the other details of the bizarre murder. He said the actor had been flailed with a silver-handled cane — a memento of one of his early movies. He was struck on the head, on the penis and on the testicles. His nose was broken and one of his teeth was knocked out. When he was in danger of losing consciousness and would be unable to tell the brothers what they wanted to know, he was led to a shower and revived.

Ideman said that at some stage of the beating his hands were tied behind his back and thus he was unable to ward off the blows that were rained down on the most sensitive areas of his body.

Ideman told the jury, "He was placed on his back on the bed, his hands tied behind him. In that position, unable to

307

move, and bleeding, he ultimately lost consciousness. And the blood that dripped into his throat from his broken nose unable to swallow because he was unconscious, the blood drained down into his lungs.

"He drowned in his own blood!"

Ideman said that while Novarro lay dying on his bed, the brothers ransacked the house looking for anything of value they could find. He said they found the wallet, took the $45 from it and placed it under a corner of the rug in the bedroom. Then they stripped off their bloody clothing, replaced it with items taken from Novarro's home and disposed of their own clothes in a nearby lot where they were recovered by police.

He said the pair hitchhiked back to Hollywood, dined on a hamburger steak in a Sunset Boulevard restaurant where Paul tried to make a date with a waitress, bummed $8 from a friend, and took a cab to their apartment in Gardena.

Prosecutor Ideman declared in closing, "When I get through presenting the evidence, it will show Mr. Novarro was murdered. It will show who did it. It will show that the Fergusons did it and it will show why it was done.

"It was done for robbery."

The defense attorneys waived their rights to make opening statements and the prosecution opened its case by calling, among others, a wealthy real estate man with whom Paul Ferguson admittedly had lived at one tune. The man testified that on October 29th, Paul called him, "and said he wanted some names—faggots to hustle." Questioning by the prosecutor brought out that "Larry" (a brother-in-law) would receive phone calls at the real estate man's home from potential "customers" and that these were the names that Paul Ferguson was seeking. And among the names that were given to him was that of Ramon Novarro, along with

308

his phone number. He said, "Paul wanted to make some money so he only wanted names of people who had some money."

The real estate man testified that the brothers came to his Hollywood apartment late on the night of October 30th or early on the morning of the 31st. He said Tom was lying down in another room and Paul said, "Tom went to bed with Ramon. Ramon tried to screw him and he hit him several times and he is dead."

The real estate man testified that he asked Paul, "Where were you at the time this happened, Paul?" and that Paul replied, "I was in another room sleeping on a couch." (Up to this point it was thought Paul had killed Novarro; that is what police concluded after questioning the brothers.)

The witness testified that when Tom woke up, Paul said, "Tom, I told what happened." The witness said he asked Tom, "How could you do such a thing?" and the younger brother told him, "The guy made improper advances toward me. I just hit him several times and he is dead."

The Chicago girl whom Tom had called the night of the murder was extremely nervous the day she was called to testify against the younger brother.

Under questioning by Ideman, the girl said Tom called her and told her he was at the home of Ramon Novarro. When she told him that she didn't recognize the name, Tom had to explain to her that Novarro was an old-time actor. And after some general conversation he told her that there was $5,000 hidden behind one of the pictures in the big house.

She said Tom told her that Paul was "up with Ramon" trying to get Novarro to tell where the money was. The girl quoted Tom as saying, "My brother Paul told me there is $5,000 in the house and we are going to tie him up and make him tell us where it is."

At times during the conversation, she testified, Tom would leave the phone to get cigarettes or beer and she said she asked Tom what was wrong and he said Paul was just trying to find the location of the money.

Throughout her testimony Tom Ferguson stared at the witness but not once did she look at him.

The young girl's testimony appeared to establish Ideman's case that Novarro was beaten and tortured in an attempt to get from him the money the brothers thought was in the house.

On August 25th, Paul Ferguson took the witness stand in what shaped up as a struggle between the brothers as to who would actually take the blame for the fatal beating of Ramon Novarro. Paul faced the gas chamber. Because of his age, Tom could not be executed. If Tom would admit that he actually administered the fatal blows, he could save his brother from the gas chamber with no danger to himself.

However, if Tom could convince the jury he had nothing to do with the actual murder, it was possible that he could get off with manslaughter or second-degree.

Previous testimony had established that Paul had been involved in homosexual activities with older men for pay since he was 9 or 10 years old. He been married three times, the first time at age 16 to a woman of 42.

One witness, Dr. Vernon Miller, told the jury that Paul suffered from a sociopathic disturbance and a chronic brain disease when he drinks. He said that although Paul was legally sane when Novarro was beaten to death, Paul was mentally ill and a danger to himself and others. He said Paul, when he is drinking, was unable to form the intent necessary to commit first-degree murder.

Questioned by his attorney, Cletus Hanifin, Paul was asked:

Q—Did you ever work as a male prostitute?

A—Yes, sir.

Q—How long?

A—Three months and one week. Two and half months in 1964, a week in 1965, and four or five days in 1968. (He said he had been separated from his wife since October 28, 1968.)

After telling how he got Ramon Novarro's name and phone number, Paul was asked, "What was the reason you wanted those particular names?"

He replied tersely, "To hustle." And asked what he meant by that, he answered, "Prostitute." But he denied that he ever heard there was $5,000 in the Novarro home or that he went to the house in the Hollywood Hills with the intention of robbing the actor.

He said he contacted Mr. Novarro by phone on the afternoon of the 30th and that the actor gave him the address and said he would expect him about 6 p.m. Asked if he knew anything about Mr. Novarro's career, Paul said, "I never heard of Ramon Novarro as any kind of actor."

Q—What was your real purpose in going to Ramon Novarro's home?

A—To earn some money.

Q—How did you expect to earn that money?

A—Hustling.

Q—By that you mean male prostitution.

A—Yes.

Q—You mean you were going commit some kind of sexual act with Mr. Novarro and in exchange he was going to pay you a certain amount of money.

A—No certain amount. Nobody said anything about a

311

certain amount.

Paul Ferguson said he had liked Novarro and thought he was "a nice guy" and had been told by the actor that he might become a superstar. "He said I could be a young Burt Lancaster, a superstar, another Clint Eastwood." This would tend to support the defense contention that Ferguson would have had no reason to kill a man who might become his benefactor.

He testified that when he and his brother arrived at the house, Novarro greeted them wearing a bathrobe. He said the actor led them to an L-shaped couch where they sat on either side of the aging actor. During the evening they chatted, played the piano and "horsed around" with castanets. Paul Ferguson said that he himself drank more than a full bottle of vodka and said that Novarro was also drinking quite a bit.

Paul Ferguson said Novarro even called his publicity agent who, he said, knew Fess Parker and could help Paul get a part in a picture Parker was making in Mexico. He said Novarro arranged for him (Paul) to return to the house in three days and meet the agent.

Ferguson said that at one stage Novarro had read his palm. He was asked by his attorney, "Did he tell you whether you were going to have good luck or bad luck?"

Ferguson replied with a grimace, "He wasn't a good palm reader. He said he thought I could be a star like Burt Lancaster . . . you know, that sort of stuff."

Ferguson said that while he and Novarro were playing a duet at the piano, Novarro asked which of the two brothers was going to stay and which was going to leave. Paul said he told the movie star he was drunk and that he had to hitchhike about 30 miles home and asked if he could sleep off the drunk.

312

Novarro said he could stay. Paul testified that just before he passed out he saw Novarro and his brother go out onto the patio together.

Q — Did someone waken you?

A — Yes. Tommy.

Q — What did he say to you?

A — He said, 'This guy is dead.'

Q — What did you do next?

A — I followed Tommy into the bedroom. Tommy said, 'See, this guy is dead, He's turned blue.' I touched him (Novarro) on the shoulder. It was starchy-like, you know, tight-like. Stiff. Starchy. Like paper.

Paul testified that he and his brother lifted Novarro onto the bed and it was then, for the first time, he said, that he noticed the actor's hands had been tied. However, he denied that he tied the hands or that he had even assisted in tying them. Paul quoted his brother as saying, "I didn't mean to do it," and then Tom suggested that they make the death look like a robbery.

Paul testified that Tom wrote on the mirror with a grease pencil while he himself wrote the word, "Larry," on the bed and on the memo pad, but he denied that he had his brother-in-law in mind when he wrote the name.

He said his brother sat on Ramon Novarro's chest and scratched four marks on the actor's throat with a knife to make it appear that he had been scratched by a woman.

Attorney Hanifin asked Paul if he expected to get any money from Novarro other than what he was to be paid for a sex act. The older brother replied in the negative. Then he was asked, "Did you have any sex act with Mr. Novarro that night?"

Paul replied, "No, sir."

Q — Is there some reason you went along with Tom to

313

make this look like robbery?

A—Stupidness.

Taken on cross-examination by Prosecutor Ideman, Paul was asked:

Q—What do you mean by being a hustler?

A—All right, I'll tell you. A hustler is someone you can talk to. Not just a man. Women, too. They can cook, keep company, wash a car. Lots of things make up a hustler. It is not just that you are like a bug or something. There are lots of lonely people in this town, man.

Q—Is that what you meant when you said you were going to hustle Mr. Novarro? You were going to wash his car?

A—No, no, no. That was strictly sex. He paid for what he wanted to do.

Q—You sell your body to men for money, is that right?

A—Yes. That is right.

Q—Do you consider yourself a homosexual?

A—No.

Paul told the prosecutor that a friend had told him Novarro was "a soft touch" and that he understood this to mean that Novarro paid well. Asked how much he thought he was going to get from Novarro, Paul replied, "About $20 to $25."

Asked why he wrote the name Larry on the sheet, Paul replied simply, "Goofy."

During the cross-examination, he held to his story that he had passed out on couch and that when he woke up, his brother told him Novarro was dead. He also denied that he had gone to the house to rob Novarro, or that he had any knowledge of $5,000 being hidden in the house.

Paul told Prosecutor Ideman that he "lied and lied and lied" to the police after his arrest because he was "trying to get out of this thing." Ideman tried to point out the discrepancies between the story he told the police and what he told the jury, but Paul simply said that what he told the police was a lie and what he told the jury was true.

Under cross-examination by Walton, the young attorney defending Tom Ferguson, the older brother admitted that the thought had occurred to him that he might have killed Novarro during one of his drinking blackouts but that doubt disappeared when Tom told him he had committed the murder. Clinging to his previous testimony that he did not kill Novarro, Paul declared:

"I didn't kill him. It was my brother."

Paul said that most of the lies he told to the police were told to protect his brother, but he said the detectives broke him down after four or five hours of questioning.

Asked Walton, "Then you decided to lay it on Tom?"

Paul replied, "I guess I did."

Walton got back to the subject of hustling and asked Paul just what a hustler is. The older defendant replied, "A hustler is a lot of things. He is a companion, mostly, not just a sexual thing. That is part of it, of course, but a hustler is a companion . . . for money. There are lots of homos who don't particularly care for being homos but they still like the company of other men for the simple reason that they don't feel they have anything in common with a woman. Sometimes there is no sex in the hustler-homo relationship."

Asked what kind of a hustler he was, Paul replied, "Just a guy who gets along, who doesn't believe in beating up fags or stealing from them. Lots of hustlers fleece the faggots."

During his questioning of Paul Ferguson, Walton suggested that Paul was trying to "con" the jury into believing that his younger brother had actually committed the murder because he thought the courts would go easier on a juvenile.

Paul denied that after he and his brother left Novarro's home he ever discussed with Tom that the younger brother should take the blame for the murder because he could not get the death penalty.

The jury got to hear the other side of the story when Tom Ferguson was called to the witness stand and gave his version of what happened in Ramon Novarro's home and during the days that followed.

Under the expert questioning of Defense Attorney Walton, Tom insisted that it was his brother Paul and not he who had administered the fatal beating to Ramon Novarro. He said he was on the phone for nearly an hour talking to the girl in Chicago while Paul was alone with Novarro.

Q—Did you murder him?

A—No.

Q—Did you kill him?

A—No.

Q—Did you participate in his death?

A—No.

Asked why he thought Novarro was a homosexual, Tom said that the actor was sitting between them on the couch and grabbed each one by the leg. Said Tom, "He just kept moving his hands up. I moved from the couch right away."

Tom Ferguson said that once during evening when he wanted to use the bathroom, he went through the master boom and there saw his brother and Ramon Novarro naked together. When he completed his phone call to Chicago, Tom said, his brother called him from the bedroom. There, he said he saw Ramon Novarro lying on the bed "alive and conscious" but he appeared to have been beaten about the nose and mouth. Tom said Paul directed him to help Novarro to the shower. Tom said when he and the elderly actor were alone he warned him not to say anything to Paul because his older brother would get violent.

Tom said he handed Novarro a towel and after the actor dried himself, he helped him back to bed, warning him again not to say anything to Paul. Meanwhile, said Tom, Paul had donned a hat and, clad only in his shorts, was posing in front of a mirror and talking about vaudeville.

Tom said he left the bedroom and when he returned seven or eight minutes later and saw Novarro lying on the floor; he looked as if he were dead. Tom testified that he never saw Paul actually strike Novarro but he swore that he never hit the elderly man himself. Tom said Novarro was tied up when he and his brother lifted him on the bed. Asked if he remembered who tied up Novarro, Tom answered, "I had a recollection that Paul tied him up but over the months he keeps telling me that I did."

Tom admitted that it was his idea to mess up the house to make it look like a robbery-murder, that he scratched the throat of the dead man, and that he placed a condom in the dead man's hand.

Tom said he and his brother heard the news of Novarro's death the following morning on a cheap radio they bought. They took a long walk to the beach and during that walk, Tom testified, Paul reportedly told him that he didn't mean to kill Novarro but that the booze had gotten the best of him. Tom testified that Paul persuaded him to accept the blame for the killing because the older brother would face the gas chamber.

He said Paul told him that because of his age, Tom would get only about six months in a juvenile facility. Said Tom, "He told me that's the most I would spend and that he would get me a lawyer and send me money." Asked if the gas chamber was mentioned in the conversation, Tom said, "Yes, he said he was facing the gas chamber and all I was facing was six months."

Tom said he changed his mind about taking the blame for the murder of Novarro when he learned in court that the actor had been viciously flailed with the cane. He said he never saw the cane in the house and when the details of the beating were revealed in court, Tom said, "It turned my stomach against Paul."

However, like Paul, Tom denied there was ever any mention of $5,000 in the Novarro home and claimed he never told his girl friend in Chicago anything about it.

Cross-examined by Prosecutor Ideman, Tom said Paul had told him that when he went into the bedroom with Mr. Novarro, the elderly actor tried to kiss him and at that time a vision of his estranged wife flashed in front of him. He assertedly told his younger brother that he shoved Novarro away from him, causing the actor to fall, injuring himself. It wasn't until much later that Tom learned the actor had been beaten with the cane.

Ideman asked Tom how many times Paul had reminded him that he was facing the gas chamber and Tom replied, "About 300 or 400 times — maybe more." Tom also said that he (Tom) told about 1,000 persons in the county jail during the months he spent there that he had killed Novarro. Asked why he told people he committed the murder, Tom replied, "For two reasons: 1, My brother told me if I did this the DA would pick up on some of them and have them brought into court, and, 2, I thought it was my obligation to — you know — just take it for him."

Ideman asked, "Did Paul ever tell you you would be a big man at Tracy (a California Youth Authority Facility)?"

Tom replied, "Yes, he did. Because of murder. They tend to make it, you know, like . . . I don't know. It's just a big thing. They leave murderers alone and stuff like that. This is a highly publicized case and it would tend to make everybody look up to you and stuff like that."

Questioned on the witness stand by Paul's attorney, Tom recounted that when he helped the bleeding actor into the shower, he heard Novarro mumble through his battered lips, "Hail Mary, full of grace . . ."

Tom also said he had been pressured by different persons, including his mother, to take the blame for the Novarro killing.

When he returned to his place at the counsel table, his older brother flew into a rage and threw a ball point pen at him, shouting, "You punk liar! You son of a bitch!" Judge Brandler rapped for order and threatened to gag and bind Paul if he disturbed the proceedings again.

The mother of the accused murderers, said she received several letters from Tom in which he said of the murder, "He deserved to be killed. He was nothing but an old faggot," and that "we killed him."

In a letter to Tom she wrote, "Paul wrote the first trial day and said everyone seems out to save his own skin and he is in a corner now. Tom, when you testify, think, think about what you are saying. I guess you are the only one who really knows the score. You are holding Paul's life in your hands . . . I'll keep my fingers crossed and remember after the sentencing it is too late to change the story so make sure you realize what you are doing."

Another time she wrote, "I hope something happens for the better and lets Paul off the death sentence that he feels he is going to get."

But despite the tone of her letters, she denied under oath that she was attempting to persuade her younger son to take the blame for his brother so that Paul could escape the death penalty.

Despite all the allegations, Tom refused to change his story on the witness stand. He insisted he had nothing to do with the death of Ramon Novarro. And although he never saw Paul strike the elderly actor, he implied that it was Paul who had killed the actor, not him. He said he had told a number of people that he had committed the murder but only because Paul persuaded him to do so.

In his final argument to the jury, Prosecutor Ideman said there was evidence of bad things as well as good things about Mr. Novarro. He described him as a person who had made great contributions to the entertainment industry, that he was well liked by his associates, was a nice person and was non-violent. The prosecutor also brought out that the victim had "homosexual tendencies and drank to excess" but he cautioned the jury, "I hope sincerely you will not put Mr. Novarro on trial. He has paid for whatever he did and now it is the Fergusons' turn to pay for whatever they may have done."

Ideman said, "The girl from Chicago is the closest thing to an eye-witness that we have. You will have to decide whether or not she was telling the truth. Three people know what happened in the house that night. Novarro is dead, so he can't tell us. Neither of the Ferguson brothers will admit striking Mr. Novarro even once. As a matter of fact, after listening to the Fergusons testify, I was beginning to wonder if what we were dealing with was a suicide. Perhaps Mr. Novarro wrapped himself in that electrical wire and beat himself to death with the cane."

He said, "The brothers tell us a lot when they tell us about each other, but not one word about $5,000 because they know the consequences of robbery-murder."

He added, "They are hustlers — I don't know why I keep

using those nice word. That means a male whore. That is what they are. They sell their bodies to other men for money. What kind of a person do you think does that?"

Ideman stressed to the jury the agony Mr. Novarro must have endured as he lay tied on his bed and was beaten on the most sensitive parts of his body with a cane to force him to tell where his money was supposedly hidden. The prosecutor pointed out, "I don't think the killing was premeditated. None of the specific injuries would be fatal . . . Novarro was trussed up like an animal and beaten to death. I don't think you would treat an animal like that.

"This is deliberate torture. You don't strike a man on his genitals and split his scalp with a cane unless you are torturing him."

Attorney Hanifin told the jury that Paul had two defenses: 1, simply that he did not kill Ramon Novarro, that he went to the house strictly to hustle him; and 2, that he suffered from a mental illness brought on by alcohol. Hanifin said there was no evidence to show that Paul participated in any act that would constitute torture and asked why in the world Paul would kill a man who could have been his benefactor, who could have given him an entree into the movies.

Defense Attorney Walton insisted that Tom had played no part in the murder of Ramon Novarro and that he, like his brother, went there on a hustling job. He asked the jury to consider why Paul was nagged by the thought that he might have committed the murder and why he was so obsessed with the thought of the gas chamber if he did not kill Ramon Novarro.

Then he asked, "What would have happened that night if Paul had not gotten drunk on Novarro's booze, at Novarro's urging and at Novarro's behest? Would this have happened if Novarro had not been a seducer and a traducer of young men? The answers to those questions will determine the issue and degree of guilt of Tom Ferguson and the issue and degree of guilt of Paul Ferguson."

Walton argued that the elder Ferguson beat the victim after blacking out and that he could not have formed the intent necessary for either first or second degree murder. To courtroom observers, the defense counsel's strategy at this point seemed to be to persuade the jury that his client, Tom, should not be convicted of any more serious charge than his older brother was.

The jury deliberated for three days and returned verdicts of guilty of first-degree murder against each brother. This meant that automatically Tom would draw a sentence of life in prison. The fate of Paul would be determined at the penalty phase of the trial, which would be held immediately.

When the penalty phase opened, Tom took the stand and promptly reversed his field. Questioned by Attorney Hanifin, Tom was asked, "Did you kill him. (Novarro)?"

A—It was my fault that he died.

Q—Did Paul participate in Ramon Navarro's death?

A—No, sir.

And thus, for the first time under oath, Tom Ferguson indicated that older brother did not kill Ramon Novarro, even though he already stood convicted of the charge.

Tom testified that in the earlier phase of the trial he lied about some things. He testified that he got mad at Novarro—"He made me sick"—and hit him repeatedly with his fists while his brother was sleeping.

He said he tied the unconscious victim and woke up Paul. He testified that after he and Paul "messed up the house," he took money from Novarro's wallet and the victim's cane from a closet. He said, "At first I was just goofing around, twirling it like a baton and then I walked into the bedroom and hit Novarro across the face with it."

When he was asked, "Why?", he replied, "Just because I was mad. He was just like an old punk." Tom told the jury that he finally decided to tell the truth because "I don't want it on my shoulders if I send Paul to the gas chamber and I sit up there (in prison) like Mr. Cool."

Asked by Prosecutor Ideman if it didn't bother his conscience during the first phase of the trial to blame the killing on Paul, Tom replied cockily, "Not a bit. He was supposed to get manslaughter and I was supposed to get off. It's not our fault that we got a dumb jury."

Ideman asked Tom if he thought his confession would make him a big man in prison and the younger brother answered, "I'm big already. I've been big all my life."

When the cross-examination was completed, Judge Brandler asked several questions to clear up some points of Tom's testimony. "What did you mean," he asked, "when you said you didn't kill him but that you were responsible for his death?"

Tom replied, "He wasn't killed. He died of a broken nose and I'm the one who busted his nose."

"Did you murder him, kill him, or participate in his death?" pressed the judge.

"I caused his death . . . he caused his death . . . we caused his death," Tom replied. "He was as much part of it as I was."

"Who's the we?" asked the judge.

"Mr. Novarro," replied the cocky teenager.

In his closing argument to the jury, Prosecutor Ideman labeled Tom's confession "a last minute scurrying about to create a doubt in your mind," and he urged the jury to vote the death penalty for Paul, "the man who in my opinion deserves the ultimate penalty."

Said Ideman, "It was done for money by torture, done cruelly by a man — Paul — who has no respect for himself or others, who has no remorse, no compassion, no regrets, who tried to frame an innocent man (his brother-in-law) and who got his brother to perjure himself."

Attorney Walton said later that he had advised Tom not to testify at the penalty phase for three reasons — It would hurt his chances for a new trial, it could be used against him at a retrial if the conviction should be reversed, and it would hurt his chances for an early parole.

But if Tom's scheme was to keep his brother from going to the gas chamber, it was successful. The jury deliberated for 2½ hours and brought back a verdict of life imprisonment. Paul was spared the death penalty.

Through the tangled web of admitted lies, admissions and denials, the strange case of the Ferguson brothers came to an end. Both have been sentenced to life in prison. Normally in California they would become eligible for parole after they served seven calendar years. But Superior Court Judge Mark Brandler, who formally sentenced them, recommended that they never be freed on parole saying that the two-month trial "established convincingly and conclusively to the jury and the court the guilt as to each of the defendants in the brutal, vicious, torture-killing of Mr. Ramon Novarro."

The sentence seems little enough to pay for taking in a most callous way not only the life of a man whose name was synonymous with Hollywood stardom for decades but for destroying his good name.

A Most Likely Candidate
For Murder

by Charles Walker

"If you wanted to collect all the suspects and put them all in one place," said one sleuth who worked on the case, "you'd have to hire Yankee Stadium."

From time to time in various published accounts of homicides, the reader encounters this compelling comment about the unfortunate person who has been slain: "He (or she)," the story often goes, "was a most unlikely murder victim." Almost immediately, the words conjure up graphic mental images of the unfortunate who was dispatched by violence — a kindly old lady beloved by all who knew her; the neighborhood good-deed champion whose greatest pleasure was helping others; the old-fashioned doctor who never sent bills to his patients; the dedicated clergyman whose sole purpose in life was extending a helping hand to one and all . . .

To the cynical, such people may sound like stereotyped characters in a movie, or perhaps a soap opera, but they exist nonetheless, and at least one specimen of each of the categories cited can be found in virtually every community in the country. Regrettably, moreover, they do get murdered with distressing frequency.

The opposite of the unlikely murder victim, of course, is also a fact of life — and death — yet rarely if ever does one encounter the published comment that so and so was "a most likely candidate for murder." Anyone who has reached voting age can probably think of countless examples of such people within their own field of experience, victims whose violent demise came as no surprise. Shock, perhaps, but not surprise. People whose deaths evoked such comments as, "He had it coming to him," or "Sooner or later, it had to happen," or "He was asking for it."

Serge Rubinstein was such a man. January 27, 1975, was the twentieth anniversary of Rubinstein's murder, but for a wide variety of reasons it remains one of the most memorable homicides in the history of New York City. Rubinstein was the White Russian emigre who, by devious means, burst upon the American scene a few years before World War II, emerged as the *enfant terrible* of Wall Street and other financial marts and added to an already impressive fortune by destroying an appalling succession of companies and their stockholders, became the most notorious draft dodger of the great war, and culminated his unsavory career by getting himself strangled, to the surprise of virtually no one.

Not the least of Serge Rubinstein's outstanding qualities was his talent for success. It is scarcely a generality to say that everyone hated him, with the possible exception of perhaps a half dozen people linked to him by blood relationship.

If this bothered him, he never showed it. His record in the business world was garishly successful, despite repeated onslaughts by powerful and righteous forces massed against him. He was the refutation incarnate of those nacient precepts that the good are rewarded and the evil are punished.

Paradoxically, even his murder was one of Rubinstein's

successes, albeit his final one. It was a success because his career was a lifelong preparation for the fate that finally overtook him. Just as a youth spends years of study to become an engineer or a scientist, Serge Rubinstein assiduously devoted his life to an unbroken series of acts — psychologists would call it a behavior pattern — that made his murder inevitable. You might say he worked hard, consciously or unconsciously, to become a murder victim, and he achieved that goal with the same spectacular flair that characterized most of the accomplishments of his life.

Rubinstein's killer — or killers — have never been caught. The homicide dossier in the New York City Police Department is designated as Case 432, 1955. The cops would like to nail someone for the slaying — even at this late date — because it is embarrassing to the crack professionals who direct New York Homicide to have the murder of a celebrity, even an infamous one, remain unsolved. With them, it is a matter of professional pride.

Beyond that small group of pros, however, it is probably safe to say that no one really gives a damn whether Rubinstein's murderer is ever brought to justice. When you talk to persons involved in his life, or in the investigation into his violent departure therefrom, the attitude almost unfailingly is: good riddance. Let sleeping dogs lie. The killer did the world a favor.

Traditionally, clergymen intone pious words of sweetness and light over even the most reprehensible rascals when they are laid to rest. The remarks of a Rabbi from Temple Emanu-El on Fifth Avenue, at graveside rites for Serge Rubinstein, were rather more pointed:

"He possessed a brilliant mind, but was utterly lacking in wisdom . . . He wanted friends and never had them, because he never realized that to have friends, one must be a friend.

"He wanted love, but never knew that love must be earned, and cannot be bought . . . . He feared death, because in his heart there was no faith. The irony of his life was that death should have come to him in so brutal a guise."

How does a man qualify himself as a murder candidate? A study of the career of Serge Rubinstein gives an unparalleled opportunity to find the answer.

Rubinstein was born in St. Petersburg, Russia, on May 18, 1908. His father, Dimitri Rubinstein, was a moneylender and privy counselor to the Czar. In later years, Serge was fond of saying that his old man was financial advisor to Rasputin, the notorious confidant and power behind the throne of the last of the Romanoffs. This may have been true, but more likely it was not; history makes it fairly clear that the Mad Monk dished out a lot of advice but never took any.

Serge spent his boyhood in court circles, highly privileged, but with well-defined limitations on those privileges because he was not of the blooded nobility. These limitations became a galling spur to the boy's ambition. He once said he was eight years old when he decided: "I wanted to be a grand duke, because they had the longest and blackest limousines and the tallest and blondest women."

He added that later he found out that neither the limousines nor the blondes "were all they were supposed to be." Yet he never could abandon his pursuit of either.

When Serge was ten, the Bolsheviks overthrew the Czar and murdered every nobleman in sight. The Rubinsteins, exhibiting the fancy footwork for which Serge later became so noted, had made careful preparations well in advance of the event. Papa Rubinstein had invested the family fortune in foreign holdings, and when young Serge escaped over the snowy Russian border, he had a goodly portfolio of these solid foreign stock certificates sewn into the lining of his coat.

Trying to establish himself, however, Serge's father went bankrupt in the Balkans, where he later died. One way or another, though, he salvaged enough to make it possible for Serge to be educated at Cambridge. At that hallowed institution he was remembered for a brilliant scholastic record, and as being an aggressive social climber who used scions of the war-made nouveau riche for his ends when he was rebuffed by members of the entrenched Establishment.

Upon graduating from Cambridge at the age of twenty, Rubinstein found himself penniless; the last of the family hoard had been exhausted to insure his education. So Serge went to Paris and tried to get a job in a French bank.

In this he failed, but it was not for lack of trying. He was foiled by French law, which had rigid restrictions barring emigres from such positions.

His desperation at this time inspired Rubinstein to a display of the resourcefulness that was later to become his trade mark. Many of the Russian nobility, sensing disaster before it came, had transferred the bulk of their cash reserves to Swiss banks before the revolution. A great many, unfortunately, never lived to escape from Mother Russia and reclaim their fortunes.

Serge's operations in this area remain one of the great mysteries of his life. He never disclosed how he pulled it off, except for the cryptic, unrevealing comment, "It was a percentage payoff."

The fact is that somehow or other, he managed to get his hands on a list of the unclaimed accounts of three Swiss banks in Geneva, from which he compiled a careful roster of dead Russians whose names were recorded thereon and the amounts of their bank balances.

Considering the traditional secrecy with which Swiss banking institutions guard their dealings, even from foreign governments pressing criminal investigations against citizens suspected of hiding illicitly gained money in foreign banks, this was an accomplishment of the highest order.

At one period when the United States Government was fine-combing Rubinstein's background, there was a story circulating behind the scenes which might explain how Serge managed his extraordinary coup. According to this unconfirmed report, Rubinstein, during the days when he was trying to land a job in a French bank, met a young Swiss who, he somehow learned, had embezzled money from a financial clearing house in Geneva and fled to Paris, where he was doing his best to squander his ill-gotten gains and drink himself to death.

Serge, the story goes, attached himself to the embezzler primarily for one reason: it provided him with a meal ticket and a place to live. He made himself indispensable to the young profligate, acting as a sort of major domo-butler-companion in his wild sprees. He often had to carry the man home in a drunken state, undress him and put him to bed. It also gave him the perfect opportunity to examine his host's papers at his leisure, and among them he found the list of the unclaimed accounts of foreign depositors in the three Geneva banks.

As stated earlier, this story was never confirmed, but it remains as an interesting possibility. American investigators established that such a Swiss embezzler was at large in Paris during the period when Rubinstein was struggling to gain a foothold there. They confirmed, too, that Serge had known the man, but they could never get proof positive that they had lived together for a time.

One federal agent who worked on the case says that when the story was laid before Rubinstein, Serge merely threw back his head and laughed. He started to say something, but then thought better of it and, with a crafty look in his dark eyes, he simply shrugged and said, "It's a marvelous story, isn't it?"

In any event, there is no questioning the fact that he did have a list of dead Russians who had deposits in three Geneva banks, together with the outstanding balances credited to each. Armed with this information, Rubinstein hunted up the emigre heirs to these fortunes. Many were living in abject poverty, working at the most menial jobs in Paris and elsewhere to eke out a bare existence. In their desperation, they were ripe for the proposition that Rubinstein put to them. In effect, his pitch went something like this:

"Make me your agent. I will arrange for your inheritance to be delivered to you. All I want is ten percent of the gross, plus expenses."

The ten percent was certainly a legitimate fee. Rubinstein denied reports that many of his prospective clients, wildly excited when first approached with the proposition, vowed to give him a third, or even a half of all the money he could recover for them. He had something else going for him. The "expenses" stipulated in his proposition, his pigeons soon found, were nebulous, large, and based entirely on what Serge said they were.

The climate of intrigue of that postwar era, of course, worked in his favor and made credible his claims that he had to pay off a large percentage to his Swiss "contact."

Suffice to say that in less than two years, Rubinstein made himself a millionaire with the gambit, and with this bankroll he was off and running. In 1931, at the age of 23, he formed a holding company with which he swiftly wrested control of the Banque Franco-Asiatique. In no time at all, he extended his operations to obtain control of a large hotel in Paris, several investment companies and a handful of industrial plants.

His future in French finance was assured, until he made a grievous mistake. Throughout his life, Serge's proclivities as a lusting tomcat were exceeded — but just barely — only by his avarice. Now his roving eye settled on a countess whose beauty enthralled him. Rubinstein's vigorous youth and even more vigorous bank account enthralled her.

There was, however, one flaw in this idyllic situation. The lady happened to be the mistress of Pierre Laval, Premier of France, who did not take kindly to competition on his mattress. Laval turned a few agents loose on Monsieur Rubinstein.

Bum rap or not, it did not take them long to find evidence that the Premier's rival had violated numerous chapters of the Napoleonic Code, and that Rubinstein's residence in the country was a blot on the fair name of France.

Rubinstein was deported forthwith.

Never a man to limit his operations to one country or continent, Rubinstein already had heavy financial investments in England. Thus, when he became *persona non grata* in France, he simply transferred his base of operations to London. There he laid the foundation for his later fortune by acquiring control of the Chosen Corporation Ltd., an English company with 87 square miles of gold-rich land and mines in Korea.

To solidify his control of Chosen, Rubinstein persuaded the directors to vote him an extra 150,000 shares of stock, with payment deferred until the future. Lawsuits through the years were to contend that the only payment he ever made on this deal was by rigging the books to make it appear he had paid when he hadn't.

In any case, when Japan took over Korea, Rubinstein went to the Orient. In his first encounter with the Japanese, it must be said, he was eminently more successful than General MacArthur. In effect, Serge accomplished the impossible, for despite the vigilance of his Nipponese watchdogs, he found a way to smuggle out $1,200,000 in blocked Japanese yen, to the great distress of Emperor Hirohito's finance ministers.

Having thus outmaneuvered some of the best financial brains in France, England and the Orient by his lightning sleight-of-hand smuggling, Serge Rubinstein decided at last to favor the United States of America with his genius.

For a man of his devious resourcefulness, the fact that he was a stateless person was only a minor obstacle. It was perhaps foreordained that one with his special interests would discover a loophole in Portuguese law which conferred citizenship on illegitimate offspring of a Portuguese national.

So Serge went to the Portuguese island colony of Macao, sitting in the Pacific near Hong Kong. There, spreading money around where it would do the most good, he wangled a Portuguese passport on the claim that he was the bastard son of a Portuguese nobleman who, conveniently, was deceased and thus unable to dispute the claim.

Serge Rubinstein apparently was not at all concerned about the light in which this maneuver cast his doting mother, a woman of impeccable virtue, who was still very much alive.

In any event, in 1938, sleek, matured, and the picture of the ultra-sophisticated cosmopolite, Rubinstein entered the United States by way of Ontario, Canada, bearing a Portuguese passport which gave his name as Sergio Manuel Rubinstein de Rovello. He was still listed by that name in the Manhattan telephone directory when he was murdered.

American immigration officials eventually made a federal case of this transparent fraud, but Rubinstein, whose millions always bought him the shrewdest legal experts to be had, tied the government in knots in protracted court battles that still had not been settled at the time of his death.

In the meantime, the boy wonder who had helped himself to tasty dishes from the financial marts of Paris and London now plunged into Wall Street and discovered it was precisely his dish of caviar. Setting up corporations so fast that no one could keep track of them, he pulled off one colossal coup after another.

He made a fortune out of the Postal Telegraph-Western Union merger. In 1940 he cornered the stock of New York's BMT Subway and came out with better than a million dollars net profit when the New York subways were unified.

Even more dazzling was his feat in obtaining control of Panhandle Oil and Refining, a Texas company he picked up at a Houston auction for $1.25 a share. The company became an important producer of aviation gasoline in World War II and its stock zoomed to $12 per share, at a reputed $3,300,000 profit to Serge Rubinstein.

With his forays in high finance producing millions for him in such profusion, it was a cinch for Rubinstein to indulge his passion for the longest and blackest limousines and the tallest and blondest beauties. And he was never a man to stint himself.

In fairness to the man, it must be said that even without the added attraction of his wealth and sinister reputation, a quality which rogues throughout history have proved to be irresistible to some women, Rubinstein very likely would have been a successful ladies man.

In appearance he was not unattractive; he bore a striking resemblance to comedian Alan King, or vice versa, if you prefer. His 184 pounds were distributed over a stocky frame. Although he stood about 5 feet 8 inches in height, his muscular build made him look shorter. He never smoked, he exercised regularly, drank sparingly and kept himself in excellent physical condition.

He spoke with a clipped Cambridge accent in a high, reedy, somewhat flat voice. When he chose, Rubinstein could be the most captivating, charming, persuasive man in the world. His manners were completely Continental; he kissed a lady's hand with the easy naturalness with which other men might say "Hiya, honey." As a conversationalist he had few peers, exhibiting a mind and wit that struck brilliant sparks.

But when his charm and savoir faire failed to win a female objective, Rubinstein could change in a flash and resort to the technique of the pimp.

"Everyone has a price tag," he was fond of saying contemptuously, and the record shows he believed this passionately.

It mattered not whether the girl who refused to go to bed with him was a virgin or a tart, he reacted to refusals as if they were flung gauntlets. "How much do you want?" he'd ask bluntly.

If the girl waxed indignant and declared she couldn't be

bought, Serge would laugh contemptuously. In his later years he made it a habit not to carry much money with him preferring to sign tabs, but for many years he always carried a sheaf of big bills in his left pants pocket.

He'd reach into the pocket, pull out the greenbacks, unfold them slowly. The top bill was usually a C-note. His gray-green eyes would dart from the hundred-dollar bill to the girl, and he'd smirk, "Not enough, eh?"

Then he'd flip the bills over and peel off a $500 note from the bottom of the stack. "How about that, my dear? Think of it as taxi fare home."

He seldom had to go higher, but one of his flunkies swore he was present at a table in Broadway's Latin Quarter nightclub on one occasion when Rubinstein temptingly peeled off ten of those $500 bills before a famous New York showgirl capitulated.

At other times he was less crude. Upon occasion he was known to send a girl a mink stole as a gift *before* their date. Such tokens of largesse, with their inferential promise of more to come for a girl who knew which side her bed was buttered on, almost inevitably produced the desired results.

There is one instance of record when Rubinstein failed to conquer. Stopping at a hotel in Miami Beach which was playing host to a tennis tournament, he was smitten by a vibrantly fresh young blonde player in her teens. The hotel manager arranged a meeting, but the blonde brushed off Rubinstein after five minutes in his company.

Never a man to take no for an answer, Serge sent her an expensive jeweled bauble in a bouquet of flowers, with a note asking her to have dinner with him. She sent back the posies *and* the jewels.

Rubinstein thereupon exercised the time-honored prerogative of the rich: He complained, in effect, to the manager, or to some equally influential official. In any case, someone hastened to the girl's room and impressed on her how important it was to be nice to a man like Mr. Rubinstein. The girl agreed to meet him for dinner.

Neither she nor he would ever reveal precisely what transpired at the table, but in full view of hundreds of people, the young blonde abruptly rose and stalked indignantly out of the dining room.

The next morning she was notified that she was ineligible to compete in the tennis tournament. She packed at once and left Miami.

For all his avid antics in the boudoir, there is evidence that Serge Rubinstein may not have been the great lover he aspired to be. The prime witness, whose perfection of figure was matched by her candor, was a girl he romanced for several months. Working as a model when she first met Serge, she made no claim to having been an innocent young thing seduced by the rich tycoon.

Police records show, though, that she graduated to the ranks of Mickey Jelke's call girl stable within a year after her fling with Rubinstein ended. Still she felt no rancor toward him.

"He was very generous and he always treated me well," she said. She had but one complaint, which she confided with a shrug:

"He was lousy in bed."

Long before this, however, Rubinstein met one girl who disproved his precept that everyone had a price tag. She was the girl who could not be bought, the tall, blonde, beautiful and glamorous model who, some insist, was the one genuine love of Rubinstein's life.

Early in March of 1941, she and Serge were guests at a

dinner in the White House hosted by then-President Roosevelt. Two weeks later they were married at a glittering wedding at Alexandria, Virginia.

Among the guests in attendance was a dazzling galaxy of senators, congressmen, cabinet members, foreign ambassadors and other luminaries from the international set.

This may or may not have been the one true love of Rubinstein's life, but it soon became apparent that Serge was constitutionally incapable of monogamy. He continued indulging his appetites for blondes, brunettes and redheads with unrestrained impartiality. Finally, after he was sentenced to prison as a draft dodger in 1974, his wife divorced him.

Rubinstein's conviction for draft evasion was the lone legal battle lost in a career choked with lawsuits. True, he lost the early rounds to avoid deportation when the United States Immigration authorities uncovered the shabby fraud of his Portuguese passport, but by hook or by crook he staved off execution of the deportation order for some eight years, and the government was still trying to kick him out of the land of the free and the home of the brave when he was murdered.

It was at one of the deportation hearings that a United States Attorney excoriated the draft-dodging multimillionaire with the words:

"Any man who would go into court and say that he is the bastard son of his own mother has sunk to such a depth that be deserves no consideration."

When Rubinstein entered prison in 1947, he liquidated his stock holdings. He then controlled 17 corporations representing oil wells, mines, banks, construction companies, real estate and aircraft manufacturing. When the final tally was in, Rubinstein's accounts added up to $6,000,000 in cash. And in Wall Street the smart boys were saying this represented only his worth in American holdings, that he had at least as much more in foreign investments.

Even while serving time in Lewis Federal Penitentiary, Rubinstein could not be stopped from adding to his fortune. During the latter months of 1947 and early 1948, he had his broker buy him 200,000 shares of Boeing Aircraft stock. On the day Rubinstein was found strangled in his bedroom, that stock alone was valued at $15,000,000 at current market prices!

Feared as he was in the world of finance before he went to prison, Rubinstein became even more terrifying when he got out in 1949. Now, added to his natural cupidity, was a lust for vengeance — a driving compulsion to make everyone pay for those lost years behind bars. Previously he had been known by the time-worn epithet of "Wolf of Wall Street." In his post-prison years he swiftly earned a new title, "The Cobra."

It was not a nickname spoken in jest.

In many ways, Serge Rubinstein was a living caricature of the villain in an oldtime melodrama, the evil-hearted Mr. Slime who chortled and twirled his mustache as he gave pure Little Nell the choice of a frolic in the feathers or eviction from the old homestead for her and her ailing grandma. He manifestly relished the role, and he took no pains to conceal his motives.

He was utterly candid, in fact, about his corporate modus operandi:

"Get control, then liquidate. If you have to wash out the stockholders in the process, that's too bad."

With a happy smile on his face, he would confide, "A company's earning power, to me, is meaningless. I want to know only one thing: Is the liquidation price of its assets

339

higher than the price of its stock?

"I want to know *how much a company is worth dead, not living*."

Rubinstein likewise made no secret of how he went about getting control of a company. Over a period of months he would use a host of dummy agents to buy up its stock quietly. At the exact right moment, he would then announce that he held the controlling interest.

His next move was strictly a take-it-or-leave-it proposition: He would give minority stockholders the option of fighting him—at the risk of losing everything they owned—or selling out to him on his own terms and bailing out with whatever they could still salvage out of the debacle.

If they were smart, they settled for the half-loaf he offered and got the hell out.

He once blackmailed a highly respected broker who controlled a crucial block of stock into selling to him with the threat of spreading the word that the man had been a secret associate in Rubinstein's operations for years. The broker had no choice but to comply; the lie would have destroyed him long before be could ever have hoped to disprove it.

Such tactics inevitably earned Serge Rubinstein an army of enemies. Yet he was inured to threats. Only once did he ever suffer physical violence. That happened a couple of years before his death when he was the victim of an attempted shakedown.

A couple of thugs worked him over, but it was a once-over-lightly sort of mauling, with the promise of much worse to come if he didn't pay off.

Serge Rubinstein didn't pay off. Instead he went to the law, a trap was set, and the culprits ultimately were sentenced to prison terms to ponder their folly in their choice of a victim.

Lawsuits were thrown against Rubinstein literally by the hundreds. They bothered him no more than a speck in the eye. Beautiful women came and went in his life in an unending parade. When they were in favor, he gave them keys to his six-story mansion at 814 Fifth Avenue, in the heart of Manhattan's Gold Coast. When one fell out of favor, he had the front door lock changed and distributed a new set of keys.

Regardless of how many blondes he bedded, Serge could be viciously possessive with those engaging his current interest. Once he suspected that one of his girl friends was two-timing him with a cafe society hanger-on. His reaction was typical of the man.

Serge simply sent for a man renowned for his expertise in wire-tapping and surreptitious electronic surveillance. He explained his problem and announced that he wanted a very special sort of job done in this instance.

When the bugging expert heard what Serge had in mind, he said very frankly that he'd never done anything like it before, but he was confident he could pull it off.

He did, too. Gaining entrance to the two-timing doll's apartment was simplicity itself, inasmuch as Serge was paying the rent on the place and was able to supply a key. The electronics wizard simply picked a time when Serge took the girl out for an evening to make sure he could work undisturbed, and then, at his leisure, he planted a tiny transmitter in the chick's mattress.

Serge had already arranged for the guy to set up a listening post, complete with tape recorder, in a nearby apartment in the same building. After that, the operation was a piece of cake. Other operatives staked out the girl's apartment, and when they saw her return home late at night with the other man, they flashed the word to the men on duty at the listening post. They turned on the equipment and obtained a tape recording of the sounds being broadcast from the transmitter concealed in her mattress.

When the tape was delivered to Rubinstein, he invited the cheating blonde — *and* her secret love — to his home the very next night. After serving them cocktails like the perfect host, he announced he had some rather special entertainment for them, at which point he turned on the tape and played back to them the sounds of their amour.

The gal's partner in two-timing, who was half a head taller than Serge, thought it was pretty dirty pool, so to speak, and threatened to knock Rubinstein's block off.

Serge stood up, hands at his side, and dared him: "I don't think you've got the guts. Go ahead, I'll let you throw the first punch."

The man backed down.

But although Rubinstein was a robust man and no physical coward, he was harried by a morbid fear of death. On repeated occasions he said: "I will never die a natural death. They'll murder me yet . . .

"I'll be walking on the street — going into my house, my office, maybe a night club. A big limousine will come by . . . *bang, bang!* That will be finis for Rubinstein."

He used to say it lightly, but real dread lay behind his words. There were nights when he refused to go home, fearful that assassins were lying in wait for him to appear there. On such occasions he usually spent the night at the Savoy-Plaza.

On one of those nights he ordered an associate who happened to be the same height and build as himself to go to the house for some papers. The man refused.

"I knew what he had in mind," he later told police. "If somebody was laying for him, they'd have thought I was Serge and I'd have gotten it in the back."

For all his brilliant acumen, Rubinstein was only partly right about the way he would die. He didn't get shot down in the street. He was strangled in his own palatial home. The end toward which he had been moving inexorably all his life came within the comforting, presumably safe, confines of his own bedroom.

On the night of Wednesday, January 26, 1955, Serge Rubinstein had a date with a blonde. Even he must have lost count of all the blondes he had dated, and this one is memorable only because she was the last, but her name is of no importance. They had dinner at Nino's La Rue, an expensive restaurant in East 58th Street.

They went back to Rubinstein's mansion shortly after one o'clock on the morning of Thursday, the 27th. Rubinstein fixed the girl a nightcap at the bar in his study on the third floor. His 78-year-old mother was asleep in her room on the fourth floor. His aunt, who was 82 years old, was sleeping in a room on the fifth floor.

The blonde did not stay long. Serge took her downstairs in the elevator, walked her to the door, gave her a $5 bill for cab fare and kissed her goodnight. He then went back to his bedroom, undressed and got into a pair of mandarin pajamas.

Lolling in a big comfortable chair, he read for a little while, then dropped his book, picked up the telephone and dialed a number in the Trafalgar 9 exchange.

In the bedroom of an apartment on East 79th Street, the ringing phone roused another blonde from her slumbers. She answered sleepily.

"Sweetheart, it's Serge," a voice said in her ear. His voice was soft, with a note of urgency. "Hop in a cab and come over, sweetheart, I'm lonely . . ."

"I can't, Serge," the blonde responded. "I've been out. I'm just too exhausted."

"I'll meet you at the door," Rubinstein said, as if he hadn't heard what she said.

"No, Serge. Not tonight. I'm sorry."

Unless his killer spoke to him, the last voice Serge Rubinstein ever heard was that of the blonde. There would be something grimly poetic about it, if that's the way it was, for blondes, to Serge Rubinstein, had been a way of life.

At a few minutes after 8 o'clock in the morning, Rubinstein's butler brought a breakfast tray to his master's bedroom. The master was not eating that morning.

He was dead.

Still wearing his black pajamas, Serge Rubinstein lay sprawled on his back, his hands and feet bound tightly with venetian blind cord. Plastered across his mouth and wound around his throat were strips of adhesive tape two inches wide. It was obvious he'd been strangled, and at first it was thought that the killer had accomplished his deed with the adhesive tape.

The autopsy, however, disclosed that this was an error in deductive judgment. Serge Rubinstein had died by *manual* strangulation. Someone had throttled him with a pair of powerful hands.

It was a very personal, very intimate method of murder. Whoever did it probably derived a great deal of pleasure from the act. Some criminologists contend that strangling can be a powerful sexual stimulus. Many stranglers have confessed that they had orgasms while choking the life out of their victims.

No other homicide in recent history evoked such a concentration of police activity or such protracted efforts to find the killer. A horde of Rubinstein's business contacts, friends, enemies, associates, prison mates, past and current girl friends were hauled in, questioned and eventually released to writhe their way out of the limelight as best they could.

When all else failed, New York detectives tracked down and interrogated every one of several thousand persons whose names Rubinstein had written in several loose-leaf notebooks. It appeared he made a habit of writing down the name of every person he met who might ever be useful to him, either romantically or in business.

These prodigious efforts have failed to turn up Serge Rubinstein's murderer. Even the precise motive remains unclear, although countless motives existed. Attempts to narrow down the motivation present these alternatives:

It might have been a murder of reprisal; a preventive murder to keep Rubinstein from achieving some objective; or an elimination killing if Rubinstein was a stumbling block in the path of some desired end.

In the matter of suspects, homicide detectives suffered from an embarrassment of riches. "If you wanted to collect them all in one place," said one of the sleuths who worked on the case, "you'd have to hire Yankee Stadium."

The one indisputable fact in a horrendous welter of confusing factors in the case is that Serge Rubinstein fulfilled his destiny. He spent virtually his entire life making people mad enough to kill him.

And, finally, someone did.

The Texas Killing
Caused A Political Earthquake

by Bill G. Cox

The shooting of J.R. Ewing on the television series, "Dallas" — that exaggerated prime time soap opera about the loves and sins of a wealthy Texas family — was nothing compared to the real-life drama that shocked the big state of Texas on Monday, January 19, 1981. It happened in a rambling, posh ranch home just outside the little town of Liberty, Texas, located 45 miles northeast of Houston in the southeastern part of the state.

The episode that rocked Liberty and soon the rest of the sprawling state involved one of the oldest and most politically famous families in Texas. It also involved homicide.

It came to public light through a frantic telephone call made to Kerstin Memorial Hospital in Liberty. The caller was a hysterical woman. Crying and screaming, she called for an ambulance for her husband who, she said, had been shot. The woman identified herself as Vickie Daniel. At one point during the highly emotional phone call, it sounded to the hospital employee taking the call like the sobbing woman dropped the phone, and screamed, "Price, get up!"

The hospital dispatched an ambulance to the Price Daniel ranch six miles north of town. The Liberty Police Department also was notified. Because the Daniel ranch was outside the city limits and within the county jurisdiction, the police dispatcher relayed the shooting call to the Liberty County Sheriff's Department.

The mere mention of the Daniel name sent a current of excitement along the phone wires. Everyone in Liberty County knew that Vickie Daniel was the pretty, blonde wife of handsome Price Daniel Jr., a wealthy attorney-businessman whose political career had included one term as Speaker of the Texas House of Representatives in Austin and an unsuccessful bid for the office of Texas Attorney General.

Price Daniel Jr., 39, was the son of former Texas Governor Price Daniel Sr., who also had been Texas Attorney General, a justice of the Texas Supreme Court, a U.S. Senator and an assistant to President Lyndon B. Johnson.

Moreover, the family traced its roots back to the very founders of the Republic of Texas. Price Daniel Jr. was a great-great-great-grandson of General Sam Houston — the first president of the Texas Republic — who as a general had routed the forces of Mexican General Santa Ana at the Battle of San Jacinto after the Mexican troops earlier had defeated and slain Davy Crockett, James Bowie and other legendary Texas heroes at the Alamo in San Antonio.

Now, Sheriff C. L. "Buck" Eckols headed the sheriff's department officers who sped to the Daniel Ranch. An ambulance already had arrived at the one-story rambling ranch home nestled in the bottomlands of the Trinity River amid huge oak trees draped with Spanish moss. The ambulance had departed for the hospital after strapping the hysterical Vickie Daniel to a stretcher.

Entering the posh ranch home, Sheriff Eckol found Daniel, Jr. lying on his left side on the floor of a small hallway leading from the kitchen to a carport. Blood was oozing from Daniel's mouth and nose. It appeared he was dead from at least one gunshot wound in the stomach. In the kitchen, spaghetti and green peas were simmering on the stove as if dinner were being prepared.

A .22 caliber, bolt-action rifle was discovered on a bedroom floor about 25 feet from Daniel's body. Officers also found two spent .22 shells nearby.

Surveying the house interior and checking all doors and windows, the investigators found no evidence of forced entry. They did observe some broken glass on the floor that indicated an altercation could have taken place. The officers also saw several packed cardboard boxes in the house. The investigators also noted a freshly-mixed drink, which appeared to be Scotch and water, sitting on a washing machine in the hallway near the spot where the body was found.

The officers were unable to locate any bullet hole in the walls or other surface areas in the home.

Continuing his inspection of the ranch home, Sheriff Eckols noticed a trap door to an attic-storage area was open and a light was on in the attic. It looked to the sheriff as though Daniel might have been putting up Christmas decorations in the attic-storage room. A nylon jacket later identified as Daniel's was hanging from one of the springs on the folding ladder leading to the attic trap door.

As the large home was photographed and processed for possible evidence, Sheriff Eckols learned from attendants at the hospital that Vickie was being treated for apparent emotional shock and had been given sedation. She apparently was not injured in any way otherwise, according to the cursory examination made upon her admittance to the hospital.

At this point, the investigators could not say what had happened in the Daniel home, or who had fired the shot that killed the popular political scion.

Liberty County Justice of the Peace I. B. Carrell, who was called to the shooting scene in his role of acting coroner, ordered that an autopsy be conducted. For this purpose Daniel's body was sent to a hospital in Houston, where the autopsy would be done by the Harris County Medical Examiner's office.

Sheriff Eckols determined that the Daniel couple's two children, one and three years old, and Vickie Daniel's 11-year-old daughter by a previous marriage, had been in the home at the time of the shooting, but apparently had been watching television in another room. The children had been picked up by a brother of Daniel's, who had been phoned by a neighbor who had seen and wondered what all the flashing lights were doing at the Daniel place, the sheriff learned.

None of the children had been harmed in any manner.

As news of the tragic shooting spread, relatives, friends, officials and newsmen from the newspapers and television stations in the nearby major cities converged on the Daniel Ranch located on Farm-to-market Road 1011 and nicknamed "The Governor's Road" because the large home of former governor Price Daniel Sr. was located only a few hundred yards from his son's place. The Daniel ranch that was home for father and son spread over 3,000 acres. It also was the site of the Sam Houston Regional Library and Research Center housing official family papers of the Daniels' famed ancestors and other historical figures.

Reporters were pressing for details of what happened on this cold, rainy night, but investigators and officials at the scene were mum.

However, Sheriff Eckols told reporters, "When a husband is shot, and the only other person around is his wife, well, you have to question her. We feel like she was involved. She was quite hysterical, and they took her to the hospital, gave her a sedative, and we haven't talked to her yet. We ex-

349

pect to talk to Mrs. Daniel later today."

Meanwhile, the sheriff posted a deputy at the young widow's hospital room.

Although the shooting death undoubtedly was the most sensational Texas story to break in many a month, the newsmen covering it were well aware they were competing for front-page space with two other national and international headline grabbers: The inauguration of President-Elect Ronald Reagan and the freeing at last of America's hostages in Iran.

Meanwhile in Liberty the investigators, under the direction of District Attorney Carroll Wilburn Jr., knew they had their work cut out for them. For one thing, the minute-by-minute day's activities of both Price Daniel Jr. and his 33-year-old blonde wife, Vickie, had to be pinpointed from the time they got up Monday morning until Daniel died in a pool of blood on the hall floor. The officers hoped to question Vickie later when her condition permitted, and also the oldest child who had been in the house, the 11-year-old daughter by a previous marriage.

One of the persons who came to the Daniel home after news of the fatal shooting broke was the former husband of Vickie. They had been divorced in 1976 after nine years of marriage. The ex-husband said he came to the Daniel place to get his daughter after learning that Daniel had been killed.

Later, the ex-husband threw some light on the .22 caliber Remington rifle found on the bedroom floor and believed to be the death weapon. He told reporters the gun usually was kept in a hall closet of the Daniel home.

"They had a garbage barrel out back, and possums and 'coons always were getting in it," the former spouse said. "Price used the .22 to shoot them. He was a pretty good shot."

The ex-husband said also that Vickie was "damn good with a rifle."

"We used to go hunting together, and she was extremely good with a .22 rifle," the blonde's first husband told newsmen. He said that he had visitation rights after the divorce and that he frequently went to the Daniel home to pick up his daughter. Usually, he said, he just honked his horn and the daughter came outside.

The times that he did go inside, there never was any unpleasantness, even though Vickie had married Daniel only a short time after divorcing her first husband.

"Price was always very polite and civil," the ex-husband said.

Daniel himself had been married before. His first wife, a pretty, tall, brunette from a refined and cultured family background, was a descendant of another Texas chief executive, Gov. Thomas M. Campbell. She had divorced Daniel in 1975, after nine years of marriage, citing "conflicts of personality."

It was no secret in Liberty, a town of about 9,000 residents, that young Daniel's second marriage to Vickie was a stormy relationship. He had met her while she was a waitress in the local Dairy Queen, a fast-food outlet specializing in malts and burgers. The second marriage was a contrast in personalities and family backgrounds.

Vickie had been born in Baytown, located 25 miles from Liberty, the 11th of 12 children. Her parents were divorced when she was about 10, and her mother later remarried. Vickie had attended Waxahachie High School, south of Dallas, but dropped out in 1967 before graduation. She had met and married her first husband that year, when she was 20 and he was 18. They settled down in Dayton, a town that adjoins Liberty, and had two children during their marriage. When they divorced, Vickie got custody of both children, a girl and a boy, but the father later was given custody of the boy.

Her ex-husband recalled to reporters later that Vickie was a "good mother" but problems developed during their marriage and they fought. "She used to get down in a cold rage and attack," he said.

Friends said Price Daniel Jr. was "lonely" when he met Vickie at the Dairy Queen. Daniel was her lawyer when she filed for divorce from her first husband in June, 1976. The divorce was final on August 16.

On October 1, 1976, Vickie had applied for a marriage license to remarry her ex-husband; the remarriage never came off. Only a month later, she married Price Daniel Jr. The high-spirited, attractive blonde, who had been dubbed in private by some local residents "The Dairy Queen," had become through marriage a part of one of the most famous and politically-astute families in the Lone Star State.

The Daniel family had stepped out of the pages of history books. Daniel's ancestors had settled Liberty, Texas in the 1820s, having come from Liberty, Miss. and bringing the town's name with them. Liberty was one of the first three Anglo settlements in Texas. Price Jr.'s mother was Jean Houston Baldwin Daniel, whose great great grandfather was Sam Houston, first president of the Texas Republic and later governor of the state. Price Daniel Sr., was serving his second term in the Texas House of Representatives when Price Jr. was born.

During the next 38 years, Price Daniel Sr. rose to the top as a political figure. His spectacularly successful career saw him as Speaker of the Texas House of Representatives, governor, state attorney general, state supreme court justice,

U.S. Senator and later assistant to native Texan President Lyndon Johnson. He was the only person ever to serve in all three branches of the Texas government and two of the three Federal branches. He had retired in 1980 to look after numerous business interests, leaving the political stage to his son.

Price Jr. also was out of politics at the time of his death, but friends believed he was interested in some day returning to the field of public service.

Price Jr. as a youth had divided his time between Austin and Liberty. In later years he told friends that he made his first political speech at the age of 11 in behalf of his dad's campaign for the U.S. Senate. He received his bachelor and law degree from Baylor University at Waco. He matured into a handsome young man with a taste for the better things of life, including rare books — especially those on Texas history.

In 1966, Price Jr. graduated from Baylor, married, began his private law practice and took his first public office — justice of the peace of Liberty County. Two years later he was elected to his father's old post as state legislator from the Liberty area. It didn't seem he was setting the world on fire — not until 1971, that is.

That was the year the Sharpstown Bank scandals sent shock waves through Texas political circles, engulfing a number of high placed politicos.

Among those affected by the Sharpstown scandals was the then Texas House Speaker. A group of legislators chose Price Jr., a "decent young fellow" to replace the speaker. He won the spot as the presiding officer of the House after a year-long campaign, and moved immediately for a package of reform legislation to offset the effect of the political scandals on state government.

Through Daniel's energetic leadership the Texas Legislature passed the Open Public Meetings Act, Open Records Act, laws requiring campaign finance disclosures, ethics rules and lobby registration and disclosure regulations. In 1974 Time magazine cited Price Daniel Jr. as one of the "200 faces of the future."

But for all of Daniel's professional accomplishments, friends said they never really felt they knew the man that existed in the political figure. "I don't think I ever saw him totally relax," one associate told reporters. "There was always a mask, as though there was something pent up inside."

There were people in Liberty who thought that the marriage of Price Jr. to Vickie — "The Dairy Queen" — was doomed from the start. Certainly the romantic waters appeared troubled, judging from Vickie's plans for remarrying her first husband only one month before she became Mrs. Daniel.

And in October, 1977, a month after Price Jr. declared his candidacy for the office of Texas Attorney General, Vickie sued him for divorce, citing as grounds "conflict of personalities."

But she withdrew the divorce petition two days later.

The man who served as Price's executive assistant at that time told reporters, "I spent 12 hours on the phone with her and Price that day (when the divorce was filed). That situation happened because Vickie was politically naive and political campaigns are demanding. They place pressures on the best of marriages, and Vickie had never been close to politics before."

The Daniel marriage survived the crisis, but Daniel lost his bid for state attorney general to a lesser known opponent, Mark White. Many political observers blamed Daniel's defeat on "overconfidence."

Then, on New Year's Eve, Dec. 31, 1980, Vickie Daniel again brought suit for divorce, alleging the same "conflict of personalities." She also asked that the court restrain Price from "dissipating" the assets. Price Jr., was served with the divorce papers on Jan. 15th—four days before his death by gunshot. A court hearing on the divorce suit had been scheduled for the next Thursday.

On the same day that the court hearing was set on the disposition of assets, Vickie had planned to move out of the brick ranch home to an apartment in Liberty, officers learned from talking to friends of the couple. Vickie had intended to rent an apartment until she could buy a home in Liberty, it was reported, and Price Jr. was supposed to have given her the down payment for the apartment on Thursday.

Vickie even had asked her first husband to drop by and help her move that day, and he had agreed, investigators were told. The investigation being pressed by the officers and reporters unearthed other details of the marital rift. Although Price and Vickie had separated on December 29, 1980, neither of them had moved from the ranch home. Apparently they just shifted to different parts of the big house.

Friends said that the couple had reached an amicable type of settlement, as marriage breakups go. Price would pay Vickie $700 a month child support, buy her a car and give her $15,000 as a down payment on a house. Price also had agreed to pay rent for an apartment until her new home was ready.

For some time there had been signs that a bad marital storm was brewing, signaled by more recent events over and above the earlier divorce suits filed by Vickie and then withdrawn. Friends related that she had complained of boredom, that Price was neglecting her, beating her, harassing her. But investigators turned up no evidence that Vickie had ever sought medical or hospital treatment for any injuries.

The investigation brought forth stories of some friends that Vickie had complained her husband didn't give her any money, that he personally did the household shopping to keep her from having any cash. Even friends of Price acknowledged that he was a "workaholic" who didn't spend a lot of time with his blonde wife. But they had an explanation to the effect that "she couldn't come to understand that in the upper bracket of life you have to devote a lot of hours to business."

In May 1980, Price Jr. had made a will that didn't mention Vickie, but left his property to a trust fund for his three young children until they reached age 21. The will made no estimate of the value of the estate.

One newspaper reporter was told by Liberty residents and associates that Price Jr. — since his return to private life after departing the political arena — had sometimes neglected his businesses, on occasions went on unexplained trips for periods of time, and had a quick temper. Yet, others related he seemed to be pleased and content with his real estate business, his investments, his community interests and his law school teaching at the South Texas School of Law, Texas Southern University and the University of Houston, all located in the Houston area.

Certainly Price Jr.'s outward appearance changed after he returned to the private business world from state politics. Where coat and tie had been his uniform, Price switched to blue jeans, shirt and boots as his regular attire. He dressed in casual Western clothes most of the time and was wearing them the night he was shot to death in his ranch home.

Price Jr. was popular in his home community, where his

private law practice and businesses were going well, from all outward evidence. He moved his law firm-real estate office to a portable building on North Main next to one of his mobile home developments. Associates said Price Jr. spent 12, 14, 16 hours a day on business — trying cases, selling homes, working on real estate developments.

Through questioning friends, associates and relatives, officers were able to fill in most of the activities of both Vickie and Price on Monday. The Daniels seemingly had started the fateful day in good moods. Price spent most of the day at his office in Liberty, and Vickie apparently stayed to herself at the ranch home, going out about 4 p.m. to pick up her 11-year-old daughter at a Liberty school.

Vickie had phoned a Liberty mobile home dealer, with whom Price was a partner in the business, later Monday afternoon to talk about a possible mobile home purchase. Vickie had mentioned during the phone conversation that she was going to ask her husband for the down payment for an apartment that night.

A friend related that he had talked with Price on the phone Monday evening, probably around 5:30 p.m.

"I talked to him a couple of hours before it happened, and he was in high spirits, very upbeat," the friend recalled. Price left his office about 6:30 p.m. in his blue pickup truck. Normally, it would be about a five minute drive from office to the ranch home north of town.

Since the first call on the shooting had been received at 7:43 p.m., that meant the events that culminated in the tragic shooting of Price Daniel Jr., had taken place in slightly over an hour.

In reconstructing the evening's happenings, Sheriff Eckols learned that the crying, screaming Vickie Daniel had been on the phone about 20 minutes when reporting the

357

shooting.

An ambulance bearing two medical technicians was the first vehicle to reach the ranch, followed closely by a local radio station owner who had heard the siren, called police and learned an ambulance had been sent to the Daniel place. The radioman was an acquaintance of the family. Minutes later sheriffs officers had sirened up to the ranch home, the first being Deputy John Stapleton and reserve Deputy Steve Shelburne.

They saw that Daniel's blue and silver pickup was parked in the driveway, the passenger-side door standing open and the dome light on. Two cars belonging to the couple were parked in the carport.

Bill Buchanan, the owner of Radio Station KPXE, saw Vickie Daniel struggling with the two ambulance attendants, who were trying to restrain the obviously hysterical blonde.

"She was trying to bite . . . she scratched . . . She was babbling like a child," Buchanan said later. Buchanan himself received a scratch on his forehead when he tried to assist the ambulance men in controlling Mrs. Daniel, he said. She was strapped to a stretcher and rushed to the hospital in Liberty.

Upon arrival and entering the house and finding Daniel's body on the hall floor, one of the deputies had asked Vickie Daniel where the weapon was, the radioman recalled.

According to Buchanan, the wife had answered, "In the frog room." The officers at first thought Vickie was talking about the children's playroom, but they discovered that the "frog room" was a guest bedroom near the kitchen, a room that had been decorated with pictures of frogs, big and little. The .22 caliber bolt action Remington rifle was on the floor of the "frog room."

On the kitchen table were clothes that appeared to have just been picked up at a dry cleaning plant. The bag that the clothing apparently came from, along with some legal papers, were found on the front seat of Daniel's pickup. The door on the driver's side of the pickup was locked.

A search of the house showed no evidence of attempted robbery or burglary. No dresser drawers were open, no valuables appeared to have been disturbed.

Whatever had happened in the Daniel home after Price Jr.'s arrival seemingly had happened quickly and certainly violently, and at this point the direction of the investigation was pointed right at the blonde wife.

District Attorney Wilborn told reporters:

"Our investigation has led us to believe that the injury was inflicted by Vickie Daniel, and therefore our investigation at this time is focusing upon . . . the crime scene, scientific analysis, and trace-metal tests on both the decedent and Vickie Daniel's hands."

Sheriff Eckols, his face grim under his broad western hat, said, "It was not an accident and not self-inflicted."

On Tuesday, District Attorney Wilborn drove to Houston to get the report on the autopsy, and then returned to Liberty. The pathologist found that the fatal slug entered Daniel's stomach just below the navel, traveling from front to back and upward at about a 20 degree angle. A fragment of the bullet had ruptured the small intestine and severed the aorta artery, causing death, the autopsy showed. The slug lodged against the spine. It was estimated the shot had been fired from more than two feet away.

What had happened to the other bullet fired remained a mystery for a while. After a search of several hours, however, it finally was discovered that the slug had apparently gone through the ceiling and out the roof, investigators said.

The house was gone over for evidence by crime scene technicians from the Harris County Sheriff's Department at Houston.

Sheriff Eckols was not happy about the fact that he hadn't been able to question Vickie Daniel up to this point.

"Mrs. Daniel's attorney said she fired one warning shot, before the fatal shot that killed her husband," the sheriff told reporters. The sheriff said Daniel apparently was moving toward his wife when the fatal shot was fired, but pointed out that no weapon had been found on Daniel or near his body.

Eckols said he had tried to talk to Mrs. Daniel, but she refused on the advice of her attorney.

But Sheriff Eckols told newsmen, "By God, I'm going to talk to her, I'm going to talk to her in the morning. She knows me, and I'm going to ask what went on out there."

The outspoken sheriff had some doubts about the defense theory apparently being advanced by Vickie Daniel's lawyer.

"If she was afraid of him, she could have run," Eckols said. "As long as she doesn't talk to me, she's in worse shape. She's hiding something, don't you think? I told her she can't go back into the house until I talk to her. I knew him (Price Jr.) all his life. He's not a violent person. He's got a great personality. There's no way he could be violent and hide it from me. I'm not taking up for him. I'm telling the truth."

Early Wednesday morning, Sheriff Eckols did get to talk briefly with Vickie Daniel in her hospital room. However, the sheriff later told reporters, "She said she did not want to discuss it."

Investigators revealed that a trace-metal test had been made on Vickie's hands to determine if she might have fired a shot from a gun recently. The test was made several hours after the shooting and did show that she had "held metal," officers said, but it was not disclosed whether the test conclusively showed she had fired a gun. It also was revealed there were fingerprints on the .22 rifle, but District Attorney Wilborn said it had not been determined whose prints were on the weapon, at that point in the probe.

As the investigators continued to sift through the evidence and interview friends of both Price Jr., and Vickie, District Attorney Wilborn again answered the questions of reporters as to whether charges would be filed in the shooting death.

"The investigation thus far has led us to believe the fatal wound was inflicted by his wife," said the prosecutor. "But we have yet to determine whether it was a homicide, in self-defense, provoked or an accident." He said the case would be presented to a county grand jury the following week.

Meanwhile with the overcast, gray, cold day matching the occasion, hundreds of mourners packed the First United Methodist Church in Liberty for funeral services for the state's popular young ex politician whose death still was shrouded in mystery. Present for the final rites, although friends said later they had tried to dissuade her from coming, was the blonde widow, Vickie. Dressed in a dark navy blue suit, shielding her face from photographers and crying quietly, the woman suspected of firing the fatal shot arrived on the arm of a relative. She sat in a pew near the back of the church — 17 pews behind the Daniel family whose members apparently were not aware of her presence until after the services.

In his eulogy the Rev. Marvin D. Agnew described Price Jr. as "the epitome of life, a person who always thought there would be a rainbow in the sky, and always believed there was good in everyone."

"He loved to be around children, they fascinated him," the minister said. "Price Daniel had on occasion said he wanted to be the director of an orphanage or work in a day camp with children."

Vickie Daniel left the church to return to the hospital immediately after the services and did not attend the graveside rites in the Daniel family cemetery on a quiet hill on the Daniel ranch. An attorney representing Vickie would not permit her to talk to reporters. But the lawyer told newsmen, "I hope toward the end of the weekend she can be released from the hospital. But until such time as the sheriff's investigation is complete, she does not want to make any statements that might impede the investigation."

On Feb. 4, 1981, the Liberty County grand jury met and returned a murder indictment against Vickie Daniel in the shooting death of her husband. When arraigned on the murder indictment before District Judge Clarence Cain, she answered softly "not guilty" when asked to enter a plea to the charge. She was clad in the same navy blue suit she had worn to her husband's funeral.

Following the five-minute court proceeding, Mrs. Daniel told reporters, "I did not intentionally shoot my husband."

Later in February, Mrs. Daniel retained famed Texas criminal lawyer Richard "Racehorse" Haynes to defend her on the murder charge and also to represent her in custody suits by her sister-in-law and her first husband seeking custody of her three children. Haynes told newsmen that facts behind the murder charge will show that Vickie Daniel was a "battered wife."

During a child custody hearing for his client conducted at Houston on Feb. 24th, Haynes dropped a bombshell during cross-examination of Daniel's sister-in-law when he asked if Vickie Daniel had ever confided in her whether

362

Daniel ever had problems with marijuana or "young boys . . . bringing black boys around who stayed there."

The witness denied any knowledge of such information, and the presiding judge ordered Haynes to abandon that line of questioning. But later Haynes told reporters he did not ask the questions frivolously but had a definite purpose in mind.

"I don't want to give away any secrets at this point," Haynes said, "but suffice it to say the questions were not just off the wall. You didn't see the tip of the iceberg. All I can tell you is that we intend to develop the factual situation as fully as we can do it, put it in the proper context."

The defense lawyers were reported to have possession of about 200 letters Price Jr. had written to persons other than his wife. The letters are sealed evidence and filed with the court.

The attorney for Price Jr.'s sister-in-law rejected Haynes' suggestions of impropriety by Daniel. He said, "I am certain when the evidence is in Price will be shown to be a good, decent citizen and all the innuendoes cast at him will be shown false. It is regrettable that he is dead and can't answer for himself."

During the hearing that still was underway when this story was written, Vickie Daniel took the stand and tearfully testified, "I am a good mother and I love my children."

She took the Fifth Amendment when asked if she had shot her husband in self defense and when questioned about letters removed from a warehouse that contained Daniel's belongings.

Vickie Daniel is free on $50,000 bond on the murder charge, and must be presumed innocent of the charge unless or until proven otherwise at a later trial after due process.

Kid McCoy's Own Story of the Mors Death Mystery

by Norman Selby

After a lifetime of triumph came tragedy. Norman Selby—"Kid McCoy"—champion of the prize-ring, became the idol of thousands of sport fans—only to run afoul of the law. He was tried for the murder of Mrs. Teresa Mors. A jury of "twelve men and true" brought in a verdict of manslaughter against him. Did he kill the woman who shared his home? Here he tells his own dramatic story of what happened that fatal night last August.

Norman Selby, known to prize-fight fans everywhere as "Kid McCoy," was held in Los Angeles County Jail awaiting trial for murder. On November 20th, 1924, an investigator for his defense, Mrs. Pearl Antibus, sat with him. To her he told his story. Here it is:

I put a leg of lamb and vegetables in the oven at 4 P.M., August 12th, for our dinner, Teresa's and mine. At 5:30 P.M. Teresa phoned me to bring the car to Seventh and Carondolet Streets, Los Angeles, where I met Emden and Teresa walking up from the Mors art store. She told me to wait for her as she wanted to see Kay Rosenthal at her store about one block west, so I turned the car about and waited down the street until Teresa came out.

She and Emden got in the back seat, Teresa remarking

that she wanted to talk over something with Emden, and for me to drive them out to see Mr. Jones, her attorney.

When we arrived there, I stopped in front of Mr. Jones' house — with my car facing the wrong way, as there was no traffic. I left the car standing in that position until Jones arrived. Then the three walked up a few doors away and stood talking. I decided to turn the car around, and as I did they came back to Jones' house and went in. I looked at a clock and saw it was after six, and remembered I had left the fire burning under our dinner, so I drove to the apartment and turned out the gas.

I took a shower and changed my clothes. Before I left, a fellow brought me three bottles of Scotch, for which I paid him. I had ordered it that afternoon. When I looked at the time, I saw it was after seven, and as Jones did not have a phone, I walked down to the store. As no one was there, I went to Alvarado Street, got a cigar, and walked back to the store. (Teresa and I had an agreement always to meet at the store if separated.)

I saw Teresa entering the store, and Jones and Emden sitting outside in Jones' car. They saw me and called: "Come here."

I went over, and one of them asked me: "Why didn't you wait?"

"I'm not in the habit of being treated like a chauffeur," I said. "I wouldn't treat you like that."

I had taken them all to lunch that day, and paid for it myself.

I told them I was damn sore about it. They both apologized, and said they didn't mean anything by it.

I started to walk across the alleyway and wait for Teresa when Jones got out of the car and came over. He asked me in a confidential way not to say anything to Teresa about it (about the way I felt) as she had more trouble than she could stand ordinarily, and that her nerves might give out. I told him "All right."

Then Teresa and I bid Jones and Emden good night and walked down Seventh to Hoover. While she waited on the corner I got the car. "I'm too upset to eat," she said and so we drove around to Wilshire Place and talked things over.

Then I remembered I had an appointment with a Mr. Gentz of the United Studios at the drug store at Seventh and Hoover, so I told Teresa to drive the car around through Sunset Place and pick me up on the corner, as it was just eight o'clock.

I walked back to the drug store and asked a stranger if he was Gentz. He said "No." I waited ten minutes, then told the owner of the drug store that if a fellow called, to say I waited ten minutes. Then I left.

As I got to the corner, Teresa came along and stopped. I got in and we drove past her store, then up Alvarado to Eighth Street and out to Leeward Avenue, a few doors west of Nottingham, where we sat and talked over the different things.

Teresa said: "Let's go to the apartment and eat, then go to bed. My nerves are terrible!" She put her arms about my neck and kissed me many times.

I drove back. She went in alone, as usual. I put up the car and went upstairs to the apartment. Teresa was in the kitchen eating a sandwich when I entered.

I took a .32 gun out and put it on the living-room table as usual. I told her to sit at the table, and I would make a nice sandwich and bring in a drink, which I did. She told me her feet were hurting her, so I pulled her shoes off.

The sandwich was too big. "Where is the bread knife?" she asked. "I want to cut this thing in half."

I brought the knife and cut the sandwich in two and laid the knife on the table between us.

We talked and smoked some cigarettes. It was then around 11 P.M. I suggested we get to bed early, as she had only a few hours' sleep the night before.

"I'm too worried to sleep! I wish I could go to sleep and never, never wake up!" she said.

She was very despondent, and as I gave her a hug and kissed her eyes, she began crying and sobbing as if her heart would break.

I took the dishes out to the kitchen, but never thought of the bread knife that she had been playing with in front of her. When I returned, she was still crying. I tried to cheer her up. I brought her another drink of Scotch and seltzer, but she pushed it away, and I drank it.

Then I said: "Suppose I jump to New York until things blow over. I don't like to go around keeping away from the store" — as per her agreement with Mors. I had just lit a cigar and was sitting down in the big chair when she said: "Norman, would you leave me now?"

"Well, dear," I replied, "it will only be for a few weeks, and then everything will be over. Mors will be gone, and we can do as we planned."

"Oh, I can't stand it any more! I'll just end it all!" and as she talked she grabbed the bread knife and tried to run it through her heart.

I grabbed her right wrist and almost knocked the table over trying to get the knife away from her. She was twice as strong as I was, and I had to get rough. I shoved her head back and finally got hold of her right hand that held the knife. In the struggle I jerked the hand upward, and the handle struck her in the mouth. She gave a little scream as I got her hand back in my grip and got her over to the sofa.

I pulled her fingers off, and as I got the knife I saw that she had my gun in her left hand, holding it backward, pointing at our heads!

I tried to grab it, but missed. She had hold of my coat. I grabbed her left arm about the elbow. She pulled the trigger with her thumb, and I closed my eyes and shook my head as I felt the flame in my face.

I didn't know if I had been hit or not until she wilted. In her nervous condition and excitement the gun was discharged. It was pointed toward our heads. As I grabbed her arm the gun was discharged, and I closed my eyes and shook my head to find out if she had struck me. Then I felt her wilt and her arms dropped. As she wilted the gun fell on the floor.

I caught her under the arms, held her in a sitting position. I laid her head back on the sofa and run to the bathroom for a towel, wet the end of it, and come back and wiped away the blood and kissed her. "Speak to me! Teresa, speak to me!" I cried.

Then I became faint, and I went to the kitchen and took a tumbler of Scotch whisky. It gagged me, and I spilt nearly half of it on the outside of my face. It ran down my throat and saturated my clothes. Then I went back to Teresa. She had toppled over to the side of the sofa, and the blood was streaming out. I washed if off again and tried to put her on the sofa, but she was too heavy.

I caught her under the arms, and half carrying her, her feet dragging, I got her to the side of the bed, but could not lift her into it.

I took another tumbler of Scotch and got my big gun, intending to shoot myself in front of the mirror. I saw the knife lying on the floor. I picked it up and tried to straighten out the blade. I cleaned up the place the best I could and wrung out the towels, then as I stood with gun in hand I thought I heard a voice telling me: "Go get Mors! Go get Mors!"

I went in and lay down by the side of Teresa. In so doing I saw my picture by her right side, and I put it on her breast. I kissed her several times. I put my arm across her and kissed her again and again — and that is the last I remember until I was in an automobile with a policeman by my side.

Looking across the street, I saw George Home in front of the Nottingham Apartments. Then Captain Cline came over and told the officers to take off the handcuffs, and he took me across the street to an apartment in the Nottingham and sat me on a sofa in a room downstairs where I lived. I looked on my hand and saw a ring that I knew was not mine, so I took it off and put it under the cushion I was sitting on. I knew something was wrong, but could remember nothing that had happened — not even Teresa — so I sat there until they took me to the station.

Murder of Bob ("Hogan's Heroes") Crane

by Thomas Grass

Scottsdale, Ariz., June 29, 1978

Virginia Berry was young actress whose career was just beginning to blossom. She had felt it was a major break in June of 1978 when she had been contacted by her agent and offered the female lead opposite Bob Crane in a touring dinner theater play called, "Beginner's Luck." The actress who had been portraying the part had left for another engagement, and Miss Berry was hired to pick up in the middle of a scheduled five week engagement at the Windmill Dinner Theater in Scottsdale, Arizona.

Crane, a 49-year-old star who had gained prominence during the six-year television run of the series, "Hogan's Heroes," owned rights to the marital farce called "Beginner's Luck," and he was touring around the country with the play.

After a week of stage performances with Bob Crane, Virginia Berry had discussed her acting ambitions with the star. An active video-tape hobbyist, Crane had suggested she video-tape a performance of "Beginner's Luck" and use the recording as part of an advertising brochure for her agent to help in obtaining other acting jobs, possibly some in television and movies.

As suggested, a video-tape recording was made of the play's performance on Wednesday, June 28, 1978.

Shortly after two o'clock on Thursday, the following afternoon, Miss Berry headed for Crane's $365-a-month rented apartment in the Winfield Apartment Complex in the seventy-four hundred block of East Chaparral in Scottsdale. The two-bedroom, ground-floor apartment was leased by the Windmill Theater for use by actors playing there.

Miss Berry had an appointment for two-thirty with Crane to re-tape the soundtrack on the video recording from the previous evening. The picture portion of the tape had turned out well, but the sound had been muffled. Crane had agreed to work with her closeup on the microphones to re-dub the sound-track.

Miss Berry knocked at the apartment door. There was no answer. Realizing that actors worked until late at night and often did not retire until the early morning hours. Miss Berry thought Crane might still be asleep. She tried the door and discovered it was unlocked and opened it carefully, calling his name.

The apartment was dark, curtains in the living room closed. There was enough light, however, for the woman to notice a half-empty bottle of scotch and a bottle of vodka on a coffee table.

The actress, who'd been in the apartment a few times earlier in the week to talk over the play and rehearse lines with Crane, crossed to the bedroom door, which was open.

A few seconds later, shortly before two-thirty on Thursday afternoon, June 29, 1978, the halls of the apartment complex were pierced by a series of screams. A resident of another downstairs apartment heard the screams, noticed they were coming from the Windmill apartment and entered the open door to find an attractive young lady sobbing hysterically. When she indicated an open bedroom doorway, he crossed the room and clicked on a light switch. A body, the head smashed and bloody and unrecognizable, was lying on the bed in the room. The resident notified by telephone the Scottsdale Police

371

Department of the apparent homicide, then tried to comfort the crying woman.

The city of Scottsdale, a suburb of Phoenix, has only about two or three homicides a year on the average. The city does not maintain a central detective bureau or homicide unit.

Instead, the city is divided into three geographical areas, each area covered by a separate team of uniformed officers and detectives. The same detectives who investigate burglaries, robberies, grand theft auto and other crimes, also handle the murder investigations.

Lieutenant Ron Dean is the officer in charge of Scottsdale's district three, operating out of a unit headquarters building only seven blocks from the site of the murder. Lieutenant Dean directed a crew of seven officers to eventually work on the case. His top aide during the investigation was to be Dennis Borkenhagen.

Detective Borkenhagen and Lieutenant Dean were at the scene of the reported murder within minutes of the arrival of the first two patrol cruisers to answer the emergency call from the radio dispatcher.

Though thoroughly upset, actress Virginia Berry told the officers of her scheduled appointment with actor Bob Crane, of finding the apartment unlocked, and of entering the bedroom. She saw blood on the bed, she told Dean, but didn't recognize Crane because the dead person had been battered so severely. At first, she said, "I thought it was a woman . . . a woman whose hair was standing on end."

Miss Berry said at that point she had yelled Crane's name, then had realized the victim was a man. Finally, she claimed she recognized Crane's wristwatch on the arm of the dead man and had screamed.

By three o'clock in the afternoon, the apartment was crowded with police technicians taking photographs, dusting for fingerprints and searching for other possible evidence. Detective Borkenhagen and Lieutenant Dean walked through the apartment together. They paused before the coffee table with the two bottles of liquor. "Looks like he had company last night," the detective said to Dean.

Dean nodded. The actress who had found the body had mentioned the scotch and vodka. Crane, she had said, drank little. When he did, he only drank vodka and orange juice and usually no more than one glass.

At this time, the officers were relatively sure the dead man was the famed actor, but a positive identification could not be made. Miss Berry said she was not sure. The victim had been lying on his right side. There were deep head wounds, crushing the skull, and the face was totally unrecognizable. It was to be some two hours before fingerprints would positively identify the slain man as Bob Crane.

Lieutenant Dean looked around the living room. The actor had apparently hung his pants neatly over a chair in the living room. His shirt was on a hanger. The first officers to respond to the homicide call had found Crane's glasses on a table beside the fatal bed.

Other detectives had found his billfold and keys on the kitchen table. The key to the front door of the apartment was still on the key ring. There had been a black bag, a photographer's equipment bag with several zippers, on the bed beside the body at the time it was discovered. Members of the lab crew were going through the bag, which apparently contained several personal effects of the actor. Dean discovered that the 1977 Chevrolet Monte Carlo, a rental car driven by Crane during his stay in Scottsdale, was parked in its normal spot at the complex.

Then came the discovery that was to drive this murder into the realm of the truly sensational. The first detectives to give a cursory search of the apartment had noted expensive video-tape equipment, its presence explained by Miss Berry when she told of the reason for her appointment with the actor that afternoon. In a closet, officers found expensive photography gear which indicated that Crane developed his own pictures, using a bathroom as a darkroom. Several loose large glossy black and white photographs were found, along with several albums of mounted photographs. All were sexually explicit, many of them showing nude women and others obviously taken with a time-delay mechanism on a camera of Crane involved in various sexual acts with many different women.

"It's going to be a bucket of worms," breathed Detective Borkenhagen. The investigators made no mention of the pornography to the news media when first information on the murder was released. If there could be an early solution to the crime not connected with the sexual "art," there would be no need to drag it into the case. If the solution proved difficult, the investigators knew that the photographs, if the women depicted could be traced, might serve as eventual clues. Late that afternoon, Lieutenant Dean reported on his findings thus far to his immediate superior, Captain John Pratt of the Scottsdale PD. "We think the killer could have been someone he knew since there were no signs of a struggle and no sign of forced entry into the apartment," Dean said.

In response to a question from the captain, Dean said that it was possible, at least it looked to be a possibility, that a woman could have struck the blow that killed the television star. "He was wearing shorts and an undershirt. When we found him, a sheet was pulled high around the head. It took us a little while to identify him," noted Dean. "He had been lying on his side and his head was smashed in so it was hard to get a good view of his face."

The preliminary check by a man from the county Medical

Examiner's office had indicated death had probably been caused by the blow to the head. However, a length of electrical cord had been tied around Crane's neck. "We think the cord came from the apartment, off the TV set. The plugs had been pulled out of the wall and the back of the TV set and the cord we found around his neck matched."

Officers were dispatched to the Windmill Theater to talk to the manager and others involved in the production of the play. Other officers were detailed to the grim work of contacting relatives and friends of the slain man in Los Angeles and in Seattle, where they learned his estranged wife was living.

Lieutenant Dean talked to newsmen late Thursday concerning the murder. He told the media, "We have no prior reports of burglaries or robberies in the apartment and the neighborhood is not plagued with these crimes. But there was a report by a neighbor that loud noises and some door-banging were heard in Crane's apartment sometime Thursday morning."

The officer said that since announcement of the murder had been made many people had contacted the police department voluntarily and that his detectives had questioned numerous people concerning where and when they had last seen the actor.

It had been discovered that it was Crane's habit to frequent several night spots in the area after the performances of his play concluded each evening and police had received several reports that he was seen at a nightclub after his theater performance Wednesday evening.

"I understand that he did go to the nightclubs and was very personable, giving out autographs and all that," Dean told newsmen. "But I heard he was not much of a drinking man and not into drugs at all."

To Captain Pratt, Lieutenant Dean discounted the possibility the motive for the slaying had been robbery. Quite a bit of money was still in the actor's wallet, found on the kitchen table, and the apartment had been full of the expensive camera and video-tape equipment. Even though the car keys had been available to the killer, the vehicle had been left untouched in the parking lot. The detectives investigating the case were to continue their work throughout the night. They had opportunity during the evening hours to talk to his co-stars in the play and the management and staff of the Windmill Theater, since the performance of "Beginner's Luck" had been canceled for the evening. A taped recording answered all telephone calls to the theater: "Due to the untimely death of Mr. Bob Crane, the run of his show has been canceled."

The theater's public relations director was crushed when she learned of the brutal murder.

"He was such a pleasant person," she said. "He was always — he was very physical. He always gave you a little kiss and a little hug. It was a closer kind of relationship than the stars who come in and sit across the table from you and say, 'Well, what have you got for me?'

"The last time I saw him, Monday night, he kissed me good-bye."

An autopsy was conducted on the remains of the slain actor Friday morning by Maricopa County Medical Examiner, Dr. Heinz Karnitschnig. Dr. Karnitschnig called Dean to report on his findings. He said that in his opinion Crane was struck on the left side of the head as he was asleep and "never knew what hit him."

"Have you been able to establish anything about the time of death?" the lieutenant wanted to know.

The ME said the nearest he could pin-point the death was sometime Thursday.

Lieutenant Dean also discussed the examination with Eloy

Ysasi, an investigator with the Medical Examiner's office and former homicide detective with the Phoenix Police Department. Dean questioned Ysasi about the electrical cord found around the neck of the dead man.

"It didn't strangle him," said Ysasi. "The cord was put on after he was dead, but it was put on tight. It looks like somebody walked in on him while he was in bed and smacked him on the head a couple of times."

On Friday, Captain Pratt and Lieutenant Dean began a modern process called "charting." Charting involves the laying out of a case graphically, a relatively new technique used in homicide investigations. As Captain Pratt describes the technique, "It's designed to give you a picture of what is happening as opposed to having to read it all in a printed report."

As reconstructed by the investigators who had examined the murder scene, this is the way it is believed Crane met his death.

The murder weapon was heavy, probably the handle from an automobile jack or a lug wrench. The weapon used to slay Crane measured somewhere between a half to three-quarters of an inch in diameter.

At the time of the attack, Crane was asleep on his right side facing away from the bedroom windows. Detectives questioning friends of the actor had determined this was a sleeping habit he had, so that morning light would not wake him up.

The first blow from the killer cut open Crane's scalp, covering the weapon with blood. According to the medical report, that first blow would have been sufficient to render Crane totally unconscious, even if the noise of the attack had started to awaken him. The second blow was delivered with a short arc, slinging only a couple of droplets of blood onto the ceiling and table lamp near the bed.

The Scottsdale detectives theorized that if the killer had been a woman, she would have had to swing the heavy weapon in a wider arc, which would have splattered more blood onto the ceiling. It would have taken considerable strength in the forearm and wrist to hit the second blow with the short arc described by the coroner's report.

The wounds were deep and the skull was totally crushed, indicating the blows were delivered by a strong person.

Lieutenant Dean and his men theorized that the killer was probably a man who knew Crane, and he took his time in the killing. There were no signs of haste or excitement in the apartment. The killer had even taken the time to wipe the blood off the weapon and take it with him. The material used to clean the weapon had been the sheet on the bed.

By Monday, four days after the slaying, detectives were no closer to a solution of the crime then when they had first arrived on the murder scene. It was felt that officers would have to delve further into the messy situation involving the sexually explicit photographs found in the apartment. Lab technicians had also checked the video-tape equipment and had found dozens of video-tape cassettes of Crane performing sex acts with different women. The actor, said one detective in a wry comment, liked to watch himself perform.

"He was really into pornography. But he was completely open about it," one friend of the slain actor said.

Police, through their questioning of many witnesses, had learned that Crane apparently never forced his photographic interests on his women friends. In other words, according to the information developed, all of the female subjects had done their posing voluntarily.

But did one of the women have a boyfriend or a husband who took exception to the posing? The chore of identifying the women was long and involved.

Checks also had been made into the actor's relationship with his estranged wife, a blond actress herself who had appeared occasionally with him in his "Hogan's Heroes" TV series.

Crane and his wife had separated in November of 1977, and he had been hit with divorce papers while getting off a plane in Cincinnati toward the end of that year.

The investigators learned that Crane and his wife had talked by telephone a couple of times per week, but there were apparently no attempts being made to save the marriage.

The detectives also discovered that two weeks before his murder, Crane's wife and seven-year-old son had arrived in Scottsdale without warning for a visit. Reportedly, Crane had been furious about the sudden visit. The wife and child had left Phoenix by plane the next day.

Early Wednesday morning, just a few hours before the killing, neighbors reported overhearing Crane talking loudly over the telephone. It was discovered that the telephone argument had been with his wife, who was on vacation in Seattle at the time.

A possible new complication was uncovered when it was determined Crane had just begun a relationship with a young, pretty and blonde Phoenix woman. He had been dating the young girl for the two weeks prior to the slaying.

The major undertaking of the team of detectives was an attempt to reconstruct the actor's movements immediately prior to his death.

It was learned that a woman friend of the actor had watched the Wednesday evening performance with a girl friend of hers at the invitation of Crane. The actor had not gone out with the two women after the play, instead returning to his apartment alone. He had been joined at the apartment by a friend of his, a sales representative for an electronics firm who had known Crane for some years. The friend had left Scottsdale the next morning, reportedly flying to his home in Los Angeles long before the discovery of the slain actor's body. On Saturday, Lieutenant Dean and Detective Borkenhagen flew to Los Angeles to meet with the sales representative, and to question him pertaining to the events of that evening.

On Monday, the friend returned with the officers to Scottsdale to attempt to aid in the investigation. The man told the detectives he often traveled on business to the cities where Crane was appearing, and that he had been with Crane the day before the actor was murdered. The friend's assistance was requested in an attempt to identify some of the women in the photographs found in the murder apartment.

The sales representative said he had been in the apartment with Crane at the time he had received the phone call that had erupted into the loud conversation reportedly overheard by neighbors. The witness told officers the call was from Crane's wife. He described the conversation as "loud, but not necessarily an argument."

About a half hour after the call, the friend said that he and Crane met the two women who had been at the performance of the play the previous evening as the actor's guests, and the four people went together to an all-night coffee shop. They spent about forty-five minutes in the restaurant, with Crane leaving alone for his apartment at about two-thirty in the morning. The electronics salesman said he had gone from the coffee shop to the airport to catch an early morning plane to Los Angeles but that he had called Crane from the airport shortly before his flight had left, and that the actor was apparently in good humor and alone at the time of that conversation.

That, apparently, was the last time anyone had seen or talked to Crane before his murder.

Another trail followed by the investigators had led to a bit of confusion. The apartment was maintained by the management of the Windmill Dinner Theater for actors appearing in the regular plays throughout the year. A set of keys was given to he current user of the apartment, with a duplicate set kept in a ocked drawer in the theater itself some miles away. When police tried to obtain the keys kept at the theater, the housing manager reported after checking that the set normally kept at he theater was missing.

Since so many people had used the unit over the past couple of years, police felt that many other duplicate copies could have been made at various times, and that it would be practically impossible to track down all who might possibly have a key to the apartment.

Using the identifications made by the electronic salesman friend of Crane's, detectives contacted and interviewed many of the women depicted in the pornographic pictures and videotapes found in the murder apartment.

All said that the photographs and video-tapes had been made voluntarily, that no force had been involved. And police were able to clear most of the women and their boyfriend/husbands of any possible implication in the crime when they were able to provide adequate proof of their whereabouts on the morning of the murder.

An intensive search was carried out for the murder weapon. Investigators had searched the entire apartment complex and the surrounding grounds on the day the body was discovered, without uncovering the weapon which the coroner had believed to be the handle from an automobile jack or a lug wrench.

Two weeks after the slaying, Lieutenant Dean again talked to news reporters.

"We feel we're making headway, but there are so many people to interview both in and out of the state. Police agencies in California and other states have been extremely cooperative, assisting us with interviews in their area."

The lieutenant said that each witness questioned "seems to

lead to another," and he said until all the interviews were completed the probe would continue.

"We cannot know all that is needed to make the investigation complete until the loose ends are tied up," he added.

"Right now we're stepping it off and pursuing as many leads as possible. Unless we get some kind of a break . . . such as the killer walking in and confessing . . . we expect to take whatever time it requires to make our investigation as complete as possible."

When the slaying had first been announced it made a big splash in Los Angeles, where Crane had enjoyed his greatest success. Top-rated disc jockey Gary Owens, the one-time mustachioed announcer on "Laugh-In," reported in an Associated Press interview that Crane had been earning almost $100,000 annually as a disc jockey when he left the security of radio to test his skill as a full-time actor in "Hogan's Heroes."

Said Owens, "He always wanted to be an actor as much as he wanted to be in radio. I remember a comment he made to me one day when we were having lunch sometime in the early 1960s. He said 'I want to be the next Jack Lemmon.'"

Gary Owens and Bob Crane had both begun their careers as disc jockeys in the Los Angeles area at about the same time. "He got a big name for himself in radio on the west coast," said Owens. "He used to interview stars and producers like Frank Sinatra and Otto Preminger. He was truly a talented man and he's going to be missed. He was a fine actor and also a fine drummer."

While still maintaining his radio show in Los Angeles, Crane had made guest appearances on the old "Dick Van Dyke Show" and then had a continuing role on the "Donna Reed Show" in the 1950s.

Yet he continued his full-time radio employment until he was offered the starring role as Colonel Hogan, leader of a group of American prisoners in a German prison camp during World War II, "Hogan's Heroes" was on television for six years. After that series folded, he also stareed in a short lived, "The Bob Crane Show," which lasted only a single season.

In the two years before his death, Crane spent most of his time on the road with touring plays, with most of his success in the six months prior to his death with the property called "Beginner's Luck."

On Thursday, July 20, Scottsdale police made an unsuccessful attempt to obtain either a complaint or an arrest warrant for a suspect in the slaying of the actor.

The next day, Friday, Maricopa County Attorney Charles Hyder confirmed that investigators working the Crane case had sought a complaint from his office, but he told newsmen the information was insufficient "Even to show probable cause."

He continued, "Some of our people talked with the Scottsdale detectives, but the matter was referred back for further investigation."

Dean, speaking for the Scottsdale Police Department on Monday, July 24th, said that he was only asking for issuance of a complaint and that he believes the evidence he has is sufficient to show "probable cause."

"But the suspect is out of state and therefore we can't make an arrest without the proper paperwork," added Dean. "Our investigation will continue long after any complaint is filed."

Dean revealed that a representative from the County Attorney's office had accompanied investigators when they had traveled to Los Angeles a few days earlier to serve subpoenas they had obtained from a judge in Maricopa County based on information garnered from the investigation.

"We could not serve the subpoenas for certain documents because they were faulty and not legal in California," explained

Dean.

Maricopa County Attorney Charles Hyder told the news media he had hoped the subpoenas would be honored without going through a lengthy interstate process and added, "We don't have a case to issue subpoenas at this time."

The County Attorney added, "What they (police) think and what can be proved in court are two different things." The prosecuter indicated that he would not issue a complaint until he believes the evidence is sufficient to stand up in court.

On Friday, August 4, 1978 representatives from the County Attorney's office and the Scottsdale police department met to review evidence in the case.

The meeting was attended by Scottsdale Police Chief Walter M. Nemetz and Lieutenant Ron Dean.

Said Hyder after the meeting, "We just reviewed the evidence they had presented and we discussed some areas we felt had to be explored and requested some other material.

"We were just trying to get some general direction as to where we are going to go to assist them in the case. We are going to give them the legal assistance they need."

Asked by newsmen on that Friday afternoon whether any complaint is likely to be filed in the near future or if there are any additional suspects in the Bob Crane murder, Hyder's answer was: "No comment. My policy is not to discuss active cases."

Since that date investigation of the case had been carried out in secret. Neither the County Attorney's office nor detectives from the Scottsdale Police Department have divulged further information on the investigation.

Only two items of immediate interest have been disclosed since this point in the investigation. Witnesses have been found who report that the photographic equipment bag found on the bed by the body of the victim had normally been kept in a closet. Apparently the killer had taken the bag from the closet, placed it on the bed, unzipped it and removed something from the bag before leaving.

Although hundreds of sexually explicit photographs were found in the murder apartment, police have learned of the existence of at least one other album, a complete book of glossy black and white photographs of sexually explicit acts, that is now missing.

Friends of the slain actor report seeing the album, describing it to police and describing in detail some of the photographs contained, but who verified that that particular album was missing in a complete inventory of the apartment after the murder was not revealed.

So it is possible the killer took two items from the scene after the brutal bludgeon murder; something from the black equipment bag and an album of sexually explicit photographs that in some instances showed the actor engaged in intercourse with at least three different women.

The murder of Bob Crane is still definitely wide open and under intensive, but secret, investigation.

Murder Of The
Beloved Actor

by Bill Ryder

A little more than 100 miles northwest of Santo Domingo, (the capital of the Dominican Republic) lies the minuscule town of Sosua. If you searched a map of the West Indies, you'd be hard-pressed to locate Sosua. But rest assured that once you had spotted it, you'd have discovered a tropical paradise.

In an era marked by stress, Sosua offers the type of ambiance which is tonic to body and soul. Here there are the bucolic delights of well-tended dairy farms. There are the expanse of pristine beach and the clear azure waters of the Atlantic Ocean.

Sosua is a serene area. In its environs, one can contemplate items in his life for which he seldom, if ever, has time under other conditions.

Best of all, for all its otherworldliness, Sosua is only a short flight's distance from the American mainland and an easily accessible refuge from the ratrace there.

At age 68, George Rose had grown increasingly contemplative. Four years earlier he'd begun thinking of a future without the glories and tensions which went with being an internationally acclaimed luminary of stage, screen, and television.

It was then that the magnet, which is Sosua, had attracted him. Rose was beginning to have feelings that the time to think about such things as retirement was almost at hand. A few more stellar roles such as that of the master of ceremonies in "The Mystery of Edwin Drood" (Produced by Joseph Papp) and Rose would be ready to bring down the curtain on his 40-year career as a brilliant actor.

Thus it was that in 1984 he had purchased a magnificently furnished beach house in Sosua. The home, which was just a stone's throw from the warm and inviting Atlantic surf, had contained such niceties as a swimming pool and three master bedrooms.

In the years between 1984 and 1988, Rose had stolen whatever time he could to repair to his West Indies retreat. However, "Edwin Drood" had been one of the great Broadway hits of the decade and it had demanded the lion's share of the actor's time and energy.

The payoff had been big. From 1985 on, "Drood" had played to near sell-out crowds on Broadway as well as on the national company's tour. Rose, who had won a coveted Tony Award for his lead performance, had agreed to stay on for the coast-to-coast swing.

However, the British-born star had become ever more committed to retirement. He had told intimate friends that once the national company tour ended (later this year in California) he was going to call it quits. He would settle permanently in Sosua with his beloved household pets and his huge record collection.

In the meantime, the highly respected thespian continued to occupy a spacious loft in Greenwich Village.

On the first weekend of May 1988, "Drood" finished its Washington, D.C., run. Taking advantage of the three-week break in the show's schedule, Rose had boarded a plane for the Dominican Republic and his beloved Sosua homestead.

Outside of an ugly dispute with household servants that climaxed with their being fired, Rose had settled in to the relaxed and restoring country life. He'd seemed in good health and spirits through the early part of the week.

That's why the shock was so great when his closest friends got the word.

It came at 6:30 a.m., on the morning of Thursday, May 5th. At that very moment, a passerby noticed a red Suzuki car lying upside down in a six-foot roadside ditch about a mile east of Sosua.

Peering into the vehicle's wreckage, the passerby felt his stomach churning at the sight of the balding, gray-haired man pinned there. Fighting back the panic within him, the good Samaritan, knowing that the person in the car was beyond medical help, did the only helpful thing he could. He put in a call for police assistance.

First on-site officers, under the direction of Sergeant Eladio Gomez Morales arrived at the ditch and began their probe into what had caused the apparently fatal accident and a determination of who the victim had been.

The answer to the second question was far more positive than that to the first one. There was no doubt that the person in the rented red vehicle was George Rose. How he and the car had wound up upside down in the ditch along a little used road just a mile from his home was something else.

Morales' first theory was that Rose had been returning from a day trip and had fallen asleep at the wheel. The police sergeant's best guess was that the Suzuki had been traveling at a moderate rate of speed. There was nothing to indicate that it had hit another vehicle or roadway obstruction before careening off the road.

Rose's corpse had been wedged in the front seat. A search of his clothes showed that he had been carrying his passport and $4.14 in American and Dominican currency in his pocket. Of particular interest to the Dominican police officers was the recovery of a plastic bag containing a small quantity of white powder.

Still, there was nothing to indicate that Rose's demise had been anything but the result of an accident which had been caused possibly by a fatal or near-fatal coronary seizure.

For their part, local authorities refused to consider any possibility of violence in the Rose case. Their position was given added weight by the preliminary autopsy report offered by Dr. Anibal Sygal. Dr. Sygal held that the actor had died of a "cardiopulmonary attack of the lungs and the heart." A deep wound in Rose's head was believed to have occurred when the Suzuki overturned. It was thought that the eyeglasses the actor had been wearing had gouged out the flesh. In addition, two 5-to-10-inch-long gashes were noted by forensic experts.

Yet there were those who felt the "accidental death" theory was a little too pat.

Sergeant Morales was one of those. Said the Dominican police officer, "It's possible that his car was pushed with him in it, so we're still investigating a possible murder."

Those who had worked alongside of Rose could not conceive of the fact that Rose might have been the victim of a homicide.

Papp, who had produced one of Rose's great professional triumphs, added, "He was a consummate gentleman who set a standard of conduct that the rest of the acting company always followed.

"To lose him now is unconscionable. He was an old-timer, but his energy made every 21-year-old breathless."

The man the theatrical world was mourning had seen his name in lights in London's West End and New York City's Great White Way for over 40 years. In that time he had won two Tony Awards, the most coveted recognition given by the legitimate stage. He'd also been nominated for three others.

In addition to his "Edwin Drood" role, Rose had appeared in Gilbert and Sullivan's "Pirates of Penzance," and the 1976 revival of "My Fair Lady."

Born in an English village near Oxford, he'd left school at the age of 16 to become a secretary at Oxford University. During World War II, Rose had served three years in the British Army. After that, he began the serious study of music and acting. He then joined the prestigious Old Vic Company and made his New York City debut with them in "Henry IV," in 1946. Critics began heaping praise on him for the ability he showed in various supporting roles with the Royal Shakespeare Company.

Typical comment was that of New York drama critic Brooks Atkinson. Speaking of Rose's efforts in "Much Ado About Nothing," the highly respected *New York Times* reviewer said, "Mr. Rose's Dogberry makes it unnecessary for anyone to play the part again."

During the 1960's, Rose became the favorite of Big Apple audiences. He received his first Tony nomination in the musical, "Coco" in 1969. For his role as Alfred P. Doolittle in the revival of Lerner and Loewe's "My Fair Lady," he received his first Tony Award for best actor in a musical play. "Edwin Drood" marked his second such award.

In addition to his stage work, Rose appeared in more than 30 films. On television, he appeared in the mini series, "Holocaust."

A caring man, the actor also made numerous recordings for the American Foundation for the Blind.

And now he was dead and the probing into the whys and wherefores of his demise were moving inexorably forward.

Dominican lawmen began digging more deeply into recent events in Rose's stay on the historic inland once known as Hispaniola.

Lieutenant Colonel Morilla reported that his people had been checking into reports of trouble within the Rose household. The dead actor had recently been the victim of a robbery. However, Morilla was holding fast at this point to the belief that the cause of Rose's death had been a roadway accident.

But an American woman who had been a close neighbor and friend to Rose's in the Dominican Republic reported that the actor had recently dismissed several members of his household staff at his vacation home following a bitter dispute.

The woman said that when she had viewed the dead man's body at the scene of the car wreck, the injuries she had seen did not seem to be consistent with those which might have occurred in an automobile accident.

The woman's comment brought this rejoinder from Lieutenant Manuel Raposo: "There was absolutely nothing to support the belief that this was a murder."

Assurances from Dominican officials that Rose had not died at the hands of parties unknown did little to lessen the mystery surrounding his death or still the suspicions of American residents of the West Indian island.

On Friday, May 6th, the United States Consulate in the Dominican Republic entered the case. On the basis that a United States citizen had died under somewhat suspicious circumstances, consular officials opted for launching a probe of their own.

Said Peter Brennan, a consular official, "There are many suspicions and theories we must look at. This is a real mystery."

What concerned the State Department representatives was whether drugs or murder had been the primary cause of Rose's death. Because of these misgivings, a woman consul had been dispatched from the capital city of Santo Domingo to the northwest coast community of Sosua to dig for more information on the mysterious slaying.

Under the mandate issued by Brennan, "we need more answers," the dispatched investigator, whom Brennan refused to name, would be looking into these aspects of the baffling case:

First: Talk by stunned neighbors of the dead man that he had been beaten and strangled.

Second: The discovery of the small bag of what had been determined to be cocaine on Rose's body.

Third: Reports of Dominican officials that preliminary autopsy findings had revealed injuries to Rose's skull and spine and that he had died of heart and lung failure. However, more detailed tests remained to be made and the United States Government was anxious to learn what they would reveal.

Fourth: The dismissal by Rose of his domestic personnel in what had been termed "a bitter dispute."

Fifth: The fact that two of Rose's favorite pets — a dog and a parrot — had been slaughtered mysteriously recently.

Sixth: The fact that one of Rose's arms had appeared to have been almost severed when his corpse had been removed from the overturned Suzuki. This wound seemed inconsistent with the crash.

In commenting on the consulate's action in launching its own check, Morilla said, "Public rumor had it that he (Rose) was murdered. The people are talking about it on the streets. We won't know until more tests are made."

Meanwhile, those directing the consular probe said they had already quizzed neighbors of the dead man. They also planned to grill known drug dealers over the weekend of May 13-15.

One item coming in for a share of attention was Rose's homosexual activities and the fact that he had recently adopted an 18-year-old boy as his son.

On this point, Brennan said, "We're trying to establish if he was ever legally adopted or not. If he were, he obviously would be Rose's only living kin."

The consular official added cryptically, "We've expressed

our concerns to the police."

On Sunday, May 8th, new elements were added which only served to deepen the mystery surrounding Rose's death.

These concerned the whereabouts of the actor's corpse. There were conflicting accounts about where the cadaver was currently being held.

In Puerto Plata, where Rose's home was situated, Dominican police spokesman said the body was now in Santiago.

However, police officials in Santiago replied that Rose's remains were on their way back to Puerto Plata for burial.

In the Dominican capital of Santo Domingo, local authorities said the more detailed autopsy on the victim had been completed and the body would be shipped to the United States mainland for interment.

However, Anselmo Silverio, a reporter for the newspaper, La Informacion, said he had been told a complete autopsy had been "set for today (Sunday)" because there were "questions" about how Rose had died.

Said the newspaperman, "The corpse was disfigured as if it had been burned and beaten.

"It was confirmed by Francisco Bencosme, the medical director at Jose Maria Cabral Baez Hospital in Santiago, that Rose's body was sent to a hospital in Santo Domingo for an autopsy to be done (today.)"

Countered a Dominican Police Lieutenant, "They did the autopsy in Santo Domingo on Saturday and this morning they took the body back to Puerto Plata. It is all in the hands of the American embassy now."

At this point in the case, American officials could not be reached for comment.

On Monday, Dominican spokesmen took an even more positive stance that Rose's death had been accidental. They pointed to findings of the Dominican Medical Association that the injuries suffered by the actor had been the result of the crash rather than foul play.

For their part, some of the dead man's close friends felt a sense of relief at this news. From New York, where she was appearing in "The Phantom of The Opera," a women said, "It's a relief to know that. I'd rather think that he died in an accident than been murdered."

While the veritable army of close friends and associates of Rose waited and speculated during the days that followed, the probe in the Dominican Republic continued. Under scrutiny were possible motives which would have driven a killer or killers to slay the man whose life up to the moment of his death had appeared to have been so free from violence.

The general public was not privy to one vital piece of information which would represent a pivotal turn in the case. This was that a second autopsy had been performed and this time results had tilted sharply towards homicide.

The grisly findings would later be described graphically by Dr. Sergio Valdez, president of the Pathologists' Commission of the Dominican Medical Association.

Speaking at a hastily called news conference Thursday, May 12th, Dr. Valdez said, "They beat him, gave him several knocks, and then put him in the car to make it appear as if it were an accident."

The physician also revealed that urine tests carried out on Rose's body had shown small amounts of cocaine.

Reporters who had gathered in the Santo Domingo police offices had one major question on their minds at the police presentation. It was, "Who were they?"

The answer was quick, in coming. "They" consisted of . . .

Domingo Antonio Rafle, 18.

Juan Antonio Vasquez, (Rafle's father).

Maximo Vasquez Padilla (Vasquez's brother and Rafle's

uncle).

Luis Manuel Toribio (allegedly a co-conspirator who had been paid somewhere between $350 and $2,000 to participate).

According to police allegations, Rafle, Vasquez, and Padilla had all allegedly signed confessions as to their role in the Rose killing. The three were now in custody and would shortly recite their alleged complicity to the eagerly waiting press members.

Toribio was still at large and the search for him was continuing. At the news conference, Rafle said that he had planned the murder along with his father, Vasquez, on April 20th, two days before Rose had returned to the island on his vacation.

Taking up the story, Vasquez said that he had enlisted his brother, Padilla, and the friend, Toribio, to carry out the killing.

The stark chronology needed sorting out to create a modicum of sense out of the relationships and events that had led to a triple confession of murder.

According to the written oral statements made by the suspects, the twin motives for Rose's murder had been as old as time. They were passionately jealous and greedy. The fact that Rose had been old enough to have been Antonio Rafle's grandfather had not precluded the development of a torrid gay romance between the pair.

According to the suspected killers, Rose had first met the then 12-year-old Rafle in 1982. As the association had grown more involved, Rose had approached Vasquez in 1985, volunteering to adopt the youngster.

Vasquez had been agreeable to the plan and had given his consent. (Whether the purported adoption ever was legalized is still in question at this writing.)

Be that as it may, Rose was generous financially to Rafle and the boy's male relatives. All of them had lived in Sosua at the actor's expense.

Nor would have the financial largesse of the short term be anything compared to the long-term benefits Rafle stood to reap should his love affair with Rose continue until Rose's death.

According to those acquainted with Rose's financial position, the estate of the highly successful actor would be worth in the neighborhood of $1 million. What's more, Rose had no other known living relatives who might become his heirs. The package of major holdings which Rafle might inherit included the sprawling Puerto Plata beach house and the Greenwich Village, Manhattan, super-loft.

The monkey wrench in the six-year affair was tossed in when, according to the three who had made statements, Rose's eyes began to wander towards the direction of an unnamed 14-year-old boy who had become part of the household.

There were fears that the 14-year-old might be adopted by the aging homosexual and as a result Rafle would find himself cut off from his inheritance.

There was also another element in the troubled romance between Rafle and his erstwhile benefactor. This concerned a relationship between Rafle and an unnamed 24-year-old woman of which the stage star reportedly disapproved.

Putting the best possible light on his motive for allegedly participating in the slaying, the elder Vasquez said in his statement to the police, "What I really wanted was to take revenge on the American Rose, because of his homosexual activities since he was hurting a lot of boys in this sector — in addition to mine, whom he had already prostituted since the age of 13."

Vasquez did not attempt to sweep the money motive under the carpet, however. The police say he confessed that both he and Rafle had been afraid that Rafle would lose his inheritance should Rose go ahead with his plans to adopt the 14-year-old.

Vasquez was quoted as saying, "If Rose died, it would be all inherited by my son.

"For this reason, on the second of the month, I began to prepare my plan."

The intrusion of the unnamed 14-year-old into the knotted relationship between Rafle and Rose again was pointed out by Vasquez. He commented, "I felt bad because he (Rose) felt a certain weakness for a minor . . . who lived in our house."

Turning to the techniques used to set Rose up for murder, Rafle reportedly said in his confession that he felt jealousy over the 14-year-old (whom he referred to merely as Juli). For that reason he had agreed to drive Rose in the red Suzuki to a spot where the older members of the homicidal conspiracy waited.

"When we joined up at the indicated spot, they pulled out a pistol which I had previously bought," Rafle said. "I got out of the car and went to one of the minibuses that go from Cabarete to Sosua and headed for an apartment outside of Sosua."

Vasquez then took up the story, telling how he and the others had taken Rose into a field and "gave him blows to the back of the head." After that, he said, they put him in the car and pushed it into a ravine.

The accounts given by the alleged participants in Rose's slaying appeared somewhat self-serving in that they attempted to picture the victim as the arch villain in the piece. However, others who had been privy to the sordid events over the years placed a different construction on them.

The American woman, a close neighbor and friend of the dead man, claimed that Rafle had been adopted by Rose in January of this year because the actor had wanted an heir. She charged that later on Rose had become disenchanted with Rafle because the 18-year-old was not attending to a business in which Rose had invested $25,000.

Two days before his death, Rose had told the woman he wanted to make changes in his will.

Another neighbor noted that while Rafle had not been wealthy, he had traveled with moneyed interests on the island.

"The guy was well connected," the source said, "although he did come from the lower class of Dominican society."

To back up his contention, the anonymous neighbor noted that Rafle had a girlfriend who was the daughter of a wealthy disco owner.

Those who had been close professional and personal friends of the dead man remained appalled at the savagery of his killing.

Stated a well-known actress and comedienne, "You don't think of a guy like George leaving the world, especially in that manner. It's just unbelievable."

Summed up another, "It's hard for me to understand it because as far as I could tell, he (Rafle) was never denied anything. George doted on him."

A business associate of Rose's expressed shock at Rafle's confession. He said he had considered the boy "a very nice person, very pleasant."

The American woman who had been a long-time Rose friend and confidant and had been in a position to watch the relationship of Rose and Rafle over the course of the years from her vantage point as a close neighbor, spoke of the unrequited hopes the older man had held for his teenage protegee.

Acknowledging that the actor had indeed been a homosexual, she noted that his motives in becoming Rafle's benefactor had been more selfless and complex than had they been purely sexual.

Said the woman, "Rose had adopted the boy because the man was never married. He wanted an heir.

"He was 68 years old," she continued. "He never put a hand on that boy, like a father loves a son.

"George wanted this boy to go further in life. The boy refused, he was not functioning. The boy had a girlfriend. He was all taken up with this girl and George was angry."

As new information surfaced, the brutality of the killing became all the more evident.

Dr. Rafael Estevez, the medical examiner in the case, told press representatives that Rose had been beaten numerous times on the head and chest with a wooden object. The medical examiner also claimed that the overturned Suzuki in which the actor's body was discovered had been moving too slowly when it had gone into the ditch to have caused the injuries suffered by the victim.

According to police sources, Rose had been held a captive for eight hours after Rafle had turned him over to his older accomplices. Pathologist Sergio Valdez reported that at the end of his captivity, Rose was clubbed over the head three times, placed in the rented sports car, and the Suzuki was then rolled into the roadside ditch.

Reliable police sources claim that in addition to beating the actor to death, the captors had ripped a gold chain from his neck and taken $500 he'd been carrying in his pocket. After seizing a diamond ring he'd been wearing, the three men had allegedly demanded more money.

Said the police source, "When he couldn't produce, they beat him and clubbed him.

"They drove the car with his body in it . . . and pushed it into a ditch, but . . . there was a witness who saw it.

"The witness watched as they went over to a mud puddle and washed Rose's blood off their hands."

From the beginning of the probe, the accident had appeared phony to some of the lawmen. This was because the

Suzuki had been only slightly dented. No car windows had been broken. The gear was in "park." The ignition was off. And despite the minor damage to the vehicle, Rose's body was a bloody pulp.

Then, too, the actor had been stripped to the waist. A fastidious and conservative dresser, Rose would not have been driving his automobile while half-naked.

Actions of the four alleged murder conspirators in the days that followed had aroused the suspicions of a number of civilians.

Said a real estate broker, "They (the four suspects) all went drinking and got very drunk. They were nervous like they were hiding something. The son was drinking rum in great amounts."

The woman who had supplied many other details of the alleged slaying, claimed she had spent the entire day following the discovery of Rose's body with Rafle. She commented; "I was with Juan the whole day. He never shed a tear. He was like a cucumber, not a tremble."

Another witness has come forward, according to sources, to say that Rafle was seen entering his girlfriend's house on the night of the murder. The teenager was told of the discovery of Rose's body at dawn of the next day.

Rafle, Vasquez, Padilla, and the still missing Toribio have all been charged with Rose's murder.

Should they be found guilty of the charges against them, they face a maximum penalty of 30 years in prison, according to Dominican officials.

Until such time as they have been convicted under due process of law, they have the right to be considered innocent.

The Unpublished Truth about the Thelma Todd Extortion Case

by Andrew J. Viglietta

"Thelma Todd Gets Threat Letter."

It was this headline that first drew my attention to the story.

I smiled as I picked up the Hollywood paper to read additional details. The story sounded and read exactly like another publicity stunt — the brain-child of a high-pressure press agent.

There was nothing unusual in the letter itself. According to the newspaper article, the writer of the extortion note demanded $10,000 from the glamorous blonde movie comedienne under threat of bodily injury. There was the usual reference to bodyguards, an investigation by local police, and a report of a "scare" among others of the motion picture colony. Stars are often annoyed by such notes.

That was on February 15th, 1935. At that time I was in Hollywood — an unemployed newspaperman, and broke. Nine months later, in New York, it was my fate to be personally drawn into this amazing case, for it did turn out to be amazing.

In Hollywood I had seen Thelma many times. I had attended parties at which she was a guest. I had spoken to her. I knew her press agent and I knew others who worked for and with her. So for nine months I kept a constant, vigilant watch for news of the case, but it was not until November 4th, 1935, that I was drawn into it personally.

On February 7th, Miss Todd received the first of a series of extortion notes. The letter was postmarked February 2nd and had been sent from Long Island City, N.Y. It was hardly legible. It read:

> "Pay $10,000 to Abe Lyman in New York and live if not our san francisco boys lay you out. This is no joke Thelma Todd Ruby Schaeffer Abe Lyman Harvey Priester Roland West."

That was all. The letter carried no signature except a crudely drawn Ace of Hearts.

All of the persons mentioned in the note are Hollywood or Broadway celebrities. Some I know personally. Others I knew only by sight.

Scores of such letters are received each year by members of Hollywood's famed movie colony, and at first Miss Todd appeared inclined to treat the message as the act of a crank. For several days the letter lay in her desk in her palatial Santa Monica home. Finally she sought the advice of friends.

"Take it to a newspaper," suggested one. And Miss Todd did.

Up to this time neither Miss Todd nor her secretary had notified the police, still believing that the letter and its threat was a joke. But when the Hollywood papers, on February 15th, printed the contents of the note in a story under an eight-column headline, Federal agents and local police began an immediate investigation.

Familiar with the work of Hollywood publicity men, authorities themselves at first were doubtful that the letter was genuine.

But if Department of Justice agents themselves had any such idea or belief during the first few weeks of their investigation, it was dispelled on March 4th when the second letter arrived. This letter also was postmarked from Long Island City and repeated the demand for $10,000.

"Don't forget the $10,000 for our san francisco boys and pay to Abe Lyman," read the second note.

Miss Todd was now genuinely alarmed. She hired a special bodyguard of three men. Hollywood and Santa Monica police were detailed for special patrol duty at her home. Federal agents kept constant watch — even over her brown phaeton automobile in which she drove to and from the studios.

The newspapers never received word of the second letter. I heard of it in the studios where I had managed to obtain a job in a clerical office. I, too, now was convinced that the extortion notes were authentic.

Within two hours after the second note was received, Federal agents had it in their possession, comparing the writing with that of the first letter. Microscopic examination by handwriting experts revealed that the writing matched — matched perfectly in every detail. So did the crudely drawn Ace of Hearts.

Now authorities were convinced that they were dealing with a real extortion plot. Photostatic copies of the two letters were sent to Department of Justice headquarters at Washington, D.C., for comparison with the handwriting of known extortioners, and word of the letters also was flashed to field headquarters in New York City.

All immediate trails led to blind alleys. There was but little information to work with. The comparison between the writing of the extortion letters and the writing of known extortioners and blackmailers had negative results.

Then Federal agents questioned those whose names were mentioned in the threat letter — Schaeffer, Priester, West and

Lyman, in the hope that they might possibly furnish a clue to the writer of the letter. The Federal men paid particular attention to Abe Lyman, well-known orchestra leader, although they made it emphatically clear that Mr. Lyman was in no way connected with the case other than that he had been mentioned in the letter and by some remote chance might be able to identify the writing.

But Mr. Lyman knew nothing of the writer or the letter—except what he had read.

On March 27th another threat reached Miss Todd. This time it came in the form of a postal card. It read:

"Hurry up with the $10,000."

That was all. And again the brief command was signed with the Ace of Hearts. This time, however, the card had been sent from Grand Central Station, New York City, instead of from Long Island City (part of New York City, located in the Borough of Queens). The writing again checked with the previous letters, but who the writer was or where he lived was not a matter for merely police routine.

Eight million persons live in New York City and its immediate suburbs, in what is generally known as the metropolitan area. One of them MIGHT have written the extortion threats.

Very little of what Department of Justice agents know reaches the newspapers. I had kept in contact with the case through friends of Miss Todd whom I knew through my newspaper experience. Sometimes I turned back to my original theory that the entire matter was a publicity stunt or a hoax. At other times I would sit for hours attempting mentally to picture the writer of the letter, what he was like, who he was, and if he really hoped to get the $10,000 he demanded.

To the snatches of information I received from those close to Miss Todd was added an occasional newspaper article. Nothing much in the way of startling news. Most of the headlines and stories were hackneyed repetitions — "Police Still Working On Todd Extortion Case," and "Police Seek New Clues In Extortion Attempt."

Certainly there were no choice morsels of information there.

Meanwhile Miss Todd still was under guard. She had been questioned repeatedly. She insisted she knew of no one who would send her threats and she was adamant in her opinion that the writer of the notes was insane.

More letters, all signed with the mysterious Ace of Hearts, came in April and May. Each letter was written in the same hand and each repeated the demand for $10,000. Also, each letter had been sent either from Long Island City or from Grand Central Station.

As rapidly as the letters were received by Miss Todd, they were seized by the Department of Justice, compared with the others, processed for fingerprints, and then filed in the Todd case dossier.

The Federal agents were baffled. They were bucking a solid wall — and they admitted it.

Special agents were detailed to watch certain letter boxes at Grand Central Station. Others were stationed at the more important postal districts in Long Island City in an attempt to apprehend the criminal. But it was a futile, almost ridiculous, effort.

Then, quite suddenly, came the first tangible clue. It came in the form of a letter to Abe Lyman. The writer demanded an unspecified amount of money "for protection against harm." The letter was signed "Tad Dorgan" or "Tad Dugan." The poor handwriting made it impossible to tell which.

Mr. Lyman called Department of Justice agents. He was not alarmed, believing that the letter had been sent by a friend as a practical joke. He assumed that it was merely coincidence that he too should receive an extortion threat. But the Federal agents were struck by the similarity of the handwriting with that in the Todd notes. They submitted the Lyman letter to experts, who expressed the opinion that the writing was the same, although cleverly disguised.

How shrewd the writer of the letters was in conducting his game was indicated first in the disguised handwriting and secondly by the fact that the Lyman letter had been sent from the City Hall post office. The letter had been sent on July 15th.

A few New York newspapers carried the story about two days later. At that time I was working for the Long Island *Daily Star*, having left Hollywood early in June.

One of my duties on The *Star* was to clip other newspapers for "local" news. I was engaged in this work when I chanced upon two paragraphs buried at the bottom of an inside page. It said merely that Mr. Lyman had received an extortion letter. There was no mention of the Todd case at all. I clipped the article and placed it with the other clippings and typewritten data I had accumulated on the case over a six-month period.

I reasoned that the Lyman letter dovetailed too neatly into the Todd case to be a coincidence. I expected and hoped for a "break." But the "break" came first to the Department of Justice agents.

In questioning Mr. Lyman they found the one employee of the restaurant where the orchestra leader was engaged at that time lived in Astoria, a section of Long Island City. For reasons of their own they became interested in this man. Quickly but quietly the Department of Justice threw out its net. They obtained the address of the employee, 31-18 Newton Avenue, Astoria. For almost a week they watched the house in relays.

Then they obtained samples of the suspect's handwriting. But the handwriting did not match with either of the two sets of extortion notes.

Federal agents were not dismayed. It was possible, they argued, that someone in the apartment house at that address had sent the note to Mr. Lyman, knowing that one of the tenants was an employee at the restaurant where Mr. Lyman was playing. Thus every tenant in the dwelling was brought under suspicion.

The next step was to obtain specimens of the handwriting of the tenants of the apartment house. Obviously it could not be done by a door-to-door canvass. So the Federal agents went to the office of the renting agent. There they took by photograph the handwriting of some of the tenants — mostly names affixed to leases and to applications for apartments.

This procedure was far from satisfactory. For one thing, the application cards or leases were not signed by all of the tenants. In most cases only the husband had signed. In other instances where adults were living with relatives or other families, there was no signature at all.

One signature resembled the writing in the Todd notes and compared with the writing in the Lyman letter. But arrests cannot be made merely on resemblances and comparisons. The Federal men were seeking more substantial evidence, but they were getting nowhere.

The one signature which "resembled" the writing in the Todd notes was placed under a microscope no less than twelve times. And each time experts differed in their opinions.

Then the Federal agents decided upon a bold stroke. They would take samples of the handwriting of the tenants in the apartment whose writing compared most favorably with that in both sets of letters. They did, and again the handwriting of the man whom they suspected by reason of his signature came closest to the writing in the threat letters.

The man was Harry Schimanski, the thin, nervous and slightly timid superintendent of the apartment house.

But still sufficient evidence was lacking. The Department of Justice was not interested in only an arrest. They believed that if an arrest was to be made, the arrest should be buttressed by evidence strong enough to send the suspect away to prison.

For the next week Schimanski was shadowed. He was followed to and from stores, into moving picture houses and into beer taverns. Even his mail was watched. And again the careful plans of the Department of Justice led to a negative result.

Discouraged and almost convinced that Schimanski was innocent, the Department of Justice decided upon one last move. They sent a telegram to "Tad Dorgan" at the Astoria address.

"If Schimanski wrote these letters, he'll accept the telegram," Mr. Lyman was told. "When and if he does, we'll grab him."

Whether Schimanski accepted the telegram or whether he refused it, has never been made quite clear. Schimanski says he told the messenger boy that no one by the name of "Dorgan" lived in the apartment house. Department of Justice agents say he accepted the telegram in the hall of the apartment house and then, recognizing a Federal agent outside in the street, handed it back.

But whatever happened in the hallway of the apartment house — there were no witnesses except the messenger boy and he could not remember what happened — Schimanski was seized and arrested, then and there.

Bewildered and stunned by his sudden arrest, Schimanski was at a loss to answer the flood of questions put to him by the arresting officers. He was permitted to put on a coat and hat and then, despite the screaming protestations of his wife was whisked to Department of Justice headquarters.

There he presented a pitiful picture. Too shocked, too afraid to answer interrogations, Schimanski sat huddled in a chair. His head was buried in his hands. He wept a little. He answered mostly in monosyllables. But he stoutly denied any connection with the case.

"Gee," he kept repeating. "I don't know nothing about the case. I only saw Thelma Todd in the pictures and I never heard of Abe Lyman."

Authorities were perplexed. Schimanski's background — one of eighteen children of a poor family, deprived of even an ordinary education — did not seem to coincide with the shrewd, clever manner in which the extortion notes had been written and mailed.

"I'm poor," he pleaded again and again. "I need money, sure. But I don't want to get it that way. I didn't have anything to do with the case. I'm innocent. Can't you see that!"

Schimanski was arrested on the evening of August 18th. The arrest was not made public until the next day when he was brought in court. When I saw him in court that morning, he was a weary, red-eyed, bedraggled figure. It was obvious that he had had no sleep.

Without a hat, his collar tieless, without socks and in a worn, almost thread-bare suit he stood before U.S. Commissioner Garrett W. Cotter in New York's Federal Court for arraignment.

Commissioner Cotter himself was shocked at the defendant's appearance.

"This man is a pitiful object," Commissioner Cotter said, addressing the Department of Justice agents and Assistant U.S. Attorney John A. Burke. "Do you think he is guilty?"

At the word guilty Schimanski's body gave a nervous twitch and his eyes eagerly sought an answer from the Department of

409

Justice agents.

"I repeat," said Comissioner Cotter, "do you think this is the guilty man?"

Only a nod was given in answer.

"How do you plead?" Commissioner Cotter asked Schimanski.

For a moment it appeared that Schimanski was not going to answer. He gulped and grew red. His eyes remained glued to the floor and his hands played with the pockets of his threadbare suit.

"Not guilty," he whispered.

Commissioner Cotter fixed bail at $10,000. Schimanski was led away to a cell in the Federal House of Detention, Manhattan. I telephoned the story of the arraignment to my newspaper and then walked out of the courtroom.

I could not erase the picture of Schimanski and his arraignment from my mind.

"Schimanski is *not* the guilty man," I kept repeating over and over.

Now, if ever, I was determined to solve the case, if I could, and bring the guilty man to justice. But could I? I had nothing more to work with than a hunch, imagination and plenty of ambition.

My first step was to interview Schimanski's neighbors and family. I found Schimanski's wife heartbroken. She told me her husband was a "hardworking, poor man, the victim of circumstance." The Schimanskis had lived in the Astoria apartment house for three years and their neighbors characterized the family as "poor but honest." Some charged that Schimanski was the victim of a frameup.

Next I went to see the owner of the apartment house, Fred Motl of Astoria. He knew of Schimanski's arrest, having heard the story from Mrs. Schimanski.

"I honestly believe in Schimanski," he told me. "I don't believe he could do such a thing. I may raise the bail for his release."

I agreed with him. The evidence against Schimanski, in my opinion, was far too flimsy to be substantiated in court, even in an indictment. But I was wrong. For on September 2nd a Federal Grand Jury indicted Schimanski on an attempted extortion charge. The indictment no doubt was returned on the strength of the opinion of some Department of Justice handwriting experts that Schimanski had penned the letters to Thelma Todd and therefore might be said to be based on a technical reason. The indictment omitted reference to Abe Lyman.

Several days later Commissioner Cotter, on application of Schimanski's attorney, reduced the bail to $7,500. On the same day Schimanski was released on a bail bond furnished by Mr. Motl, his landlord and employer. Also on that day I interviewed Schimanski, not for my paper but for whatever personal knowledge I could obtain about Schimanski and his family.

But my self-appointed task of helping to clear the indicted man and to nab the real criminal appeared hopeless. Through Schimanski's lawyer I had obtained photostatic copies of Schimanski's handwriting and also the handwriting of the original extortion notes. These I took to a handwriting expert. He assured me there was a resemblance but would venture no other opinion.

"I know of no two experts who judge handwriting on the same basis," he told me. "There is a resemblance between Schimanski's handwriting and the handwriting used in the extortion notes. But I would not suggest that the letter to Miss Todd was written by Schimanski. On the other hand, I would not suggest that Schimanski did not write it."

411

Back I went to the office of Herman Siegal, Schimanski's attorney.

"I have the opinion of a handwriting expert that Schimanski did not write these letters," he said.

I left his office feeling more than discouraged. The whole case seemed to hinge on the testimony of handwriting experts. The weight of testimony along these lines appeared to be heavily in favor of the prosecution unless some unexpected development occurred or unless I personally, through my knowledge of the case, could assist in producing the real criminal. Unless this occurred I knew that Schimanski would be sent away to jail.

On the morning of September 4th, two days after Schimanski was indicted, Ernest Kremer, city editor of the Long Island *Daily Star*, received a government postcard. It had been sent from the City Hall post office and had been mailed on the previous day. It was addressed, Editor, *Daily Star*, Long Island City, N.Y.

Written on the back in a shaky scrawl, were these words:

"Here is prove that man held in Todd case is innocent.

"Pay $10,000 to Abe Lyman in New York and live if not our san francisco boys lay you out. This is no joke Thelma Todd Rudy Schaeffer Abe Lyman Harvey Priester Roland West."

There was no signature but after the word "out" there was a crudely drawn Ace of Hearts.

Knowing that I was familiar with the case, the city editor turned the card over to me with instructions to deliver it to the Department of Justice office in Forty-second Street, New York City. I was told to obtain a photostatic copy of it and to find out if the handwriting compared with the Todd notes.

412

"With the exception of the first sentence, this is a copy of the original letter," I told him.

"Who but the writer of the original letter, Department of Justice agents and Miss Todd and a few newspapermen know that?" he asked. "The original letter never was published in any New York newspaper."

"Then this must be the man who wrote the original letter," I replied. "Furthermore, it is postmarked from City Hall station. Several of the original letters came from that station. And what's more, the man who sent it must live in Long Island City, otherwise he would not have sent it to *The Star.* Few residents in Manhattan, Brooklyn or the Bronx ever heard of *The Star.* It is strictly a Long Island newspaper".

But the city editor was skeptical.

"I doubt it," he said. "This is probably the work of a crank. Or maybe Schimanski sent the letter himself. We can't be sure of anything until the letter is checked with the original notes."

This was the opportunity I had been waiting for. Now, at last, I was definitely in the case. I went to the Department of Justice headquarters and gave the postal card to one of the agents working on the case.

"The writing is disguised," was his first comment. "But we'll send it to Washington for comparison."

"Suppose we get another card?" I asked. And without giving the G-man an opportunity to reply, I supplemented this question with another:

"Or a telephone call?"

The G-man smiled.

"Do you think there will be telephone calls?"

"There may be," I persisted.

He gave me his telephone number.

"If telephone calls are made, call me up."

With that I was dismissed. That night I dug out all my clip-

413

pings and typewritten data on the Todd case. For more than four hours I compared clippings and data and made my own deductions. I then was sure that the man who had sent the postal card to *The Star* that morning was the writer of the Todd notes — the real criminal.

On the following day and on each day during the next two weeks I visited Department of Justice headquarters, constantly hoping to get a new slant on the case. But what the Department of Justice had learned — if anything — from the card which I delivered to the bureau was kept a closely guarded secret. Perhaps I appeared to be over-talkative or over-zealous. Anyhow, always I was cut off with the same terse comment:

"There is no report from Washington."

Nevertheless my enthusiasm was not lessened in the slightest degree. Each day I perused all of the city's newspapers for some news of the case in Hollywood. In that city, however, the investigation had been dropped entirely. The arrest of Schimanski had placed the case entirely in the hands of Department of Justice men working in the New York area. There was nothing of importance in the papers except a small dispatch from Hollywood in which Miss Todd was quoted as saying she was "happy" that the criminal had been arrested.

Naturally I was eager for a break — and also a story. I wanted to be in on the solution. I had a hunch that the "break" when it did come would be in the nature of a surprise, for now I was more firmly convinced than ever that Schimanski was not the guilty man.

Finally the telephone call which I expected would follow the postal card did come — on September 29th. On that day I was on another assignment. The call came at three o'clock in the afternoon. City Editor Kremer answered it.

"Is this the editor?" queried the caller.

Assured at once that it was, the caller then reminded Mr.

Kremer of a "postal card sent September 3rd in connection with the Schimanski-Todd case."

Alert at the possibility of tracing the call, the city editor attempted to engage the caller in conversation. But apparently sensing such a move, the man on the other end of the wire rang off with a plea to have the postal card he sent turned over to the Department of Justice.

That evening when I returned to the editorial rooms I was told of the telephone call and the next day I submitted this information to the Department of Justice agent whom I had contacted previously. He seemed not at all impressed. I asked him again while I was there what report had been made by the handwriting experts on the postal card sent to *The Star*.

"The experts tell us that the writing is disguised," he said, "but that it is undoubtedly Schimanski's."

For more than a month the case remained at a standstill. Schimanski's trial had been set for November 10th and once more it appeared that the task of tracing the mysterious caller, the man who had sent a copy of the original threat letter to *The Star*, was hopeless.

Then at nine o'clock in the morning of November 3rd came the second call. Unfortunately I again was out of the office on assignment. And again City Editor Kremer answered the call. Bluntly and coldly the voice at the other end of the wire said:

"Are you going to help me or not? This is the man who wrote the extortion notes to Thelma Todd. Schimanski is innocent. I can't give myself up to the police. But you can help me if you want to. Will you?"

Pretending that he could not hear, Mr. Kremer ordered another reporter to trace the call.

"I can't hear you," Mr. Kremer said. "Will you repeat?"

The caller obliged.

"What is your name?" asked Kremer.

"Richard Harding," came the reply after a moment's hesitation. "Please put a piece in your paper that Schimanski is innocent. He had nothing to do with the case. I did it to give Thelma Todd publicity."

"Are you the man who sent the postal card to *The Star?*" was Kremer's next question.

"Yes, on September 3rd," was the answer.

"Do you know Schimanski?" the caller was asked.

"Sure I know Schimanski . . ." were the first few words of his reply. Then apparently realizing that he might have given a clue to his identity, the man added: "Not personally, you know. I only know what I read about him. But I must go to work now. Good-bye."

The caller hung up. All efforts to trace the call were futile.

Within the next half-hour I was relieved of my assignment and was directed to relay the conversation to the Department of Justice. I did. But the Federal Agents received the news without comment.

When I returned to the Editorial rooms of *The Star*, I was ordered to remain "glued to the telephone."

"If he really is the man and is anxious to clear Schimanski, he'll call again," said the city editor. "You know more about this case than any newspaperman in the city. We'll need you if he calls again and he probably will."

Shortly after one o'clock that afternoon the call came through. This was the first time I had spoken to the mysterious "Ace of Hearts" or "Richard Harding."

"Keep him talking," Mr. Kremer ordered. "Say anything, do anything, but keep him talking."

I had the call switched to one of the booths in the editorial rooms. As I stepped into the booth, I realized that here at last was my opportunity to solve the case of which I had first heard on February 15th in Hollywood when I picked up an evening newspaper. And I was determined not to muff the chance.

The conversation, as best, I can remember it, ran something like this after I had reassured the caller that he was speaking in the strictest confidence.

"What is your name?" I asked.

"Richard Harding," he replied. The voice was low and gruff.

"Speak in confidence," I continued, "I am your friend. My name is Charles Brown. I couldn't understand yours."

"My name is Richard Harding."

My only chance, I knew, was to win this man's confidence, to make him speak freely, and I used all my experience as a newspaperman and as an actor to do it. I knew also that luck would play a big part but that my ability to continue the conversation while the city editor was attempting to trace the call would play an even greater one.

"My name is Richard Harding," he repeated for the third time (apparently with the idea of impressing the name upon me) "and I am the man who sent those letters to Miss Todd. Do you know about that? Honest, I didn't mean any harm. I love the girl. I wanted her to get publicity out of it. I want to free this man Schimanski who is charged with the crime."

"Dick," I said, "I think you are telling the truth. I think Schimanski is innocent. Now I want you to tell me the whole story and I'll go to bat for Schimanski and leave you out of it."

Either it was the tone of my voice or the fact that I had called him by his first name that won his next reply.

"I think I can trust you, Mr. Brown. So here's the story. I mailed those letters to Thelma Todd. Honest, I'm in love with the girl. I tell you I'm in love with her and I had to do something to let her know that I am her admirer. Why, I spent my last ten bucks to wire her orchids for her birthday (a statement

417

later found to be false). So you see I'd rather starve if I could only give her something."

I sympathized with him.

"I know, Dick," I said. "I knew Thelma Todd when I was in Hollywood. I can't blame you for being stuck on that girl. She's a swell looker. I've watched every picture she's been in. In fact, I saw her make pictures in Hollywood."

The word Hollywood appeared to have a magical effect on him. For the next two minutes he kept repeating demands that I describe Hollywood, the screen stars, the directors and the producers.

I became suspicious. Was this man really a dangerous criminal? Was he the real writer of the extortion letters? Was he a crank? Or was he playing a shrewd game to make it appear that he was merely a simple-minded individual who had sent the letters to Thelma Todd for "the sake of publicity."

At that moment there was plenty of doubt in my mind. But there was no need for me to prolong the conversation now. He burst into another flood of questions concerning Hollywood and Thelma Todd.

My answers were lengthy. I had received specific instructions to keep talking. I did. Meanwhile City Editor Kremer had not gone to sleep. He had called Department of Justice headquarters and had notified the agents that the mysterious "Richard Harding" was on another wire.

The keys to both telephones — the one on which I was talking and the other on which the city editor had contacted the Department of Justice — were open. Very carefully and slowly the operator at the office switchboard transferred my line to the wire connecting the city editor and the Department of Justice agents. And now the G-men were listening to my conversation with Richard Harding.

In the meantime two other reporters were attempting to

trace the call. Up to this point our only information was that the call was being made from a booth in John Street, New York City. It was impossible immediately to obtain the address of the place where the booth was located or to get the exchange number.

In the interim the conversation continued. But now there appeared a faint note of suspicion on the part of Harding.

"I wonder whether I can trust you," he said. "I don't want to be arrested. It'll be too bad for you if I am."

For the moment I was nonplused. This was his first threat of violence.

"I know it will be too bad for me," I answered. "But I'm not a fool. I don't want to be bumped off. I'm not going to tell the cops. All I want is a story. I believe you. I want you to trust me just as I am trusting you."

There was a brief silence. Then he said:

"I think you're all right. I want you to put a piece in the paper about Schimanski. Tell them I did it. My name is Richard Harding (again note the repetition of his name) and I want it put in the paper today."

Then he rang off abruptly, so abruptly, in fact, that I was startled to hear another voice almost immediately.

"Nice work, Viglietta," the voice said. "That was a great piece of work."

It was the voice of the Department of Justice agent who had been listening in on the conversation. Before I could reply, he continued:

"Have you traced the call?"

I inquired of the city editor and then informed the Federal agent that the call had come from a public pay station in John Street.

"We are attempting to get the number now," I added.

The Federal agent asked me to call him immediately after I

obtained the number. Within five minutes this information came through. The address, however, was missing. I gave the G-men the information. They received it with the request that I remain available at the office of *The Star* for the remainder of the afternoon.

Frankly I was a bit disappointed. I thought that my last chance to collar the mysterious Richard Harding and solve the mystery was gone. I blamed the telephone company for its tardiness in tracing the call. I blamed the city editor for not having "pressed" telephone officials to trace the call. And I blamed myself for allowing the caller to ring off before I had obtained all of the necessary information.

But my hopes were suddenly buoyed when the G-men called back fifteen minutes later with the news that they had obtained the address of the public pay station from which the call was made.

"We are going to that address now," the Department of Justice agent said. "Keep yourself available. We will let you know of any immediate developments."

My hopes ran high. But at five o'clock that afternoon I again was doomed to disappointment. Department of Justice agents called and informed me that they had processed the telephone booth for finger-prints but that all of the prints were smudged, the smudges having been caused by the fact that several persons apparently had used the booth after the mysterious Mr. Harding.

A clerk in the drugstore where the booth was located had described one of the persons using the telephone as a "tall, dark and skinny man." The clerk said he had noticed this particular man because of the length of time he had remained in the booth.

"I am not positive and I don't want you to think that it is so," the Department of Justice agent said, "but the voice on the telephone this afternoon sounded strangely like Schimanski's. It is possible that it was he who called. He is out on bail and he is in a tough spot."

I agreed that it was possible, although not probable.

"If Schimanski is innocent, he wouldn't dare take such a chance," I argued. "Besides, the general run of the conversation this afternoon doesn't fit in with Schimanski."

"Have you ever heard Schimanski speak?" I was asked.

I replied that I had but that I was not too familiar with his voice. Whereupon it was suggested that I interview Schimanski for the purpose of attempting to determine whether I could recognize the voice of the man on the telephone as that of Schimanski's.

This I agreed to do. That night I went to Schimanski's house. He met me at the door, dressed in a paint-spattered shirt and trousers. I bluffed my way into an interview, giving as an excuse a rumor that he had engaged a new attorney.

"That's a new one on me," he replied with a weak grin. "I haven't been out of the house for the last two days. I'm painting apartments." And he pointed to his smeared clothing.

As he spoke, I listened intently to each word. And I was amazed at the striking similarity of speech between Schimanski and Richard Harding, particularly the pronunciation of certain words.

Both men spoke in a low voice. Each slurred words ending in "ing," using the expression "in." Also each used the word "me" in place of "my."

I was perplexed. After all, my belief that Schimanski was innocent was based on nothing firmer than a hunch. But I could not bring myself to the point where I was convinced beyond all reasonable doubt that Schimanski was the guilty man.

True, his handwriting resembled the writing in the threat

letters. His voice was almost identical with that of Mr. Harding who had called me, and his handwriting again resembled the writing of this same Mr. Harding — if there was a Mr. Harding.

Later that evening I again talked with the Department of Justice agent.

"I am not sure that it is the same voice," I told him. "There is a similarity, a strong resemblance. But I am not positive."

"Neither am I," the G-man replied. "Frankly I think Schimanski is the guilty man. But I want and intend to give him every possible chance to prove that he is not. I don't want to send a man away to prison without being absolutely sure and we are going to be very careful on this. These telephone calls are complicating matters. If there is a second man in the case he writes and talks enough like Schimanski to be Schimanski himself or his twin brother."

The next morning, November 5th, was Election Day in New York City. Because I had been working on the Schimanski case I had been relieved of routine assignments and I was detailed only to office assignments in the expectation that another call would be made and that I would be available to take it.

At three o'clock that afternoon the city editor's telephone rang. The city editor had left for the day and I answered. The caller asked for Charles Brown. I recognized the voice immediately.

"This is Charles Brown," I acknowledged. "Who is this calling?"

"This is Richard Harding, Dick Harding," he answered. "I called you yesterday. Why didn't you put that piece in your paper like I asked you to."

"I can't speak to you here, Dick," I said, attempting to regain his confidence. "There are too many people around. Wait until I get into a booth."

My mind was in a whirl. Should I call the Department of Justice immediately? Should I again attempt to have the call traced? Or should I handle this man myself? Something told me that this was my last opportunity. It was now or never. In a flash I remembered that evening in Hollywood when I first saw the newspaper headline and I remembered my vow to "get the criminal."

After I had the call transferred to a booth, I was profuse in my apologies.

"I am very sorry, Dick," I said. "The editor would not permit the article to go in today's paper. He said he wanted more of a feature story. He wants me to get the human interest angle. I want to help you and Schimanski in every way possible. But I can't unless I see you personally."

"I think you're kidding," was his reply. "Why do you want to see me personally? You know I can't do that."

I repeated my reason.

"You're not double-crossing me?" he asked. "I warn you not to. It'll go bad for you."

I was trembling with excitement, anticipation—and fear.

"All I want is a story," I said assuringly. "I saw Schimanski last night and I know that he is entirely innocent. I don't want to put anybody in jail. But I want to free an innocent man and I want a good story for my newspaper."

"Let me think," he said. For almost a minute he did not speak. Then he said:

"O.K. I'll trust you. I'll meet you."

What my thoughts were at that moment I cannot remember. Here was the opportunity for which I had been waiting for nine months. I grasped it.

"Tonight?" I asked.

Perhaps it was my noticeable eagerness which again made

him suspicious.

"No," was his slow answer. "Not tonight. Maybe tomorrow or the next day. I don't know when or where."

"That will be too late for tomorrow's paper," I said. "You must meet me tonight. Otherwise we cannot carry your story tomorrow. Don't you think the sooner we publish your story the better it will be for you and Schimanski."

He agreed. He said:

"Meet me this afternoon. Meet me in one hour at the out-of-town news stand in the back of the Old Times building at Times Square."

"Aren't there too many people there?" I asked. "We ought to be alone. I don't want anyone to know about this."

"I don't want anyone to know about it either," he replied. "But no one will bother us there. I go there every day to buy out-of-town newspapers, papers from Hollywood, so I can read news about Thelma Todd."

"How will I know you?" I asked.

"Never mind about me," he quickly retorted. "You just give me your description. How will I know you?"

I told him I would be wearing a black overcoat and a black fedora.

"And I'll be carrying a paper in my hand," I added.

The rendezvous was set. Without waiting to call the city editor at his home I rushed out of the office. It was exactly 3:30 P.M. I had just thirty minutes to tip off the Department of Justice and then meet the "criminal." I hailed a taxi. In fifteen minutes I had crossed the Queensboro Bridge and arrived at the Department of Justice office which happens, incidentally, to be directly across the street from the office of this magazine. There I told the story.

The G-men heard my story with a look of amazement on their faces. At first, I knew they didn't believe it. One of them

424

scoffed at the idea that "Mr. Harding, the mystery man," would keep the appointment.

"Isn't worth trying," I argued desperately.

"Of course it's worth it!" the head of the department said. He assigned three of his agents to go with me.

With sirens screaming we streaked toward Times Square from the Department of Justice agents headquarters at Forty-second Street and Lexington Avenue. As the car wove in and out of heavy city traffic, I took careful notice of the arsenal in the rear of the car—machine-guns, rifles, revolvers and an abundance of ammunition. Evidently these men were prepared for trouble.

We parked the car in Forty-second Street near Times Square. The commanding officer had ordered the driver to stop the siren.

"We had better separate now," I suggested. I glanced at my watch. "It's just four o'clock. I'm late. Just what do you want me to do?"

"If he shows up," I was told, "talk to him. Don't be afraid. We'll have you covered. When you are sure that he is the right man, just tip your hat. That's all."

Then we separated. I walked straight toward Times Square. Two of the agents crossed the street. Another walked a few feet in back of me.

I felt strangely afraid. It was not fear of injury. The fear came from anticipation and the thought that perhaps I was the victim of a hoax, that my persistent hope of capturing this man was to be dashed and that I was to be made the butt of never-ending jokes

When I reached the out-of-town news stand in back of the old Times Building, the focal point of the so-called Great White Way, I looked around. No one was there except a wizened old man, crouching over a small portable stove, warming his hands. Even the three G-men had disappeared.

I took a copy of *The Star* from my overcoat pocket and started reading, more from sheer nervousness than anything else. Suddenly I looked up. There, standing near the entrance to the subway, was a tall, thin man. I walked toward him, remembering that although he had given me no description of himself, the mysterious Richard Harding had once been described by a drugstore clerk as a "tall, thin man."

At the same time he saw me and approached a few steps.

I held out a copy of *The Star*.

He took it quickly from my hand and looked at me. Then he looked at the paper. He had not yet spoken. He glanced around and then looked at the paper again. Without looking up he asked:

"Your name is Brown?" The question was almost a whisper.

"Yes," I replied. "And you are Richard Harding?"

"Yes," he whispered again. "I am Dick Harding. Are you alone?"

I assured him that I was. A feeling of disgust came over me as I studied the man's features. Tall, thin and dark, walked with a slight shuffle. His face was pock-marked and almost completely covered with pimples. His clothes were ragged and dirty. His lips were sensuous and he had a queer look in his eyes. And when he shook hands with me I shuddered at his touch. I was staring at him when he asked his next question.

"Do you want to eat? We can't talk here. I want to tell you the whole story."

"O.K.," I responded. "Let's go."

A creepy feeling came over me. There was something queer about this man, something behind his eyes I could not fathom. I felt afraid of him.

Then I lifted my hat.

The next instant I saw "Richard Harding" attempt to run,

to struggle free from the heavy grasp of two G-men. A second later he was in handcuffs.

"You . . . . ," he screamed. "I'll get you for this." His profanity was cut short by the curt command of one of the G-men. He became suddenly quiet.

"All right," he said. "Let's go."

All during that short ride back to Department of Justice headquarters I wondered if it really was true — that I had succeeded in trapping the criminal who had evaded the G-men for nine months.

At headquarters the prisoner confessed. The name Richard Harding was of course, a fake. His name was Edward Schiffert and by coincidence which later proved to be not so amazing he was a tenant in the apartment house of which Schimanski was superintendent.

"How could I be so dumb, so stupid as to make an appointment with that newspaperman?" he said. "But he tricked me. He made me believe that he was my friend, that all he wanted was a story for his paper.

"Yes, I did it," he continued. "I gave you guys the runaround for nine months. But when you arrested that poor guy Schimanski for a crime which I committed, I couldn't rest. I couldn't see an innocent man go to jail. See?

"But that newspaperman Brown! He's smarter than all you guys put together. If it hadn't been for him, I'd still be laughing at you."

The next morning Schiffert was arraigned before Commissioner Cotter, the same Commissioner who three months before had held Schimanski in $10,000 bail.

Schiffert pleaded not guilty.

"I did it as a joke," he said.

"The joke is on you," answered Assistant U.S. Attorney Burke.

427

"Bail is set at $3,500," added the Commissioner.

Schiffert remained in the Federal House of Detention, Manhattan, for one day. Then he was sent to the observation ward at Bellevue Hospital.

Schimanski called at my home and my office three times to offer his thanks. There were tears in his eyes.

On November 14th Schimanski's attorney filed papers with Commissioner Cotter to have the indictment against his client nolle prossed. Assistant U.S. Attorney Burke concurred in the application and the court dismissed the indictment against Schimanski on November 19th. Schimanski was completely innocent of any connection with the crime.

Schiffert was kept in the observation ward at Bellevue Hospital. In the meantime Department of Justice agents checked and rechecked all evidence in the case against him. Each check and recheck dovetailed with Schiffert's statements.

Specimens of Schiffert's handwriting taken during his incarceration were declared to be identical with the writing in the extortion notes. Experts now declared that there was not a scintilla of doubt that Schiffert had written the notes. But they also pointed out that his handwriting and Schimanski's were almost identical.

On December 3rd, Assistant U.S. Attorney Burke appeared before Federal Judge Alfred W. Coxe and submitted a report of alienists that Schiffert was insane.

"There is not the slightest doubt that Schiffert sent those notes to Thelma Todd," the Prosecutor told the Judge. "To substantiate that charge we have the opinion of handwriting experts and Schiffert's confession when he was arrested."

Several days later Schiffert was committed to an institution for the insane on Ward's Island, New York City.

I cannot finish the story of this case without paying respect to the unbounded enthusiasm and co-operation of Mr. Ernest

Kremer of the Long Island *Daily Star*.

It also occurs to me as I end this tale that someone might misunderstand the facts, or the way I expressed them, and get the idea that the G-men are in the habit of jumping at conclusions and make mistakes easily.

The exact opposite is true.

For this strange Schiffert case is conceded to be one of the convincing coincidences. The voices of the two men are identical; their handwriting practically the same and they are living in the same house. Had this case been in the hands of a less skillful police organization than the Federal Bureau of Investigation, an innocent man would have been sentenced to prison in my opinion, before the real perpetrator was revealed.

Note:

Walter Winchell stated in his column in the New York Daily *Mirror:* "Great credit is due a reporter for the Long Island *Star* in the arrest of Schiffert, the extortionist, who confessed that he, not the superintendent of his dwelling, sent the threats to Thelma Todd and Abe Lyman. . . . The reporter is Andrew J. Viglietta. He trapped Schiffert near the out-of-town newsstand behind the Times edifice and phoned the D of J men. . . . Ironically enough, Viglietta appeared in a Chamberlain Brown opus last season. It was 'Idle Tongues' and he portrayed Public Enemy No. 1. . . . Now the G-men call him Public Hero No. 1."

Killing Of The Scarsdale
Diet Doctor

by George Carpozi Jr.

The rumble of thunder and crackle of lightning gave the driving rain an eerie chill on that night of last March 10th. But the storm raging over New York State didn't disturb the gathering at the dinner table in Dr. Herman Tarnower's palatial glass and brick mansion in the exclusive Westchester County community of Purchase.

His guests at the evening repast that Monday were his sister, Mrs. Billie Schwartz, a niece, and Mrs. Marjorie Lynn Brundage Tryforos, who was the bachelor doctor's nurse, secretary, and in recent years his companion at an increasing number of professional and social functions.

It was his relationship with Mrs. Tryforos, a divorcee, which will hold increasing significance in this story. But it is much too early to discuss either his affair with this sweet, warm, adoring young woman or his romance with the other beautiful older woman, the very opposite of Mrs. Tryforos — the brilliant, strong-willed, witty, and very social Mrs. Jean Struven Harris.

We shall also return to the supper table later and join the conversation, which was about murder. Not about the killing that would be committed in the house later the night, but about three women who kill their husbands in the pages of a novel.

Entertaining guests at the evening repast was one of life's great pleasures for the 69-year-old heart specialist and internist. His zest for good food was matched only by his desire for the pleasurable companionship of a good woman. But before we talk about his women, let's get into Dr. Tarnower's gusto for nutriments.

No less an authority on food than *The New York Times'* Craig Claiborne tells us that Dr. Tarnower not only had "a lean and leathery and definitely unhungry look . . ." but also that he believed "good food is one of life's great arts and great pleasures and should not be bypassed even by dieters."

The comments were occasioned by the publication of Dr. Tarnower's first book, The Complete Scarsdale Medical Diet, a regimen for dieters that advocates a high protein intake and lesser amounts of fats and carbohydrates than conventional plans for weight loss. It was not the publication of the book alone that prompted Claiborne to write about Dr. Tarnower. The story was also influenced by the spectacular reception the volume received.

On that Monday night when the now widely-celebrated author sat down to supper with his guests, *The Complete Scarsdale Medical Diet* had become a runaway best-seller. The hardcover edition sold more than 750,000 and the paperback over 2,250,000, earning for Dr. Tarnower and his co-author, Samm Sinclair Baker, an estimated $2,500,000 — with additional earnings from sales to book clubs, serializations, condensations in newspapers and magazines, and foreign sales.

But income from the book that promised its readers they could lose 20 pounds in 14 days "and keep them off" was not the catalyst which led to Dr. Tarnower's present comfortable station in life. Long before he put a single word on paper for the manuscript, his reputation had preceded him as an eminent physician, renowned around the world for his contributions to medicine. While the book did add more than $1,000,000 to his wealth, its most telling impact was that it

431

made the doctor a celebrity.

Therefore, it was not the book but his medical practice that enabled Dr. Tarnower to live in a Japanese-styled $500,000 home nestled in a 6-acre wooded tract on Purchase Street, a country-like road which is the address for many imposing estates in that affluent community.

The doctor's taste for beautiful works of art also was acquired long before the book was written. His home was filled with many valuable paintings and sculptures. The collection stressed Buddha statuary, but the one he treasured most was brought by him from China during a trip in 1973, when he also met the late Premier Chou En Lai.

The Premier was but one of scores of world leaders whom Dr. Tarnower knew both professionally and socially. Even his friends were drawn from the high echelons of the privileged classes. Closest of those associates was Joseph F. Cullman III, chairman of the board of the Phillip Morris Company, also a frequent golfing partner.

All who knew Dr. Tarnower agreed that he was an aristocratic, distinguished, and a highly-professional physician. His practice was in neighboring Scarsdale, where he founded the Scarsdale Medical Center. He was also on the staff at St. Agnes Hospital in White Plains and Westchester Medical Center in Valhalla as consulting cardiologist.

This portrait of a gentlemanly, illustrious, and eminently skilled medical scientist is also shaded by the bold and incongruent strokes of a brush that depicts Dr. Tarnower in the most unlikely and improbable pose of a "woman chaser." In and of itself such a reputation must not be interpreted as a derogation of his character. For he was unmarried and never had wed. He was a true bachelor. But in his pursuit of feminine companionship, more than one observer noticed, the good doctor had a penchant for young women, even women in their twenties who could have been his granddaughters.

However, it can be said with reasonable certainty that Dr. Tarnower's interest in the tender souls and flesh of fresh and bright-eyed maidens was merely a passing fancy. It could be no secret as to why liaison with blooming misses had to be impermanent. Herman Tarnower, or "Hi," as his friends called him, had practiced the ritual of pairing with only one mate at a time. In marriage it's called monogamy. In the single state it has no identifying label.

Dr. Tarnower was a firm believer in permanent relationships. Yet a woman with whom he maintained such an arrangement in a prior time and over a span of many years learned one day to her grief and desolation that her amour with the doctor would not, after all, thrive everlastingly.

She got the message slowly and by degrees beginning in 1966. That was when Dr. Tarnower's heart began to beat for tallish, blue-eyed, blonde-haired Jean Struven Harris. What Mrs. Harris brought into Dr. Tarnower's life at that point in time was the very same combination of attractions which his then slightly-aging mistress had carried over the threshhold of her lover's home when she came into his affections years before — youth, buoyancy, verve, and an elegant bearing.

Mrs. Harris also bore another just-right ingredient that made her a glittering attraction to Dr. Tarnower. She had already been divorced from James Harris, a Detroiter, who fathered her two sons, the one now 29, and the other 27, both born in Shaker Heights where the family lived for many years. James Harris later died.

It was in neighboring Cleveland where Jean Struven was born 57 years ago, in 1922, one of three girls and a boy in the family. From earliest childhood, her roots were planted in soil that influenced her growth into a young woman of sophistication, charm, integrity, and above-average intelligence. She was graduated with honors from prestigious Laurel School, which couldn't be anything less than exclusive and far-famed since it was, and still is, a landmark institution in swank Shaker Heights.

Then it was on to Smith College where the ivy grows even thicker than at Yale. Jean Struven majored in economics and was graduated magna cum laude in 1945.

Only months after she received her degree, some 9,000 miles away, General of the Army Douglas MacArthur entered triumphantly into Tokyo. One of his first acts was appointing Army Major Herman Tarnower to the Atomic Bomb Casualty Survey Commission.

"This was the most significant and important experience in my entire medical career," Tarnower was to say at a later time after studying first-hand the effects of the atomic bombing of Hiroshima and Nagasaki which brought Japan's immediate capitulation and the end of World War II.

Dr. Tarnower had a more prosaic upbringing than Jean Struven. His education was received at schools highly rated for their academics but which were not in league with the "blue blood" institutions of learning that his future friend attended.

While his background had little of the elegance and tone of the upper crust environment in which Jean Struven grew up, the Brooklyn-born son of the late Harry and Dora Tarnower was no slouch in radiating refinement and polish. He did so in everything he said, in everything he did. At Syracuse University, where he was a member of Phi Epsilon Pi fraternity, one of the more affluent and weightier campus brotherhoods, he was remembered for his politeness and intelligence.

In sharp contrast to his gravitation toward women at a later time, as a student at Syracuse the youthful Herman Tarnower didn't appear attracted to coeds. He was a bookworm, and his grades reflected his seriousness — an A student in most of his courses.

After graduation with his M.D. degree from Syracuse, Tarnower returned to New York City and served his internship and residency in internal medicine at Bellevue Hospital. In 1936 and 1937, he traveled abroad and visited numerous medical facilities in Europe on a New York Academy of Medicine fellowship, one of the most prestigious honors that can be conferred upon a young doctor.

On his return and before enlisting in the Army Medical Corps, he served as director of cardiology at Grasslands Hospital in Valhalla (which later became the Westchester County Medical Center), attending cardiologist at White Plains Hospital, and an assistant physician at New York's Presbyterian Hospital. Then upon leaving the Army he became an associate professor of clinical rehabilitation medicine at New York University and a clinical professor at New York Medical College. Thereafter, he founded the Scarsdale Medical Center and renewed his associations with Westchester hospitals.

Jean Struven's career took a totally different turn than she expected after graduation from Smith. Instead of pursuing post graduate studies as she intended, she got married in 1949 and had two children. It wasn't until after the divorce and the youngsters were able to fend for themselves that Mrs. Harris returned to her studies and finally obtained a master's degree in education from Wayne State University in Michigan.

With her master's, Mrs. Harris made significant new strides in education. However, she had not been without experience in the teaching field. For when her husband's interests shifted from Ohio to Michigan and the family moved to Grosse Point — the word "posh" has been greatly overworked in describing this community, but not unjustly so — Mrs. Harris sought even then to advance her own career. While her sons were still adolescents, she founded a nursery school. Later she taught at the Grosse Point University School.

After Wayne State conferred the master's degree on her, Mrs. Harris brought her teenage sons East where she was employed by the Allied Maintenance Company in Manhattan for a year and a half as sales administration manager. But her big ambition was to re-enter her principle discipline. That finally came to pass when she was engaged as headmistress of the Thomas School in Rowayton, Connecticut. Then she went on to become director of the middle school at Springside School in Philadelphia's suburbs.

In that fateful year of 1966 when she earned her master's, she also had her very first encounter with Dr. Herman Tarnower. The well-traveled Mrs. Harris made an instantaneous impression upon the Scarsdale physician. And he stuck out in her consciousness just as strongly.

With such chemistry stirring the early bloom of their acquaintanceship, it was only a short time before they became good friends, better friends, then still better friends. When the prevailing winds of their romance finally gusted, Tarnower's previous inamorata got the hint, finally and at last, that she had been replaced in his affections by the attractive 42-year-old educator.

With the other woman out of the way now, Jean Struven Harris took center stage in Dr. Tarnower's life. Her privileged background, her brightness, wittiness, intellect, strong character, and other attractive attributes made her a perfect companion for practically all occasions. She went with him to intimate dinner gatherings and to Westchester Heart Association fund-raising banquets. She was at his side on the golf links. And she accompanied him on vacations to many exotic spas around the world.

For ten years, Mrs. Harris played that gratifying role in Dr.

Tarnower's existence without the slightest hint that she could ever be phased out. Yet in that time, the doctor's eye for a young woman became an occasional distraction. But it was only for the briefest time. No serious fling ever interfered with the warm, friendly, caring, and loving romance shared by the lady from Shaker Heights and the heart specialist from Brooklyn.

Yet a day finally came when Dr. Tarnower was introduced to a pretty, blonde, fashionably slender woman in her middle twenties. Unlike the time he first made Mrs. Harris' acquaintance at a social function in Westchester, his initial meeting with Mrs. Marjorie Lynne Brundage Tryforos was on a professional plane. She had applied to the Scarsdale Medical Center for a job. After an interview with Dr. Tarnower she was hired as a medical assistant in 1972.

That's how it started for Mrs. Tryforos in the 29th year of her life, a life that began in the Westchester village of Ossining, home of Sing Sing prison.

Little Marjorie Lynne Brundage didn't spend many days of her childhood in Ossining. Her parents moved to Eastchester, where she attended elementary school. But her stay there was also brief. Her parents divorced and her mother re-married. The new husband, a man of means, moved the family into a $90,000 one-family home on Edgemont Road off Ardsley Road in a "middle-class" section of Scarsdale.

Marjorie Lynne, or just Lynne to her friends, was graduated from Edgemont High School with "just average grades." She went on to Endicott Junior College in Beverly, Massachusetts, whose reputation is that it's a "rich girl's school, and for girls who aren't very good students."

After her freshman year, Marjorie Lynne dropped out to marry Nicholas Tryforos, a florist. Because Miss Brundage was a Protestant and her future husband was a member of the

Greek Orthodox Church, and since both wanted to be married in their own faith, two ceremonies were held — one in a Protestant church, another in a Greek Orthodox church.

Her marriage was sunny for a time. Mrs. Tryforos bore her husband two daughters and she also helped out in Peter's flower shop on Garth Road in Scarsdale. Tryforos and his partner, doing business under the trade name of Tryforos and Pernice Florists, also had a branch shop in Bronxville.

Mrs. Tryforos' labors in the store came to an abrupt end when Dr. Tarnower employed her at the Scarsdale Medical Center. Her duties at the outset and for some years afterward were administering electrocardiograms. But in more recent times her responsibilities became more diversified until in the present scheme of things she was functioning as the medical center's office manager, combining duties of a secretary and of a nurse, as well as being Dr. Tarnower's Girl Friday. She was programming his day for him and was even preparing his daily lunches, usually yogurt with a mixture of fresh fruit and walnuts.

It was sometime in 1976, after being around him for four exciting years, that Mrs. Tryforos began to mean more to Dr. Tarnower than just a faithful, dutiful employe. Those who observed the change in the relationship when it began happening could understand how the doctor became attracted to this pleasant young woman radiating a fresh, warm, and uncomplicated personality.

Whether Jean Struven Harris, then approaching her 53rd birthday, sensed her man's interest in his 33-year-old employe isn't known. But we're told that was the turning point in Dr. Tarnower's affair with Mrs. Harris. It did not, of course, end abruptly. The erosion was slow, in a sense like the weathering of granite. Indeed when Mrs. Harris finally faced the bitter truth, one could say she insulated herself with a layer of the igneous rock to cushion the staggering blow of seeing a woman 20 years younger taking over—just as she herself had done a dozen years before when she replaced Dr. Tarnower's other love.

One can wonder whether Mrs. Tryforos could have supplanted Mrs. Harris completely in Dr. Tarnower's affections if the latter lady had not taken the job in 1977 as headmistress of the Madeira School, the exclusive and very conservative private preparatory school for girls high on the banks of the Potomac just south of Washington, D.C., in McLean, Virginia.

Some 300 miles separated the couple. Now instead of seeing each other every day, as they had been doing for all those many years, it was only on weekends that they could get together. Often several weekends went by before Mrs. Harris journeyed to Scarsdale and Purchase, or Dr. Tarnower would meet with her at her second home which she opened near the school. Her other residence was a small red frame house with white shutters in Mahopac, just north of the Westchester County line in Putnam County.

Ironically, that home was situated on Bullet Hole Road.

We are rapidly approaching a day when Mrs. Harris will walk into the Irving Sports Store in Tyson's Corner, Virginia not far from the school in Greenway, and place an order for a .32-caliber Harrington & Richardson revolver with a two-inch barrel. Although the store had the weapon in stock, Mrs. Harris had to wait about a week to take it home because her application to own a gun had to be approved by authorities. The request was routinely reviewed and accepted by the Fairfax County police chief.

When Mrs. Harris returned to the store, she took possession of the gun and of a box of .32-caliber bullets which she had also ordered. In Fairfax County, no reason is needed to buy a gun and there are no requirements for firearms registra-

439

tion.

What motivated Mrs. Harris to pack a gun at that point in time isn't known. The year was 1978 and a long time before she'd finally decide that there was, after all, a use for a gun.

Whether she carried the weapon to Scarsdale whenever she visited Dr. Tarnower also is not known. But what we are aware of is that at that juncture her relationship with the doctor was deteriorating at an accelerating pace.

Mrs. Harris was now being referred to by Dr. Tarnower's friends and associates as his "summer girlfriend," and Lynne Tryforos was called his "winter girlfriend." Those distinctions were dictated by the obvious — the headmistress could only spend fulltime in her lover's company when school was out and during the Easter and Christmas-New Year's recesses. At all other times, it was clear to all, Lynne Tryforos had become the doctor's woman friend of the hour.

The situation deteriorated still more for Mrs. Harris at the beginning of 1979 when Dr. Tarnower began flaunting his friendship with his lady. Until then he'd exercised a modicum of discretion in the amount of exposure given to Mrs. Tryforos in his presence. She had almost never accompanied him to the fancy and elaborate gatherings and he rarely introduced her to persons of prominence or high standing. Attending such events and experiencing such presentations had always been Mrs. Harris' exclusive province.

Then, all at once, that changed. Dr. Tarnower could be seen with Lynne Tryforos at his side, whereas in the past only Jean Harris could be found beside him, winter, spring, summer, fall. Then people in his exclusive circle began to see more and more of Mrs. Tryforos at elegant affairs, winter, spring, summer, fall. He had taken her out of the closet, in a sense, and was showing her off to the world.

Mrs. Tryforos also began serving as hostess at some of the

doctor's sumptuous dinner parties, assisted by his live-in housekeepers of the past 14 years, Suzanne and Henry van der Vreken. Until then it had always been Mrs. Harris' function to be mistress of ceremonies at those gatherings.

Another season arrived on December 21, 1979, and this truly was to be Mrs. Harris' winter of discontent. One would think it should not have been an unhappy time for her because she was in Miami, holidaying with her one and only. But the interlude with Hi Tarnower was shattered devastatingly the morning after she and the doctor had joyously celebrated New Year's Eve. Dr. Tarnower should not have tried to keep up with the news that day, nor should Mrs. Harris have.

He saw it and she saw it. They both saw it. It was in *The New York Times*. It was on page 1, at the very bottom where two-and-three line agate type advertisements and notices regularly appear in the columns. "Happy New Year Hi T," read the first line. "Love Always Lynne" said the second line. It cost $150 to send that greeting, but its effect was no less devastating than if she had taken out a full page ad for $2,500 and sent her message in 5,000 words of text in 8-point news-column type.

Finally and at last, Jean Struven Harris had to have realized that the thing Dr. Tarnower had going with Lynne Tryforos was for real. For very real . . .

On the afternoon of Friday, March 7th. Mrs. Harris put the finishing touches to her week behind the desk at the Madeira School and prepared for a weekend at home. She had a number of chores to perform and these would keep her from yet another visit to Purchase. Anyway, there hadn't been many of those lately. Indeed, when there were trips to Westchester in these days, they were hardly like old times. Yes, Mrs. Harris drove along familiar, meandering Purchase St., but she didn't venture into Dr. Tarnower's driveway on those occasions. She simply got out of her car on the road, stood in the wintry cold, stared at the living room and dining room windows, where now and then she'd catch a glimpse of the doctor, and he a glimpse of her. There'd be no sign of recognition from him. On one or two occasions she even spotted Lynne Tryforos in the house. When she was through looking, Mrs. Harris would get behind the wheel and either drive to her Mahopac home on Bullet Hole Road or make the five-hour return trip to Virginia.

That Friday afternoon at Madeira School was a busy one for Mrs. Harris. She was a dedicated headmistress. Her efforts to remodel the school in her image had met with considerable success in the three years she'd been in charge. She was managing to emancipate the school from its starchy finishing school reputation and to give it some modern sophistication. But that didn't mean to allow permissiveness to creep in. In fact, that very same day, Mrs. Harris expelled four seniors after a search of their room disclosed a quantity of marijuana and drug paraphernalia at the bottom of a laundry bag.

Mrs. Harris' weekend was onerous. She devoted herself to the writing of letters. Writing on endless pages. Mostly messages she would leave in sealed envelopes around the house. There were letters to friends and to relatives. But the most important correspondence of all was addressed to Hi Tarnower.

Early Monday morning, Mrs. Harris took the envelopes and mailed them at the post office. She sent Dr. Tarnower's bulky envelope by certified mail. Then she went to her office at the school.

In early afternoon, she dialed Dr. Tarnower's home and spoke with one of the housekeepers. She learned inadvertently that Dr. Harris was giving a dinner that evening for his sister, his niece, some friends — and Lynne Tryforos. Mrs. Harris put the receiver down and mulled over what she'd just learned.

442

She placed another call now. This to the Scarsdale Medical Center offices occupied by Dr. Tarnower. "I'm coming to see you tonight," she is said to have told the doctor. He was reported to have agreed to entertain her, but asked that she come after ten o'clock.

If it had been like old times for Mrs. Harris and the doctor and the most ideal driving conditions had prevailed, there could have been no way to arrive in Purchase before 10 o'clock — not so long as the headmistress planned to finish the day behind her desk until her normal 5 p.m. quitting time.

As it was, Mrs. Harris didn't begin her journey from the school. Instead, she returned home briefly. Very briefly. Just as long as it took to fetch the Harrington & Richardson revolver and the box of .32-caliber bullets. Then she carried the weapon and ammunition to her 1972 Chrysler Newport and locked them in the glove compartment. Now she could start her trip . . .

Dinner started punctually at six at Dr. Tarnower's house. The conversation was casual. Complaints about the heavy rain and gusty winds. Expressions of an eagerness to tolerate the rain because . . . "Imagine if this had been snow," someone said. "We'd be buried under a foot." Then came the talk about the murder — the three wives killing their husbands in the novel the dinner guests were discussing.

Dr. Tarnower, who almost always directed conversations at the table or later in the two-level living area, was particularly vocal that evening. He was also in a humorous mood. He reflected on the three wives doing in their mates and he quipped:

"I imagine that's one of the advantages of being a bachelor. Something like that could never happen to me . . ."

Dr. Tarnower checked his watch several times that night. Undoubtedly he must have had the thought in the back of his

443

mind that Jean Harris was coming up to see him. But he had no concern that his guests — most particularly Lynne Try-foros — would cross paths with his late-night visitor. The dinner gatherings at the doctor's house on weekday nights, unless special occasions, seldom lasted later than 9 o'clock. And on that Monday night of March 10th, the last of the guests had departed well before nine.

Some 15 minutes later, Dr. Tarnower said goodnight to his housekeepers, who were cleaning up the living room, and went upstairs to the master bedroom.

The doctor couldn't have known what Jean Harris wanted to talk about. She hadn't told him. Nor had he any awareness that Mrs. Harris had written him a long letter because she hadn't mentioned that to him either in their brief phone conversation. So he couldn't have known he was the target of a posthumous message from a letter-writer. That Mrs. Harris intended to bait Dr. Tarnower into killing her — with her own gun!

She reportedly had told all this in her letter to him as well as the other letters she left around the house and the ones mailed to friends and relatives.

If that was Mrs. Harris' intention, then so be it. But things didn't work out quite the way Mrs. Harris intended them to happen . . .

She arrived at Dr. Tarnower's house at about 10:30 pm. She didn't have to unlock the garage door because it was open. She knew she could reach the doctor's bedroom quicker through that route than by the front door, for which she also had a key.

The housekeepers, now in their living quarters, didn't hear Mrs. Harris arrive. Their ears picked up no sounds, in fact, until shortly after 11 o'clock. Then they were startled by the noises coming from Dr. Tarnower's bedroom. Banging and scuffling. Alarming noises.

Suzanne van der Vreken dialed the city police in White Plains and reported that burglars apparently had broken in and were ransacking the house.

The desk officer then phoned the Harrison Town police, who have jurisdiction in the area, and relayed the alarm. A radio dispatch was transmitted to a cruiser manned by Patrolman Brian McKenna. When he arrived at the house, he found Mrs. Harris getting into her Chrysler. But on seeing the police car, she got out and approached McKenna.

"There's been a shooting. The phone in the house isn't working. I was going somewhere to call . . ."

But there was no need for Mrs. Harris to phone, nor was it necessary for McKenna to ask headquarters for an ambulance and assistance. He found that out when he called and was told that Mrs. van der Vreken had phoned the police a second time and reported that Dr. Tarnower had been shot and was gravely wounded. McKenna also was told an ambulance and other help were on the way.

Mrs. van der Vreken learned from her husband about Dr. Tarnower. That came after they both heard a series of shots, followed by the sounding of the servants' buzzer in their quarters, triggered in the doctor's bedroom. Van der Vreken found his master lying unconscious on the floor between the twin beds, his beige pajamas soaked with his blood.

As McKenna entered the bedroom, he saw all the classic signs of a struggle. An overturned chair, a tilted night table, the phone torn from its wall outlet. That was why Mrs. Harris couldn't dial the police. The housekeeper had used the extension in her quarters.

The condition of the room was of least concern to the policeman. His only thought was to assist the victim. But there was little McKenna could do. Dr. Tarnower's eyes were closed. And although his breathing was labored, he didn't appear to be in need of mouth-to-mouth resuscitation. McKenna's main concern of the moment was stanching some of the bleeding. And as he applied that procedure, Patrolman Daniel O'Sullivan arrived, followed by other officers and Harrison police surgeon Dr. Harold Roth.

The surgeon administered further medical attention to the doctor, then supervised his removal in a stretcher to the ambulance that took him to St. Agnes Hospital. In the emergency room it was determined that Dr. Tarnower had been struck by four of the five bullets which were later determined had been fired from the six-shot revolver. He was hit in the right hand, right arm, and upper chest. That last wound proved to be the fatal one. Dr. Tarnower expired at 11:58 p.m., before he could be wheeled into the operating room for surgery that might have saved his life.

Back at the house, Mrs. Harris spoke freely with her police questioners. Patrolman O'Sullivan elicited statements from her that she had left notes in Greenway, sent letters to friends, and mailed a certified letter to her former lover outlining her plan—to have him kill her.

"I had no intention of going back to Virginia alive," she confided to O'Sullivan.

"Where's the gun?" the policeman asked.

"In my car . . ."

O'Sullivan nodded to McKenna. He went downstairs and found the revolver, one live bullet in the chamber and five spent cartridges in the cylinder. He also recovered the box of ammunition from which six live rounds had been removed.

O'Sullivan wanted to know how Mrs. Harris sustained the bruises around her mouth.

"He did it when we were struggling. He kept hitting me and shouting, 'You're crazy! Get out of here!'"

Mrs. Harris was taken to Harrison police headquarters,

booked for murder, and lodged in the lockup. The next afternoon, she was taken before Harrison Town Justice Harvey Fried for arraignment. By now the headmistress had retained attorney Joel Aurnou, a former Westchester County Court judge. He was in court defending her.

Pointing to the bruises on his client's face — one over her upper lip was most evident — Aurnou told Justice Fried:

"Nothing I've heard would apply to intentional homicide. This is not a second-degree murder and I'm challenging the prosecutor on that score."

Justice Fried ordered Mrs. Harris bound over for a hearing in Westchester County Court the next day and remanded her to the county jail without bail. On Wednesday, Mrs. Harris appeared before Judge John C. Couzens, who heard arguments from both sides.

Assistant District Attorney Joseph Rakacky stated to the court:

"It's apparent this arose from a romantic relationship."

He didn't explain further. But Aurnou argued:

"I don't think that's the way the case is going to go. Any discussion of a possible love-triangle is off the wall. There was no three-way romance here. Furthermore, I'm not going to speculate on what a 69-year-old man does in his spare time."

Judge Couzens ruled that Mrs. Harris could go free in $40,000 bond, but admonished her not to leave Westchester County. Her bail was posted by her brother, U.S. Navy Captain Robert Struven, who put up two $10,000 Certificates of Deposit, and $20,000 from a sister, Mrs. Margaret Lynch, who came from Shaker Heights to give comfort and aid to her sister. Mrs. Harris' other sister, Mrs. Virginia McLaughlin, also came to White Plains and was in court during the arraignment, as was the defendant's son. Her other son, a lieutenant in the Marine Corps, could not be there.

447

As Mrs. Harris was escorted from the court by her family and lawyer, she was heard to say, "I want to go to the funeral." But the next day when 300 relatives, associates, and friends attended Dr. Tarnower's last rites in Larchmont Synagogue, Mrs. Harris was nowhere to be seen. She'd been whisked away to an undisclosed Westchester hospital and placed under psychiatric care.

In the eulogy given in the red-carpeted synagogue, Rabbi Leonard Poller, the spiritual leader, said about Dr. Tarnower:

"His life's song was broken off halfway. How grieved we are at the loss of this poet of a person, this skilled physician . . . No one in control would attempt to reduce his personal independence. Perhaps someone tried to do that at the last."

Dr. Tarnower was interred in Mount Hope Cemetery at Hastings-on-Hudson, where only some 20 persons attended the private burial rite.

The most dramatic post-playing development occurred when one of Aurnou's law partners, John Killigrew, went to the Scarsdale post office at 5 o'clock Wednesday afternoon and presented Postmaster Samuel Morrison with a properly executed form called a "Senders Application For Recall of Mail." Killigrew had first appeared at the post office on Tuesday with a notarized request signed by Mrs. Harris, recalling the letter she mailed to Dr. Tarnower. The lawyer was given the form, which had to be filled out and signed by the addressee. Mrs. Harris had every right to recall the letter before it was delivered — that's the way the postal regulations read.

The ten-page letter, which had been mailed in a 14" x 4 1/2" beige envelope, was recovered just one step ahead of a Town of Harrison detective. He got to the post office on Thursday, although Mrs. Harris had told her questioners about the letter early Tuesday morning.

But that was not the last word on the letter. Westchester

County District Attorney Carl Vergari subpoenaed Killigrew to obtain the letter. The prosecutor demanded it be turned over to him because it conceivably contained evidence in the case. The letter's content, Vergari strongly insisted, could make the difference in deciding to charge Mrs. Harris with second-degree murder or manslaughter.

Aurnou said the letter was Mrs. Harris' property and that he needed it to defend her, to support his contention that Mrs. Harris was acting under an "extreme emotional disturbance" and had not intended to shoot Dr. Tarnower. "It's not up to the district attorney but the psychiatrists to determine whether the letter supports my argument," he said.

Under New York State law, a person killing another intentionally is charged with murder, a crime punishable by a minimum term of 15 to 25 years and a maximum of life. A killing committed in that heat of passion or in a highly emotionally state can result in the lesser charge of manslaughter, which carries a lesser penalty.

As Official Detective went to press, the wheels of justice in the case of the love-triangle murder of the Scarsdale Diet doctor were turning slowly but inexorably toward the day when his killer was to have her day in court.

There is a lesson we can draw from this case before the verdict is finally rendered. The lesson is twofold . . .

First, we have the awful realization that authors, like all mortals, are vulnerable to violent death. In that respect, we may duly note that this was the first time in all the decades that best-seller lists have been kept when an author enjoying a prestigious rating on that roster was murdered.

Then we can also take comfort in the knowledge that three can never go into two. Or put another way, there is no mathematical equation to solve the eternal love triangle, started when Biblical David sent Uriah to die in battle so he could marry Bathsheba and have her deliver his son, David.

There were no children, not even marriage for Dr. Tarnower and Mrs. Harris on that tragic day when the latest version of the love triangle was orchestrated to its fortissimo finish.

And before the sounds of the last bullets fired into Dr. Herman Tarnower's body had subsided, his book rose from No. 4 on *The New York Times* paper-back bestseller list to No. 3 in the mass market softcover book category.

The headlines helped to reactivate interest in the book. But we can be certain of one thing—that was not how Dr. Tarnower would have wanted to spur sales of his runaway best-seller.

The press, which had been having a field day with the sensational case, was filled with speculation that the state would settle for a manslaughter charge from the grand jury, but before this issue could be resolved, the fast-moving developments surrounding the fate of the genteel socialite accused of killing her lover produced yet another bombshell. Moreover, it was a bombshell that, at the very least, clouded the reports that the motivation for the fatal shooting had been Dr. Tarnower's callous dismissal of the suspect from his affections in favor of a younger, more attractive woman.

There seems little doubt that the Scarsdale Diet doctor did, indeed, transfer his affections, but when Dr. Tarnower's will was filed in Surrogate's Court in White Plains on March 27th, it became clear that he must have retained considerable regard for Jean Harris, the longtime lady friend who had been "replaced."

In this will, which Tarnower had signed as recently as January 21st, a mere seven weeks before his death, the doctor had bequeathed $220,000 to Jean S. Harris, his accused murderer!

And in the same will, he had left the sum of $200,000 to Lynne Tryforos, the lady who allegedly had taken Ms. Harris' place in his life. Additionally, the two young children of Ms. Tryforos were left $20,000 each for their education.

In the light of events that followed Tarnower's signing of this will, there is a certain irony in the position in which Jean Harris now finds herself. For one thing, it is logical to assume that she was wrong if she believed Dr. Tarnower no longer cared a damn about her; if that had been true, it is hardly likely that he would have left her $220,000.

And for another thing, there was the question about Jean Harris' chances of collecting this handsome bequest. Under the laws of New York State, she would forfeit the inheritance if she is convicted of Dr. Tarnower's slaying.

On March 26th, the speculation as to whether Jean Harris would be charged with murder or manslaughter ended when Westchester County District Attorney Carl Vergari filed an indictment returned by the grand jury which charged Jean Struven Harris with second-degree murder and two counts of criminal possession of the pistol which allegedly was the weapon used to kill Dr. Tarnower.

On March 28th, in a two-minute arraignment before Judge John C. Couzens in Westchester County Court, Ms. Harris pleaded not guilty to the three-count indictment.

Actor Tom Neal's Fight to Prove He Didn't Murder His Wife

by Chris Edwards

Twice in 14 years triangles have complicated the life of Tom Neal and plastered his name across newspaper front pages in lurid headlines. Each time he emerged relatively unscathed. And each time it was the woman who paid.

In the Barbara Payton-Franchot Tone-Tom Neal affair in Hollywood in 1951, it was the voluptuous blonde who took the toboggan ride from beauty and near stardom to dissipation and professional oblivion.

And in Palm Springs in 1965 it was pretty Gail Neal, the attractive 29-year-old wife of the ex-actor who paid — with her life. Neal's life was spared by a jury of nine women and three men who had been asked to believe he had fired a .45 caliber slug into her head as she slept because she had allegedly told him of her affairs with other men.

Tom Neal, a handsome, muscular, ex-amateur boxer was never any great shakes as an actor, but he had a way with women and headlines that many a more successful actor envied.

On May 30, 1944 a two-paragraph story appeared in a Los Angeles paper announcing that two young Hollywood couples had been married in a double ceremony in a Las Vegas wedding chapel. One of the grooms was identified as Tom Neal, "a young leading man." The bride was Vickie Lane, a "film starlet."

When the marriage ended in divorce five years later—no

community property, no children and no alimony—the story rated three paragraphs.

In the years that followed Neal pursued a movie career that was distinguished by small roles in big movies ("Another Thin Man" and "Flying Tigers"), and a few big roles in small movies ("The Unknowns" and "First Yank in Tokyo").

Then he met Barbara Payton.

The way the sexy blonde actress told it, she "knew in a minute" she "loved" Neal after seeing him standing on a diving board in his swimming trunks. A week later they announced they would be married.

From that time on the flickering, lackluster film career of Tom Neal really hit the skids, but his reputation as a lover grabbed him headlines even in some of the nation's most conservative newspapers.

But during the few weeks she had to wait for a final divorce decree from her first husband, an Iowa car dealer, the 23-year-old Miss Payton didn't confine herself to dating the 32-year-old Neal. She also dated 45-year-old Franchot Tone, handsome veteran star of major importance.

Franchot Tone had the Hollywood reputation and recognition. Tom Neal had the muscle and the virility. And Barbara wanted a little of what both men had to offer.

To make a long story short, the showdown came on September 15, 1951, when Barbara came home with Tone to find Neal waiting for her. When the smoke cleared, Franchot Tone was lying semi-conscious with a broken nose on the steps of Barbara's apartment.

Said Neal, "Barbara threw her arms around Tone and kissed him right in front of me. That's what touched it off. The sight of the girl I love kissing another man made me see red."

This was a far cry from the Tom Neal of 1965 who told a Superior Court jury that he was not jealous of his wife's shar-

453

ing their apartment with another man while he was out of town.

Neal won the fight with Franchot Tone but he lost the girl; she married Tone on September 28, 1951. The union lasted for 53 days before Tone filed for divorce, accusing his wife of committing adultery with Neal. Miss Payton's attorney threatened to file counter charges accusing Tone of "worse than adultery"—but he never did.

Tone had threatened to file felonious assault charges against Neal, but he gave up the plan in the "best interests of my family, my friends and my profession."

The triangle marked the end of the Hollywood careers of Tom Neal and Barbara Payton. Barbara drifted downhill into a life of booze and dissipation. Neal headed for Palm Springs, where he started life anew as a gardener.

There was a rumor that Barbara showed up in the Riverside Superior Court in Indio during Neal's trial for the slaying of his wife, but if she did she eluded the newsmen who covered the trial.

Neal married for the second time in the mid-1950s and became the father of a son, now 8. But that marriage ended in tragedy in 1958 when his wife, Patricia, died of cancer.

By 1961, Neal was no longer a gardener but a landscape architect and a respected member of the Palm Springs community. In June of that year he married Gail Evatt, then 25, a striking brunette who was a receptionist at the swank Palm Springs Tennis Club.

Neal was then 48—three years older than Tone was at the time of the Hollywood affair. By April 1, 1965, it was as if the tables had been turned. Neal was cast in the role that Tone had played—the middle-aged lover. And Gail, like Barbara Payton, was seeking companionship among younger men—or so Neal alleged.

454

That triangle was shattered with a single blast from a .45 caliber pistol that sent the heavy slug coursing through the head of Gail Neal as she lay on the big red couch in the living room of their Palm Springs apartment.

The phone that jangled in the office of the radio dispatcher for the Palm Springs Police Department at 6:30 a.m. on April 2, 1965, heralded the return of Neal's name to the nation's headlines. Few could remember any of the films he played in, but most readers would never forget his role in the Payton-Tone affair.

The man who called the police identified himself as James Cantillon, a prominent Beverly Hills attorney. He asked that a radio car be sent to North Palm Drive and Via Edcuela regarding "a party dead or seriously injured."

The dispatcher asked, "From natural causes or otherwise?"

And Attorney Cantillon replied tersely, "Otherwise."

At the intersection Patrolman Joe Jones found Attorney Cantillon, another attorney, James Kellem, and Tom Neal waiting for him in a blue Lincoln Continental. A few minutes later Police Lieutenant Carl Youngberg arrived and all three cars proceeded at Cantillon's direction to the Neal apartment at 2481 Cardillo Road.

Lieutenant Youngberg said that when Attorney Cantillon opened the front door of the Neal apartment with a key, the first thing he saw was the body of Gail Neal, 29, lying on the couch, partly covered with a light blanket. She was clad in green Capris and a green sweater. The Capris had been ripped below the zipper; they were unzipped and were pulled low on her hips. In her left temple was a gaping wound.

Lieutenant Youngberg said he felt Mrs. Neal's forehead and wrists, seeking some sign of life, but found none. He concluded she had been dead for hours.

A closer examination showed that the bullet had struck

Mrs. Neal in the head, about one inch above the right temple, and exited at the nape of her neck. The slug tore through the three pillows under her head and was found in the upholstery of the couch.

While the front door of the apartment had been locked, the rear door was kept ajar with a rock to allow the family pets, two cats, to come and go as they pleased.

A search of the apartment produced no sign of the murder weapon and Tom Neal, on the advice of his attorney, refused to make a statement. Wearing brown slacks, a white sports shirt, and with a topcoat draped across his shoulders, Neal was taken to the police station and booked on suspicion of murder.

Pending his arraignment the following Monday in Indio, he was held without bail.

Under the direction of Captain Robert White and Lieutenant Youngberg, the Palm Springs police were faced with the task of unraveling what appeared to be a murder — without an admission of murder, a witness to the crime, or a death weapon.

The account of the slaying of Gail Neal had hardly reached print before rumors were being whispered about that the Neals had not been getting along and that there had been some talk of divorce between the ex-actor and his wife. There were rumors, too, that Mrs. Neal had been seeing other men while her husband was out of town.

Police learned that Neal went back to Evanston, Illinois with his son in January, 1965, and returned alone on the afternoon of March 31st. Less than 48 hours later his wife was found shot to death under — to say the least — mysterious circumstances.

An autopsy indicated that Gail Neal had been dead about 12 hours when police found her body. Autopsy surgeons also found alcohol in her blood, which indicated she had been drinking before she was slain.

In questioning friends of the couple, the police learned that Mrs. Neal had worked at the Tennis Club Wednesday afternoon and went home at the usual time. She and Neal were at home together late that afternoon and were seen in some of the Palm Springs night spots that evening.

The following day—April Fool's Day—they were seen at about 1:30 p.m. lunching in a Palm Springs steak house. A businessman who knew the couple said they appeared amicable and had nothing to drink with their lunch.

And so far as police could determine, Gail Neal was never again seen alive. It was estimated that she was shot about 4 pm. that afternoon.

The man who saw them together in Mrs. Neal's apartment on the afternoon of March 31st was a real estate broker who brought some letters of recommendation to her home. He said Mrs. Neal had wanted them duplicated to seek employment in Los Angeles—another indication that Mrs. Neal was preparing to leave her husband. The real estate man said that while he was in the apartment, Neal appeared to be nervous and tense.

What happened between 1:30 and 6 p.m. on April 1st remained a mystery, but the story picked up at 6 p.m. miles away in an exclusive restaurant in Idyllwild, high atop the San Jacinto Mountains overlooking Palm Springs.

The police had learned that Cantillon, the Beverly Hills attorney, had been summoned to help Neal by Robert Balzer, one of the owners of the Tirol Restaurant at Idyllwild. Balzer, an esthetic looking man who had spent some time in a Buddhist monastery and was a Buddhist monk, also was socially prominent in the Los Angeles area and extremely wealthy.

He and James Willett owned the Tirol and were surprised to see the front door open on a blustery, snowy night of April

1st and to see Tom Neal walk in wearing only a light sports jacket to protect him from cold. It was 6:15 p.m.

As disclosed at a grand jury hearing a few days later, Balzer testified Neal told him he had shot his wife with a .45 caliber pistol as she lay on the couch taking a nap. Balzer also said Neal told him he had brought the death weapon with him from Chicago when he returned to Palm Springs the day before the shooting.

Mostly on the strength of Balzer's testimony, the grand jury indicted Neal for murder and remanded him to jail where he was held without bail to await trial. The gun was not found, nor had Neal made any statement to the police about the shooting or what had happened to the death weapon.

Neal was to be defended by Leon Rosenberg, a prominent Palm Springs criminal attorney, considered by his associates as one of the best in Riverside County. Up until the day of the trial he made every effort to have the trial moved to another county because of the newspaper publicity given to the case.

"The headlines have already convicted my client," Attorney Rosenberg contended.

But he was unsuccessful. The trial began in the Indio branch of the Riverside County Superior Court on October 11th before Judge Hilton H. McCabe.

Strikingly rugged looking and handsome and still in top physical shape, except for his graying hair, Tom Neal appeared little changed from the day he battled with Franchot Tone. Dressed in a neat dark gray suit and wearing horn-rimmed glasses, he looked every bit the distinguished businessman as he pulled his chair up to the counsel table when the trial began.

It opened with a warning from Judge McCabe who said, "The defendant stands before you with a presumption of innocence. If you had to vote right now you would have to vote, 'Not guilty.'"

A panel of 130 prospective jurors was all but exhausted before a panel of nine women and three men were sworn in to hear the case. Many were excused because they felt they could not vote for a death penalty in this trial or any other. Others were excused for various reasons, one because he had built the building in which the slaying had taken place.

In his opening statement, Prosecutor Roland Wilson told the jury that he expected to prove that Tom Neal had deliberately shot and killed his wife as she slept on the afternoon of April 1st and later that evening Neal had admitted the slaying to Balzer and Willett.

Technical testimony introduced by the prosecution showed the autopsy revealed that the bullet wound was not necessarily fatal. It was revealed that the gases entering the victim's head from the muzzle of the gun, held at close range, had "almost completely fractured" her skull. It was pointed out that the gun had been held within six inches of the temple, apparently while Gail Neal was asleep. The heavy slug that killed her was found in the upholstery of the couch, the ejected shell casing was found on the floor under the coffee table.

Other witnesses told of seeing the Neals together on March 31st and on April 1st up until three hours before the time of Mrs. Neal's death. All agreed that the couple seemed to be in a good mood and very friendly.

Police officers testified as to how they were informed of the crime, how they found the body, and the disarray of the master bedroom when they examined the Neal apartment on April 1st.

On October 27th, the prosecution called its star witness, Robert Balzer, the Buddhist monk and restaurant owner, who had told the grand jury that Neal confessed to him that he had killed his wife. There was an attempt to keep Balzer from testifying on the grounds that the communication between the

459

monk and Neal was in the nature of a religious confession and therefore could not be violated. This was overruled, however, by Judge McCabe.

Balzer took the stand. During his testimony, the slender, balding Balzer wept openly as he said he could not, "if my life depended on it," quote the exact words Neal used in telling of the slaying of his wife. And as it turned out, it was on the exact words that the credibility of the statement hinged.

Balzer said he was standing in the foyer of the restaurant at 6:15 p.m. on April 1st when Neal walked in. Balzer said he told Neal, "It's good to see you," and chucked the ex-actor under the chin.

He said Neal replied, "This is the kindest gesture showed me in some time." Balzer said Neal's reply to him indicated that the former actor was upset.

"Then I suggested we have a drink," Balzer said, "and we went to a corner of the cocktail lounge and had a drink. I don't remember what Tom ordered. I drink Scotch and water. Neither of us finished the drink."

Asked if Neal seemed intoxicated, Balzer replied, "No. He seemed disturbed. On all previous occasions he was merry and bright. This time he seemed depressed and disturbed." He said Neal told him he had taken his son back east. Balzer told the jury that when the boy's mother died of cancer in 1958, "Tom devoted himself to his son and to the study of science and philosophy. For two and a half years he was a celibate.

"He said he had met Gail and fallen in love with her and she became his whole life. Then he told me they were separated. I observed he was distressed. I recognize there was some kind of a problem. I mentioned the Buddhist philosophy in which one is taught to face problems as they are — as a tiger at the door. "If there is a tiger at the door you must face it."

Balzer said Neal replied, "If I told you I was a tiger you

would call the police."

Balzer said he answered, "Under no circumstances."

Balzer said it was then that Neal told him Gail was taking a nap when he shot her in the head about 4 p.m. that afternoon.

Balzer testified, "I didn't believe it. I assumed it was a fantasy. When I realized it was probably true I asked him if he knew a lawyer or had one." He said Neal answered by saying, "She is alone now," and that he intended to kill himself but he didn't have the courage.

Balzer said he told Neal that if he wanted legal counsel he would call James Cantillon of Beverly Hills, one of the finest criminal attorneys in the country. He said they went to his office where they placed the call for Attorney Cantillon. He estimated it took about 45 minutes for Neal to reach the decision to agree to calling the lawyer.

Balzer said he tried to give Neal "what comfort and courage I could." He said he told him, "If it is true and Gail is dead she is gone now and we must be concerned with the present. Ring down the curtain of razzle dazzle."

Balzer said later that evening, Neal repeated the story of the shooting to Willett. "Willett said he didn't believe it. He said it must be some kind of an April Fool joke. Then Tom repeated that he shot her in the head with a .45 and said 'Pow, Pow!' extending his arm." Balzer said he was startled when Neal made the "Pow" sound and extended a pointed finger.

Balzer said he and Neal went to the dining room for dinner between 8 and 9 p.m. and that during dinner a phone call was received from Attorney Cantillon's son, Richard, also an attorney.

After talking to him, Balzer said, he and Neal finished their dinner. Then, he said, Neal went to Balzer's office to take a nap. While Neal was sleeping, Balzer said, James Cantillon called and said that he and Attorney Kellem were on their way and expected to reach Idyllwild about midnight.

Meanwhile a blizzard struck and it was 3 a.m. before the attorneys arrived at the mountain top restaurant. Before Neal left with the lawyers, Balzer said, he gave the former actor his blessings and "he received them."

Asked, "Was there any gesture of farewell?"

Balzer replied, "I embraced him."

Willett later corroborated Balzer's story and added, "Neal said he thought of killing himself but felt he didn't have the courage. He said he would permit the State to do it for him."

Prosecutor Wilson asked, "Did he use the phrase, 'he would permit the State to do it for him?'"

Willett replied, "Maybe he said he would let them do it." Willett said Neal told him that the gas chamber would be easier because it takes only 10 seconds.

That was the nub of the prosecution's case — that Tom Neal had admitted killing his wife while she slept and that he expected the State to execute him for it. Medical testimony, however, declared it was impossible to determine whether or not Mrs. Neal was awake or asleep when she was slain. But it was determined that she did not have sexual intercourse immediately prior to her death.

Immediately after Balzer and Willett had testified, the prosecutor rose and announced, "The people rest."

The suddenness of the move caught the defense by surprise and Defense Attorney Rosenberg was given until the following morning to open his defense of Tom Neal. It had been expected that the prosecution would call some 30 witnesses. The prosecution rested after but eight were called.

When Tom Neal was called to the stand in his own defense, he broke down and wept as he publicly related for the first time the lurid and shocking details of a love-making session that preceded his wife's death.

He related that his wife was "surprised but glad" to see him when he arrived home unexpectedly on the afternoon of March 31st and they went out on the town that night and did quite a bit of drinking in night spots. He said he had landed at Los Angeles International Airport and rented a car for the drive to Palm Springs. He said his wife wasn't home when he got there but that she arrived about an hour later.

Neal said it was about 1 a.m. when they finally called it quits at the Rim Rocks night club and headed for her apartment on Cardillo Road. He said he offered to get a motel room but his wife said it wouldn't be necessary, that he could use the extra bedroom in the apartment.

He said both he and his wife were "feeling pretty good, but not smashed." He said they spent the night in the separate bedrooms. The next morning, Neal said, Gail told him of a number of affairs she had with men during his 10-week absence and also while they had been living together.

He said she also mentioned that she had been followed home from the tennis club on several occasions and that once someone had followed her right to the front door. Neal said he asked her what had happened to the gun he had given her and she replied, "I have it." Neal said he went to the bedroom closet and brought out the weapon.

He said his wife told him she had been having trouble loading the gun and asked him to do it for her. Neal said he put the safety on but she asked him to release it because "it was hard for her to get the safety off."

Neal told the court he put the weapon on the coffee table beside the red couch in the living room and continued their conversations until lunch time. He said she spoke of what she had been doing and of the men in her life. "It was a semi-confessional," Neal said.

After lunch at a steak house, Neal continued, he and his

463

wife returned to her apartment. Neal testified, "She brough out pillows and a white spread from the bedroom. I sat along side her on the couch and kissed her. She kissed me back."

Neal said he moved down to unzip her Capris and ther pulled down her panties. "She liked me to undress her in the physical act," he told the court. He said when he began kissing her more intimately, she murmured, "I don't know whether we should be doing this."

Neal said he replied, "I've been away for ten weeks and you've been banging all my friends. I'll bet you didn't even draw the color line."

Neal said he felt his wife's body tense and she screamed, "I'll kill you — you son of a bitch!"

Neal said, "I looked up to face the .45 in her hand. It was pointed at my head. I was down on one knee. I said, 'Gail, you're out of your mind,' and I shoved the gun with both hands. The gun went off and Gail was hit."

Neal said the gun had been on the coffee table since he put it there before lunch and she apparently had reached for it as she lay back on the sofa during his lovemaking. The former actor wept as he told the jury how dumbfounded he was when he realized his wife had been shot.

"I couldn't believe what I saw with my eyes," he said. "I took her hand and called her name. I kept talking." He told how he ripped his wife's Capris as he tried to straighten her clothing. Then, he said, he partly covered her with the light blanket that had slipped to the floor.

Neal testified that he packed an overnight bag, returned to the living room beside the body of his wife, prayed and left. He said he thought of going to Los Angeles because he had to talk to someone and he had friends there. He said when he found no train available at the Palm Springs railroad station he decided to drive his rented car to Los Angeles.

When he came to the Idyllwild cut-off at Banning, Neal said, he decided to drive to the Tirol Restaurant to talk with Balzer. He said it was dark and snowing when he arrived.

Neal contradicted Balzer's and Willett's version of his alleged confession to them and said that his conversation with the two men ranged from discussions of metaphysics and "the material approach" to spiritual things. Regarding the shooting he said he told Balzer:

"She's been shot and I feel that I am to blame because if I hadn't come back she'd still be alive." He said that when Balzer asked him if he had shot Gail he replied, "Literally, I didn't shoot her, but she's been shot. I loaded the gun."

Neal denied any knowledge of the death weapon and denied telling Balzer that he brought the gun with him from Chicago.

And so the jury was faced with the other side of the coin. On the one hand a Buddhist monk had sworn under oath that Neal told him he shot his wife in the head while she was sleeping. Neal swore under the same oath that he never told Balzer this, that the shooting was accidental and that in effect Gail shot herself.

Stephen Peck was called to the witness stand by the defense. His name had cropped up in the case from time to time and his belongings were found in the Neal apartment at the time of the slaying. From the witness stand he testified that he had been sharing the apartment with Mrs. Neal during Neal's absence, but with Neal's approval. Peck said he moved into the apartment complex in October, 1964, and moved into the Neal apartment in January, 1965.

Peck was asked, "At any time was there any discussion as to rent?" He replied, "I was told I would pay half of Gail's rent." Asked who was to occupy the premises with him, Peck replied, "Gail."

When Neal was asked if he was jealous of Peck, he replied

465

that he was not, adding, "I knew Steve. Gail and I discussed the move over the phone. I was not really concerned, knowing Steve, but when a man and a woman live under the same roof, who knows what may happen?"

Asked, "Did you have some concern about him living there?" Neal replied that he did not. Asked, "You were extremely jealous?" Neal said, "No."

Fourteen years before he had flattened Franchot Tone because Barbara Payton had kissed him. Now he admitted he felt little concern over his wife, a woman whom he described as being his whole life, sharing her apartment with another man.

While he was on the stand for the defense, Peck described a struggle over a gun between Gail and Neal which took place in the Neal apartment in November, 1964. At that time Gail said to Neal, Peck testified, "I'll kill you—you son of a bitch!" By coincidence, these were the same words Neal said she uttered on April 1st when she leveled the pistol at his head.

Peck said he had been watching TV in the Neal apartment with Gail and Tom when Tom got up and said,. "Let's go to bed, Gail." When she refused, Peck said, the couple got into an argument and Gail began packing to leave.

"The next thing I knew," Peck continued, "Tom and Gail were in the hallway struggling for the gun she was holding. She had the gun in her left hand and Tom was holding her wrist. His other arm was around her waist. It was then that she threatened to kill him."

Peck said he moved behind the couple and disarmed Gail.

When the defense rested, Prosecutor Wilson called H. R. Gumber, assistant county clerk for Riverside County, who produced evidence to show that Gail Neal had begun divorce proceedings on March 11, 1965. It appeared that Neal knew nothing of this until he heard it in the courtroom.

Also called as rebuttal witnesses were the dead woman's

mother and aunt, Mrs. Betty Bennett and Mrs. Margaret Casper. The women related how they searched the Palm Springs apartment for a gun after Neal left home to go to Evanston. Mrs. Bennett said Neal called her the night before he left and told her that Gail had left him and that there was nothing for him to live for. The following Sunday, Mrs. Bennett testified, she visited her daughter in Palm Springs and was told that Tom had moved everything out, with the single exception of his young son's bike.

Mrs. Bennett said she asked her daughter if Neal had taken the gun and Gail replied, "Oh, Mother, I didn't think about that."

Mrs. Bennett said they searched the house but could find no trace of the weapon. Earlier in the trial, Neal had testified that the gun was in the house when he left for Evanston.

Mrs. Casper said she visited her niece Gail over the Lincoln's Birthday week end and helped Mrs. Bennett and Gail search for the gun, but it was never found.

Also called as a rebuttal witness was Ray Pinker, former forensic chemist for the Los Angeles Police Department, and currently a professor of criminalistics at California State College in Los Angeles.

He testified that his examination showed the woman was lying on her back when she was shot and that the muzzle of the gun was practically against her head. Pinker said that due to the position of the woman's head and the prominence of the back of the sofa "it would not have been possible to discharge the weapon the way Neal said."

But under cross-examination by Defense Attorney Rosenberg, Pinker admitted he was not on the premises during the investigation of the crime, had never seen the corpse and based his conclusions on photographs furnished by the Palm Springs Police Department.

Three co-workers of Mrs. Neal were called on rebuttal to testify that Gail had been in fear of her life from Neal. Mrs. Neal was quoted as telling the witnesses, "I'm not going to be an idiot. I'm afraid of him." They said Gail told her Tom had a gun and on two occasions Neal had beaten his wife and blackened her eyes.

On November 16th, the opposing lawyers made their final arguments with Prosecutor Roland Wilson thundering that in his 30 years as an attorney he had "never heard a more dirty, foul-mouthed or vulgar description of a homicide between a husband and wife." He added, "The version Mr. Neal gives of the way in which his wife died is not supported by the evidence. The young lady (Gail Neal) is not here to give her side of the story — at least not physically.

"But she is here in the blood on the pillow and in the photographs introduced in evidence."

Calling on the jury to return a verdict of first-degree murder Prosecutor Wilson declared, "If you do not reach this decision you will be turning a murderer loose on the streets."

Defense Attorney Rosenberg argued that the jury must believe that Mrs. Neal was shot in self-defense after she pulled the gun on Neal and threatened him with it.

Judge McCabe spent an hour instructing the jury, telling them they could bring in any one of five verdicts ranging from first-degree murder to innocent by virtue of justifiable homicide.

The jury filed out of the courtroom at 10:23 a.m. on November 17th to begin its deliberations. They deliberated until 9:30 p.m. when they were locked up for the night.

The following day they asked Judge McCabe to read to them certain instructions pertaining to the two degrees of murder and manslaughter. It was 9:30 p.m. on November 18th when the jurors announced they had reached a verdict. The court was in readiness at 9:53 p.m. and the clerk read the verdict — guilty of involuntary manslaughter, punishable by not more than 15 years in prison.

The jurors evidently had chosen to believe Neal's version of the slaying, rather than the one he purportedly gave Balzer and Willett on the day of the murder.

When the verdict was read, Neal closed his eyes and breathed an audible sigh of relief and said, "It's been a long, tough road."

Smiling broadly, Defense Attorney Rosenberg gripped Neal's hand and said, "Tom Neal's deep religious faith carried him through."

Prosecutor Wilson appeared to be surprised at the verdict, but he declined to comment on the findings of the jury. He said, "The average time difference between a sentence on manslaughter and one for second-degree murder is only about eight months, anyway. The jury voted the way they thought it should be."

Although Prosecutor Wilson had asked for a conviction for first-degree murder, he told reporters during deliberations that he would be satisfied with a second-degree conviction.

Defense Attorney Rosenberg said he did not expect that his client would serve much time in prison, pointing out that many persons convicted of manslaughter serve less than a year and that Tom Neal already had served more than seven months in jail.

The defense attorney said, "We have a longer way to go in this case than did the prosecution. We started the trial with a presumption of guilt, not a presumption of innocence."

The judge set sentencing for December 10th. But on Tuesday before Thanksgiving, Neal got a present: He was released on $2,750 bail pending his appearance in court for sentencing.

On December 10th, in Indio Superior Court, Judge Mc-

Cabe announced his sentencing of Tom Neal: One to 15 years in prison. The California Adult Authority will determine how much Neal will have to serve of the 1-15 rap, but under state law it must be at least a year — and contrary to Defense Attorney Rosenberg's prediction, the seven months Neal served in jail while awaiting trial will not count toward his prison term.

Prior to sentencing, Neal had expressed confidence that he would not be imprisoned. "There would be no sense in putting me back in jail," he said. "My atonement is complete. I've seen the light."

When the prison sentence was announced, he commented: "Even God has to answer to Judge McCabe, I guess. This is His vengeance."

But District Attorney Wilson had a comment of his own:

"When that jury returned the involuntary manslaughter verdict, Neal got all the breaks anyone is entitled to."

PINNACLE'S TRUTH IS STRANGER THAN FICTION — REAL LIFE GREED AND MURDER!

THE BEAUTY QUEEN KILLER   (345, $3.95)
by Bruce Gibney

They were all attractive, vulnerable, ambitious. They fell for his promises of glamorous careers in modeling. And they died slow, horrible deaths at the hands of one Christopher Wilder.

Chris Wilder: successful businessman, sportsman, convicted sex offender. Author Bruce Gibney traces the six week, cross-country odyssey of sexual sadism and murder. This is the chilling account of one of the greatest and all-encompassing manhunts this country has ever witnessed. The search was for the man with a perverted mind and a murderous rage, a man who loved beauty queens . . . loved them to death!

MONEY TO BURN   (408, $4.95)
by Michael Mewshaw

On July 9, 1985, a terrible explosion ripped through the silence in the exclusive Naples, Florida community. Pipe bombs blew apart the Benson family car, killing millionaire tobacco heiress Margaret Benson and son Scott. Steven Benson, the sole remaining son and heir, had exited the car moments before, escaping death or injury. After an extensive investigation, Steve Benson was charged, convicted and sentenced to life in prison.

Award winning author Michael Mewshaw gives us the blood-chilling account of this notorious case of heartless, premeditated murder. More than a story of murder, MONEY TO BURN reveals the fall of the super-rich, a family torn assunder by hate, greed, scandal and drugs.